THE SCULPTURE AND SCULPTORS
OF THE GREEKS

THE METROPOLITAN MUSEUM OF ART

THE
SCULPTURE AND SCULPTORS
OF THE GREEKS

BY

GISELA M. A. RICHTER

NEW REVISED EDITION

NEW HAVEN AND LONDON, YALE UNIVERSITY PRESS

Ρητὸν γὰρ οὐδαμῶς ἐστιν ὡς ἄλλα μαθήματα, ἀλλ᾽ ἐκ
πολλῆς συνουσίας γιγνομένης περὶ τὸ πρᾶγμα αὐτὸ καὶ
τοῦ συζῆν ἐξαίφνης οἷον ἀπὸ πυρὸς πηδήσαντος ἐξαφ-
θὲν φῶς ἐν τῇ ψυχῇ γενόμενον αὐτὸ ἑαυτὸ ἤδη τρέφει.

PLATO, EPISTLES VII. 341 C.

*"There is no way of putting it into words like
other studies, but after much communion and
constant intercourse with the thing itself suddenly, like a light kindled from a leaping fire,
it is born within the soul and henceforth
nourishes itself."*

PREFACE TO THE FIRST EDITION

THE immediate incentive for writing this book was the preparation of a course of lectures on Greek sculpture given under the auspices of The Metropolitan Museum of Art, Columbia University, and New York University in 1925 and 1926. It was a welcome opportunity to try a somewhat novel scheme for the presentation of this subject: the concentration first on the study of the sculpture itself and then on that of the sculptors who produced it. The abiding interest of Greek sculpture lies in the objects themselves. Their proper appreciation and understanding are a source of unending interest and enjoyment. It seemed desirable not to confuse this study with constant digressions concerning possible attributions to known artists; and it was likewise easier to give a consecutive picture of the great personalities who determined the development of Greek sculpture without continually interrupting the narrative by the consideration of other material. The opportunity thus afforded of giving our undivided attention to the sculpture as a purely artistic manifestation has suggested the consideration of a number of new aspects not usually treated in our histories of Greek art. In addition to making a consecutive, chronological study of the various types of the human figure I have tried to trace the development of drapery, of composition, and of the treatment of relief; and have added a chapter on Animals and one on Forgeries.

In the second part of my subject—The Greek Sculptors—I have endeavored to give the evidence pure and simple, carefully sifted to the best of my ability; for the time seemed ripe to present the foundation we now have to build on without questionable superstructures. When we consider the large number of sculptors known to us practically only by their names[1] the pastime of assigning the extant sculptures to a small group of familiar masters appears precarious. And I have omitted the absorbing question of "schools" as equally unprofitable in a book of this kind. In spite of certain diversities of style in various localities (cf. p. 6) the common characteristics are by far the more distinct. And

---

[1] E.g., Amphion, Diodoros, Skymnos, Askaros, Arkesilaos, Kleoitas (first half of fifth century B.C.); Pison, Kolotes, Theokosmos, Styppax, Demetrios, Pyrrhos, Pyromachos, Kleiton, Nikodamos, Kallikles, Telephanes (second half of fifth century); Apellas, Xenophon, Polykles, Sthennis, Polykrates, Kalliades, Telesias, Ktesikles, Exekestos, Strabax, Nikomachos, Demetrios (fourth century); Telephanes, Telesias, Ktesikles (dates uncertain); etc., cf. Overbeck, *Schriftquellen, passim.*

especially is this true from the beginning of the fifth century when communication among the Greek states became more constant. Artists traveled from place to place and local traditions became merged in an international Greek style. This homogeneity of Greek art is convincingly brought out by a study of the coin types of the various Greek cities, where we should expect such diversities but where local characteristics of style are seldom observable—except in the broad divisions of Peloponnesian, Athenian, and Ionic. Though our archaeological literature abounds in discussions regarding the geographical origins of extant sculptures the varying theories held by different archaeologists have shown how difficult it is to draw the dividing line. I have therefore spared my reader such attributions and concentrated my attention on the salient characteristics common to Greek sculpture.

For the convenience of the student I have added a chronological table, rendering myself thereby particularly vulnerable to attack, since many dates are disputed.

The translations of the Greek and Latin texts are taken mostly from the Loeb editions and H. Stuart Jones's *Select Passages from Ancient Writers Illustrative of Greek Sculpture*, with occasional slight variations.

The large number of illustrations in proportion to the text will, I know, be acceptable; for reproductions are more eloquent than words and make, in fact, many words unnecessary. Photographs of casts have been used in preference to those of originals only when the casts could be photographed in a better light or from a more convenient angle than was possible with the originals.

My debts for help rendered are so numerous that I can acknowledge them only in a general way. Throughout the years that I have been at work on this book I have invariably found a ready response from my fellow archaeologists in the giving of desired information, in the opportunities of study afforded, and in the supplying of needed photographs. I gratefully acknowledge herewith this friendly assistance. I am under special obligation to Mr. E. T. Newell, who has generously helped me with information regarding coins; to Mr. J. D. Beazley for many important suggestions particularly in the chronological table; to Mr. M. N. Tod for help in inscriptions; and above all to my sister, Irma Richter, an artist by profession, who has revised the whole first part of my MS. and made innumerable suggestions and corrections in

my text; I owe to her also the advice that I take up modeling and
stone-cutting, an experience which proved invaluable.

Greek sculpture is a theme so much vaster than the interpretation of
it by any one individual that it can never be a closed subject. Every
fresh mind can make a new contribution by approaching it from a different angle and devoting to its analysis his own individual faculties.
No apology is therefore needed for adding yet another volume to our
histories of Greek sculpture. The mine on which we are working is in-
exhaustible; for its ore is not gold but the highest aspirations of a
gifted people.

G. M. A. R.

New York, October, 1928.

PREFACE TO THE SECOND EDITION

THE smaller format of this second edition has necessitated the repag-
ing of the text. The figure numbers of the half-tone and line illustrations are, however, the same as before. The colored plates have been
omitted. A few alterations in the illustrations have been made: figures
72, 203, 466, 564, and 644 are I hope now clearer; 418 and 689 have
been corrected; and in 575 and 577 the statue (Harmodios) has been
made to lean slightly further forward. In the text I have been able
to profit by some criticism and have tried to correct various mistakes
and misprints. It is hoped that having the illustrations all at the end
and a reference for each figure to the page where it is discussed will
facilitate the use of the book. For the same purpose an index to the
illustrations has been supplied and additions have been made to the
index to the text.

G. M. A. R.

New York, May, 1930.

PREFACE TO THE NEW REVISED EDITION

TWENTY years have passed since the second edition of this book appeared. In the two reprintings of 1941 and 1946 no changes were made. In this third edition I have been allowed to make alterations that seemed essential if they could be fitted into the old pagination. These changes, however, proved extensive, for much has happened in archaeology in the last two decades. I have tried to embody the most important new discoveries, to correct antiquated theories, and have largely rewritten the portions dealing with the archaic and the Hellenistic periods. The chronological table and the bibliography have been revised, and about forty-five substitutions have been made in the illustrations. In the footnotes I could only insert recent publications where space allowed; they are supplemented, however, by the new bibliography.

I have not tried to change the style of the text, since this would have necessitated rewriting most of the book; for one's style changes with the years—for better or for worse. I hope, however, that the improvements that I have been able to make will give the book a new lease on life.

I am indebted to many colleagues for help in various ways, especially to Professor Alfred Bellinger for drawing my attention to additional dated coins; to Dr. Margarete Bieber for improving the section on Greek dress; to my sister for many suggestions; and to several members of the Metropolitan Museum staff for timely assistance and several photographs. Above all, I am grateful to the Yale University Press for making this new edition possible.

G.M.A.R.

New York, November 1949

CONTENTS

LIST OF ILLUSTRATIONS

FIGURES

Unless otherwise stated the material of the sculptures is marble.

[1] The objects in the Metropolitan Museum have been photographed by Edward Milla, the Museum photographer.

THE FOLLOWING ARE THE CHIEF ABBREVIATIONS
OF PERIODICALS USED

Arch. Anz. = Archäologischer Anzeiger (Beiblatt zum Jahrbuch).
A.J.A. = American Journal of Archaeology.
Arch. Ztg. = Archäologische Zeitung.
Ath. Mitt. = Mitteilungen des deutschen archäologischen Instituts, Athe-
nische Abteilung.
B.C.H. = Bulletin de correspondance hellénique.
B.S.A. = Annual of the British School at Athens.
Εφ. Ἀρχ. = Ἐφημερὶς Ἀρχαιολογική.
Δελτ. Ἀρχ. = Δελτίον Ἀρχαιολογικόν.
Jahrbuch = Jahrbuch des deutschen archäologischen Instituts.
J.H.S. = Journal of Hellenic Studies.

PART ONE

GREEK SCULPTURE

CHAPTER I

THE HISTORICAL BACKGROUND OF
GREEK SCULPTURE

L IKE every art, Greek sculpture was largely conditioned by the
history of its time; and the four chief phases in its development clearly reflect the outlook and conditions of the four
outstanding periods in Greek history. The archaic, classical, and Hellenistic periods in Greek sculpture may be elucidated by contemporary events. It is essential, therefore, to view Greek art against its
historical background.

(a) Early Period (1000–500 B.C.)

AFTER the fall of the "Minoan" and "Mycenaean" civilizations there
followed everywhere in Greece an obscure period during which the
brilliant monarchies of the Aegean chieftains were replaced by
"feudal" aristocracies. It is during these "dark ages" of the tenth
and ninth centuries that the Greek nation—that is, the Aegean
people reinforced by successive invasions of northern tribes—
slowly prepared for the phenomenal rise of the classical Greek
civilization. Its earliest manifestation was a widespread colonial
movement. The expansion was first westward. As early as in the eighth
century colonies were founded all over Sicily and Southern Italy—
at Cumae, Naxos, Syracuse, Katane, Megara, Rhegion, Sybaris,
Kroton, Tarentum, Poseidonia, etc. The movement continued during
the whole of the seventh century, reaching in 600 as far as Marseilles
and Spain and spreading also northeastward to Thasos, Chalkidike,
Thrace, and the cities of the Bosphorus. At the end of this period of
discovery and adventure we find Greece consisting of a number of
powerful city states each with its colonies and dependencies, ranging
from Asia Minor to Italy and Spain. All these cities were independent
units, knit together by a common religion, similar institutions and
customs, and the consciousness of the same origin. To symbolize this
unity there had arisen religious centers in various localities—Dodona,
Delphi, Olympia, Delos, Cape Mykale—to which all Greeks jour-

neyed to worship or consult the oracles. And, periodically, great religious festivals were celebrated—at Olympia, Corinth, Nemea, and Delphi—and hither Greeks from all parts of the world came to compete in athletic and musical contests while "barbarian" outsiders were strictly excluded. And thus were fostered the two dominating loyalties of the ancient Greeks—an intense local patriotism for the individual city state and the consciousness of a common Hellenism amid a "barbarian" world. Throughout Greek history we are aware of these two important factors which intermittently combined and separated the Greek city states.

Another element which constituted a bond among the Greeks was the creation of new forms of political institutions unknown in the powerful East—of democracies in the place of the old aristocracies and monarchies. The first stage in this transformation was the appearance of "tyrannies." In one Greek state after another we note in the later seventh century and during the sixth century the downfall of the powerful families and clans which had held the power for several centuries, and the substitution of the rule of one powerful man risen generally as champion of the people. This change began in Sikyon, Corinth, Megara, and in the Ionian cities and spread from city to city. Kypselos and Periander of Corinth, Orthagoras of Sikyon, Thrasyboulos of Miletos, Polykrates of Samos, Peisistratos of Athens are names which stand out with many others as the founders of the greatness of their respective cities. Under the rule of most of these tyrants, as well as of some of the early aristocrats, the arts flourished. It was then that Greek monumental sculpture began.

After centuries of modest production in small bronzes, terracottas, and ivories (see p. 51) there suddenly appears all over the Greek world an enthusiastic activity of temple building with sculpture in relief and in the round. We can catch a faint reflection of this brilliant dawn of Greek sculpture in the remains which have survived to this day. In Corfu, the ancient Kerkyra, a temple has come to light with an amazingly impressive pediment, dominated by a central Medusa (figs. 76, 374). In northern Thermos has been found another early temple with painted metopes (figs. 401, 402). The head of Hera at Olympia (fig. 138) is perhaps part of the cult group of Zeus and Hera of the old Heraion. At Delphi the Treasury of "Sikyon" (figs. 358, 404) and the splendid dedicatory

MAP OF GREECE AND THE AEGEAN ISLANDS

statues of Kleobis and Biton by [Poly]medes (fig. 17) bear witness
to the growing wealth of the Greek states and the increasing importance of the common sanctuary of Apollo. On the Akropolis in
Athens there arose a number of early temples, large and small, of
which the gaily painted limestone pedimental sculptures are now in
the Akropolis Museum—the "Achilles and Troilos" group (p. 120,
note 13), the Herakles and Hydra (fig. 376), the introduction of
Herakles to Olympos (fig. 380), the splendid bull attacked by lions
(fig. 377), and above all the "Bluebeard" or three-headed Typhon,
and the Herakles fighting Triton (figs. 378, 379). We do not even
know where some of the respective temples were situated, but we can
visualize nevertheless the splendid effect of the whole. Furthermore,
impressive single statues, like the colossal kouroi of Sounion (fig. 16)
and the calf-bearer dedicated by Rhombos (figs. 5, 6), show the boldness and skill of these early sculptors.

Farther east in the Islands and Asia Minor there is the same activity. At Ephesos a temple is built to Artemis with the help of
Kroisos, king of Lydia (560–546 or 555–541; figs. 265, 266). The
row of seated statues which lined the Sacred Way at Didyma (figs.
62, 264), the statues from the early temple of Hera at Samos, and
the reliefs from Xanthos and Assos (cf. fig. 403) are typical east
Greek products of the first half and third quarter of the sixth century. The flying Nike from Delos (fig. 77) and the Naxian Sphinx
at Delphi are two distinguished island products. In the West the
metopes from two temples of Selinus[1] (fig. 405) and the terracotta
sculptures from the temple of Athena at Syracuse (fig. 79) show
that Sicily kept pace in this artistic production.

This widespread prosperity and interest in art reach their acme
in the second half of the sixth century, which forms indeed the climax
in the first act of the drama of Greek civilization—the period when
Greece was as yet undisturbed either in the East or the West and
could work out her novel experiments unhampered. Athens under
Solon (594–593) and Peisistratos (c. 561–527) had risen to a powerful state. The marble pedimental sculptures representing the battle of
gods and giants (figs. 112, 385), the fine array of marble maidens
erected as dedicatory offerings on the Akropolis (figs. 270–273),
the statues of the later athletes and "Apollos" (figs. 20, 23), the

---

[1] Benndorf, *Metopen von Selinunt*, pls. I–IV; Gabrici, *Mem. Acc. Napoli*, V, 1924.

large number of splendid tomb monuments (figs. 423 f.) reflect this prosperity and show a high degree of refinement. But Athens was only one of many art-loving, prosperous states. The temple of Apollo at Delphi was rebuilt after a fire at an enormous expense in which the whole of Greece took part. The "Treasury" of the little island of Siphnos at Delphi (about 525) with its pediment (fig. 382) and magnificent frieze (figs. 418, 419, 487) and karyatids bears eloquent testimony to the widespread wealth of the time and the fine achievements of its artists. The Treasury of the Megarians at Olympia (fig. 383), the other great common sanctuary of the Greeks, is another example. Boeotia appears to have been particularly active, to judge from the beautiful series of "Apollo" statues (fig. 28) found in the Ptoan sanctuary and elsewhere. Even Sparta has presented us with a fine series of reliefs of the period (fig. 468).

In comparing these sculptures from so many localities with one another we note certain distinctions—a sturdiness, for instance, in the Peloponnesian products (cf. the Argive Athlete, fig. 17) and a softness and elaboration in the Ionian works (cf. the Didyma and Samos statues, figs. 62, 264, 110). Nevertheless, it is the common characteristics that stand out—their buoyancy and freshness, their dignity and decorative quality. They present us indeed with a spirited picture of this early civilization and help us to visualize it as a time of eager quest—when philosophers were trying to understand the physical structure of the universe, when political experiments were everywhere being tried, when new forms of literature were being evolved; and also as a time with a strictly local outlook. The Greek states were self-contained, actively content in their respective spheres, with a brilliant and yet limited activity. Their sculpture, however, with its sense for volume and design, and its progressive development toward the representation of nature has a universal quality shared by them all.

(b) Fifth Century

In the fifth century a new direction is given to the history of Greece. Her expansion had already stopped a century before. Now, at the end of the sixth century, she is herself threatened. The danger of Persia, the irresistible conqueror, looms in the East; in the West, Carthage and Etruria have risen as powerful rivals. Meantime the political aspect of the Greek states has again changed. The descendants of the beneficent tyrants, having abused their power, have in many places been overthrown and in their stead aristocracies and democracies have been established—the latter a novel form of government in the ancient world and one which we now regard as typically Greek. It fostered that sense of individualism and independence which was of the essence of a Greek city state, and thereby made more apparent both its weakness and its strength. Its weakness was shown when the danger of invasion threatened and its inability to present a united front became almost fatal to the common cause. On the other hand, it doubtless made possible the rapid rise to power of men of obscure origin like Themistokles, whose remarkable foresight turned the scale at a critical hour. The whole early part of the fifth century is taken up with the Persian danger. The attack on the Greek Islands began in 499. By 493 most of the East was subdued. The expedition against Greece proper was started in 492. Then came Marathon (490), Salamis (480), Plataia (479), the three great victories which decided the fate of Greece; in the West, Himera (480), which disposed of the Carthaginian danger in Sicily; and in the East the battles of Mykale (479) and the Eurymedon (467 or 466), which freed Miletos and the Eastern cities.

These were strenuous days in which all energies were devoted to the safeguarding of the state. Naturally it was not the time for the erection of many important buildings and monuments. We have a few precious examples just preceding the cataclysm, for instance, the sculptures of the temple of Apollo Daphnephoros at Eretria (figs. 281, 284), which probably still belong before the turn of the century; and a few private dedications on the Akropolis (fig. 159). The pediments of the temple of Aphaia at Aigina (figs. 388, 389, 103, 113, 114), begun perhaps about 500, were brought to their completion about 480, an eloquent testimony to the prosperity of the island at that period (shortly before her subjugation by Athens in 456), and also of the protection from the Persian danger which her outlying position afforded her. But otherwise there is little artistic activity to record during the actual years of the war and for a decade or so later, except a few memorials by which Greece showed her gratitude to the gods for her delivery: a platform with trophies erected by the Athenians in front of the Athenian Treasury at Delphi as a dedicatory offering after Marathon (p. 126); a snake tripod in the same precinct, dedicated as a joint offering of the

Greek states to commemorate the victory of Plataia; and a new
group of the Tyrannicides (fig. 571) set up in the Athenian market-place (477) to take the place of that carried off to Persia by
Xerxes. All more ambitious undertakings had to bide their time.
Athens could not be expected to restore her temples when she was
straining every nerve to fortify her city and to strengthen her
navy.

In the second quarter of the fifth century we find the Greek world
recovering. The great temple of Zeus was begun at Olympia
(c. 468); Sicily under her tyrants (who retained their power there
longer than elsewhere) was becoming more and more prosperous.
Temple E was built at Selinus (figs. 410–413). A fine bronze
chariot group (of which a charioteer [fig. 285] and other fragments have survived) was dedicated at Delphi by a Syracusan
prince. Athens, too, was bestirring herself and was finding time at
last to erect her important war monuments. The colossal Athena
Promachos (fig. 596) by Pheidias was set up on the Akropolis, "an
offering from the spoils of the Persians who landed at Marathon,"
and at Delphi was dedicated a group of deities and heroes "with
one human figure, that of Miltiades, the general," another work of
Pheidias and it, too, in memory of Marathon.

Not only is there in this period a general revival of artistic production, but a new element has entered Greek sculpture. The Greek
horizon has been enlarged, the long struggles with representational
problems have borne their fruit, and Greek sculpture now assumes
an idealistic, spiritual character which gives it a new grandeur. In
literature we perceive it best in the works of Aischylos; in sculpture
perhaps in the pediments and metopes of the temple of Zeus at
Olympia (figs. 390–393, 355, 414, 319). And inevitably there arose
now artists of the first rank, able to perpetuate in their work the new
outlook. Of Pythagoras and Kalamis we have only the enthusiastic
comments of those who had the good fortune to know their works
(pp. 199–204); of the rhythmical sculptures of Myron we can form
some conception by a few Roman copies which have survived (figs.
578, 584).

The second half of the fifth century is the climax of the second
period in Greek sculpture, as the second half of the sixth was of the
first period. At first, it was a time of comparative peace and material
prosperity. In 454–453 the treasury of the confederacy of Delos

MAP OF SOUTHERN ITALY AND SICILY

was transferred from Delos to Athens; that is, the funds contributed by the members of the League for the upkeep of a strong navy as a protection against Persia were virtually at the disposal of Athens. In 446–445 a thirty years' peace was signed between Athens and the Peloponnesians. The outward circumstances were thus favorable for artistic activity. Moreover, the elimination of the Persian danger, which had for a long time threatened annihilation, brought as a reaction a certain exaltation and a new dignity and importance to Greece. Athens, under the guidance of Perikles, seized her opportunity and spent her large resources for the beautification of her city. And thus arose the Parthenon (447–432; cf. figs. 415, 416, 131, 486, 488, 489, 356, 291, 394–396, 91, 292, 351) with the chryselephantine Athena by Pheidias (438; figs. 595, 597–605), the Propylaia as a palatial entrance to the Akropolis (437), the new Hall of Mysteries at Eleusis (c. 430), the temple by the Ilissos (c. 450; fig. 420), the temple at Rhamnous with a cult statue by Agorakritos (c. 435–421; figs. 633, 634), and many other memorials, large and small. The leading sculptor in Athens was Pheidias. The idealism and majesty of his works, especially his chryselephantine Zeus at Olympia (figs. 606, 607), left an abiding impression on Greek art and determined its character thenceforth. Greek art now assumes a universality consistent with its broadened horizon. Pheidias had many distinguished associates and followers—Alkamenes (pp. 237 ff.), Agorakritos (pp. 240 ff.), Kresilas (pp. 233 ff.), etc., whose works in Athens and elsewhere gained wide renown. His greatest contemporary was Polykleitos of Argos (pp. 246 ff.), whose sense for harmonious composition we can appreciate even in the Roman copies which have survived of his Doryphoros (figs. 645–649) and Diadoumenos (figs. 650–652). Besides works which can be connected with prominent sculptors, there are others to which we can attach no names but which are among the finest that have survived. The Niobid in Rome (fig. 4) and the two figures in Copenhagen (figs. 92, 118) perhaps come from a pedimental composition shortly after 450.

If Athens had been allowed to carry out her imperialistic policy, if she had succeeded in subjugating completely, first the tributaries to the Delian League and then the Peloponnese, the history of Greece might have been that of Italy, with Athens in the rôle of Rome. But Athens was stopped in mid-career. After she had safely established her sea empire the trial of strength between herself and the Peloponnese began (431). It lasted first for ten years until the peace of Nikias (421) and then again from 419 to almost the end of the century. For a long time the result remained in question, but the disaster which overtook the Athenian expedition to Sicily (415–413) had much to do with the ultimate downfall of Athens. The decisive battle was won by the Spartan Lysander at Aigospotamoi in 405. The dream of empire which had come to Athens, as it has to many nations, was over. She was merely a small city state once more.

The immediate influence on art of the Peloponnesian war was a stoppage of various building activities such as the Propylaia on the Akropolis. But as the war dragged on in a sometimes rather desultory fashion, normal life asserted itself and art regained a place. We have many fine monuments by which to judge this art of the last third of the fifth century—at Athens perhaps the Hephaisteion frieze (fig. 293), the Erechtheion (c. 421–413; fig. 502; and c. 409–406; figs. 296, 728), and the temple of Nike (c. 426; figs. 295, 297) with its "balustrade" (c. 410; figs. 504, 506); at Sounion the temple of Poseidon (c. 423); at Argos the temple of Hera (c. 420; fig. 165); and farther afield the temple of Apollo at Bassae in mountainous Arkadia (figs. 197–199, 201–204, 298–301); the flying Nike of Paionios at Olympia (figs. 637, 642); and in the East the Nereid monument at Xanthos (figs. 302–304), and the Heroön of Gjölbaschi (figs. 421, 422, 326). And besides this architectural sculpture, single statues like the Idolino (figs. 43, 44) and exquisite grave reliefs like those of Hegeso (fig. 429) and Glykylla (fig. 306) testify to the beauty of private memorials of the period.

The delicate character and refinement of these monuments hardly suggest that they were created against a background of bitter warfare (we may except the tumultuous Phigaleia frieze). They are rather the logical development of the art of the preceding period, showing the continuance of artistic appreciation and well-being. As so often in history, the events of the time influence not contemporary but subsequent art. Indeed the soft, transparent draperies of many of the sculptures, evidently reproducing some fine and precious material (cf. p. 100), suggest an era of luxury. The same impression is gained by the continued output of chryselephantine temple statues (e.g., the Hera of Argos by Polykleitos [fig. 654]), the expensive dedications, the splendid character of the festivals and processions, and the defrayal by private citizens of costly state duties. The mental outlook may be gauged by the fact that this is the time of Euripides, Thucydides, Sokrates, and Aristophanes, following upon that of Herodotos and Sophokles. The old acceptance of traditional religion and customs is waning and there appears in its stead a new spirit of inquiry and scepticism, no longer confined as it had been in the sixth century to investigations of physical phenomena, but active now in the moral sphere. A time of individualism has begun.

(c) *Fourth Century* (400–323 B.C.)

THE end of the Peloponnesian war was not followed—as had been that of the Persian wars—by an era of peace. Sparta's domination was even more distasteful to the Greeks than had been that of Athens; and when, after the battle of Leuktra (371), Thebes assumed the leadership, hostilities continued until her leader, Epameinondas, was killed at Mantineia (362), and therewith her power ended. It was clear that no one Greek city was able to impose her will on the others. Local independence was too deep-rooted. In the meantime a new experiment was being tried. The old idea of the city state was being enlarged and various confederations and leagues gradually formed round the most prominent states—for instance, the Athenian, Boeotian, Arkadian, Achaean, and Thessalian. Unfortunately this proved no solution. Local jealousies and bickerings continued until Macedonia under Philip (359–336) and Alexander (336–323) at last subjugated the whole of Greece.

As we review the art of the fourth century we realize how these long-drawn-out hostilities gradually impoverished Greece. Compared with the great periods of public building in the sixth and fifth centuries the output of the fourth century appears modest. In the first quarter of the century we can cite the temple of Asklepios at Epidauros with its small pedimental groups (figs. 716–718) and its delicate akroteria (figs. 710–713). The temple of Tegea with sculptures probably by Skopas (figs. 690–693, 696) was a magnificent undertaking, perhaps built to celebrate the overthrow of the Spartan yoke soon after 371. The temple of Apollo at Delphi, which had been destroyed in 373, was rebuilt shortly afterward by an international subscription. But the majority of artistic enterprises at this time were either private dedications and grave monuments (cf. figs.

317, 428)—for private fortunes do not always decline with public ones—or were undertaken outside of Greece proper by the princes of Asia Minor. The Mausoleum at Halikarnassos (figs. 720–722, 729, 730, 735, 313, 314, 228), the temple of Artemis at Sardes, the temple of Artemis at Ephesos (figs. 705, 703, 328), even such single master-pieces as the Aphrodite of Knidos by Praxiteles (fig. 668) were all commissioned in Asiatic Greece. And the prominent sculptors of the time had to go eastward to find important work. But that Greece was still capable of great things is proved by the appearance of three such geniuses as Praxiteles, Skopas, and Lysippos in the sculptural field and of thinkers like Plato and Aristotle. Prose became a high art with such writers as Lysias and Demosthenes, and drama took a new lease on life at the end of this period with the comedies of Menander. We are clearly still in a creative period. The individualism initiated by such men as Euripides and Sokrates is reflected in the personal note of fourth-century sculpture. The impersonal grandeur of fifth-century art gives place to a gracious charm and delicacy.

(d) Hellenistic Period (323–100 B.C.)

WITH Alexander we have reached the so-called Hellenistic age. By a series of brilliant campaigns he conquered the old kingdoms of Asia Minor, then marched victoriously farther and farther east until he reached distant India. It was a remarkable achievement, the more so as it was consummated in the brief thirteen years of Alexander's reign (336–323). If he had lived he would doubtless have consolidated his empire and the consequences of this Greek penetration would have been even more far-reaching. But his premature death was the signal for revolts and disaffections everywhere and Alexander's vast structure crumbled immediately. But not entirely. After more than twenty years of continuous warfare and intrigues there emerged in 301 four large monarchies under Macedonian generals—Macedonia and Greece under Kassandros; Thrace and Asia Minor under Lysimachos; the Oriental provinces under Seleukos; and Egypt under Ptolemy. These four kingdoms, with some independent states like Pergamon and Rhodes, continued in existence for two or three centuries, marked by great undertakings but also by constant warfare. The Greek inability to form powerful political units again showed itself in these altered circumstances.

Endless quarrels and hostilities characterize the history of these kingdoms, until all-conquering Rome annexed one territory after another and finally in 30 B.C. included them all in her great empire, and thereby initiated a long era of peace.

The art of this Hellenistic period (323–100 B.C.) is a remarkable phenomenon. Though politically Greece has become a mere adjunct of Macedonia, from the point of view of culture she is still paramount. The small Hellenic city states have been enlarged to embrace the "Hellenistic" world; artistic activity has shifted to new centers —to Pergamon, Ephesos, Rhodes, Tralles, Alexandria; but the artists are still Greek and their products continue in the Greek tradition, modified both in scope and in spirit to correspond to the new outlook. In contrast to the earlier periods the majority of Hellenistic sculpture is not architectural. Commemorative single statues and groups predominate, and a new importance is given to portraiture (p. 83). Though in this long epoch of two or three centuries production was constant and extended over a wide area, it is difficult to trace any consecutive development. There are obvious borrowings and adaptations from the past side by side with important original creations. It is also difficult to distribute the material among local schools, e.g., of Pergamon, Rhodes, and Alexandria, though the attempt is constantly made. We note, to be sure, various tendencies, but they appear in different localities,[2] and inscriptions teach us that artists from all over Greece and Asia were at work at the same place (e.g., in Pergamon and Rhodes).[3] Individual styles apply to certain monuments, but not to localities.[4] In other words, Hellenistic art is truly international. For a general survey it is better therefore simply to enumerate some conspicuous datable works of this period.

The so-called Alexander sarcophagus from the royal burial place at Sidon (figs. 748, 176) is a product of the last quarter of the fourth century. The Tyche of Antioch by Eutychides, a pupil of

[2] E.g., the "Alexandrian morbidezza" is found not only in sculptures from Alexandria but in a considerable number from other sites (Priene, Chios, Athens, etc.).
[3] Cf. Loewy, *Inschriften*, Nos. 170 ff. Artists at work in Rhodes, for instance, hailed from Crete, Halikarnassos, Antioch, Laodikeia, Soloi, Miletos, etc.
[4] The vigorous "Pergamene" style is characteristic of the Galatian groups (see below), but is conspicuously absent from such statues as the Hermaphrodite from Pergamon in Istanbul (fig. 53) or the relief No. 90 also in Istanbul. Furthermore, many sculptures in the vigorous "Pergamene" style have been found elsewhere than in Pergamon (e.g., the giant's head, No. 2506 in the British Museum, in Trebizond, etc.).

Lysippos, made after the foundation of Antioch in 300, is preserved in Roman copies (figs. 753–755). The portrait of Demosthenes by Polyeuktos (fig. 757) was erected c. 280. All three are characteristic products of the early Hellenistic age.

Pergamon supplies us with valuable material for the succeeding period. Attalos I, king of Pergamon, won a momentous victory over the invading hordes of Galatians or Gauls who had long constituted a danger comparable to that of Persia more than two centuries ago. This achievement was commemorated in two splendid dedications. One was a group of statues erected either after the decisive victory in 241 or after the end of the war in 228. Marble copies of this group are preserved in the famous Dying Gaul in the Capitoline Museum, and the Gaul killing himself and his wife, in the National Museum in Rome (figs. 108, 178). The other memorial consisted of a group of statues, two-thirds life-size, of Gauls, Amazons, Persians, giants. They were set up on the Akropolis in Athens probably on the occasion of Attalos' visit there in 200 B.C., and were seen by Pausanias in the second century A.D.[5] From his description, copies of these originals have been recognized in several small statues in Naples, Rome, Venice, and the Louvre (cf. fig. 120). Eumenes II, son of Attalos, enriched his city with a series of splendid buildings, one of which was the great altar of Zeus with its famous frieze representing the battle of gods and giants (cf. figs. 177, 334, 335) and the smaller one with the adventures of Telephos (196–159). These three sets of sculptures give us a vivid picture of Pergamene activities during the second half of the third and the first half of the second century B.C. We know that for their production artists were employed not only from Pergamon, but from Athens, Ephesos, and Rhodes;[6] so that we must beware of claiming as Pergamene qualities which may be characteristic of their time rather than of one place.

As examples of second-century work from other localities we may mention the sculptures of the temple at Lykosoura by Damophon (figs. 757–760), the statues from Priene,[7] and the coarse reliefs from Magnesia in the Louvre.[8] A series of portrait statues found at Delos (recently published in *Délos*, XIII) dates from the middle of the sec-

---

[5] I. 25. 2.

[6] Fraenkel, *Inschriften von Pergamon*, pp. 70–84; Pliny, *N.H.* XXXIV. 8 a.

[7] Wiegand-Schrader, *Priene*, pp. 366 ff.

[8] *Catalogue sommaire des marbres antiques*, No. 2881.

ond century to about 88 B.C., the year of the sack of Delos (cf. fig. 240). The first century B.C. was an age chiefly of copying and adapting former creations. The Borghese Warrior (fig. 107) signed by Agasias of Ephesos, the Belvedere torso (fig. 771) and the bronze boxer (fig. 770) signed by Apollonios of Athens, once thought to be first-century originals, more probably reproduce second-century works by able copyists.

It is difficult even in the third and second centuries to trace a consecutive development. On the whole we may say that the earlier traditions are still strong in the late fourth and the early third century, while the later Hellenistic age is characterized both by a baroque realism and a rococo style with genre subjects. But there is also a constant harking back to earlier types, so that we get classicist and realistic work side by side. Taken as a whole the Hellenistic period presents a singularly confused spectacle compared with the steady trend of the earlier epochs.

As a matter of fact with the subjugation of Greece by Macedonia and the loss of independence the city states seem to have lost the mainsprings of their existence, and henceforth there is merely an outward show of what was most characteristic in Greek life—their constitutions and law courts, their festivals and games, and their religion. Though their culture spreads triumphantly eastward, at home the sources of creation gradually dry up. Fortunately an impetus was given to art by the activities of the Hellenistic princes in Pergamon, Alexandria, Rhodes, and elsewhere. In these products we observe an enlargement of sympathy and so of scope (cf. pp. 82 ff.). Allegorical subjects, rustic scenes, figures in violent movement, languid women, old men, and children are favorite themes, and they are moreover treated with a new realism. The art of portraiture is developed. It was not until Rome conquered the Greek states one by one that creative Greek art practically stopped.

When we blame Greece for her inability to combine into one political unit, and when the constant strife and bickerings between the various Greek states contrast unfavorably with the steady purpose of Rome, let us remember that there is another side to the story. The same spirit which created trouble in Greece, that love of local independence which would not brook the overlordship of a neighbor, is also responsible for the individualistic artistic output of these city states. The friendly rivalries among the artists, poets, and philosophers of the different states who were allowed to develop their genius in an atmosphere of freedom must be set against the bitter political animosities. And the fact remains that Rome with all her political genius was a beggar and borrower in art. Since nations no more than individuals combine all the qualities, we must choose what appears of the most permanent value, or at least appreciate the circumstances which allowed each people to make its particular contribution. And with Greece it was essentially the spirit of freedom that stimulated artistic enterprise. "We have received from our ancestors a free state" is the proud boast of Perikles to his fellow Athenians.[9] With no other form of government would the buoyant, idealistic sculpture of Greece have been possible.

(e) The Greek View of Life

In conclusion, before we pass to our next chapter and to the consideration of the sculpture itself, let us pause a moment to consider what was the view of life that was evolved by this Greek civilization. What was the background of ideals against which Greek sculpture was created?

CIVIC IDEAL   The civic ideal of Athens at the height of her power (431 B.C.) is admirably brought out in the famous funeral speech of Perikles as recounted by Thucydides[10] in his succinct, pregnant style. Briefly and with restraint Perikles enumerates the things that Athens values, that make up her creed of life. They are, first, a democratic form of government where "the administration is in the hands of the many and not of the few," where "the law secures equal justice to all alike," and where "the claim of excellence is recognized," so that "when a citizen is in any way distinguished, he receives public advancement, not as a matter of privilege, but as the reward of merit"; in short where "a man may benefit his country whatever be the obscurity of his condition." It is not a blatant democracy: "A spirit of reverence pervades our public acts; we are prevented from doing wrong by respect for the authorities and for the laws, having an especial regard for those which are ordained for the protection of the injured as well as for those unwritten laws which bring upon the transgressor of them the reprobation of the general sentiment." And in this democracy it is individual responsibility that is fostered: "We regard a man who takes no interest in public affairs, not as

9 Thucydides II. 36.				10 II. 35 ff.

harmless, but as a useless character; and if few of us are originators we are all sound judges of a policy." Courage and skill in warfare are encouraged, not, as at Sparta, by intensive military training but by an all-round education: "Whereas they from early youth are always undergoing laborious exercises which are to make them brave, we live at ease, and yet are equally ready to face the perils which they face." "And thus our city is equally admirable in peace and in war. For we are lovers of the beautiful, yet simple in our tastes, and we cultivate the mind without loss of manliness. Wealth we employ, not for talk and ostentation, but because of the opportunities for action which it affords." (And let us remember here that the wealthy were called upon to bear heavy expenses for the state, such as the defrayal of trierarchies [i.e., the maintenance of warships], of the *choregia* [the equipment of the costly choruses of tragedies, etc.], and of embassies to Delphi, etc., which the patriotism of the city demanded to be in a fitting style.) The brilliant festivals with their colorful processions, the contests of athletic prowess, music, and literature, the unsurpassed art of the Periklean age are thus simply described: "We have provided for our minds very many relaxations from toil; we have regular games and sacrifices throughout the year;[11] our personal establishments are handsome; and the delight which we daily feel in these things banishes vexations." An amazingly concise and eloquent description by someone who does not believe in long speeches; for he proceeds with this beautiful appeal: "Instead of listening [to a discourse on a brave defense] I would have you day by day fix your eyes on the greatness of Athens, until you become filled with love of her."

As a preparation for this civic life the young Athenian was trained in athletics and in music (cf. p. 25). We know that athletic prowess was encouraged by the games at Olympia and elsewhere and that to the victor was given great honor (cf. p. 29). Even in our days of sport enthusiasm some of Pindar's odes in praise of these young athletes seem somewhat excessive in tone. But we must remember that to the Greeks, at least to the enlightened ones, a perfect body was also a means to a higher end: "In keeping the harmony

ATHLETICS

---

11 There were about seventy feast days in the year. The great Panathenaia took place once every four years and lasted six to nine days. It consisted of musical and athletic contests, warlike exercises, torch and boat races (at the Peiraieus), and an impressive procession immortalized for us on the Parthenon frieze.

of his body in tune, his constant aim is to preserve the symphony which resides in the soul."[12]

MUSIC   This "symphony" was fostered by music: "The music master makes rhythm and harmony familiar to the souls of boys, and they become gentler and more refined and having more rhythm and harmony in them they become more efficient in speech and in action. The whole life of man stands in need of good harmony and good rhythm."[18]

Greek literature is full of this ideal of harmony and temperance: "A day can prostrate and a day upraise all that is mortal; but the gods approve sobriety and forwardness abhor."[14] "God has everywhere assigned superiority to the mean, though the ways of his administration vary."[15] The underlying theme indeed of most Greek tragedies is the punishment of ὕβρις. The procession of maidens in the Parthenon frieze (fig. 291), and such figures as the Idolino (figs. 43, 44) and the Farnese Diadoumenos (fig. 621) show us this ideal of reverence and temperance embodied in art.

LOVE OF   But what the Greeks considered most characteristic of themselves
KNOWLEDGE   was love of knowledge: "The spirited element . . . is attributed . . . to the natives of Thrace, and Scythia, and generally speaking of the northern countries; the love of knowledge would be chiefly attributed to our own country; and the love of riches people would especially connect with the Phoenicians and the Egyptians."[16] This "knowledge" comprised, for the elementary education, reading and writing (included in music, μουσική), mathematics, and the study of the poets, especially Homer (the average Greek seems to have known his Iliad and Odyssey by heart). A promising youth would proceed to natural science, rhetoric, grammar, and above all philosophy; for his nimble mind was ever ready for speculation. Plato in the Academy, Aristotle in the Lyceum, and the prominent Sophists supplied this need for higher education. The quality of this speculation is shown by the saying which Plato had put over the Academy: "Let no man ignorant of geometry enter here." And the wide range of knowledge covered by the educated Greek is suggested by the variety of subjects on which he wrote. Not many learned men of today would write authoritatively on Law, Kingship, Piety, and the

12 Plato, *Republic* IX. 591.   18 Plato, *Protagoras* 326 B.
14 Sophokles, *Ajax* 131 ff.   15 Aischylos, *Eumenides* 520.
16 Plato, *Republic* IV. 435.

Origin of the Universe,[17] or combine the professions of an astrono-
mer, a geometer, a physician, and a legislator.[18] In Greece this was
the rule rather than the exception.

And then the Greek loved spectacles and sights. It was part of   FESTIVALS
his joy of life and of his aesthetic sense: "Does he [the tyrant] not
bury himself in his house and live for the most part the life of a
woman, while he positively envies all other citizens who travel
abroad and see grand sights?"[19] It is to satisfy this love of "grand
sights" that the many processions and festivals were instituted in
Greek life.

It has often been noted that the Greeks rarely speak of art. Compared with us, indeed, they are strangely inarticulate on the subject. But then they were an extraordinarily artistic nation in whom
art was evidently taken for granted. Even so their power of analysis
enabled them here, too, to judge clearly. Art to them was an end in
itself, not a means to teach something else. "Have the arts severally
any other interest to pursue than their own highest perfection?"[20]
How refreshing is this objectivity after the subjective estimates of
many of our writers!

Interwoven into each one of these Greek ideals was religion. There   RELIGION
was the religion of certain prescribed rites and sacrifices in the worship of the various gods and goddesses, a merely formal observance
day by day, and yet one which continually connected life with im-
material values; and there was the religion which transcended current beliefs and found its popular expression in the Eleusinian mysteries or produced a mystic like Plato to whom the objective world
was merely a symbol of reality. But however deep or shallow, however analytical or unquestioning, this religion stirred the Greek soul
to aspiration and creation.

Public life, then, service to the state in time of peace and war, the
cultivation of the body and the mind by athletics, music, poetry,
mathematics, and philosophy, relaxation in games, the theatre and
processions, and a reverent worship of the supernatural—these
made up the chief activities of an Athenian citizen. It is a radiant
picture which Athens presents to us of a full and rounded life, perhaps the sanest that man has evolved; but in fairness we must re-

---

17 Like, e.g., Akellos, cf. Diogenes Laertios VIII. 80.
18 Like, e.g., Eudoxos of Knidos, cf. *op. cit.* VIII. 86.
19 Plato, *Republic*, IX. 579.   20 *Ibid.*, I. 341.

member that this life was only for the select—the male Athenian
citizens—and that women, metics (resident aliens), and slaves were excluded from much of it. It has been computed[21] that in Perikles' time
there were in Athens 150,000 to 170,000 citizens, 35,000 to 40,000
metics, and perhaps 80,000 to 100,000 slaves (the totals comprise men,
women, and children). The metics were not allowed to vote or hold
political office. The slaves, though from all accounts generally well
treated and allowed considerable independence of action, had not, of
course, the same privileges as the citizens. And the women mostly led a
quiet life indoors, apart from the intellectual and athletic life of the
men. This exclusion of part of the population from what was most
valuable in Greek life we must always remember in our estimate of it.

[21] No actual statistics are available; cf. Tod, *Cambridge Ancient History*, V, p. 11;
Gomme, *Population of Athens*, pp. 21 f.; Westermann, *Harvard Classical Studies*,
Special Vol., 1941, p. 469.

CHAPTER II

THE GENERAL CHARACTERISTICS OF
GREEK SCULPTURE

BEFORE studying Greek sculpture in detail we must view it as a whole and analyze its general characteristics. Perhaps nothing could bring home to us better the difference in horizons between the Greeks and ourselves than the comparison of a work such as Bourdelle's Beethoven (fig. 1) with, let us say, the head of Kladeos from Olympia (fig. 2). Both are great works of art. In each the sculptor has been able to sum up the spirit of his age, and to lift it to a spiritual plane. But what a contrast between the fresh, forward-looking purity of the one and the brooding comprehension of the other! The life that was simple and joyous has become infinitely complex. For we must remember that when the Greeks of classical times began their career civilization was still young. Everything that has happened in the last three thousand years was to them non-existent. It is difficult to realize at once what this implies. It means that their artistic background was confined to the products of Egypt, Western Asia, and, in part, of Crete; and even of these their knowledge was limited, especially in literature, for what existed of Eastern writings was not easily accessible. Their own past was dimly remembered in the form of myths and legends. So practically the only literature they knew was Homer; the only history they were cognizant of was the Trojan war. In religion they had come in contact in the East with beliefs in heterogeneous gods and monsters, and from this they had developed the anthropomorphic religion found in Homer and Hesiod. In other words, most of the influences —artistic, intellectual, and religious—which act upon the modern man were as yet unformed. The background was simpler and the human mind had the freshness of youth.

In the centuries in which the classical Greek civilization was developed great changes happened. From its primitive beginning it passed through many stages to a more complicated outlook, and during this time it created a large part of what constitutes our

Western culture. Nevertheless, it is possible to view the Greek mind as a whole. We will endeavor to do so and to see how its quality determined the character of Greek sculpture.

THE GREEK MENTALITY

The three outstanding characteristics which strike us when we analyze the Greek mentality applied to art are directness, agility, and a feeling for beauty.

Directness

The directness was no doubt largely the result of a simpler outlook. It is a quality which we with our more complicated natures have lost; and when we come in contact with it, it affects us like a fresh breeze on a sultry day. It enabled the Greeks to keep their eyes on the essentials without the distraction of superfluous details. In literature this shows itself in their vivid similes, their keen observation, and also in a bald sincerity in stating facts.[1] Take such a description as Aischylos': . . . ταχύπτεροι πνοαὶ, . . . ποντίων τε κυμάτων ἀνήριθμον γέλασμα, παμμῆτόρ τε γῆ,[2] "Swift winged winds . . ., and numberless laughter of waves, and earth the mother of all." Could there be a truer and more beautiful description of the much-besung wind and sea and earth? It reaches out to the chief quality of each, transforms it into poetry, and creates thereby something fundamental and permanent. Or take Klytaimnestra's analysis of her emotions (in Sophokles' Elektra[3]) when she hears of the death of her son Orestes, whose vengeance she dreaded: "Are these glad tidings? Rather would I say sad but of profit." It is a simple statement of the case, without pretense or blinking of facts; and perfectly concise. Greek literature is full of these pregnant, clear-eyed sayings. The much-quoted epitaph, "His father Philip laid here to rest his twelve-year-old son Nikoteles, his high hope,"[4] is another example of this combination of sincerity and conciseness. What could be added to the essential facts conveyed in "laid to rest," "twelve-year-old," and "high hope" which would not be a superfluity? And let us remember Aristotle's definition of superfluities, "That which makes no perceptible difference by its presence or its absence is no real part of the whole."[5]

It is this feeling for the whole unencumbered by superfluities which gives Greek art its peculiar greatness. At the very beginning

1 For an excellent discussion of this subject, cf. Livingstone, *The Greek Genius and Its Meaning to Us.*
2 *Prometheus Bound* 88 ff.   3 766.
4 Kallimachos, *Epigr.* 19.   5 *Poetics* 8. 4.

of his career the Greek sculptor went straight to the essentials. In the early "Apollo" statues (cf. figs. 15 ff.) why is it that in spite of their stiffness and faulty construction they are full of life? Because the important functional parts of the body are properly accented, the details are omitted, and each and every part passes into and connects with the adjoining part. In the Apollo of Melos, for instance, what a clear realization we obtain of the anatomical structure—the chest, the abdominal region, the pelvis, the kneecap, and ankle; the arms are not suspended from, but seem to grow from, the shoulders, the legs from the trunk, the head from the neck; and so on with every member. Moreover, the rendering is simplified; the important parts are made to stand out and there are no incidents, no superfluities. The result is that we have the impression of an organic whole which can function and live. And this is true of all Greek sculpture during its best periods.

The second outstanding characteristic of the Greeks we may take *Agility* to be their agility. It was stimulated doubtless by the geography of the country. For the combination of mountains and sea tended both to separate the Greek peoples from one another and to stimulate emigration. The mountains acted as barriers and the sea invited adventures. Hence the formation of a number of separate communities distributed over a large area including Greece, western Asia Minor, the Aegean Islands, southern Italy, and a few outlying places in Spain and France. This double circumstance insured on the one hand compact community life in small city states, on the other the variety of stimulus derived from heterogeneous peoples; all of which made for lively activity, because individual responsibility in a small state and rivalry with other states are apt to invite energy. This striving for adventure and for knowledge led the Greeks into many untried paths. It is responsible for the amazing number of their discoveries in almost every field of intellectual activity. "To be learning something is the greatest of pleasures, not only to the philosopher but also to the rest of mankind, however small their capacity for it," is Aristotle's definition of happiness[6] of which Plato's more imaginative rendering is, "He whose heart has been set on the love of learning and on true wisdom and has chiefly exercised this part of himself, this man must without fail have thoughts that are immortal and divine."[7]

6 *Poetics* IV. 4.   7 *Timaios* 90 A.

In sculpture this agility of mind and this love of knowledge are likewise responsible for a great deal. They meant progress and development. Without them Greek sculpture might have remained stationary, never surpassing the attainments of Oriental artists. The Egyptian sculptor, for instance, with all his wonderful feeling for the value of essentials, practised his art for thousands of years without solving some of its difficulties. He followed throughout the old law of frontality,[8] his knowledge of anatomy remained primitive, and in his reliefs proper perspective was never attained. The agile mind of the Greek determined to wrestle with these problems. Not content with what had been accomplished before him, he was eager to solve new problems, and so he started out on his adventure of representing a human body in all manner of postures, constructed according to nature, with its parts in proper relation and perspective, both in the round and in relief. To a pioneer in the field it was a formidable task. But with remarkable perseverance the Greek artist accomplished it, and his solution of these problems was like the removal of shackles which had hampered the free development of art for generations. The human figure, by its movements and gestures, could henceforth express action and emotion. In a century or two we pass from the Apollo of Tenea (fig. 22) to the Idolino (figs. 43, 44), from the Nike of Delos (figs. 77, 78) to the Nike of Paionios (figs. 637, 642), from the Spartan ancestor relief (fig. 468) to the Hegeso stele (fig. 429).

Feeling for Beauty   A love of truth and of knowledge could easily have made realists of the Greeks; but their realism was transformed into idealism by their third great characteristic—their feeling for beauty. Beauty to them was not something apart from daily life but interwoven into every phase of it. The beauty of their own landscape undoubtedly quickened their sensibilities in this direction. Its grandeur and suavity, its rich colors and fine contours, its elusive, subtle quality would inevitably influence a young, impressionable people. It would incline them to regard beauty as an integral part of their lives and to find their happiness in the loveliness of their immediate surroundings. And their sense for beauty grew so strong that it became the underlying principle in their lives. For they made a great discovery—one that we have lost since, perhaps through Puritan interpretations, but

[8] Frontality I take to mean a perfect symmetry in the two sides of the body, i.e., the equal distribution of weight on the two legs. This admits of the torsion of the body which we find adequately rendered in some Egyptian sculptures.

are beginning to realize again—that goodness and beauty are identical, not only figuratively but actually. "Virtue it appears will be a kind of health and beauty and good habit of the soul; and vice will be a disease and deformity and sickness of it," says Plato in his Republic;[9] and with the Greeks it was a generally accepted principle. "Then good language and good harmony and grace and good rhythm all depend upon a good nature, by which I mean a mind that is really well and nobly constituted in its moral character," Plato says again in his Republic;[10] and in his Symposion:[11] "From the love of the beautiful has sprung every good in heaven and earth." Most eloquent of all is the current Greek expression for a "gentleman"— καλὸς κἀγαθός, "beautiful and good." As we have seen (p. 17), Greek and especially Athenian education was planned directly with this end in view; and athletics and music were given the most prominent places, one to foster the beauty of the body, the other of the mind. That exercise develops the body is easily accepted by us today; but that art and music make men good is not so generally believed. Yet the Athenians practised this creed with good results; at least they won a reputation, Plato tells us, "throughout Europe and Asia" "for the beauties of their bodies and the various virtues of their souls."[12] Let us learn from Plato how this can be accomplished. In dealing with the education of his guardians in his Republic,[13] he gives us a specific account. Sokrates asks: "Ought we not to seek out artists who by the power of genius can trace out the nature of the fair and the graceful, that our young men, dwelling as it were in a healthful region, may drink in good from every quarter, whence any emanation from noble works may strike upon their eye or their ear, like a gale wafting health from salubrious lands, and win them imperceptibly from their earliest childhood into resemblance, love, and harmony with the true beauty of reason?" And when Glaukon assents Sokrates continues: "Is it then on these accounts that we attach such supreme importance to a musical education, because rhythm and harmony sink most deeply into the recesses of the soul, and take most powerful hold of it, bringing gracefulness in their train, and making a man graceful if he be rightly nurtured?" And finally he sums up, "There can be no fairer spectacle than that of a man who combines the possession of moral beauty in his soul with outward beauty of form, corresponding and harmonizing with the former, because the same great pattern enters into both." Translated into conduct this aesthetic ideal became a reverence for sobriety and temperance. As an imaginative, southern people the Greeks no doubt had strong feelings difficult to control; but they recognized that temperance was a kind of harmony, and therefore desirable. So μηδὲν ἄγαν, "nothing too much," became their motto, and ὕβρις, "insolence," their abomination.

Naturally in the art of sculpture the Greek sense of beauty found a fruitful field. It is directly responsible for the most characteristic quality, idealism. The creation of beauty was the sculptor's chief interest and his types are selected with this end in view. "But when you want to represent beautiful figures," says Sokrates to the artist Parrhasios, "since it is not easy to find everything without a flaw in a single human being, do you not then collect from a number what is beautiful in each, so that the whole body may appear beautiful?" And Parrhasios admits that such is their practice. This sums up very simply the Greek point of view. It is not realism and truth to nature but perfection of form that the Greeks consciously strove for. And this beauty of form was further enhanced by their feeling for design, which gave to their work a highly decorative quality. It is particularly strong in the archaic period when stylization took the place of correctness of modeling, but it was not lost even in the more naturalistic periods, and always gives style to the whole—the style which distinguishes art from nature. Indeed it is this sense of composition which the Greek regarded as perhaps the most important element in a work of art. It is clearly brought out in the definition of beauty quoted by Plotinus (as the opinion of some) :[14]

What is it that impresses you when you look at something, attracts you, captivates you, and fills you with joy?

The general opinion, I may say, is that it is the interrelation of parts toward one another and toward the whole, with the added element of good color, which constitutes beauty as perceived by the eye; in other words, that beauty in visible things as in everything else consists of symmetry and proportion. In their eyes, nothing simple and devoid of parts can be beautiful, only a composite.

[14] *Ennead* I. VI. i. Though Plotinus lived in the third century A.D. his teachings are often borrowed from Plato and other philosophers of the fifth and fourth centuries B.C.

This joy in "symmetry and proportion" can be clearly detected in all Greek art.

Another important factor in the "idealism" of Greek sculpture is its simplification. The Greek sculptor felt that to translate the human body into a work of art he must harmonize the multiformity and restlessness of nature and create a unity. We have spoken of his subordination of parts to the whole, his elimination of superfluous details, his restriction to the essentials. Equally important was his simplification of the design. His statue was contained in a unified space,[15] that is, a space with restricted depth. For instance, if the kouros of Melos (fig. 19) were placed between two sheets of glass the space occupied by the statue would be uniform; no part would unduly protrude; the whole figure is designed as a compact whole. This becomes specially noteworthy in groups or in figures in motion. In the Rhombos statue[16] (figs. 5, 6) a sheet of glass applied to the front would strike the calf's head, the man's head, and the forearms. One applied to the back would touch the calf's body and the man's body. In the fifth-century Niobid in the National Museum in Rome[17] (fig. 4), the farther arm and leg are in one plane, the nearer arm and leg are in another; the volume is conceived as a relief. That such compactness is not true to nature we realize when we think of how a man carrying a calf would look in reality—how his arms, the calf's legs and head would extend in different directions, considerably beyond the plane of his head and body. Or if a living human being were to take the pose of the Niobid sinking down on one knee and lifting one arm to extract an arrow from her back, her legs would probably be in one direction, her arms in another. We should get an effect similar to the Falling Gladiator by Rimmer (fig. 7), where the arms and legs are designed in opposite planes; so that if we should apply our imaginary sheets of glass the depth occupied would be considerable. For this real air space the Greek sculptor substituted an ideal space unity. It is important to understand and realize this characteristic of Greek sculpture; for it is very largely through this conception of space that a Greek statue acquires its dignity and grandeur. A figure thus carved can be taken

[15] Cf. on this subject Hildebrand's remarks in his illuminating book, *Das Problem der Form.*

[16] Dickins, *Catalogue of the Acropolis Museum,* No. 624.

[17] Paribeni, *Le Terme di Diocleziano e il Museo Nazionale Romano,* No. 369; Arndt, in Brunn-Bruckmann, *Denkmäler,* pls. 706–709.

in by the human eye without distraction, and thereby attains that sense of quiet and detachment which makes art a refreshment to the spirit.

This "relief conception," as it has been called by Hildebrand, was inherited by the Greeks from the Egyptians; it was stimulated by the universal practice of stone carving, in which both the figure and the space surrounding it were potentially enclosed in the block, by the demand for architectural sculpture with its uniform depths of pediments and metopes. That the Greeks recognized its importance from an artistic point of view is shown by their practice of it even when working in bronze or with figures in which no background had to be considered. It is not until the very latest period, in such creations as the Dirke monument (fig. 772), that this conception is given up, and the result is, we feel immediately, restlessness and confusion.

Still another determining element in the idealistic impression of Greek sculpture is beauty of contour. So much of Greek sculpture was out in the open to be viewed from a distance that the outline counted for much; and it is the lovely undulating outline of a Greek statue which impresses us from the first. Indeed this feeling for contour was so strong in the Greek artist that it shows itself in all his work, not only in the design of the whole figure, but in every part of it—the oval of the face, the swing of the eyelids, the curve of the lips, the drawing of the muscles and of the folds of the drapery. It is an extraordinarily strong sensitivity for rhythmic line—which found expression also in the shapes of vases and in vase painting.

It is, then, sense of structure, simplification of form and design, harmonious proportion, and rhythmic contour that stand out as the salient features of Greek sculpture. By them it acquires the grandeur which we feel in its presence. They give it its spiritual quality. And since art is a spiritualization of nature it is this spiritualizing quality which is fundamental, and without which representation is not art. And so Greek sculpture, throughout its development, has the distinguishing trait of great art.

CHIEF USES OF GREEK SCULPTURE
From our analysis of the Greek mind and its influence on Greek sculpture we must pass to the chief uses of sculpture in Greece; for the nature of the demand of course affects the character of the supply.

Sculpture in Greece was largely religious. Its chief use was for the decoration of temples either as pediment groups, friezes, or akroteria, for the cult statues of deities placed in the cella, and for votive statues and reliefs dedicated in sanctuaries. A large proportion of the sculpture that has survived is therefore architectural. This demand early developed the technique of relief as well as the composition of large groups (p. 117). We should never have had the superb creations of the western pediment of the Olympia temple (fig. 391) or of the Parthenon frieze but for the long history which preceded them and which gave the sculptor ample opportunities of development. But these pediments and friezes could not vie in importance with the cult statues placed in the interiors of temples. It was round them that the popular worship centered and it was by them that the people obtained a concrete realization of their gods. And so to embody his vision of the deity in a great temple statue was the highest task of a Greek sculptor. Unfortunately hardly any of these statues have survived. We have only descriptions and small reproductions by which to visualize the colossal chryselephantine statues by Pheidias, Polykleitos, and Alkamenes. In every estimate of Greek sculpture, therefore, we must remember that its finest creations have been irretrievably lost.

Another important demand for sculpture in Greek times was created by the custom of erecting statues of the victors in the athletic contests given in honor of Zeus, Poseidon, Hera, etc. The statues stood in the public places and in the sacred enclosures in which the games had taken place, and the young athletes were mostly represented nude, for that is how they had engaged in their contests. This practice and the athletic ideal which prompted it led to the development of the nude male type as a favorite form. Not only athletes but gods and heroes were so represented. In this series of nude male figures the ideal human form was gradually worked out and became one of the greatest achievements of Greek sculpture.

Commemorative sculptures which are so popular today also played an important part in Greece. A significant victory would be celebrated by the erection of a statue or group, like the Nike of Paionios at Olympia (fig. 637), or the bronze Athena of Pheidias on the Akropolis (figs. 594, 596) which was an offering "from the spoils of the Persians who landed at Marathon." The group of the Tyrannicides (fig. 571) set up on the market-place would remind Athenians every day of their liberation from the tyrants and of the value of their democratic institutions. We hear also of large groups of several figures, e.g., statues of Athena, Apollo, Miltiades, Erechtheus, Kekrops, Pandion, Aigeus, and five other heroes, another offering "from the spoils of Marathon" by Pheidias. Such groups in the round must have been remarkable achievements, and it is a grievous loss that they have disappeared. The erection of portraits of distinguished men became increasingly popular as time went on.

Besides these more or less public uses of sculpture there was a large private demand for grave monuments. The chief forms adopted in Athens were slabs with reliefs representing the departed, either alone or with sorrowing relatives, statues in the round, slabs crowned by finials, and vases decorated with reliefs. They supply us with some of the most touching and most "personal" representations we have in Greek art. These sculptured grave monuments remained in vogue until the end of the fourth century B.C. when the "anti-luxury" decree of Demetrios put a sudden stop to this artistic expression (p. 133). Their constant use during three centuries greatly furthered the development of relief technique.

SUBJECTS   It is important to become familiar also with the subjects represented in Greek sculpture; for the Greek artist had an entirely different repertoire from our own. Early Christian, mediaeval, and Renaissance art are from this point of view much nearer to us, since they need little explanation; but when we enter the Greek field we are stepping into an unknown land; and we must be careful to leave behind us any preconceptions we may have.

We have seen how the athletic ideal helped to concentrate interest in the human figure. It accustomed people to seeing the human body in all manner of postures and to appreciating its beauty. Moreover, the Greek with his love of the normal had a tendency to humanize everything. His gods and goddesses are no longer monsters, as often in Eastern art, but assume human form; so do the Nymphs, Satyrs, Centaurs, Tritons, and the other personifications of nature. Even when these start with hybrid shapes they soon lose their animal characteristics and gradually become more and more human. And so Greek sculpture consists largely of figures of human beings representing divinities, heroes, and athletes. Animals and decorative motives find a place and an important one, but they are nevertheless secondary. The human figure is the theme par excellence.

Joined to this humanizing tendency the Greeks had a love for story-telling. Much of Greek religion consists of stories about gods and goddesses and heroes; and these manifold imaginative tales would naturally make a great appeal to the artist. They supplied him with the most varied material, which he used so constantly that definite standardized types soon emerged. Plato's words about literature apply also to sculpture and painting—that art must eschew novelty and be framed after the pattern of those foundation myths which the poets have made familiar. So we must become conversant with these foundation myths. And a delightful process it is; for these stories have the freshness and imaginative quality of a poetic people. In entering this world of Greek fiction with its contests of Lapiths and Centaurs and Amazons, its wonderful deeds of heroes, and its manifold adventures of gods and goddesses, we feel very near the beginning of civilization. We sense the vivaciousness and naïveté of youth. No doubt some of the myths have a historical background; some are certainly rooted in actual experience; but the poet when he took his material transformed fact into fancy and then the artist translated this fancy into a beautiful picture. And so in our interpretation of Greek mythology in Greek art let us endeavor to catch the lovely simplicity of these spirited stories directly and concretely told. It is easy for us with our modern, complicated minds to read our own thoughts into these representations and endow them with far-fetched symbolic significance. But thereby we lose the early Greek flavor and become more like the late Latin commentators. Take, for instance, the tale of the birth of the goddess Athena from the brain of Zeus. To a later artist it would inevitably have suggested the coming of the spirit of wisdom from the thought of the mightiest god, and he would have tried to convey the idea with appropriate grandeur. The Greek instead adopted a version of almost childlike literalness (fig. 3). We have Zeus in the center, Hephaistos splitting his head open with his axe, a little Athena emerging fully armed, and the goddesses of childbirth ministering on either side; no symbolism, only a refreshing fairy tale. Or take Theseus and Herakles in their many contests with monsters. How close to us the thought of the knight purging the world of evil, how dear the wish to see this moral conveyed! But to the Greek artist the hero was al-

Mythological

ways Herakles with his lion's skin and club or Theseus with his little chiton and his sword (fig. 11) or Perseus with his distinctive paraphernalia, tackling in various ways these dangerous creatures. The whole interest lies in the contest, in the story, and in its artistic rendering. Its subjective significance was outside the artist's scope.

In this connection we may again quote Plato;[18] for in his analytical time a few learned people were beginning to lose the childlikeness of earlier days and search for far-fetched interpretations. When Sokrates is asked by young Phaidros whether he believes in the story that Boreas carried off Oreithyia he gives an illuminating answer, which it may be well to quote at length, for it states the case admirably: "If I disbelieved," Sokrates says, "as the wise men do, I should not be extraordinary; then I might give a rational explanation, that a blast of Boreas, the north wind, pushed her off the neighboring rocks as she was playing with Pharmakeia, and that when she had died in this manner she was said to have been carried off by Boreas. I think, however, such explanations are very pretty in general, but are the inventions of a very clever and laborious and not altogether enviable man, for no other reason than because after this he must explain the forms of the Centaurs, and then that of the Chimaira, and there presses in upon him a whole crowd of such creatures, Gorgons, Pegasoi, and multitudes of strange, inconceivable, portentous natures. If anyone disbelieves in these, and with a rustic sort of wisdom, undertakes to explain each in accordance with probability, he will need a great deal of leisure. Now I have no leisure for them at all. . . . And so I dismiss these matters and accept the customary belief about them."

Surely our interest also lies in these customary beliefs of the people who produced and enjoyed the art which we are endeavoring to understand. So we cannot do better than follow Sokrates' advice and not spoil a fairy tale with a laborious mind. We must remember, then, that the only symbolism we shall find in Greek art is the concrete one by which pebbles suggest the beach (cf. fig. 12), a fish the sea, a growing plant the meadow (cf. fig. 9), a pine tree the mountain (cf. fig. 10), a reed the river bank (cf. fig. 8), and a column the house. This practical symbolism was freely used, for such shorthand methods were useful and easily understood, and were thoroughly in line with the Greek tendency to simplification.

18 *Phaidros* 229 D.

The large mass of architectural sculptures—the pediments of the temples, the continuous friezes, the metopes—have almost invariably mythological representations—either legends directly associated with the deity to whom the temple was dedicated (e.g., the birth of Athena and her strife with Poseidon in the pediments of the Parthenon), or the familiar contest scenes of Herakles, Theseus, Lapiths, etc. Only occasionally is there a scene from actual life, for instance, the Panathenaic procession in the Parthenon frieze; though here too the subject is lifted to a higher plane by the actual presence of the gods on the eastern side. The almost total absence of historical representations is striking. Even in single sculptures erected to celebrate a specific victory such subjects are rare; when Miltiades is introduced in Pheidias' group commemorative of the battle of Marathon[19] he is associated with Athena, Apollo, and various heroes; the representation of Greeks and Persians on the frieze of the temple of Athena Nike is exceptional. We have not a single representation of the battles of Thermopylai or Salamis, of the Peloponnesian war, of the great plague, of the Sicilian expedition; in short, of the outstanding events which formed the chief preoccupation of the Greeks of the fifth century. How different the Romans or the Egyptians and Assyrians with their endless friezes recording their triumphs over their enemies; how different we ourselves with some of our war monuments and realistic pictures of contemporary battles! The Greeks, in order to convey the strife and stress of their time, had recourse to mythological contests, or to the semi-legendary events of the Trojan war.[20] These were far enough removed to admit of safe treatment, which with the constantly changing alignment of the Greek states was probably an important point. At all events, the Greeks knew that history with the strong partisan and bitter feeling it arouses is not an appropriate subject for sculpture. The same is true of contemporary political events. The Greek was distinctly a "political animal." Of all his contributions to mankind he prided himself most on his civic ideal. Every Athenian citizen was a representative in Congress and a legislator in the law courts. But that part of his life was passed over by the artist. And probably for

[19] Pausanias X. 10. 1. In Mikon's famous painting of the battle of Marathon, Athena and some popular heroes (Theseus, Herakles, and Echetlos) are likewise introduced (Pausanias I. 16).

[20] We have a few exceptions to this general rule in Greek paintings, for instance in the representation of the battle of Oinoe in the Poikile (Pausanias I. 15).

Daily Life

the same reason for which contemporary wars were omitted—that controversial subjects do not belong to the realm of art.

There were some other aspects of daily life, however, which found a place in Greek sculpture. Not only single statues of athletes but chariot groups were popular dedications; and occasionally even in the fifth century we hear of such "genre" subjects as the statue by Styppax of "a slave roasting entrails and kindling a fire with a blast from his swollen cheeks."[21] In the Hellenistic period such themes greatly gained in vogue, especially in bronze and terracotta statuettes (cf. p. 82). But the most frequent representations of daily life occur on the grave monuments where the departed were shown in their favorite occupations, as their families liked to remember them. To us these pictures of Greek life are singularly precious; for they are contemporary illustrations of familiar happenings and as such eloquent and trustworthy. We see here men represented as warriors or athletes; women busy with their spinning or putting on their jewelry; children playing ball or caressing their pet animals; and in the family groups we gain a realization of a happy and affectionate family life. And, always, these renderings are simple and direct—with no trace of sentimentality or exaggeration, but with the Greek note of serenity which makes of them something typical and permanent. We are reminded of Nietzsche's famous saying: "Die Griechen sind, wie das Genie, einfach: deshalb sind sie die unsterblichen Lehrer."

[21] Pliny, *N.H.* XXXIV. 81.

CHAPTER III

TENTATIVE CHRONOLOGY OF OUTSTANDING GREEK SCULPTURES

Period	Monument	External Evidence
c. 650 B.C.	Statue dedicated by Nikandre (fig. 263) Fragment of a kouros from Delos (Richter, *Kouroi,* figs. 15, 16). Statuette from Dreros (fig. 14)	Comparison with a terracotta mourner on a Protoattic vase, from the Kerameikos (Kübler, *Arch. Anz.* 1933, col. 268 f.)
c. 650–625	Reliefs from Mycenae (Karo, *Greek Personality in Archaic Sculpture,* p. 99, pl. VII) Draped woman once in Auxerre (fig. 262) Sculptures from Prinias (fig. 347)	Comparison with heads on Protocorinthian vases, placed before 628, the date given by Thucydides for the foundation of Selinus, since Protocorinthian vases have not been found there (Payne, *Necrocorinthia,* pp. 23 f.
c. 640–620	Antefixes from Thermon (Payne, *op. cit.,* pp. 96 ff., 234 f.)	Comparison with vases of the Transition Period between Protocorinthian and Early Corinthian.
c. 615–590	Sounion, Dipylon, and New York kouroi (figs. 16, 137, 18)	Comparison with plastic heads on early Corinthian pottery and with figures on early Athenian vases, e.g., the Nessos amphora (cf. Payne, *op. cit.,* figs. 470–471; Richter, *Kouroi,* p. 59).
c. 600	Head of Hera found near the Heraion at Olympia (fig. 138)	
c. 600–590	Kleobis and Biton by [Poly]medes of Argos, in Delphi (figs. 17, 142, 145)	Anatomically the statues are related to the Sounion kouroi, though they are somewhat more developed (Richter, *op. cit.,* p. 51).
c. 600–580	Pediment from the temple of Artemis at Corfu (figs. 374, 76, 96, 61, 109, 141) Head of sphinx from Kalydon (Dyggve, *Das Laphrion,* figs. 191–193)	

Period	Monument	External Evidence
c. 600–575	Seated statue from Didyma (fig. 62)	
c. 575–560	Standing Maiden from Attica in Berlin (figs. 267, 269, 139, 140)	Anatomically the statue is more developed than the Sounion group of kouroi. Comparison with figures on the François vase.
	Headless Maiden from the Akropolis, no. 593	Anatomically related to the Berlin Maiden.
	Calf Bearer dedicated by [Rh]ombos (figs. 5, 6)	Cf. Richter, *Kouroi*, p. 128.
	The Naxian Sphinx at Delphi	
	Metopes of the Sikyonian Treasury at Delphi (figs. 404, 358)	
c. 570–550	Statue dedicated to Hera by Cheramyes, in the Louvre (Buschor, *Altsamische Standbilder,* figs. 86–89)	
	Statues by Geneleos (Buschor, *op. cit.,* figs. 90 ff.)	
	Poros pediment of "Bluebeard" and Triton from the Akropolis (figs. 378, 379)	
	Metopes of the Heraion on the river Silaris	
	The Tenea and Volomandra kouroi (figs. 22, 147, 20)	Cf. Richter, *Kouroi,* pp. 125 ff.
	Statue of Chares from Didyma (fig. 264)	
c. 560–550	"Introduction" pediment from the Akropolis (fig. 380)	
c. 550	Winged Nike from Delos (fig. 77)	
c. 555–540	The kouros from Melos (fig. 19)	Cf. Richter, *op. cit.,* pp. 154 ff.
c. 555–530	Parts of the sculptured drums of the temple of Artemis at Ephesos (figs. 265, 266)	Most of the columns of this temple are said by Herodotos (I.92) to have been offered by Kroisos, who reigned c. 560–547). Part of the dedicatory inscription on the as-

Period	Monument	External Evidence
		tragal of a sculptured drum has been preserved, but it cannot be definitely associated with any of the sculptures. The building of the temple must have lasted some time (cf. p. 93).
c. 540	Metopes of temple C at Selinus (fig. 405) Maiden No. 679 in the Akropolis Museum (figs. 270, 143)	The simple scheme of stacked folds on these figures occurs on black-figured vases of the third quarter of the sixth century, e.g., on a late kylix by Lydos in New York; cf. Richter, *A.J.A.*, 1946, pp. 17 f.
	Gravestone of a brother and sister, in New York (fig. 423)	Cf. Richter, *Archaic Attic Gravestones,* p. 68.
c. 550–525	Reliefs of the temple at Assos (fig. 403) The Munich and Anavysos kouroi (figs. 20, 21)	Cf. Richter, *Kouroi,* pp. 191 ff.
c. 530–510	The Maidens Nos. 670–675, 680, 682–684 in the Akropolis Museum (cf. figs. 271, 272, 150, 144)	
Shortly before 525	Pediment and frieze of the Siphnian Treasury at Delphi (figs. 382, 418, 419, 487, 97, 123)	Herodotos III.57 and Pausanias X.ii.2 speak of an adverse oracle which was pronounced against the Siphnians while they were building their Treasury at Delphi and which was fulfilled in a Samian attack dated 524 (cf. Richter, *Kouroi,* pp. 191 f., and *Archaic Attic Gravestones,* p. 69, note 42).
c. 530–500	Athena probably by Endoios (fig. 64)	Inscriptions date Endoios in the last third of the sixth century (cf. Raubitschek, *A.J.A.*, 1942, pp. 245 ff., and *Dedications,* pp. 491 ff.).
c. 520	Marble pediment from the peristyle of a Peisistratid temple (figs. 112, 385)	Compare vases by Oltos (Langlotz, *Zeitbestimmung,* p. 34).
c. 520–510	Pediment of the Treasury of the Megarians at Olympia (fig. 383)	

Period	Monument	External Evidence
c. 510	Stele of Aristion by Aristokles (fig. 424)	Cf. Richter, *Archaic Attic Gravestones*, p. 100.
c. 513–500	Pediments of the temple of Apollo at Delphi (figs. 381, 384, 386, 387)	According to Herodotos V.62 and Aristotle, *Politeia* 19. 3, the temple (which took the place of an earlier structure burnt in 548) was begun after the battle of Leipsydrion (513). Hipparchos died 514–513. After the fall of Hippias (510) the Alkmaionids built the east front of the temple in magnificent style (Schol. Pindar, *Pyth.* 7. 9). Cf. Richter, *Kouroi*, pp. 218 f., and *Archaic Attic Gravestones*, p. 69, note 42.
c. 510–500	West pediment of the temple of Apollo Daphnephoros at Eretria (figs. 281, 284)	
	The Ptoon 20 and Strangford kouroi (figs. 28, 29)	Cf. Richter, *Kouroi*, nos. 131, 134.
	Metopes of the Treasury of the Athenians at Delphi (figs. 124, 406–409)	Cf. note 45 on p. 126.
	Frieze of mounting charioteer (fig. 275) and Hermes (fig. 276)	Compare the vases of Leagros period and early Panaitios period (Langlotz, *Zeitbestimmung*, p. 87).
	Statue base with cat-and-dog fight in Athens (figs. 283, 469)	Compare vases by Euthymides and Phintias.
	Statue base with "hockey" game in Athens	
	Metopes of the later Heraion on the river Silaris	
c. 500–490	"Harpy tomb" (figs. 472, 473)	Compare the Theseus cup by the Panaitios painter in the Louvre and vases at the turn of the century.
	Stele by Alxenor (fig. 425)	The inscription is dated at the turn of the century (Loewy, *Inschriften*, No. 7; *I.G.*, XII, 5, No. 1426).
c. 499–494	Head of Athena on a stater issued during the Ionian Revolt, perhaps by Priene	Cf. Baldwin, *The Electrum Coinage of Lampsakos*, pp. 26 ff., pl. II; Richter, *Kouroi*, p. 211, fig. 482.

Period	*Monument*	*External Evidence*
c. 500–480	Pediments of the temple of Aphaia at Aigina (figs. 388, 389, 103, 113, 114, 186, 525)	Architecturally the temple is "the most perfectly developed of the late archaic temples" in Greece proper (Dinsmoor).
Soon after 490	The statue No. 690 in the Akropolis Museum (Raubitschek, *A.J.A.*, 1940, pp. 53 ff.)	Dedicated after the Battle of Marathon.
490–480	Sparta warrior (fig. 104) The heads of Maidens Nos. 696 and 643 in the Akropolis Museum	
	Moulded head on a vase by the Brygos Painter	Cf. Richter and Hall, *Red-figured Athenian Vases in the Metropolitan Museum*, No. 43.
	Euthydikos Maiden (fig. 159) "Blond Boy" (fig. 169) Horse (fig. 348)	Found on the Akropolis in the Persian débris with colors well preserved.
c. 480	Running maiden from Eleusis (fig. 87) Seated goddess in Berlin (figs. 65, 161)	
	Reliefs with dedicatory inscription to Apollo and the Nymphs, from Thasos, in the Louvre (fig. 453)	The inscription has been dated c. 490–480 (*I.G.*, XII, 8, No. 358), "see *I.G.* XII, 8, No. 390—another inscription from Thasos dated on historical grounds 494–492, which shows considerably less developed forms of letters; so that we may choose the lower limit of 490–480 for our date of the Louvre relief and even go some few years below it" (M. N. Tod).
	Bronze statuette of a diskobolos in New York (figs. 31, 32) Bronze statuette of a horse in New York (figs 349, 350)	
c. 470	Three-sided reliefs in Rome and Boston (figs. 474–479, 183–185, 189, 289)	
479–478	The Demareteion of Syracuse (fig. 160)	Struck in commemoration of the victory of Gelon of Syracuse over Carthage at Himera (480).

Period	Monument	External Evidence
477–476	*Group of Tyrannicides by Kritios and Nesiotes (figs. 565–567, 569–577)	Erected in the archonship of Adeimantos (477–476).
476–461	Coin of Aetna (Katane) (fig. 10)	Dated by the history of the city of Aetna (Head, *Historia Numorum* [1911], p. 131).
c. 475–460	Metopes of temple E at Selinus (figs. 410–413, 187)	
c. 470	Charioteer of Delphi (figs. 285, 162)	The inscription on the base seems to indicate that the group was dedicated by Polyzalos of Syracuse (c. 478–474) in celebration of a victory.
c. 465–457	Pediments and metopes of the temple of Zeus at Olympia (figs. 390–393, 2, 66, 115, 116, 133, 134, 163, 200, 355, 414, 188, 191, 319, 343)	According to Pausanias, V. 10. 2, the Eleans built the temple out of the booty obtained in the conquest of Pisa and her vassal states (probably about 470). Pausanias, V. 10. 4, also records that the Lacedaemonians placed a golden shield on the apex of the eastern pediment of the temple after the battle of Tanagra in 457. The temple must then have been practically complete.
c. 460–450	"Mourning Athena" in the Akropolis Museum (fig. 206) Stele of a girl with casket in Berlin (fig. 427) *"Omphalos Apollo" (figs. 36, 37)	A "copy" of this statue appears on a volute krater by the Niobid Painter (*Mon. dell' Inst.*, X, pl. 54); cf. Beazley, *A.R.V.P.*, p. 418, no. 7; Richter, *Kouroi*, p. 247.
	*Herculaneum dancers (cf. figs. 260, 497)	
c. 450	Frieze of the temple of the Ilissos (figs. 420, 88) *Diskobolos by Myron (figs. 578 ff.) *Group of Athena and	

* The sculptures marked with an asterisk are Roman copies of lost Greek originals.

Period	Monument	External Evidence
	Marsyas by Myron (figs. 584–593, 190)	
c. 450–440	*Doryphoros by Polykleitos (figs. 645–649)	
	Stele of girl with pigeons in New York (figs. 426, 205) Metopes of the Hephaisteion (fig. 417) Niobids in Rome and Copenhagen (figs. 4, 196, 92, 118) "Athena Lemnia" attributed to Pheidias (fig. 614–616)	The temple was begun c. 449 B.C. (Dinsmoor, *Hesperia,* Supplement V, p. 153).
c. 447–443	Metopes of the Parthenon (figs. 415, 416, 105, 131, 192)	The building of the Parthenon was begun in 447 in the archonship of Timarchides.
442–438	Frieze of the Parthenon (figs. 486, 488, 489, 356, 291, 247)	The frieze must have been complete by 438, for, after that, work was confined to the pediment sculptures.
c. 440–430	*Perikles by Kresilas (figs. 623, 624)	After the death of Kimon (449) Perikles was the leading citizen in Athens until his death in 429.
c. 447–439	*The chryselephantine statue of Athena Parthenos by Pheidias (figs. 595, 597–605)	According to the building inscription of the temple gold and ivory were sold in 439–438 and 437–436 in large quantities, apparently the surplus material remaining after the completion of the statue. Eusebios, *Chron.,* dates the statue in the 85th Olympiad (440–436). It must, of course, have been a number of years in the making.
	*Reliefs found in the sea off Peiraieus, copied from the figures on the shield of the Athena Parthenos (Schrader, in *Corolla Curtius,* pp. 81 ff.)	
438–432	Pediments of the Parthenon (figs. 394–396, 69–71, 91,	According to the building inscription the marble for the pediments

* The sculptures marked with an asterisk are Roman copies of lost Greek originals.

Period	Monument	External Evidence
	119, 292, 351, 500, 622)	was brought to the workshops in 439–438 and the work begun the following year. For 434–433 there is an entry of the yearly wage given to the sculptors (Dinsmoor, *A.J.A.*, 1921, pp. 243, 244).
c. 440–430	Eleusinian relief (fig. 481)	
c. 435–430	* The chryselephantine statue of Zeus at Olympia by Pheidias (figs. 606, 607)	See pp. 222 ff.
	*Diadoumenos by Polykleitos (figs. 650–652)	
c. 427–424	Frieze of the temple of Athena Nike (figs. 295, 297)	The temple of Athena was planned before the adjoining Propylaia but was built subsequently about 427–424 (Dinsmoor, *op. cit.*, p. 185 f.)
c. 425–420	Nike by Paionios (figs. 637, 639–642)	The inscription on the base records that it was dedicated by the Messenians and Naupaktians to Zeus with a tithe of the spoils taken from their enemies. The campaign referred to is probably that of Sphakteria, 425 (see p. 244).
c. 420	Frieze and metopes of the temple of Apollo Epikourios at Phigaleia (figs. 106, 197–199, 201–204, 298–301)	Pausanias VIII. 41. 5 records that the temple was built by Iktinos, the architect of the Parthenon, and dedicated to Apollo "the Succorer" "for the help he gave in time of plague . . . at the time of the war between the Peloponnesians and Athenians." The most probable time, at least of its completion, is during the Peace of Nikias, which began in 421 (see p. 102).
	Statue of Nemesis at Rhamnous by Agorakritos (figs. 633, 634) and reliefs from the base (cf. figs. 635, 727)	The temple at Rhamnous belongs architecturally to c. 436, but the reliefs may be later, c. 421 B.C. (Dinsmoor, *Architecture of Ancient Greece*, 1949, pp. 182 f.).
	Sculptures of the Argive	The old temple was burnt in 423

* The sculptures marked with an asterisk are Roman copies of lost Greek originals.

Period	Monument	External Evidence
	Heraion (cf. fig. 165) including *the statue of Hera by Polykleitos represented on coins of Argos (fig. 654)	and the new building started forthwith (Thucydides IV. 133; Pausanias II. 17. 3).
	"Record" relief from Eleusis (*Ath. Mitt.*, XIX, 1894, pl. VII)	Dated by the inscription 420.
c. 421–413	The karyatids of the Erechtheion (fig. 502)	The Erechtheion was probably begun in c. 421 (Peace of Nikias); subsequently work was stopped and not resumed till 409. The karyatids must belong to the earlier period, for in the report made by a commission in 409 on the state of the building "the ceiling blocks over the maidens" are mentioned.
c. 413–400	Dekadrachms of Syracuse with female head and quadriga signed by Kimon and Euainetos (Head, *Historia Numorum*,[2] p. 176; Gallatin, *Syracusan Dekadrachms*).	Issued after the Athenian defeat of 413.
c. 420–410	Reliefs from the "Gjölbaschi" monument (cf. figs. 421, 422, 326, 516)	
c. 412–410	Head of Apollo on tetradrachms of Chalcidic League	Cf. Robinson and Clement, *Olynthus*, IX, p. 21, No. 18, pl. IV.
c. 410	Reliefs from the "balustrade" of the temple of Athena Nike (figs. 504, 506)	Built probably during the temporary successes of Athens in the last stages of the Peloponnesian war, 411–407.
410–409	"Record" relief in the Louvre (fig. 307)	Dated by the inscription in the archonship of Glaukippos.
c. 410	Portrait of the satrap Pharnabazus, on coins (Regling, *Die antike Münze als Kunstwerk*, pl. XIX, 424)	Pharnabazus was satrap of Dascylium c. 413–370 b.c. The symbol of the tunny fish shows that the coin was probably struck at Kyzikos about 410.

* The sculptures marked with an asterisk are Roman copies of lost Greek originals.

Period	Monument	External Evidence
409–406	Frieze of the Erechtheion (figs. 296, 728)	The building inscription of the Erechtheion dated 408–407 records payments made to sculptors for carving figures of the frieze.
c. 400	The Nereid monument (figs. 302–304, 490, 492, 467)	
c. 400	The Hegeso relief (fig. 429)	The earliest gravestones of this part of the Kerameikos are about contemporary with the stele of Dexileos (Brückner, *Der Friedhof am Eridanos*, pp. 24, 194); the Hegeso grave, however, may of course have existed before the building of the family monument and later been included in it.
	"Record" relief in Athens (Svoronos, *Das Athener Nationalmuseum*, pl. CCIII)	Dated by the inscription 400–399.
c. 394	Stele of Dexileos (fig. 215)	The inscription records that he fell in the battle of Corinth, 394.
c. 400–375	Sculptures of the temple of Asklepios at Epidauros (figs. 710–719)	The building inscription of the temple is dated in the first quarter of the fourth century.
c. 383–379	Head of Apollo on tetradrachms of Chalcidic League	Cf. Robinson and Clement, *Olynthus,* IX, p. 53, No. 77, pl. XI.
375–374	Relief of the Treaty between Athens and Kerkyra (*B.C.H.,* II, pl. 12)	Dated by the inscription in the archonship of Hippodamas.
c. 375–370	*Eirene and Ploutos by Kephisodotos (figs. 659–663, 499)	Erected probably soon after Timotheos' victory over the Spartans in 375 (see p. 257).
c. 370–350	Pediments of the temple of Athena Alea at Tegea (figs. 690–693, 696)	Pausanias VIII.45.4 relates that "a previous building was . . . destroyed in the . . . second year of the 96th Olympiad" (395). How much later the present temple was erected is a moot question; see p. 269.
	*"Dresden Satyr," perhaps an early work of Praxiteles (figs. 682–684)	

* The sculptures marked with an asterisk are Roman copies of lost Greek originals.

Period	*Monument*	*External Evidence*
c. 367–353	Coins issued by Maussollos with seated Zeus and head of Apollo facing	Cf. Head, *Historia Numorum*,[2] p. 629.
355–354	"Record" relief in Palermo (Diepolder, *Attische Grabreliefs*, fig. 10)	Dated by the inscription.
c. 355–352	Head of Apollo on tetradrachms of Chalcidic League.	Cf. Robinson and Clement, *Olynthus*, IX, p. 81, No. 133, pl. XVII.
c. 355–330	Sculptures of the temple of Artemis at Ephesos (figs. 705, 703, 328)	The temple was built immediately after the fire which burnt down the earlier structure in 356, but had not yet been completed in 334; see p. 269.
c. 350	Sarcophagus of "Mourning Women" from Sidon (figs. 316, 398) Demeter of Knidos (fig. 315) The Mantineia base (figs. 679–681) *Aphrodite of Knidos by Praxiteles (figs. 668–672) Hermes and the infant Dionysos by Praxiteles (figs. 664–667, 170)	See p. 264.
	Stele of Korallion (Conze, *op. cit.*, No. 411, pl. 98)	Dated from the history of the graves in the Kerameikos and the history of Herakleia on the Pontos (Brückner, *Der Friedhof am Eridanos*, pp. 64 ff., 68 ff.).
	The sculptures of the Mausoleum (figs. 697–702, 720–722, 729–730, 735, 313, 314, 228, 209)	See Pliny, *N.H.* XXXVI. 30, and pp. 271 f.
c. 350–325	*The Sauroktonos by Praxiteles (figs. 673, 675, 676) "Marathon Boy" (figs. 46–48, 172, 173)	
347–346	"Record" relief honoring three princes of the Bosphorus (Diepolder, *op. cit.*, fig. 11)	Dated by the inscription.

* The sculptures marked with an asterisk are Roman copies of lost Greek originals.

Period	Monument	External Evidence
346	Staters of Delphi with head of Demeter and seated Apollo (Head and Hill, *Guide to the Principal Coins of the Greeks in the British Museum*, pl. 23, No. 30)	Probably issued on the occasion of the reassembling of the Amphictyonic Council at the close of the Phocian war (346 B.C.).
c. 344–334	Agias (figs. 738, 740, 741)	Dedicated by Daochos II, tetrarch of the Thessalians, *c*. 344-334.
340–330	*Sophokles in the Lateran (fig. 249)	Probably a copy of the bronze statue of Sophokles set up in the theatre in Athens on the motion of Lykourgos between 340 and 330.
	*Portrait of Euripides (fig. 229)	Perhaps erected at the same time as the statue of Sophokles.
336–323	Coins of Alexander the Great (cf. fig. 747)	Alexander reigned 336–323.
335–334	Choregic monument of Lysikrates (fig. 491)	The inscription on the architrave records that it was erected for a victory by Lysikrates in the archonship of Euainetos (335–334).
c. 340–320	Dog in the Kerameikos (Collignon, *Statues funéraires*, pp. 239–240)	In the same family plot as that crowned by the dog was the grave of Lysimmachides of Acharnai, perhaps the archon of 339–338 (Brückner, *op. cit.*, p. 84).
c. 330–315	The latest Attic gravestones (Diepolder, *Attische Grabreliefs*, pls. 46–54)	The anti-luxury decree of Demetrios of Phaleron (c. 317–315) put an end to sculptured gravestones in Attica.
c. 329	Votive relief with Artemis and Asklepios (*Ny Carlsberg Glyptotek, Billedtavler*, No. 231)	Dated by the inscription.
c. 325–300	"Alexander sarcophagus" from Sidon (figs. 748, 176, 399, 400)	
	*Apoxyomenos of Lysippos (figs. 739, 742, 743)	Dated in the last quarter of the fourth century from its resemblance to portraits of Demetrios Polyorketes on coins.

* The sculptures marked with an asterisk are Roman copies of lost Greek originals.

Period	Monument	External Evidence
321–317	"Record" relief in Athens (Speier, *Röm. Mitt.*, 47, 1932, pl. 29, No. 1)	Dated by the inscription in the archonships of Kephisodoros (323–322) and Archippos (318–317).
304–285	Portrait of Ptolemy I, king of Egypt, on coins. (Head and Hill, *Guide to the Principal Coins of the Greeks in the British Museum*, pl. 28, No. 20	Ptolemy I, Soter, reigned 304–285 B.C.
306–280	Portrait of Seleukos I, king of Syria (fig. 238), on coins	Head and Hill, *op. cit.*, pp. 49 f.
c. 250–180	Nike of Samothrake (fig. 95)	The statue used to be dated c. 300 B.C. on account of its resemblance to the Nike on coins issued by Demetrios Poliorketes in commemoration of his victory over Ptolemy at Salamis, Cyprus, in 306 (cf. Newell, *The Coinages of Demetrius Poliorcetes*, pp. 32, 33). Later it was thought more probable that the statue commemorated the victory of the battle of Cos (c. 258). Recently a date in the early second century was suggested (Thiersch, *Göttinger Nachrichten*, 1931, p. 368).
After 300	*Tyche of Antioch by Eutychides (figs. 753–755)	Antioch was founded in 300.
295–294	"Record" relief in Athens (Süsserott, *Griechische Plastik*, pl. 44, no. 1)	Dated by the inscription.
280–279	*Demosthenes by Polyeuktos (fig. 757)	Demosthenes died 322. The statue was dedicated about forty years after his death in 280–279, in the archonship of Gorgias (cf. pp. 297 f.).
c. 270–250	Bronze portrait statuette in New York (figs. 230, 231, 241)	Resembles portraits of Hermarchos, who succeeded Epikouros as head of the Epicurean school of philosophy c. 270.
c. 300–250	Themis of Chairestratos (fig. 331)	The dedicatory inscription on the base is dated in the first half of the third century.

* The sculptures marked with an asterisk are Roman copies of lost Greek originals.

Period	Monument	External Evidence
c. 200–100	Aphrodite of Melos (fig. 535)	The base with an inscribed signature dated c. 100 B.C. (now lost), does not certainly belong to the statue (cf. Loewy, *Inschriften*, no. 298).
c. 240–200	*The Dying Gaul and the Gaul and his wife (figs. 108, 178)	Probably copies from a bronze group dedicated by Attalos I of Pergamon (241–197) to celebrate his victories over the Gauls.
c. 200	*Chrysippos, perhaps by Euboulides I (cf. fig. 232)	Lived c. 280–206.
	*Statues, two-thirds life-size, of Gauls, Amazons, Persians, giants (cf. fig. 120)	The bronze originals were probably set up by Attalos I of Pergamon on the Akropolis in Athens on the occasion of his visit there in 200.
	Sleeping Satyr in Munich (fig. 218)	
c. 190–160	Portrait of Eukratides, king of Baktria and India (fig. 236)	Dates of reign, c. 190–160.
197–159	Altar of Zeus and Athena at Pergamon (cf. figs. 177, 334, 335)	Built by Eumenes II, who reigned 197–159 (cf. Kähler, *Der grosse Fries von Pergamon*, p. 195, note 114).
178–168	Portrait of Perseus of Macedon, on coins	Head, *Historia Numorum*,[2] p. 235.
c. 200–150	Sculptures of the Temple of Despoina at Lykosoura by Damophon (figs. 758–760)	Inscriptions with the name of Damophon found in the temple are datable in the first half of the second century (Dickins, *B.S.A.*, XII, 1905–1906, pp. 130–136).
c. 150–125	Bronze portrait head from Delos (fig. 240)	Delos never recovered after the sack of 88 and the pirates' raid of 69 B.C.
c. 150	Laokoon by Hagesandros, Polydoros, and Athanodoros of Rhodes (figs. 768, 769, 225)	The group resembles the sculptures of the Pergamon altar 197–159 B.C. The names Athanodoros and Hagesandros occur in inscriptions

* The sculptures marked with an asterisk are Roman copies of lost Greek originals.

Period	Monument	External Evidence
		datable in the late I century B.C., but they are common in Rhodian inscriptions from the III to the I century.
	*Belvedere Torso (fig. 771) and Bronze Boxer (fig. 770), signed by Apollonios of Athens, evidently as copyist (see p. 306)	The style is that of the Pergamene altar, but the inscription is datable in the I century B.C.
	*Borghese Warrior (fig. 107), signed by Agasias of Ephesos	
	*"Hellenistic Prince" (fig. 57)	
	*Farnese Bull by Apollonios and Tauriskos of Tralles (fig. 772)	
c. 130	Head of Athena and other fragments, perhaps by Euboulides II	Found in Athens in a locality mentioned by Pausanias (I.215) not far from an inscription, with the signature of Euboulides, datable around 130 B.C.
	Statue of Gaios Ophellios from Delos signed by Dionysios and Timarchides	
c. 65–35	*Statues signed by Stephanos, pupil of Pasiteles, and Menelaos, pupil of Stephanos (figs. 773, 775)	Pasiteles was a contemporary of Pompey, 106–48 B.C.

* The sculptures marked with an asterisk are Roman copies of lost Greek originals.

CHAPTER IV

THE HUMAN FIGURE

GREEK monumental sculpture in stone apparently began in the seventh century B.C.[1] We have no reliable evidence as yet of large stone statues or reliefs from the geometric period. Though excavations have brought to light temples of that epoch in various localities the cult images in these sanctuaries were evidently small or perhaps of wood. At all events, the earliest largish Greek sculptures now extant—in stone as well as in bronze or terracotta— may be dated in the second quarter of the seventh century.

The Greek sculptor of that time had a long heritage that determined his start. He had before him on the one hand what had survived of the arts of his predecessors in his own land—the Minoans and the Mycenaeans, now considered the earliest known Greeks—and on the other hand those of his Oriental neighbors, the inhabitants of Western Asia and of Egypt. The influence of Asia (Mesopotamia, Phoenicia, Syria) is evident in the bronze, terracotta, and ivory statuettes that have come to light all over the Greek world.[2] It is seen especially in the early draped figures (cf. e.g. fig. 262), and in certain conventions, such as the spiral curls arranged symmetrically to right and left. The influence of Egypt is particularly marked in the early standing youths, the archaic *kouroi* (cf. figs. 14 ff.). The opening up of Egypt to Greek trade through its conquest by Assyria in 672 B.C. and the foundation of the Greek colony of Naukratis, probably about 650 B.C., doubtless played their part. We can imagine the sensitive Greeks beholding for the first time the impressive Egyptian sculpture and having their whole outlook changed thereby. How great this Eastern influence was we can see when we compare the "geometrized" products of the ninth and eighth centuries (fig. 13) with those of the two succeeding centuries.

In the seventh and sixth centuries, then, we find a series of primitive figures bearing a certain relation to the products of other na-

---

[1] Cf. V. Müller, *Met. Mus. Studies*, V, 2, pp. 157 ff.; F. R. Grace, *A.J.A.*, XLVI, 1942, pp. 341 ff.; Richter, *Kouroi*, pp. 43 ff., and the references there cited.

[2] Cf. V. Müller, *Frühe Plastik in Griechenland und Vorderasien.*

tions, but nevertheless highly individual. Change from this beginning was slow and deliberate. At first only a few types were attempted for single statues and used again and again with slight
variations: a standing, seated, striding, flying, or reclining figure
was represented according to an accepted scheme adhered to by
sculptors from every part of Greece. But within this scheme each
could make his individual contribution. And gradually by concentrating on his few themes, not distracted by constantly creating new
compositions, he was able to solve the difficulties which beset him.
Each new conquest became common property and formed a new
starting point. And so the forward march continued, not only in the
larger statues, but in small bronze and terracotta statuettes, and
along parallel lines in vase-painting, engraving, and goldwork. It
is an amazing feat of concentration; and could only have been obtained by that rare combination found in the Greeks of eager pro-
gressiveness and conservatism due to the blending in their blood of
the exuberant, sensitive Aegeans with the sturdy Indo-Europeans.
Eager for novelty, they nevertheless grafted the new on the old. Let
us watch the story unfold itself; for to follow it step by step is
an artistic education and pleasure of the first order. Our plan will
be to pursue the principal types adopted for the human figure
through the various centuries, restricting ourselves where possible
to the undraped examples, since we shall deal with drapery in a
separate chapter.

(a) The Standing Figure

SEVENTH
AND SIXTH
CENTURIES

In the opening chapter we find the standing figure in strictly
frontal position, with the left foot generally a little advanced, the arms
held close to the sides, occasionally bent at the elbow, the hands usually clenched. It shows the Egyptian scheme of broad shoulders,
narrow waist, and small flanks. We may take for the beginning of
our story two marble torsos from Delos and a bronze statuette from
Dreros[3] (fig. 14), of the mid-seventh century B.C. The former are
stiff and flat, almost like a four-sided plank. In the bronze statuette
there are attempts at anatomical construction, but there is little modeling, only incisions. From these beginnings we note a continuous progression toward a better realization of both the general shape and the
details of the human figure; and throughout there are retained a fine
unity and decorative sense. Indeed the simplification in the rendering

---

[3] Richter, *Kouroi*, figs. 15–18, 11, pp. 41 f.

of form imparts a grandeur to these early figures. The kouroi from
Sounion[4] (cf. fig. 16) and in New York[5] (fig. 18) and Kleobis and
Biton[6] (cf. fig. 17), of the late seventh to the early sixth century
show us the sculptural conception of that time. The shape displays
the four separate faces of the rectangular block from which it was
carved and natural forms are translated into interrelated patterns.
Thus the torso is four-sided, the head cubic. The vertebral column is
practically straight. The greatest protrusion of the back, seen in
profile, is higher than that of the chest. The forearm is turned forward,
while the clenched hand is twisted toward the body. The skull is un-
developed. Anatomical details are indicated on the surfaces of the
block by grooves, ridges, and knobs. The clavicles are generally
marked as flat ridges. The lower boundary of the thorax is indicated
by grooves forming an obtuse angle or a narrow arch. In the rectus
abdominis three or more transverse divisions are marked above the
navel, instead of the two visible in nature, and they are merely incised
in a flat pattern. The lower region is pointed obliquely, like the upper,
and is too short. The protrusion at the flanks is not indicated. The
knees reproduce more or less the symmetrical arrangement current in
Egypt, with the vastus externus and the vastus internus both reaching equally down to and bulging over the patella, whereas in nature
the arrangement is asymmetrical, with the muscular part of the vastus
externus considerably higher than the other. The kneecap takes the
shape of an approximately rectangular block and there is no indication of the pads of fat on which it rests. The shins are more or less
vertical. The feet stand squarely on the ground with long toes, more
or less parallel to one another and with ends receding along one continuous line. The malleoli are level.

The kouroi probably from Boeotia[7] (fig. 15), Tenea[8] (fig. 22), and
from Volomandra[9] (fig. 20), of the second quarter of the sixth century, and the kouros from Melos[10] (fig. 19) of the mid-sixth century
show a great development. The forms have become more rounded and
are more modelled. Instead of linear patterns volumes are coordinated,
and the artist is more alive to anatomical construction. The vertebral
column assumes a slight curve; the skull is more domed; there is a

---

[4] National Museum, Athens, No. 2720; Richter, *Kouroi*, Nos. 2–5.
[5] Richter, *Kouroi*, No. 1.
[6] Homolle, *Fouilles de Delphes*, IV, pls. I–II; Richter, *Kouroi*, No. 11.
[7] Richter, *Kouroi*, No. 33.   [8] *Ibid.* No. 58.
[9] *Ibid.* No. 51.   [10] *Ibid.* No. 72.

slight protrusion at the flanks; the inner vastus descends lower than
the outer; the shin is curved; the inner malleolus is higher than the
outer.

By the third quarter of the century further advance in anatomical
knowledge has been made. The kouroi in Munich[11] (fig. 23) and from
Anavysos[12] (fig. 21) and Keos[13] are excellent examples. The stance
is now less rigid. The curve of the thorax is indicated. Its greatest
protrusion front and back is level. The vertebral column assumes its
characteristic s-shaped curve. The abdominal region retains its early
rendering but is more modelled. The flanks are made more lifelike by
the indication of the iliac crest, with the muscle bulging over it. The
transition of the flanks to the rectus abdominis is marked by a groove.
The arrangement of the vasti muscles over the patella is asymmetrical.
The toes no longer recede along one line; the second toe projects further than the big toe and the small toe is short and turned inward.
The lovely contours in these figures and the gently undulating surfaces kept strictly within the symmetrical scheme make an impression
at once of quiet poise and extraordinary vitality. The various parts
appear proportionally interrelated and one form passes naturally and
inevitably into the next.

Since the standing female type during the archaic period was regularly draped we shall study it in our chapter on drapery; but nude
female figures occur occasionally in bronze statuettes even in the sixth
century. We may give as a good example the girl from Cyprus in New
York[14] (fig. 27).

The climax of these early struggles is reached in the Strangford
(fig. 29) and Ptoon 20 kouroi[15] (fig. 28) of about 510–500 and
the bronze statuette in New York[16] (figs. 24–26). They retain many
of the characteristics of the earlier figures. They are still in a symmetrical, frontal pose and are conceived as four-sided, with only four
principal views considered—the front, the back, and the two sides—
and the modeling is still somewhat flat. But much has been changed.
The clavicles have their characteristic s-shaped curve. The swelling of
the trapezium on the shoulder is indicated. The chest and back now
curve out considerably, sufficiently at least to make us feel that the

11 *Ibid.* No. 113.   12 *Ibid.* No. 114.
18 *Ibid.* No. 120.
14 Metropolitan Museum, *Catalogue of Bronzes*, No. 28; Richter, *A.J.A.*, XLVI,
1942, p. 324, note 21.
15 Richter, *Kouroi*, Nos. 134, 131.
16 Metropolitan Museum, *Catalogue of Bronzes*, No. 17; Richter, *Kouroi*, No. 143.

figure can breathe. The rectus abdominis at last assumes a more natural shape. The upper boundary instead of being pointed forms a semicircular arch and the transverse divisions are rightly indicated, two above and one below the navel; the lower boundary takes the shape of a semicircle as well as its proportion. The flanks are finely rounded. The interlacement of the serratus magnus with the ribs is carefully modeled beneath the arms. In the knee the vastus internus extends below the vastus externus and forms the distinctive swelling above the kneecap. The small pads of fat below the kneecap are observed. But in spite of this attention to anatomical construction the simplicity and decorative quality of the earlier statues are not lost.

Herewith the general shape of the Greek torso was achieved. It persists through later generations, merely perfected in the direction of greater amplitude of form and harmony of proportion.

The first half of the fifth century proved epoch-making in another sphere. A revolutionary change took place through the uneven distribution of the weight of the body and the consequent abandonment of the symmetrical pose. The figure is made to rest more on one leg than on the other, whereby the two sides become different and the median line of the body forms a curve instead of a straight line. It is interesting to mark the various steps in the progression. The turn of the pelvis is at first accompanied by frontal shoulders and with only a slight difference between the two sides of the body, as in the Akropolis youth (fig. 30) and the Disc-thrower in New York[17] (figs. 31, 32), both datable around 480. Presently one hip is placed markedly higher than the other,[18] as in the Apollo of Olympia[19] of about 460 (fig. 392) and the New York Adorans[20] (figs. 33–35).

FIFTH CENTURY

The variety and interest gained by this innovation are amazing. The figure suddenly acquires elasticity; it can walk and move about and is no longer confined to one place. And this change also put an end to the old four-sided conception, so that the figure becomes more rounded and natural. The "Omphalos Apollo"[21] (figs. 36, 37), the "Tiber Apollo"[22] (fig. 38), and the Boston Herakles[23] (fig. 39) of

---

[17] Akropolis Museum, No. 698; Metropolitan Museum, *Catalogue of Bronzes*, No. 78.
[18] For early tentative renderings of asymmetry cf. Richter, *Kouroi*, p. 33.
[19] Treu, *Olympia*, III, pl. XXII. [20] Metropolitan Museum, *op. cit.*, No. 79.
[21] National Museum, Athens, No. 45. The name "Omphalos Apollo" is still retained for convenience, though the omphalos base found at the same time as the statue in the Theatre of Dionysos could not have belonged to it on account of the different stance of the feet.
[22] Helbig, *Führer*,[3] II, No. 1336.
[23] Caskey, *Catalogue of Greek and Roman Sculpture*, No. 64.

about 450 B.C. show a further gain in freedom and mobility. An interplay of planes is achieved by turning the head, the shoulders, the pelvis, the knees in different directions counterbalancing one another. The lines of the eyes, shoulders, and hips are no longer horizontal but incline upward and downward in alternating rhythm. There is a lovely interplay of surfaces and yet the effect is not too variegated, for the whole is kept in a definite scheme. We have evolved from a patterned shape into a moving body. Nevertheless these statues are not a spontaneous expression, but are due to the long evolution of a type. The background of the pattern period gives them grandeur.

But even in these figures the attitude has a lingering stiffness and the shoulders are too broad compared with the rest of the body. The problem remains to give greater ease to the pose, more harmony to the composition. This was accomplished during the second half of the fifth century B.C. It was achieved by further developing the scheme of counterpoise. The counterbalancing movements are accentuated. The median curve is emphasized and the weight is borne entirely by one leg. The figure thereby acquires swing and ease of attitude. Each form is beautifully modeled, no longer in the dry, hard manner of archaic times, but with more amplitude.[24] The four-sided conception has given way to perfect modeling in the round. Each part appears to point

Fig. 45. River god Selinos, on a coin
(enlarged)

W. H. Woodward Collection

at the spectator as he looks at it, the adjoining portions retreating to the background; in other words, the sculptor no longer restricts himself to a few principal views of his figure but is able to combine a large number into a unified whole. The interrelated patterns of earlier days have given way to a balanced whole with the various parts of the body in proportional relation to one another.

[24] Cf. *infra,* pp. 245 ff.

As conspicuous examples of this developed type we may take the Polykleitan figures of the Doryphoros (fig. 645) and Diadoumenos (fig. 650); the Idolino in Florence[25] (figs. 43, 44); the beautiful bronze statuettes in the Louvre[26] (fig. 42) and New York[27] (fig. 40); and the figure of the river god Selinos on the coin of Selinus[28] (fig. 45). And for the female type we may cite the bronze statuette of a girl in Munich[29] (fig. 41). How much more natural are now the attitudes; what beautiful contours the figures have assumed! What subtle variety is introduced by the action of the arms and how harmonious is the whole composition! But we are still conscious that the figure is an interrelated scheme comparable to a carefully planned architectural design.

At this period, when the problems of construction had been fully mastered, Greek sculpture might easily have become realistic. Instead, it shows in increasing manner a quality of aloofness, of universality. The modeling is more naturalistic, but the statues have a grandeur and idealism which remove them from nature. How did the Greek sculptor accomplish this? Such things are difficult to put into words. But one of the many reasons is that in spite of his new knowledge he kept his eye on the essentials. Though he had by now a thorough knowledge of the complicated anatomy of the human body, he was not distracted by the many-sidedness of nature, but kept his modeling simple, his planes few, his volume unified; and he consciously harmonized his composition.[30] The canon of proportion which we feel underlying the early statues has been developed into a subtler scheme. And so, instead of copying closely one particular human body, merely translating nature into stone, he created something universal and typical. As is perhaps natural this quality of Greek sculpture has often been misunderstood and interpreted merely as physical beauty. But much more than the loveliness it is the impersonality of fifth-century sculpture that makes it great. Plato gives us an explanation when he speaks of painters as "fixing their eyes on perfect truth as a perpetual standard of reference, to be contemplated with the minutest care, before they proceed to deal

---

[25] Amelung, *Antiken in Florenz*, No. 268.
[26] De Ridder, *Bronzes antiques du Louvre*, I, No. 183.
[27] Metropolitan Museum, *Catalogue of Bronzes*, No. 87.
[28] Hill, *Select Greek Coins*, pl. XLI, 5.
[29] Sieveking, *Münchner Jahrbuch der bildenden Kunst*, V, 1910, pp. 1 ff. The rendering of the features and of the hair indicates a pre-fourth-century date.
[30] Cf. p. 89.

with earthly canons about things beautiful."[31] It is this recourse to
the perfect pattern for inspiration which produces the "typical" as
against the "individual," the general instead of the particular.
Fifth-century sculpture gives us a peculiar sense of exhilaration
because it can translate us from the narrow personal plane to an
impersonal one.

FOURTH
CENTURY
Naturally so lofty a standard could not be maintained forever.
By the fourth century a softening makes itself felt. The curves are
further accentuated, creating a still greater contrast of direction;
and in the modeling the number of planes has greatly multiplied,
more nearly approximating nature. All these changes are admirably
shown in the Hermes by Praxiteles (fig. 664), a statue in which we
have the advantage of studying a Greek original by a great master.[32] There is a new grace in the attitude, and in the modeling all
hard divisions have disappeared. One part now passes imperceptibly
into the adjoining, everything is gentle and soft with infinite variations. The play of light and shade on this delicately worked surface
suggests the luminous quality of flesh and we feel the envelope of
skin over muscles and bones as we never have before. And yet there
is something godlike in the quiet serenity and detachment. Nevertheless the lofty quality of fifth-century sculpture is gone. The pattern scheme out of which Greek sculpture grew and which gave it
volume and grandeur is disappearing. In spite of the increase in
grace the design harmony is lacking. And we feel we are on a different plane, more personal, less spiritual, and so less invigorating. The
same is true of all fourth-century sculpture. The Praxitelean Apollo
Sauroktonos (fig. 676) and Satyrs (figs. 51, 682), the "Skopaic"
Hermes of the Ephesos column (fig. 705), and the bronze youth from
the Bay of Marathon[33] (figs. 46–48) show a lovely composition
and modeling, but an absence of the former vigor and decorative
quality.

The new taste for grace and softness naturally awakened interest
in the female body. While in the sixth and fifth centuries undraped
female figures appear only occasionally they now become a favorite
subject. The delicate modulations of the female form were rendered
with fine appreciation, and a new realm of beauty was thereby added
to the artistic stock. We can obtain only a faint glimmer of these

---

31 Plato, *Republic* VI. 484.   32 See p. 257, note 24.

33 Rhomaios, Δελτ. 'Αρχ., 1924–25, pp. 145 ff.; National Museum, Athens, No. 15118.

fourth-century creations by the Roman copies of such famous works
as the Knidian Aphrodite (fig. 668) and the Aphrodite Anady-
omene (e.g., the Aphrodite from Kyrene,[34] fig. 50) or by bronze
statuettes like the lovely Aphrodites in the British Museum[35] (fig.
49) and from the Haviland Collection;[36] for no first-class full-size
Greek originals have survived. But even so we can form an impression of the sensuous charm of the curves and subtly contrasting
planes. And the potency of this charm can be gauged by the influence these works have exercised on all subsequent art, including our
own.

Toward the later part of the fourth century the sculptor Lysippos introduced novelty into the design by imparting a slight torsion
and "making the body more slender and the head smaller, thus giving
his figures the appearance of greater height."[37] We see this new canon
illustrated in the Apoxyomenos of the Vatican (fig. 739) with its
slender proportions, in the praying boy in Berlin[38] (fig. 54), and in
the bronze statuette of Alexander in Paris[39] (fig. 52). A new elasticity
and realism are introduced by this change. We are gradually leaving
behind us the idealistic conceptions of earlier Greek art to enter a
world of different values.

During the Hellenistic period these tendencies are still further
accentuated. The graceful fourth-century poses either become even
softer and more effeminate, as in the Hermaphrodite in Constantinople[40] (fig. 53), sometimes with an added element of picturesqueness, as in the Eros in the Metropolitan Museum[41] (fig. 121) ; or they
are completely abandoned and a new sense of movement is imparted
to the figure by "crossing the action." That is, the various parts of
the body—the head, the trunk, the legs—are placed at completely
different angles from one another, thus imparting a decided twist
to the figure. A similar change takes place in the modeling. The
planes hitherto kept fairly uniform with only subtle variations now
show violent contrasts. The original pattern scheme has been dis-
carded for a completely realistic rendering. The commanding statue

HELLENISTIC
PERIOD

---

[34] Paribeni, *Le Terme di Diocleziano e il Museo Nazionale Romano*, p. 160, No. 372.
[35] Walters, *Select Bronzes*, pl. 45.
[36] Now in New York; cf. *A.J.A.* XXXVII, 1933, pp. 48 ff.
[37] Pliny, *N.H.* XXXIV.
[38] *Beschreibung der antiken Skulpturen in Berlin*, No. 2. Both arms are restored.
[39] De Ridder, *Bronzes antiques du Louvre*, pl. 81, No. 370.
[40] Mendel, *Catalogue des sculptures du Musée à Constantinople*, No. 624.
[41] *A.J.A.*, 1943, pp. 365 ff.

of Poseidon in Athens[42] (early Hellenistic; fig. 55), the bronze
portrait statue in Rome[43] (fig. 57) and the bronze Satyr in New
York[44] (fig. 56), both later Hellenistic, are typical examples. Compared with the lofty types of earlier days they make on us a restless, almost theatrical impression; but their vitality and strength
are undeniable. And by this new realism sculpture now becomes more
human, less remote, and so easily understood by the multitude.
Therewith a new world of ideas opened up to the sculptor, and he
attempted many subjects hitherto neglected (cf. p. 82). Instead of
the portrayal of beautiful types he turned to that of individual
human beings and produced such sensitive renderings as the young
negro musician in Paris (figs. 58–60). The simple standing figure
now naturally became less common, and more intimate or complex
poses prevailed.

Much that has been said regarding the development of the standing type applies also to the other types, for the modeling of the
human figure is naturally similar in all. In our survey of these types,
therefore, we shall confine ourselves largely to a study of the development in the attitudes.

(b) The Seated Figure

THE seated figure enjoyed a great and continuous popularity in
Greek sculpture.[45] Besides the problem of representing the human
figure in a relaxed, quiet pose, we have here the further task of making it appear separate and distinct from the seat. In early archaic
renderings, like the goddess from Prinias,[46] the Branchidai statue[47]
(fig. 62), and the example on the Corfu pediment[48] (fig. 61), this has
not yet been achieved. The figure appears as part and parcel of the
throne, and the attitudes are stiff and constrained, though grandly
conceived. The statues are in strictly frontal position with both sides
exactly alike and no turn in either direction. In the examples of the
later sixth century, such as the Athena by Endoios (?) from the
Akropolis[49] (fig. 64) and the terracotta statuettes of this period
(cf. fig. 63), there is a considerable advance in the elasticity of the

---

[42] National Museum, No. 235.   [43] Helbig, op. cit., II, No. 1347.
[44] Metropolitan Museum, Bulletin XXV, 1930, pp. 40 ff.
[45] For a detailed study of the development of the seated type with numerous illustrations, cf. Möbius, Ath. Mitt., XLI, 1916, pp. 119 ff.
[46] Pernier, Bolletino d'arte, 1908, p. 459; Annuario della scuola archeologica di
Atene, 1914, p. 90, fig. 46.
[47] Pryce, Catalogue of Sculpture in the British Museum, I, 1, No. B 271.
[48] Rodenwaldt, Korkyra, II, pl. 25.   [49] Dickins, Catalogue, No. 625.

pose, which has now a quiet dignity and charm. In the Berlin goddess[50] (fig. 65) of about 480 there is a new grandeur, heralding a new era. In the transitional period (480–450) the frontal pose is abandoned and the figure begins to move and turn, just as it does in the standing type. Interesting examples are the "Penelope" of the Vatican[51] (fig. 68), the beautiful Athena of the Olympia metope in the Louvre (fig. 66), and the bronze kitharist in the Hermitage[52] (fig. 67); in the marble figures, which are really worked in high relief, the upper and lower parts of the body are placed in contrasting planes, while in the bronze statuette a pleasing variety is attained by less drastic means.

The seated figures of the Parthenon pediment (figs. 69–71[53]) show complete freedom. The poses are easy and relaxed, with a slight not too obvious change of direction in the upper and lower parts, and the seats are entirely separate so that we feel that the body can rise at will; and yet the former sense for design is still strong, imparting to these statues an imposing majesty. They make us regret the more that we have lost one of the most famous creations of antiquity, Pheidias' seated statue of Zeus at Olympia (cf. p. 220).

The reliefs of the fourth-century gravestones show many beautiful seated figures in quiet and completely naturalistic poses. As examples in the round we may mention the Demeter from Knidos[54] (fig. 315) and some Tanagra statuettes (cf. fig. 73[55]) in which the gentle charm of fourth-century art finds beautiful expression. A comparison between the girl in figure 73 with the "Penelope" (fig. 68) will bring home to us better than many words the naturalistic development of the type. In the bronze Hermes from Herculaneum[56] (fig. 72) the problem of representing a seated figure in a momentary pose is beautifully solved. This statue—a Roman copy of an original of the Lysippian circle—foreshadows the new sense of movement which became so popular in Hellenistic times. In the bronze boxer[57] (fig. 770) and the Belvedere Torso[58] (fig. 771) of the late Hellenistic period we find the same qualities we noted in the

---

50 Wiegand, *Antike Denkmäler*, III, pp. 45 ff., pls. 37 ff.
51 Helbig, *Führer*,3 I, No. 89. Cf. also the many other mourning figures of this type.
52 Waldhauer, *Pythagoras of Rhegium*, pp. 69 ff., figs. 13–15.
53 Smith, *The Sculptures of the Parthenon*, pls. 3, 5.
54 Smith, *Catalogue of Greek Sculpture in the British Museum*, II, No. 1300.
55 Metropolitan Museum, *Bulletin*, 1911, pp. 214–215, fig. 8.
56 Ruesch, *Guida del Museo Nazionale di Napoli*, No. 841.
57 Helbig, *op. cit.*, II, No. 1350.　　　58 *Ibid.*, I, No. 124.

standing types of the period—superbly realistic modeling and dramatic action conveyed by a decided twist of the body and the placing of the head at a completely different angle from the trunk. The drunken woman hugging her bottle[59] (fig. 74) and the boy extracting a thorn from his foot[60] (fig. 75) give us an idea of the manysidedness of the new outlook. But how far we have traveled from the stately Branchidai figures!

(c) The Flying or Running Figure

FROM the first the Greek sculptor was interested in motion. To represent a flying or running or striding figure, what fascinating problems it entailed, how necessary for his metope or pediment compositions, how difficult of solution with the limited powers at the command of the archaic artist! His method of coping with the difficulties is characteristic. He invented a scheme, a convention for these poses, highly decorative, far from naturalistic, but admirably serving his purpose. And the scheme once adopted was adhered to as a formula until by a greater knowledge of anatomy he achieved a more naturalistic interpretation. Thus, to show the motion of running or flying he represented the figure kneeling on one knee, with arms stretched upward, downward, or sidewise; the upper part of the body in full front, the legs in profile, with no proper interconnection between these two portions. As examples of the earlier archaic period we may cite the amazing Gorgon from the Corfu pediment[61] (fig. 76; c. 600–580 B.C.), the Gorgon in Syracuse[62] (fig. 79), the Nike from Delos[63] (figs. 77, 78; c. 560–550), and the bronze statuettes of a Nike in Athens[64] (fig. 80) and of a runner in New York[65] (figs. 81, 82). These figures, though they do not actually represent the motion correctly, certainly suggest it, and decoratively are very effective. So the scheme—adequate for the time being—continued throughout most of the sixth century, developing gradually in the direction of naturalism by a less abrupt connection of the upper and lower parts. Beautiful examples of later archaic renderings are the bronze statuettes of Nike in London[66] (fig. 83) and a marble relief in Athens (fig. 84).[67]

[59] Furtwängler, Beschreibung der Glyptothek, No. 437.
[60] Smith, Catalogue of Greek Sculpture in the British Museum, III, No. 1755.
[61] Βερσάκης, Πρακτικά, 1911, pp. 172–175; Rodenwaldt, Korkyra, II, pl. IV.
[62] Orsi, Monumenti antichi, XXV, 1918, pl. XVI.
[63] National Museum, Athens, No. 21.   [64] Ibid., No. 6483.
[65] Metropolitan Museum, Catalogue of Bronzes, No. 16.
[66] Walters, Select Bronzes, pl. 4, fig. 1.   [67] National Museum, No. 1959.

In spite of the adherence to the old scheme there is now more freedom and swing to the movement.

Side by side with this conventional scheme there appear during the sixth century more realistic representations in which the legs and arms are in more natural positions; for instance the bronze statuettes in Athens[68] (fig. 85), Berlin,[69] and London[70] (fig. 86). But they are only sporadic. Not until the early fifth century with the casting off of archaic conventions was the charming decorative motive of the early artist finally given up (surviving only in some representations on coins, where archaizing tendencies were always strong, since for practical reasons the continuity of a standard type was desirable).[71] In the small statue of a running maiden of about 480 found at Eleusis[72] (fig. 87) the body has the right forward direction, the knees are bent at the proper angle, and at last the upper and lower parts of the body coördinate. The only archaisms are a lingering stiffness in the attitude and that charming, decorative quality which is gradually lost with the conquering naturalism. We still feel these two traits, though in a slightly less degree, in the Leto of the Conservatori Palace[73] (fig. 90), and the beautiful statue from Marmaria at Delphi[74] (fig. 89) of about 460–450. Even in the figure of the Ilissos frieze[75] (fig. 88) of about the middle of the century the upper part of the body is a little too perpendicular for the motion of the lower part. But a few years later complete freedom is attained. It is difficult to imagine more adequate representations of running figures than the Copenhagen Niobid[76] (about 450–440; fig. 92) or the Iris from the Parthenon pediment[77] (438–432; fig. 91), at once swiftly moving and majestic; or of a flying figure than the Nike of Paionios[78] (about 425–420; fig. 637) gently floating through the air. There is now no

[68] National Museum, *Carapanos Collection*, No. 24.
[69] Kekulé, *Bronzen aus Dodona*, p. 32.
[70] Walters, *Catalogue of Bronzes in the British Museum*, No. 208.
[71] Thus on the coins of Kilikia a running winged female figure is shown in the conventional archaic attitude from the sixth century to the late fifth; cf. British Museum, *Catalogue of Greek Coins*, XVII, Cilicia (Mallus?), pls. XV, XVI.
[72] *Arch. Anz.*, 1925, p. 315.
[73] Stuart Jones, *The Sculptures of the Palazzo dei Conservatori*, p. 227, No. 81, pl. 85.
[74] Homolle, *Fouilles de Delphes*, IV, pl. LVI.
[75] *Antike Denkmäler*, III, pl. 36; Studniczka, *Jahrbuch*, XXXI, 1916, pp. 169 ff.
[76] Arndt, *La Glyptothèque Ny Carlsberg*, pl. 38; Brunn-Bruckmann, *Denkmäler*, pls. 712–714.
[77] Smith, *Sculptures of the Parthenon*, pl. 3, right; compare also the similar figure in Copenhagen, Brunn-Bruckmann, *op. cit.*, pl. 663.
[78] Treu, *Olympia*, III, pls. XLVI–XLVII.

longer need of formulas or conventions to suggest the idea of motion; the actual movement is successfully rendered in a naturalistic and yet artistic manner. It is a far cry from the Parthenon Iris to the schematized figures of the sixth century; but part of its greatness lies in the fact of its immediate succession from them. In spite of the consummate naturalistic modeling we are still conscious of the pattern scheme which is its background. The Epidauros Nike (fig. 713) is a graceful version of gliding motion characteristic of the early fourth century; and the forward-rushing female figure in Budapest[79] (fig. 93) is a Roman copy of a Greek work of the middle of that century. As examples of the Hellenistic period we may cite the famous Nike of Samothrake[80] (fig. 95), one of the most powerful renderings in the history of art; and the charming bronze Eros (fig. 94) of the Morgan Collection[81] typical of the new outlook of the time. The former is conceived as alighting after flight, on a speeding ship, with wings still outspread, the latter as running in a torch-race.

(d) The Striding Figure

THE striding figure, that is, one in forward though not rapid motion, likewise absorbed the Greek sculptor from very early times. It was naturally an easier action to represent than that of rapid flight, and we find a fair measure of success even in the earliest attempts: for instance in the Zeus of the Corfu pediment[82] (fig. 96), where the action of the legs and of the whole forward-leaning body is already convincing, though the modeling is still primitive, with the upper part in full front, the legs in profile. The same general attitude with legs wide apart and one arm raised holding a spear, thunderbolt, or other weapon is found again and again during the sixth century. It is a favorite one for small bronze statuettes;[83] it occurs on the coins of Poseidonia[84] from 550 to 510 (fig. 98 on p. 65), and it is that of the Herakles in the pediment of the Siphnian Treasury[85] (fig. 382)

[79] Hekler, in Brunn-Bruckmann, *Denkmäler*, pl. 640.

[80] Conze, Hauser, and Benndorf, *Untersuchungen auf Samothrake*, II, pl. LXIV. The date of the statue has been much disputed (see Chronology, p. 47). At present it is generally placed early in the second century B.C. (cf. H. Thiersch, *Nachrichten von der Geseltchaft der Wissenschaften zu Göttingen*, 1931, p. 368).

[81] Metropolitan Museum, *Catalogue of Bronzes*, No. 131 (catalogued when the statuette was there on loan).

[82] Βερσάκης, Πρακτικά, 1911, p. 167.

[83] Cf., e.g., Neugebauer, *Antike Bronzestatuetten*, No. 27.

[84] Gardner, *Types of Greek Coins*, pl. I, No. 2.

[85] Homolle, *Fouilles de Delphes*, IV, pls. XLVI, XLVII, fig. 1 a.

and of many of the warriors on the Siphnian frieze[86] (about 525; fig. 97). In all these renderings, just as in the contemporary flying figures, the upper and lower parts of the body do not coördinate; moreover, the body is often too perpendicular; and little attempt is made to show the contraction of the muscles under the strain of the action. All this is gradually corrected during the first half of the fifth century. We may mention as distinguished examples the bronze statuettes of Herakles from Mantineia[87] (fig. 99), of a warrior[88] (fig. 100) and of Zeus[89] from Dodona (fig. 101), the warriors from the west[90] and east[91] pediments of Aigina (fig. 103), the Herakles of the Selinus metope[92] (fig. 412), and the splendid Zeus (or Poseidon) from off Cape Artemision (fig. 102[92a]). In the warrior from Sparta[93] (fig. 104) the upper part of the body is inclined farther forward, a device which accentuates the action. An effective variation is introduced by Kritios and Nesiotes in the Harmodios (figs. 575–577) of the Tyrannicide group in which the right arm is brought over the head.

Fig. 98. Poseidon, on a coin of Poseidonia (enlarged)

E. T. Newell Collection, New York

All traces of archaism and stiffness completely disappear in the following period; and the type reaches its complete development in the striding Lapiths of the Parthenon metopes[94] of about 447–443

[86] *Ibid.*, pls. XXI–XXIII.
[87] Metropolitan Museum, *Bulletin*, November, 1928.
[88] Kekulé, *Bronzen aus Dodona*, pl. II, p. 13.
[89] *Ibid.*, pl. I, p. 6.
[90] Furtwängler, *Aegina*, pl. 96, Nos. 22 and 14 (Glyptothek 76 and 80).
[91] *Ibid.*, pl. 95, No. 72 (Glyptothek 86).
[92] Benndorf, *Metopen von Selinunt*, pl. VII.
[92a] Karousos, Δελτ.'Αρχ., 1930–31, pp. 41 ff.
[93] Woodward, *B.S.A.*, XXVI, 1923–25, pls. XVIII–XX, p. 253; National Museum, Athens, No. 3613.
[94] Smith, *Sculptures of the Parthenon*, pl. 19, 1.

(fig. 105) and in the Herakles of the Phigaleia frieze[95] of about 420
(fig. 106). The action is now perfectly convincing, the figures have
an amazing force and freedom and are correctly constructed
throughout. In the Herakles particularly the contraction of the
muscles of the arms and of the serratus magnus are realistically rendered. The difference between these later, finished representations
and the early attempts on the Corfu pediment is far-reaching; and
yet the kinship is close. Again we feel the tradition behind the freer
figures, which helps to give them restraint and stability. In the
fourth century, though there is a lessening of vigor, we have fine
renderings, like the warriors of the Mausoleum frieze (fig. 698). As
an example of what happened to the striding figure in Hellenistic
times we may cite the Borghese Warrior in the Louvre[96] (fig. 107)
and the superb Gaul killing himself in the Terme Museum[97] (fig.
108). Here the tradition is fading. The realism of the action and of
the modeling indicates a novel outlook. The Borghese Warrior indeed might serve as a model in an anatomy class. And yet even here
we note the observance of the unified volume, of the relief conception, one of the fundamental characteristics of earlier Greek sculpture (cf. pp. 27 f.); and the restlessness and theatrical quality are
largely neutralized thereby.

(e) The Reclining Figure

THE history of the reclining figure is one of the most interesting
in Greek sculpture. A figure in a merely horizontal position was of
course comparatively easy to represent, but the reclining posture in
which the upper part of the torso faced the spectator and the legs
were in profile presented many difficulties; and yet this attitude was
the most desirable for scenes of banquets and combats or for fitting
the figure into pediment angles. The twist of the body entailed a
strong torsion, the rendering of which required more knowledge of
anatomy than the archaic sculptor had. It is interesting to see how
the Greek sculptor tackled these difficulties. At first he simply
avoided them. He either took refuge in the completely horizontal
attitude, as, for instance, in the angle figure of the Corfu pediment[98]
(fig. 109) and in the fallen warriors on the Siphnian frieze,[99] or he

---

[95] Smith, *Catalogue of Greek Sculpture in the British Museum*, I, No. 541.
[96] Brunn-Bruckmann, *Denkmäler*, pl. 75.
[97] Helbig, *Führer*,³ II, No. 1302.   [98] Βερσάκης, Πρακτικά, 1911, p. 185.
[99] Homolle, *Fouilles de Delphes*, IV, pls. XXI–XXIII.

covered the body with armor or drapery, as in the reclining figure
from Samos[100] (fig. 110); or again he represented only the upper
part nude and covered the lower with drapery, as in the Amazon
from the corner of a pediment in the Thebes Museum[101] and in the
banqueters on the sarcophagus from "Golgoi"[102] (fig. 111). But we
see the sculptor at grips with the problem in the fallen giant from
the marble pediment of the "Hekatompedon"[103] (c. 520; fig. 112).
Here the chest is in full front view, while the hips and abdomen
are abruptly turned. Beneath the sternum where the torsion takes
place confusion reigns; the various divisions of the rectus abdominis are placed in strange positions and the median line forms several
sharp angles in an impossible manner.

In the figures of the west[104] (fig. 113) and the east pediments[105]
(fig. 114) of the Aigina temple (c. 500–480) the problem is not
yet solved; the various parts of the abdominal muscle are not rightly
related and the median line is still angular.[106] The reclining satyr by
the Brygos Painter[107] (fig. 117), datable about 490–480, shows the
same stage of development as the statues from Aigina. The rectus abdominis is rendered by adjacent ovals, the serratus magnus by a
single row of curves, and the median line is omitted.[108] But twenty
years later we find the beautiful figures of Kladeos (fig. 115) and
Alpheios (fig. 116) of the Olympia pediments,[109] both shown in reclining poses with correct construction. The action of the muscles
is rightly expressed and the necessary curve is attained; the undulating contours of the figures admirably suggest the slow stream of
rivers, and their detachment fits them well for their rôle of spectators; the only archaism left is a lingering angularity. In the Ilissos of

---

100 Buschor, *Altsamische Standbilder*, figs. 99, 100. Inscribed ". . . oche who dedicated it to Hera."

101 From Topolia; cf. *Ath. Mitt.*, XXX, 1905, pl. 13.

102 Myres, *Handbook of the Cesnola Collection in the Metropolitan Museum*, No.
1364.

103 Dickins, *Catalogue of the Acropolis Museum*, I, No. 631 A. Though the navel
itself and the portion below it are restored, the upper portion is fortunately intact.

104 Furtwängler, *Aegina*, pl. 96, Nos. 1 and 33 (Glyptothek 83 and 79).

105 *Ibid.*, pl. 95, No. 41 (Glyptothek 85).

106 Cf. on this subject Lange, *Darstellung des Menschen*, pp. 69 ff.

107 In the Metropolitan Museum, No. 12.234.5; cf. Richter and Hall, *Red-figured
Athenian Vases in the Metropolitan Museum of Art*, No. 43, pl. 43, centre; Beazley,
ARVP., p. 254, No. 137.

108 For an analysis of this development in red-figure cf. Richter, *Attic Red-figured
Vases*, p. 60.

109 Treu, *Olympia*, III, pl. XV, 2, 3.

the Parthenon pediment[110] of about 438–432 (fig. 119) and the
Niobid in Copenhagen[111] (fig. 118) the last vestige of stiffness is
conquered; each part connects naturally with the succeeding, and
together they form a beautiful and harmonious whole. The Hellenistic period has given us some splendid representations of reclining
figures, perfectly relaxed, in highly naturalistic renderings. We may
cite as typical examples the dead Gaul in Venice[112] (fig. 120), the
bronze statue of a sleeping Eros in the Metropolitan Museum[113] (fig.
121), and the marble statue of a sleeping Satyr in the Lateran[114] (fig.
122). The sculptor has not only rendered the pose naturalistically,
but has suggested the mood of each figure.

(f) The Falling Figure

THE falling figure has an interesting career. At first the motive
of a body falling backward was too difficult of achievement and a

Fig. 129. Wounded warrior, from a lekythos

Bibliothèque Nationale, Paris

(Cf. p. 233)

compromise was effected
by representing the fig-
ure as partly kneel-
ing—just as in the fly-
ing figure. We find this
device in the giant op-
posing Zeus in the Corfu
pediment,[115] of the first
half of the sixth century
(fig. 96); and in more
developed form on the
Siphnian frieze[116] (c.
525; fig. 123). In the
sculptures of the Athe-
nian Treasury (c. 510–
500), however, the fall-
ing motion is at last
attempted in the metope of Herakles and Kyknos[117] (fig. 124). In

110 Smith, *Sculptures of the Parthenon*, pl. 7.
111 Arndt, *La Glyptothèque Ny Carlsberg*, pl. 51; Brunn-Bruckmann, *Denkmäler*,
pls. 710–713.
112 Dütschke, *Antike Bildwerke in Oberitalien*, V, No. 209; Bienkowski, *Die
Darstellung der Gallier*, pp. 38 ff., fig. 50.
113 Richter, *A.J.A.*, XLVII, 1943, pp. 365 ff.
114 Helbig, *Führer*,³ No. 1176 (450).   115 Βερσάκης, Πρακτικά, 1911, p. 167.
116 Homolle, *Fouilles de Delphes*, IV, pls. XII–XIV.
117 *Ibid.*, pl. XLII.

the east pediment of Aigina (*c.* 480), at least as restored by Furtwängler[118] (cf. fig. 389), and in a metope of temple E at Selinus[119] (*c.* 470) warriors and a giant are shown falling backward at
precarious angles (fig. 413). The problem was also attempted
in single compositions, as we know from the mention of a "volneratus
deficiens" by Kresilas (cf. p. 233) and from the beautiful bronze
statuettes of Ajax in Florence[120] (figs. 125, 126) and of the warriors in Modena[121] (fig. 128) and in St. Germain-en-Laye[122] (fig.
127). These bold attempts are characteristic of the adventurous
transition period and are found also in contemporary vase-paintings (cf. figs. 129, 130[123]).

The calm serenity of later fifth- and fourth-century sculpture
hardly admitted of such restless creations of momentary poses.
When utilized in contest scenes in pediments, metopes, and friezes
the half-kneeling attitude is again adopted, but now with correct
inclinations of the body and in very beautiful postures. The metopes
of the Parthenon, and the Phigaleia and Mausoleum friezes supply
lovely examples (cf. fig. 131).[124] The striving for realism and variety in Hellenistic times made the adoption of the falling attitude
again possible. A good example is the bronze statuette in New York
of a drunken Herakles reeling backward[125] (fig. 132). The backward inclination is not nearly so marked as in the examples of the
transitional period, so that we have a better sense of equilibrium;
and the modeling is completely naturalistic.

(g) *The Crouching Figure*

THE crouching figures in the many combat scenes on pediments,
metopes, and friezes necessarily vary largely in postures, leaning
more or less forward according to the action and composition. The
favorite attitude is the half-kneeling one, with one knee on the
ground, the other bent at an angle. We can watch its development
in the pediment groups from the Siphnian and the Megarian
(fig. 383) Treasuries to those of the temples of Aigina (figs. 388,

---

118 *Aegina,* pl. 106.
119 Benndorf, *Metopen von Selinunt,* pl. X.
120 Milani, *Bolletino d'arte,* II, 1908, pp. 361 ff.
121 Bulle, *Der schöne Mensch,* pl. 94.
122 S. Reinach, *Gazette des Beaux-Arts,* 1905, pp. 193 ff.
123 Metropolitan Museum, Acc. No. 08.258.21.
124 Smith, *Sculptures of the Parthenon,* pl. 17, 2.
125 Metropolitan Museum, *Handbook* (1930), p. 195, fig. 133.

389) and Olympia[126] (figs. 133, 134). The crouching Lapiths of the Parthenon[127] metopes show us the harmonious renderings of the second half of the fifth century, and as typical examples of later times we may cite the Aphrodite by Doidalses, which has been recognized in a number of Roman copies (cf. p. 298 and figs. 135[128], 764), and the silver Satyr (fig. 556) in New York.

Such is the development of the chief types in Greek sculpture. Naturally other poses occur, at least occasionally, but they are surprisingly few; except of course in Hellenistic times, and during one other period, that of the end of the archaic epoch, when the Greek sculptor suddenly found himself able to represent the human body in all manner of postures. It was the first time in his career and he was naturally tempted to try out his powers in this new world of form. And we find him attempting such complicated poses as that of the Diskobolos (fig. 578) and the Marsyas (fig. 584), the bronze jumper in New York[129] (fig. 136) and the Niobid in Rome (fig. 4). But this indulgence was only temporary. His taste for quiet and restraint soon brought him back to his simple attitudes for standing and seated figures, with the accepted types of figures in motion for his groups of contests. And we have seen what this concentration and sculptural feeling led him to achieve.

[126] Treu, *Olympia*, III, pl. XIV.   [127] Smith, *op. cit.*, pls. 19, 2 and 23, 2.
[128] In Ostia; cf. R. Calza, *Museo Ostiense*, no. 123.
[129] Metropolitan Museum, *Catalogue of Bronzes*, No. 81.

CHAPTER V

THE HEAD

(a) *The Rendering of the Features*

THE human figure with its manifold, intricate problems was so absorbing to the Greek sculptor during his early period that he could not give the head primary consideration. He struggled with its representation, as he did with that of the rest of the body, but to him the human face was only part of a physical organism, not the chief medium for the conveyance of human emotion. Moreover, emotion per se seemed at the time of secondary interest; for the emphasis was laid on the fundamental principles of sculptural representation. So the archaic Greek sculptor, starting as he did with a primitive conception of form, had to concentrate first and foremost on an adequate rendering of the human features. Throughout the archaic period we find him absorbed in this task. At first, just as in his rendering of the torso, he was too timid to carve deeply into his block, so that the face was comparatively flat, with forehead, eyes, cheeks, mouth, and chin all more or less in one plane, the nose only protruding; the head, like the body, still retained the cubic shape of the block into which it was carved. Only gradually, in a slow and groping manner, he gave up his superficial carving and found the right relation of the different planes to one another.

It is interesting to watch him at work. The Dipylon head[1] (fig. 137; perhaps late seventh century), the Olympia Hera[2] (fig. 138; c. 600), the Delphi Youth[3] (fig. 142), the Chrysaor from Corfu[4] (fig. 141), and the Berlin standing goddess[5] (figs. 139, 140), all of the first half of the sixth century, illustrate an early stage. Everything is flat and near the surface. The eyelids are merely curved ridges, the eyeballs are apt to be flat and prominent, and there is as yet no indication of the recess (*canthus*) or the tear-duct at the inner corner.[6] The

---

1 Richter, *Kouroi*, No. 6.   2 Treu, *Olympia*, III, pl. I, pp. 1 ff.
3 Homolle *Fouilles de Delphes*, IV, pls. I–II; *Kouroi*, No. 11.
4 Βερσάκης, Πρακτικά, 1911, pp. 187 ff.
5 Wiegand, *Berliner Museen*, 1926, 2, p. 18.
6 For an early tentative rendering of this recess cf. e.g. *Kouroi*, No. 40.

two lips are sharply cut and generally horizontal, with a triangular depression at the corners. The ear is often too high or too low and lies flat against the head,[7] with a knob-like tragus and no indication of the antitragus. It has often a beautiful schematized form combining with the earring into an effective pattern.

In other words the forms of the features are conditioned by the fact that they are carved, so to speak, in relief on the flat sides of a cube instead of being modeled in the round; the front, back, and two profile views are the only ones considered. That these early heads, with all their primitiveness, often have power and great beauty is due to the feeling for design and volume. The outline of the head, the lines formed by the eyebrows, the eyelids, and the lips have a beautiful swing; and the general effect is highly decorative. Moreover, they retain the connection with the block into which they were carved and thus compare favorably with some later work where this feeling for volume is lost. Again we learn that correct rendering of nature is not a prerequisite of art.

By the second half of the sixth century much has been learned. There is now a greater difference of planes and many details hitherto neglected are observed. In the Akropolis Kore No. 679 (fig. 143; c. 540–530) and the kouros Ptoon 20 (fig. 28; late VI century), for instance, the eye is sunk more deeply beneath the brow, the eyelids are no longer mere ridges, and the upper one has considerably more width than before; the ball itself recedes downward, so that the lower lid is in a distinctly different plane from the upper; and the inner corner is carved to indicate the canthus. The eye as a whole is not yet sufficiently sunk and the ball is not felt as a separate member, but the change from the primitive rendering of fifty years before is great. The same applies to the mouth. The upper and lower lips are no longer practically identical ridges, but are differentiated, and often end in a sharp point at the corners instead of the transverse groove. The ear is assuming its natural shape and the antitragus is indicated. Moreover, the whole head is becoming rounded instead of cubic. Nevertheless, the decorative quality is retained in the simplification of the form and the sharply defined contour of each feature. A mysterious charm pervades the whole.

The decorative instinct of the early Greek sculptor enabled him

---

[7] In the Delphi Youth the ear is carved into the hair (which is brought forward) and is thereby detached from the skull.

also to deal with another great problem which confronted him, the
rendering of the hair. Since it seemed impossible with the knowledge
at his command to represent in any way approaching reality the
luminous, infinitely variegated surface of human hair, he frankly
had recourse to a conventional treatment; and utilized various designs,
often with highly pleasing results. His commonest device at first
was a series of long, vertical ridges starting from the forehead,
brought down the back, and divided by horizontal grooves or ridges
to form a chequer pattern (New York head,[8] fig. 148). The ridges
themselves are sometimes further diversified by smaller ripples (Sounion kouros,[9] figs. 146, 152, and Delphi Youth,[10] fig. 145); or the
scheme is simplified by the use of horizontal or vertical ridges only
(Tenea kouros,[11] fig. 147). Later, with greater truth to nature, wavy
ridges are made to radiate from the center of the cranium (Akropolis
Kore,[12] fig. 150). In the first half of the sixth century the hair is generally long (cf. figs. 146, 155). A few separate strands or locks are
brought over to hang down over the shoulder in front, regularly in
female statues and occasionally also in the male ones (e.g., in the
Delphi Youth, fig. 17). From about 550 B.C. the hair is sometimes
fairly short in male statues, descending only to the nape of the neck
(cf. the Munich kouros[13], fig. 151). In the late sixth century it is short
or rolled or looped up behind (cf. fig. 149[14]). To frame the brow we
often find—especially in male heads—highly stylized spiral curls, in
one or more rows arranged symmetrically to right and left of the
centre (Thera kouros, fig. 155; the Chrysaor from Corfu, fig. 153;
the Rampin head in the Louvre,[15] fig. 154; and the kouros in Kansas
City, fig. 149); or merely a wavy outline (Tenea Apollo, fig. 147).
In the female heads the hair is mostly represented waved in front,
sometimes parted in the middle, with side coils on the temples (figs.
143, 144). In some of the earliest heads, it bulges forward over
shoulder and back and is arranged in braids coiled horizontally in
layers on either side (fig. 157[16]). In both male and female heads a
fillet—either forming a closed circle or tied, with ends hanging down

8 Metropolitan Museum, *Bulletin*, 1922, pp. 148 ff.
9 National Museum, Athens, No. 2720.
10 Homolle, *Fouilles de Delphes*, IV, pls. I–II.
11 Furtwängler, *Beschreibung der Glyptothek*, No. 47; Richter, *Kouroi*, No. 58.
12 Akropolis Museum, No. 680.   13 Brunn-Bruckmann, *Denkmäler*, pl. 662.
14 *Guide of the William Rockhill Nelson Collection*[3], p. 18.
15 Brunn-Bruckmann, *Denkmäler*, pl. 552.
16 Metropolitan Museum, *op. cit.*, 1925, p. 14, fig. 1. Cf. for other examples Poulsen, *Der Orient und die frühgriechische Kunst*, pp. 137–160.

—generally holds the hair in place, adding greatly to the ornamental effect of the coiffure. It is sometimes decorated with rosettes and flame-like motives (New York head, fig. 148). Occasionally we also find a second fillet, cords and rings, or bags for tying the hair at the back (figs. 140, 146, 149). Another device sometimes employed to represent hair was the keeping of the mass plain (New York head,[17] fig. 158) or punctured (Berlin head,[18] fig. 156) with the surface, of course, painted. This treatment shows plainly how little the sculptor felt the necessity of depth, the lack of which is indeed the outstanding feature in his sculptured representations of hair; here, as in the figure and the face, the carving is flat.

FIFTH
CENTURY

In the first half of the fifth century the advance toward naturalism continues along every line. The features become more convincing. The eye is farther sunk beneath the brow; and the form and position of the eyeball are better understood; the eyelids, though still heavy, are rendered more correctly with a good understanding of the canthus. The lips glide gradually into the cheeks. But there are still continuous contours round the eye and mouth, which add to the decorative feeling and detract from their realism. The ear assumes its right place, size, and form and stands out from the skull. We can watch the progressive development in the New York head[19] (c. 500; fig. 158), the "Boudeuse" in Athens[20] (c. 485; fig. 159), the seated goddess in Berlin[21] (c. 480; fig. 161), the Demarete coin of Syracuse[22] (c. 479–478; fig. 160), the Delphi Charioteer[23] (c. 470; fig. 162), and the Olympia Apollo[24] (c. 460; fig. 163). The hair is looped up (Olympia Apollo, fig. 163) or arranged in tresses tied round the head (Akropolis head,[25] fig. 169) or simply worn short (Delphi Charioteer, fig. 162, and Brescia head,[26] figs. 166–167). It is either rendered by wavy ridges, now regularly radiating from the center of the head, as in the Barracco head[27] (fig. 164), or when worn short, by neat little ringlets lying close to the skull (Delphi Charioteer, fig. 162). There is still no depth, the surface

[17] Metropolitan Museum, *Bulletin*, 1921, p. 9, fig. 1.
[18] *Beschreibung der Skulpturen in Berlin*, No. 308.
[19] See footnote 17.
[20] Akropolis Museum, No. 686.   [21] *Antike Denkmäler*, III, pls. 37 ff.
[22] Regling, *Die Münze als Kunstwerk*, pl. XVIII, 403.
[23] Homolle, *Fouilles de Delphes*, IV, pls. XLIX–L.
[24] Treu, *Olympia*, III, pls. XXII, XXIII.   [25] Akropolis Museum, No. 689.
[26] Furtwängler, *Masterpieces*, p. 174, fig. 72.
[27] Barracco and Helbig, *Collection Barracco*, pl. 29.

being practically continuous, with nothing obtruding. The fine spherical contour of the head is left unbroken.

We arrive then by the middle of the fifth century at an approximately naturalistic rendering of the human features, but still accompanied by a strong feeling for design and volume—a combination which gives to the products of this period a beautiful, monumental quality. The general shape evolved has certain salient characteristics which have come to be regarded as typically Greek: in profile the forehead and the nose form an almost straight line; the eye is placed high up in its socket and closely approaches the eyebrow; the mouth is small with the curve of the lips accentuated; the chin is strong and the ear small; the face forms a regular oval.

The sculptors of the succeeding periods continued on the road toward naturalism. In the second half of the fifth century, the sharpness of outline gradually disappears. Attention is devoted to the study of transitional planes. In the Idolino[28] (fig. 168) and the head from Argos[29] (fig. 165) the contours of the features are softened, the upper eyelid is made to pass gently over the lower at the outer corner, the lips no longer converge to form sharp angles. Moreover, a decided rounding of the form as a whole has taken place so that every part passes naturally into the adjoining one.

In the hair too there is a marked advance toward realism. The separate strands begin to show greater variation and at last a slight feeling for depth is introduced. But the whole is still a strictly formalized design.

In the fourth century further great changes happen. We may take as representative examples the Hermes of Praxiteles[30] (fig. 170), the Marathon Boy in Athens[31] (figs. 172, 173), the Bartlett[32] head in the Boston Museum (fig. 175), and the head of a youth from a relief in the Metropolitan Museum[33] (fig. 171). The sculptor now realized that in order to convey the impression of natural form he must change it in many particulars, that is, he must translate natural form into "impressional" form. So he gives the appearance of sinking the eye much farther into the head by widening the bridge of the nose and by accentuating the brow; moreover, he greatly re-

FOURTH CENTURY

---

28 Amelung, *Antiken in Florenz*, No. 268.
29 Waldstein, *Argive Heraeum*, pl. XXXVI.
30 Treu, *Olympia*, III, pls. XLIX–LIII.
31 National Museum, No. 15118; Rhomaios, Δελτ. Ἀρχ., 1924–25, pp. 145 ff.
32 Caskey, *Catalogue of Sculpture*, No. 28.
33 Metropolitan Museum, *Bulletin*, 1911, pp. 210–211.

duces the thickness of the eyelids, particularly of the lower one (carefully modeling, however, the transitional planes), so that both now appear as members which can cover an eyeball; and he hollows out the eyeball, making it sometimes actually concave instead of convex. The mouth, too, is greatly changed. It becomes rounder and more fleshy, with the lower lip shorter than the upper. The lips are generally slightly parted with a ridge below the upper lip giving the impression of teeth. The forehead is often triangular in female heads. The modeling creates a subtly variegated surface. The head from Chios[34] (fig. 174) shows the continuation of the Praxitelean style in the direction of even greater softness. One plane now passes imperceptibly into the next.

In the rendering of hair the lesson of impressional form is also learned. After the fifth century the surface becomes more and more variegated; at last a feeling of depth is introduced. In the hair of the Bartlett Aphrodite (fig. 175), the Praxiteles Hermes (fig. 170), and the heads of the "Alexander sarcophagus"[35] (fig. 176) instead of the flat locks and strands there are irregular tufts of considerable depth creating manifold shadows. Individually these masses are less like locks of hair than their predecessors, but collectively they convey the general impression more successfully.

HELLENISTIC
PERIOD

All these tendencies are stressed and often exaggerated in the Hellenistic period. In the heads of a giant from the Pergamene altar[36] (fig. 177), of a Gaul in Rome[37] (fig. 178), and of Zeus on a cameo in Venice[38] (fig. 179) the deep sinking of the eyes, the furrowed brow, the open mouth create deep shadows and produce a dramatic effect. In the hair the depth of the separate masses further increases, the contour plane now becoming entirely broken up and uneven. The conception is naturalistic, and the execution often shows great power; but here too, as in the rendering of the human figure, the feeling for volume is lost and form is disintegrated.

(b) The Head as a Medium of Expression

WE have pursued the history of the development of the human head from the point of view of the rendering of its features. We will now turn to the subject of how the Greek sculptor used it as a medium

[34] Caskey, *Catalogue*, No. 29.

[35] Mendel, *Catalogue des sculptures du Musée à Constantinople*, No. 68.

[36] Museen zu Berlin, *Skulpturen aus Pergamon*, I, p. 27.

[37] Helbig, *Führer*,[3] II, No. 1302.   [38] Furtwängler, *Antike Gemmen*, pl. LIX, 8.

for the expression of emotion. Naturally, until an adequate knowledge of carving was attained it was futile to try to depict any range of feeling; instead, the artist had to convey his meaning by attitude and gesture. We have attempts, if attempts they be, in early Medusa heads (cf. fig. 180[39]) where presumably an expression evoking horror is intended. The so-called archaic smile may have been meant to convey happy alertness, as some hold, but it is more probably the fortuitous result of primitive carving. At all events it was not until the late archaic and transitional periods of the first half of the fifth century when the sculptor had attained an approximately naturalistic rendering, that the means were adequate for this problem. Then indeed we find a great interest in the expression of human emotion—of joy, of sorrow, of pain, of surprise, of radiance. It resembles the sudden attention given to the representation of violent action; as if the sculptor, conscious of his new powers, wanted to try them out in all directions. An early example is the graphic rendering of pain in the falling giant of temple F of Selinus (end of sixth century),[40] who is represented with wide-open mouth, his teeth showing (fig. 181). A little later there are several excellent examples, such as the mourning woman on the Boston relief[41] (c. 480–470), where sorrow is conveyed by the lowered upper eyelids and the short, drooping mouth (fig. 184); and her companion on the same relief (fig. 183), where joy is expressed by a swing of the upper lid and an upward curve of the mouth; and the triumphant Elektra on the relief in Copenhagen[42] (fig. 182), whose exultation is shown by similar means. In the "Aphrodite" of the Ludovisi relief[43] (fig. 185) we have a beautiful expression of radiance due likewise to the upward curve of the mouth and strongly curving upper lid. Another fine example of a radiant expression is the Zeus from the metope of temple E at Selinus[44] (about 475; fig. 187), where the lips are not only curved but parted and the eyes wide open. For the representation of physical pain we may cite the fallen warrior from the east pediment of Aigina[45] (about 480; fig. 525) with his contracted lips

ARCHAIC PERIOD

FIRST HALF OF FIFTH CENTURY

[39] Dickins, *Catalogue of the Acropolis Museum,* No. 701.
[40] Benndorf, *Metopen v. Selinunt,* pl. V; Collignon, *Histoire de la sculpt.* I, p. 331.
[41] Caskey, *Catalogue of Sculpture,* No. 17.
[42] Furtwängler, *Antike Gemmen,* III, p. 267. I have included this relief, for, though presumably Etruscan, it is in the Greek tradition.
[43] Helbig, *Führer,*[3] II, No. 1286.
[44] Benndorf, *op. cit.,* pl. VIII, p. 54.
[45] Furtwängler, *Aegina,* pl. 95, No. 41 (Glyptothek 85), text, p. 228.

showing the teeth between them and the deep line from the nose downward; and the head of a dying warrior from the same pediment[46] (fig. 186) in which the gradual closing of the eyes is shown in a remarkably naturalistic manner. Even more realistic renderings of pain appear in some of the Centaurs and Lapiths of the Olympia pediment[47] (about 465–460; figs. 188 and 191) where deep lines are added on the brow and round the nostrils, and the contraction of the mouth is very marked. Myron's Marsyas[48] (about 450; fig. 190) gives us an example of the expression of surprise, indicated by the long upward curve of the eyebrows, the corresponding grooves on the forehead, and the oblique setting of the eyes.

Besides emotion, age can contract the features and bring furrows to the face. This too began to interest the Greek sculptor and we have, in the transitional period, representations of old age such as the old woman on the Boston relief[49] (fig. 189). The effect is obtained by the wrinkles on the forehead and on the lower part of the face, the deep furrows from the nose downward, and the series of ridges below the chin; the hooked nose adds to the realistic expression.

It is noteworthy that we have in contemporary vase-painting a parallel interest in these variants from the prevalent types of serene and youthful beauty. On a krater in the Metropolitan Museum, for instance, there is a realistic rendering of an old man[50] (fig. 193); on a vase in Schwerin is one of an old woman;[51] and on several vases are beautiful renderings of musical exaltation.[52]

SECOND HALF OF FIFTH CENTURY

But neither in sculpture nor in vase-painting did the practice of depicting emotion become general at this period. As a rule the faces have a lofty, impersonal character. The realistic touches occur only occasionally; and in the succeeding period—the second half of the fifth century—they become if anything less frequent. For the sculptor had by now tried out his new powers; his interest in what he considered wayside experiments quickly subsided, and he put his whole effort into his great task of using the human figure, body and head alike, as an expression of lofty idealism. Representative heads of

[46] Furtwängler, *Aegina*, pl. 97, No. 93 (Glyptothek 92), text, p. 253.
[47] Treu, *Olympia*, III, pl. XXIX, 2 and 3 and pl. XXXI, 2.
[48] Walters, *Select Bronzes*, pl. XVI.
[49] Caskey, *Catalogue of Sculpture*, No. 17.　　　　[50] Acc. No. 07.286.81.
[51] *Jahrbuch des arch. Inst.*, XXVII, 1912, pls. 6 and 8.
[52] Cf., e.g., *J.H.S.*, 1922, pl. II, 1; Buschor, *Griechische Vasenmalerei*, 1913, p. 186, fig. 132; *A.J.A.*, 1923, p. 278, fig. 15.

this time are therefore such examples as the female head from Argos
(fig. 165), the Lemnian Athena[53] (fig. 614), the "Cassel Apollo"[54]
(cf. fig. 194), or the New York athlete[55] (fig. 195), which are distinguished for their detachment and serenity; or the Niobid in
Rome[56] (fig. 196), whose beautiful, composed features do not suggest in any way (except in the droop of the mouth) the physical
agony she is in.

Nevertheless it is a mistake to think that the expression of emotion in the face is unknown in the second half of the fifth century.
Instances occur particularly outside Attica, in regions which were
far from the influence of Pheidian idealism. The Phigaleia frieze
(last quarter of the fifth century) is an excellent example. In the collapsing Greek[57] (fig. 197), for instance, the suffering is indicated by
the contraction of the eyebrows, which form upward loops with the
bridge of the nose, and by the bringing of the eyelids closer together. In the dying Amazon[58] (fig. 198) this bringing together of
the eyelids and the pronounced curve of the lower lid admirably convey the feeling of faintness. A Centaur whom a Lapith has seized by
the hair[59] (fig. 199) plainly shows his physical suffering in his contracted eyebrows and open mouth. In two of the crouching women
of the west pediment at Olympia[60] (cf. fig. 200), which are clearly
later restorations, probably of the second half of the fifth century
(cf. p. 224), the contraction of the eyes and of the mouth, the deep
line from the nose downward, and the furrowed forehead effectively
indicate sorrow. Even in Attica there are examples. In some of the
Centaur heads of the Parthenon metopes (fig. 192) the wrinkles
caused by pain are indicated in an almost exaggerated manner. In
the head of Eurystheus from a metope of the Hephaisteion[61] datable
soon after 450 B.C. horror is vividly portrayed. These renderings may
be explained as late examples of the transition period, which, as we
saw, was distinguished by its experiments in the representation of
momentary action and emotion.

The commonest way for the Greek sculptor to convey emotion, how-

[53] Furtwängler, *Masterpieces*, pp. 4 ff.
[54] Bieber, *Die Antiken Skulpturen in Cassel*, pls. I–VIII.
[55] Metropolitan Museum, *Bulletin*, 1912, pp. 47 ff.
[56] Della Seta, *Ausonia*, II, 1907, pp. 3 ff., pls. I–III; Paribeni, *Le Terme di Dio-cleziano e il Museo Nazionale Romano* (1922), No. 369.
[57] Smith, *Catalogue of Greek Sculpture in the British Museum*, I, No. 542.
[58] *Ibid.*   [59] *Ibid.*, No. 526.
[60] Treu, *Olympia*, III, pl. XXXIV, 1–3.
[61] Dinsmoor, *Hesperia*, Supplement V, 1941, p. 117, fig. 44.

ever, remained the attitude of the figure, which would moreover be
equally telling near by and at the long distance at which most of the
architectural sculpture was seen.

In the rendering of feeling by gesture the Greek artist was undoubtedly helped by the emotional quality of his own people, whose
vivid gesticulations could take the place of facial expression. We
find him at all periods studying and making use of this means of
representation. How suggestive, for instance, of entreaty is the fine
group from the Phigaleia frieze of an Amazon asking a Greek warrior for mercy[62] (fig. 201). The raised arm, the upward inclination
of the head are as eloquent as any play of features could be. And
how effective a rendering of defense is the group, also from the
Phigaleia frieze, of an Amazon warding off a Greek warrior[63] (fig.
202). How vividly the feeling of collapse is conveyed in the fallen
Centaur[64] (fig. 203) and the sinking Amazon[65] (fig. 204), both from
the Phigaleia frieze. There is no need of agonized expressions in the
faces, the positions of heads and arms and legs are sufficient in themselves to indicate the sculptor's meaning. And in quieter poses we
get the same effects. The "Mourning Athena"[66] (fig. 206) has been
so called chiefly on account of the impression conveyed by the pose.
In the woman on the Boston relief (fig. 477) sorrow is suggested
even more eloquently in her bowed attitude than in the expression of
her face. It was in fact the accepted attitude for sorrow and is repeated in other mourners, for instance, in the bronze statuette in
Berlin[67] (fig. 211), the marble statues in Berlin[68] (fig. 212), the
"Penelope" in the Vatican (fig. 68), the figures on the akroterion in
Berlin[69] (fig. 210), and the Penelope on the skyphos in Chiusi.[70] In
the New York stele[71] (figs. 205, 426) the love of the little girl for
her pigeons is depicted entirely in the action and the inclination of
the head, not in the expression of the face.

FOURTH   In the fourth century, as we have already seen in our study of the
CENTURY   human figure, there is a marked change toward individualism. A
soft graciousness now takes the place of the former impersonal ideal.

[62] Smith, *Catalogue of Greek Sculpture in the British Museum*, I, No. 537.
[63] *Ibid.*, No. 538.   [64] *Ibid.*, No. 527.   [65] *Ibid.*, No. 542.
[66] Dickins, *Catalogue of the Acropolis Museum*, No. 695.
[67] Neugebauer, *Antike Bronzestatuetten*, No. 64.
[68] Berlin Museum, *Beschreibung der antiken Skulpturen*, Nos. 498, 499.
[69] No. 1707; *Amtliche Berichte*, XXXII, 1910, pp. 1 ff.
[70] Furtwängler und Reichhold, *Die griechische Vasenmalerei*, III, pl. 142.
[71] Metropolitan Museum, *Bulletin*, 1927, pp. 101–105, figs. 1, 2.

And this is naturally reflected also in the face. In the Hermes of Praxiteles (fig. 170), for instance, there is an expression of dreaminess, of gentleness which though not in itself emotional has a distinctly emotional appeal. The god has become more human, less remote, though still perfectly serene. And this same evanescent charm appears in many heads of the later fourth and the early third century, for instance, in the athlete in New York[72] (fig. 208), the Chios and Bartlett heads in Boston (figs. 174, 175), and the Goldman head in Toledo[73] (fig. 207). Feminine grace and delicacy could not find a more perfect expression.

Skopas is generally regarded as the great emotional sculptor of the fourth century; and certainly the heads from Tegea (figs. 690–693) attributed to him convey more ardent feelings than we find in the Praxitelean faces. But we have seen from our previous study that this was not an innovation; only the means of conveying it is new—by a marked projection of the lower part of the forehead, the oblique brows, and the deep-set, upturned eyes creating strong shadows. And though the expression is more intense than in most other contemporary works we can use the term "strong emotion" only relatively. According to more modern conceptions most of the Skopasian works (pp. 269 ff.) still have the Greek serenity and aloofness. We need only place them beside truly emotional sculptures of German Gothic, Italian Renaissance, and modern times to realize the vast difference. And even compared with earlier works some of the sculptures attributable to Skopas can hardly be called emotional. The dying Amazon on the Mausoleum frieze[74] (fig. 209) shows less pain in her face than do her Phigaleian sisters. It is the attitude rather than the facial expression which conveys the sculptor's intention; and this is true of the majority of fourth-century sculpture, just as was the case in the preceding period.

The sculptured gravestones might have been natural outlets for the representation of human feeling; but even here, both during the fifth and the fourth century, grief itself is seldom represented. We find instead an expression of dreamy detachment. The departed are shown as they were while alive, the men as athletes or warriors or horsemen (cf. fig. 215[75]) or students (cf. fig. 213[76]), with their sor-

72 Metropolitan Museum, *Bulletin,* 1916, pp. 82 ff.
73 Formerly in the collection of H. Goldman; *Art in America,* V, 1917, pp. 130–134.
74 Smith, *Catalogue of Greek Sculpture in the British Museum,* II, No. 1014.
75 Conze, *Attische Grabreliefs,* No. 1158.
76 Conze, *op. cit.,* No. 622, pl. CXXI.

rowing families and attendants; the women spinning (cf. fig. 214[77])
or engaged with their toilet or waited on by their handmaids or
fondling their children; and the children with their playthings and
pet animals—lovely, serene figures, their sorrow merely suggested
by a quiet pathos, by the handshakes indicating farewell, and by the
occasional mourning attitudes (cf. fig. 495). Only very rarely is
death itself represented, as in the stele of Plangon, shown fainting
on a couch[78] (fig. 217) ; or actual grief expressed, as in the weeping
siren in Boston[79] (fig. 216, once a finial of a Greek stele), in which
the contracted eyebrows and uplifted eyes, the hands tearing the
hair and beating the breasts convey acute sorrow. We see how ably
the Greek sculptor could, when he wished, express such emotion; and
we know also how harassing a whole graveyard of such scenes would
have been. The mystery and separation of death cannot adequately
or artistically be expressed by such means.

HELLENISTIC   In the Hellenistic period, with the general trend toward realism,
PERIOD   it was natural that interest in individual feelings should increase.
The complexity of human nature offered a subject full of new possibilities in an age when pure beauty was no longer the aim of the
artist; and it became the legitimate, almost exclusive interest of the
sculptor to represent the individual human being (occasionally
characterized as a god) in the manifold surroundings of his daily
life in a direct and realistic manner. We find now representations
of an Eros or a Satyr in the abandonment of sleep[80] (figs. 121, 218) ;
a boy concentrating his whole attention on extracting a thorn from his
foot (fig. 75) ; an old woman going to market with her wares[81] (fig.
219) ; a drunken old woman hugging her bottle (fig. 74) ; a little
negro child huddled up and asleep beside his wine jar[82] (fig. 220) ;
an old nurse carrying a child[83] (fig. 222) ; a young negro musician
with mobile body and sad, sensitive face (fig. 58) ; a Satyr playing
his pipes and putting his whole soul into his music (fig. 556) ; a
mischievous Eros[84] (fig. 221) ; a caricature with all the pathos inherent in a clown[85] (fig. 223) ; a dying Persian[86] (fig. 224) ; La-

77 In Berlin; Conze, *Attische Grabreliefs*, No. 88, pl. XVII.
78 National Museum, Athens, No. 749.   79 Caskey, *Catalogue*, No. 44.
80 Furtwängler, *Beschreibung der Glyptothek*, No. 218.
81 Metropolitan Museum, *Bulletin*, 1909, pp. 201, 204–206.
82 Ashmolean Museum; *J.H.S.*, VII, 1886, pl. LXIV, p. 87, No. 9.
83 Metropolitan Museum, Acc. No. 06.1066.
84 Metropolitan Museum, Acc. No. 06.1130.
85 Metropolitan Museum, *Catalogue of Bronzes*, No. 127.
86 Helbig, *Führer*,3 II, No. 1354.

okoon in agony of physical pain[87] (figs. 225, 768) ; Ge making sup-
plication for the life of her son.[88] It is a wonderfully varied world
of human moods and feelings of which the Greek sculptor now avails
himself; and he does it with remarkable understanding, using both
the attitudes and the facial expressions to convey his meaning. It is
as if, by coming down from his altitude, his sympathies had become
enlarged and he could enter more deeply into the life around him.
In our estimate of Greek art we must remember this wider region
which the Greek sculptor explored at the end of his career, when
realism in modeling and conception made him try out every theme
and represent it in a thoroughly naturalistic manner.

There is another important field in which the Greek artist distinguished himself—the art of portraiture. The archaic sculptor had
aimed at the representation of the human figure with no attempt at
individual personification. This applies to the rendering of the head
as well as of the body. On account of his strong idealizing bent the
sculptor of the fifth and early fourth centuries had produced portraits with a marked generalizing tendency.[89] The aim had been, in
the words of Aristotle,[90] "to reproduce the distinctive features of a
man, and at the same time without losing the likeness, to make him
handsomer than he is"; that is, to dispense with minor, personal traits
and create a type rather than an individual. And works like the Homer
in Munich[91] (middle of the fifth century), the Perikles in the British
Museum (fig. 624; about 440), and the bearded head by the gem
engraver Dexamenos in Boston[92] (fig. 226; third quarter of fifth century) had been the result—splendid conceptions of the general personalities of these men but without a strongly personal element.

This long tradition of generalization is still evident in the portraits of the fourth century—in the bronze Sokrates in Munich[93]
(first half; fig. 227), the Maussollos[94] (middle; fig. 228), the heads of
Plato[95] and Thucydides (second quarter),[96] and even in the finely

[87] Amelung, *Die Skulpturen des vaticanischen Museums*, II, No. 74, pl. 20.
[88] Museen zu Berlin, *Altertümer von Pergamon*, III, 2, pl. XII, p. 53.
[89] On the dating of Greek portraits cf. Pfuhl, *Die Anfänge der griechischen Bildniskunst* (1927).
[90] *Poetics* XV. 11.   [91] Furtwängler, *Beschreibung der Glyptothek*, No. 273.
[92] Beazley, *The Lewes House Collection of Ancient Gems*, No. 50.
[93] Furtwängler, *op. cit.*, No. 448.
[94] Smith, *Catalogue of Greek Sculpture in the British Museum*, II, No. 1000.
[95] Schefold, *Bildnisse*, pp. 74 f.
[96] *Ibid.*, pp. 76 f.

characterized Euripides[97] (fig. 229) and Sophokles[98] (fig. 249, third quarter). But now the time had come for a more individualistic treatment; for interest in human nature per se had arisen. And so the Hellenistic period becomes the great age of realistic portraiture. Fortunately there are a goodly number of examples preserved from which we can form a fairly adequate idea of such Hellenistic achievements; and not merely Roman copies, as is almost entirely the case in the earlier Greek portraits, but actual originals. Perhaps their greatness lies in the strange combination of the old idealism with a new realism. The Chrysippos[99] (fig. 232) and the so-called Hermarchos[100] (figs. 230, 231) in the Metropolitan Museum, the "Menander" in Lord Melchett's Collection[101] (fig. 233) and "Antiochos III" in Paris,[102] and the heads on the coins (figs. 234–238[103]) and gems[104] of the Hellenistic period are not only typical portraits of Greek thinkers and poets and statesmen, but they have become at the same time vivid character studies of individual human beings. The sculptor gives us a faithful and detailed transcription of the features of a particular man; but like a true artist he also goes over and beyond the external appearance and conveys a comprehensive picture of his sitter's character. In the late Hellenistic period the realism becomes somewhat exaggerated. We can assign to it such powerful works as the head of Homer in Boston[105] (fig. 239) and the bronze head from Delos in Athens[106] (fig. 240). They form the immediate precursors of the Roman Republican portraits, which must have been executed by Greek artists; only the physiognomies of the two are different, the Greek portraits being mostly of intellectual persons, the Roman ones of practical men of affairs.

There is another circumstance which adds considerable interest to Greek portraiture—that the sculptor did not confine his characterization to the head but took in the whole figure, and so was able to reveal his sitter's personality not merely in his features but in the attitude of the body. And this he was able to do with peculiar under-

---

97 Bernoulli, *Griechische Ikonographie,* I, p. 152, No. 9.

98 Studniczka, *J.H.S.,* XLIII, pp. 57–67, and XLIV, pp. 281–285.

99 Richter, *A.J.A.,* XXIX, 1925, pp. 152 ff.

100 Metropolitan Museum, *Catalogue of Bronzes,* No. 120.

101 Burlington Fine Arts Club, *Ancient Greek Art,* 1904, pl. XXV, No. 26.

102 Arndt in Brunn-Bruckmann, *Griechische und römische Porträts,* No. 103.

103 In the collection of E. T. Newell in New York.

104 Furtwängler, *Antike Gemmen,* pls. XXXII and XXXIII.

105 Caskey, *Catalogue,* No. 55.

106 Papaspiridi, *Guide du Musée National,* No. 14612; *Délos,* XIII, pp. 1 ff.

standing. The Sophokles in the Lateran (fig. 249), the bronze statuette of "Hermarchos" in the Metropolitan Museum[107] (fig. 241),
the Demosthenes (fig. 757), the Poseidippos[108] (fig. 242), and the
so-called Menander[109] in the Vatican are eloquent witnesses of Greek
achievements along these line. The manner in which the figures hold
and carry themselves is so consistent with their physiognomies that
it must be due to the penetrating observation of the sculptor. Unfortunately quite often the statues are fragmentary and we have
many separate heads and bodies; even then, however, the pieces retain
in a mysterious way the quality of the whole, so that even in a headless
statue we can get some realization of the character of the man.

[107] *Catalogue of Bronzes*, No. 120.
[108] Amelung, *Die Skulpturen des vaticanischen Museums*, II, pl. 54, No. 271.
[109] *Ibid.*, No. 890.

CHAPTER VI

DRAPERY

EQUALLY with the beauty of the human form the Greek felt the beauty of drapery; of large and small folds, of the differences of texture, of the composition of surfaces. To its artistic interpretation he devoted the same ability and concentration which he lavished on the study of the human body. In these studies he had a great advantage. The fashions of the day with the loosely hanging instead of closely fitting garments enabled him to watch the rich and varied play of folds of different materials. He did not have to create his opportunities artificially; he had them continuously before him. And not only did the free-hanging dresses assume beautiful folds while the figure was at rest, but they were directly influenced by the action of the body. Every motion, every mood almost of the person was reflected in the drapery. The Greek sculptor realized these possibilities fully, and after many arduous labors succeeded in making the drapery as eloquent a means of expression of the human spirit as the figure itself. It is interesting to observe the various phases through which the Greek artist passed in his efforts at artistic representation, corresponding closely to the different stages of development in the modeling of the human figure.

(a) Greek Dress

BEFORE studying the Greek sculptor's rendering of these draperies it may help to review briefly the chief garments in use among the Greeks;[1] so that we may recognize them when we see them, and understand their structure.

The chief garments of the man were the chiton, the himation, and the chlamys.

[1] This account is not meant to be exhaustive but merely a brief statement. For a study of Greek dress the reader is referred to Heuzey, *Histoire du costume antique*, Paris, 1922; Bieber, *Griechische Kleidung*, 1928, and *Entwicklungsgeschichte der griechischen Tracht*, 1934; Studniczka, *Beiträge zur Geschichte der altgriechischen Tracht*; Bieber, *Der Chiton der ephesischen Amazonen*, *Jahrbuch*, 1918, pp. 49 ff.; Kalkmann, *Zur Tracht archaischer Gewandfiguren*, *Jahrbuch*, 1896, pp. 19 ff.; Barker, "Domestic Costumes of the Athenian Woman in the Fifth and Fourth Centuries B.C.," *A.J.A.*, XXVI, 1922, pp. 410 ff.; Daremberg and Saglio, *Dictionnaire*, under *Tunica, Peplos, Pallium*; Pauly-Wissowa, *Realencyclopädie*, under χιτών, ἱμάτιον.

1. The chiton was a tunic of soft linen or of wool. It was made either of one oblong cloth, at first rather narrow, later considerably wider, folded on one side and sewn on the other; or of two rectangular pieces sewn on both sides. At the top it was either pinned or sewn over the shoulders to form the sleeves. In the archaic period the openings for the arms were regularly on the sides (fig. 243),

Fig. 243. Archaic chiton with sleeve-openings on sides

in classical times generally along the upper edge[2] (fig. 244 on p. 89), a change which made for a more beautiful fall of folds. The chiton could be worn short (fig. 245) or long (fig. 285). It generally appears with a belt (fig. 246) over which the garment was pulled to form a pouch (*kolpos*); and sometimes an overfold (*diploidion*) was introduced at the top; and now and then a second belt was worn over the pouch. Cords were occasionally placed across the back and the shoulders to keep the garment in place, especially when it was long (fig. 285). Belts, pins, cords, overfold, all helped to create a variety of folds.

A variant of this tunic is the so-called χιτὼν ἐξωμίς (*exomis*) fastened with a brooch on one shoulder only, worn likewise with a belt, but consisting merely of a rectangular cloth, not sewn, or only rarely so. As an example we may cite a rider from the Parthenon frieze in the British Museum[3] (fig. 247).

2. The himation, or the mantle, was a large rectangular piece of cloth (fig. 248[4]) about seven or eight feet long and in width about equal to the wearer's height. It was wrapped around the body in every conceivable way to suit the needs and fancy of the wearer.

[2] This important point is clearly brought out by Bieber, *Der Chiton der ephesischen Amazonen, Jahrbuch*, 1918, pp. 49 ff.

[3] Smith, *Sculptures of the Parthenon*, pl. 66.　　　　[4] From a kylix in Berlin.

The artistic arrangement of its folds thus became a great opportunity and delight to the artist.

How much the many beautiful compositions in Greek sculpture
are due to the interpretation of the artist rather than to direct
copying of nature can be seen when we compare the statue of Sophokles in the Lateran[5] (fig. 249) with living models similarly draped
(fig. 250). The drapery of the Sophokles is a harmonious composi-

Fig. 244. Classical chiton with sleeve-openings
on upper edge

tion, with the plain and the bunched surfaces consciously correlated. The actual model, in spite of every effort to imitate the happy
effect of the statue, has no artistic appeal. How clumsy, for instance,
are the folds below the right knee, interrupting the long sweep of
the outline of the leg; and how dull the large expanse of smooth surface on the lower portion, relieved in the original by contrasting
shadows; how much difference it makes when the lower edge of the
drapery forms a strongly oblique instead of a quasi-horizontal line!

3. The chlamys was the short cloak worn as a wrap when the
large himation would be in the way, for instance while hunting or
riding (fig. 251). It too was probably rectangular, and it was fastened round the neck by a brooch or button, the loose ends falling
down to form zigzag edges (fig. 253); the dimensions were probably about six to seven feet long by three and one-half feet wide.
Weights were often attached at the corners to keep the garment in

5 Helbig, *Führer*,[8] II, No. 1180.

place, as was the case also with the himation. Again, simple though the arrangement is, we can see by comparing a Greek drawing (fig. 251) with a draped model (fig. 252) how much the artist contributed to the aesthetic effect. A slight change in the zigzag edge and the different attitude of the left arm have made all the difference.

The women's dresses were similar to those of the men; that is, they were also rectangular pieces of cloth loosely worn and beautifully draped. The favorite forms were the chiton and the himation; rarely we find an additional short cloak.

Fig. 253. Chlamys

1. Of the chiton there were two varieties. The Ionic one, the chiton par excellence, was of linen imported from Egypt or the East and was generally made in two rectangular pieces, sewn together on both sides and buttoned or pinned with brooches along the upper arm to form sleeves[6] (fig. 254). The Doric one, known as the peplos, was made of wool spun and woven by Greek women in their houses all in one piece; it was often worn open on one side and was regularly fastened over each shoulder with a brooch, button, or long pin[7] (fig. 255). The width of an Ionic chiton is given by Plato[8] as three meters (seven Attic cubits). The peplos was about as wide, twice the width of the outstretched arms to the finger tips, or a little less. The length naturally

---

[6] For the openings of the sleeves, cf. p. 88 (under the man's chiton).

[7] Langlotz, *Fruehgriechische Bildhauerschulen,* pl. 16a.

[8] *Letters* XIII. 363a.

depended on the wearer's height. The former being of linen created a large number of crinkly folds,[9] the other, being of wool, fewer, massive ones. The wearing of the belts, pins, and overfolds again helped to introduce the needed diversity.

2. The himation was similar to that worn by the men and was used as an outside wrap over the chiton. It was often pulled up to cover the head to take the place of a hat (fig. 256[10]) in the manner that an Italian or Greek woman of today would use her shawl when going out of doors. Occasionally it was fastened on the shoulder with a pin.[11] A more complicated variant of this simple garment is the "Ionic" himation worn by the Akropolis Maidens (cf. figs. 271, 272, 273). This too seems to have been a long, rectangular piece of material, doubled to make an overfold, but it was regularly worn under the left arm and over the right shoulder where it was fastened by brooches or buttons, the spare material hanging loosely down. Its vertical pleats were apparently kept in place by a belt put over the right shoulder and under the left arm over which the himation was pulled up a little. The lower part was generally pulled tightly to one side and was decorated with a vertical stripe.

3. The short cloak was not nearly so common with women as with men; probably because they did not indulge so much in violent exercise, like hunting or riding, when the long coat would be an encumbrance. It occurs occasionally as an extra wrap worn over the chiton and himation like a shawl or stole (cf. fig. 257).

In addition to these loosely hanging garments we sometimes encounter sewn dresses of a similar appearance to our own; for instance, the embroidered sleeveless jacket on a vase by the Meidias painter in New York[12] (fig. 309) and the sleeved coat on a relief in Broom Hall[13] (fig. 258). In these, tubelike sleeves are sewn to the openings on the sides of the garment.[14] But such cases are few, except for Amazons, Persians, and other "barbarians" whose apparel consisted of sleeved and trousered garments (fig. 259[15]).

We must imagine these garments dyed in various colors, brilliant

[9] Whether these crinkly folds were at least partially due to an artificial pleating of the material, such as our "accordion pleating," or were wholly the result of the stylization of the artist is still a moot question.

[10] Metropolitan Museum, Acc. No. 23.73.3.

[11] E.g., on the fragment of a red-figured krater in the British Museum, No. E493.

[12] Metropolitan Museum, *Handbook* (1930), p. 155, fig. 106.

[13] Conze, *Die attischen Grabreliefs*, pl. CLVI, No. 819. Cf. also the instances figured by Bieber, *Griechische Kleidung*, fig. 8a and pls. XIV, 1-2; XXI, 1.

[14] Bieber, *op. cit.*, p. 16.   [15] Metropolitan Museum, Acc. No. 06.1021.189.

reds, browns, blues, yellows, greens, purples,[16] or plain white; occasionally with little ornaments all over the surface; and generally decorated with colored or embroidered bands. These bands—which add greatly to the artistic effect of the whole, as any practical experiment will show—generally appear only on the short sides, sometimes on one of the long sides also; not on all four sides, for the obvious reason that the composition would have lost by this excess.

The two chief materials used by the Greeks were linen and wool.[17] There is no mention of silk before the time of Aristotle,[18] but there is some evidence that it was adopted by the Greeks during the fifth century B.C. (cf. p. 100). It was known in China long before that (about 3000 B.C.). Cotton garments were worn in India and Egypt[19] but there is no evidence of their use in Greece before Roman times.

(b) *The Rendering of Drapery*

WE have seen how much the Greek artist with his instinct for composition improved on the arrangement of drapery in nature. Besides his sense for harmonious design he had the realization of two other essential requirements: that in art drapery must not hide the body beneath it; and that the folds must always clearly interconnect, so that the construction of the whole may be convincing. The female statue from Herculaneum[20] (fig. 260), wearing a thick Doric peplos with overfold, well illustrates the first quality. In the similarly draped living model (fig. 261) the outlines of the legs and breasts are completely concealed by the heavy material; and we quickly realize how much of the artistic effect is lost thereby. It is evident that art must not merely copy nature, but transform it.

The clear construction of the drapery in Greek sculpture is another source of genuine artistic enjoyment. In the many compositions of Greek drapery there is never any confusion; we do not wonder where one fold comes from or what becomes of another; the whole

---

16 That Greek garments were brilliantly colored is attested by their appearing so in terracotta statuettes and marble sculptures of all periods, and on the white lekythoi of the fifth century B.C.

17 Blümner, *Gewerbe und Künste*, 2d ed., I, pp. 106 ff., 191 ff.

18 Aristotle, *Hist. anim.* V. 19; Pliny, *N.H.* XI. 26–28. On the origin and use of silk, cf. Besnier, in Daremberg and Saglio, *Dictionnaire*, under *Sericum;* Blümner, *op. cit.*, p. 201; Richter, *Silk in Greece*, *A.J.A.*, XXXIII, 1929, pp. 27 ff.

19 Herodotos III. 47 and 106; Pollux VII. 75; Theophrastus, *Historia plant.* IV. 7.7. Cf. on this subject Blümner, *op. cit.*, pp. 199–200.

20 Comparetti and de Petra, *La Villa ercolanese*, pl. XIV, 3.

is convincing and logical. In nature that is not always so; one part
of the garment often hides another in such a way that the interconnection is not apparent. How much more clearly, for instance, do we
feel in the Sophokles statue (fig. 249) that the drapery enveloping
the arms is part and parcel of the himation than we do in the corresponding living model (fig. 250). In the model we know that the
upper shawl-like effect belongs to the himation and the cascade from
the left arm is one end of it; but if it were an unfamiliar garment
we might think that the lower part was a separate tight skirt and
that a towel was hanging over the left arm. In the statue such doubts
are impossible; each part of the mantle passes so unmistakably into
the adjoining portion and connects with it that we feel the drapery
as a whole, as a unit.

With these general characteristics of Greek drapery in mind let
us now watch the course of its development.

An early stage is shown in the Nikandre in Athens[21] (fig. 263) **SEVENTH**
and the Auxerre statue in the Louvre[22] (fig. 262), both still of the **TO SIXTH**
seventh century B.C. None of the essential requirements are as yet **CENTURY**
met. The treatment is flat, there is no attempt to render folds, only
decorative borders; and there is practically no feeling for the body
beneath. Drapery merely acts as a covering and has no independent
life. The superb standing maiden in Berlin [23] (figs. 267–269) and the
Chares statue from Miletos[24] (fig. 264), both of the second quarter of
the sixth century, mark a step in advance. The surface begins to be
broken up by a tentative, strictly stylized indication of folds. They
have as yet little depth, for the sculptor is still too timid to cut deeply
into his stone; but the essentials of the construction of the long chiton
and of the himation are understood and clearly rendered. And in each
case the decorative feeling of the artist has produced a beautiful design. The interrelation of volumes, the different directions of ridges
and grooves, the linear patterns for the edges of stacked folds all play
their part in an attractive composition. The same is true of the garments on the sculptured drums of Ephesos[25] (c. 550–530; figs. 265,
266).

21 National Museum, Athens, No. 1.   22 Revue archéologique, 1908, pl. 10.
23 Wiegand, Berliner Museen, 1926, pp. 17 ff.; Die Antike, II, pp. 30 ff.
24 Pryce, Catalogue of Sculpture in the British Museum, I, 1, No. B 278.
25 Ibid., B 90, 91, 119, 121; Pryce assigns only B 90 to the period of Kroisos and
of the dedicatory inscription, and B 91, 119, 121 to a somewhat later date; B 119 has
affinities with the Siphnian frieze.

The decorative treatment of drapery reached its climax during the second half of the sixth century. Conventions were multiplied, the scheme was enriched and enlarged. The figures on the friezes of the Siphnian Treasury (figs. 418, 419) and, above all, the Maidens from the Athenian Akropolis (figs. 270–273[26]) and from the Islands (fig. 274[27]) are instructive examples. The soft crinkly material of the linen chiton was rendered by a series of straight, or, more commonly, wavy ridges or incisions, running vertically if the drapery hung down loosely, obliquely and curving if directed sidewise. The heavier folds of the himation were indicated by straight, deep grooves or ridges rather more widely spaced, often with zigzag edges. By these means the archaic artist was able to cope with the difficult problem of representing the complicated garments of his time. The sleeved chitons and the full mantles with overfolds, borders, and little ornaments, worn over one shoulder and under the other, and generally so long that they had to be held up on one side, constituted such a mass of folds going in different directions that it was hard to simplify and to keep to the important elements. The Greek sculptor succeeded, in spite of his comparative inexperience, by his decorative sense, which enabled him to create a highly artistic design, as well as by his feeling for structure, by which he connected every fold with its neighbor, so that each had a meaning, a start and a finish, and helped to form a correlated whole.

Toward the end of the century a great change takes place. The drapery, though lying as before close against the body, begins to acquire a separate entity. We now feel that it is completely separate, that it can be taken on and off at will, and moreover that it has a life and swing of its own. We notice it best in reliefs where action is portrayed, for instance in the mounting charioteer[29] (fig. 275) and the Hermes[30] (fig. 276) in the Akropolis Museum, and in the metopes from the Athenian Treasury in Delphi[31] (figs. 407, 408). The old conventions of zigzag, radiating, and wavy grooves are still adhered to; but the direction of the folds is carefully studied in regard to the function they perform; so that they become more expressive of the action of the body. How convincingly, for instance, the mantle of the charioteer (fig. 275) clings to the back, is bunched

[26] In the Akropolis Museum, Athens, Nos. 679, 680, 674, 681.

[27] Metropolitan Museum, *Bulletin*, 1908, pp. 4 ff.

[28] Some of these conventions are borrowed from earlier arts, e.g., the wavy lines for the folds of the soft chiton occur also in Chaldaean and Assyrian sculpture.

[29] Dickins, *Catalogue*, No. 1342.   [30] *Ibid.*, No. 1343.

[31] Homolle, *Fouilles de Delphes*, IV, pls. XXXVII–XL.

over the upper arms, and where it hangs down is influenced partly
by its own weight and partly by the movement of the body! The
bronze statuette of Nike in London (fig. 83) is another beautiful
instance of drapery expressive of the movement of the figure.

For the archaic conventions adopted by the Greek sculptor in his
rendering of drapery we find interesting parallels on contemporary
vases; they follow the development step by step, and are therefore
often useful evidence for dating.[32] On the vase-paintings of the late
seventh to the middle of the sixth century (cf. fig. 277[33]) the garment more or less hides the figure, as it does in the early sculpture,
for the artist has not learned to differentiate between body and
drapery or to give each its significance; individual folds are either
not indicated or only a few of the most important are shown, and
they are composed in an effective way. In other words, these vases
show the same stage of development as the Auxerre and Miletos
statues (figs. 262, 264). In the later black-figured and earliest red-
figured vases (cf. fig. 278[34]) a conventional treatment has been developed similar to that in the more advanced Maidens: fine, wavy
lines for the chiton folds and straight, more widely spaced lines for
those of the himation; a wavy line in two tiers for the bottom edge
of the chiton; zigzag lines for the edges of the himation; and small,
wavy, radiating lines for the folds caused by the brooches or buttons in the sleeves. At the end of the sixth and the beginning of the
fifth century the draperies on the vase-paintings show the same life
and individuality that we noted in the sculpture. We may compare,
for instance, the relief of the mounting charioteer (fig. 275) with
the vase by Pasiades (510–500) in the British Museum[35] (fig. 280).
The mantles worn like shawls over the shoulder have similar bunched
folds, and there is the same suggestive treatment of drapery in motion by means of closely spaced oblique lines with zigzag edges.
Sometimes there are similar individualistic renderings in sculpture
and vase-paintings; for instance, the peculiar wavy line for the folds
of the mantles in one of the statue bases recently found in Athens[36]

---

[32] On this subject, cf. Langlotz, *Zur Zeitbestimmung der strengrotfigurigen Vasenmalerei und Plastik*, and von Lücken, *Archaische griechische Vasenmalerei und Plastik, Ath. Mitt.*, 1919, pp. 47 ff., pls. I–VI.

[33] Metropolitan Museum, Acc. No. 17.230.14.

[34] Metropolitan Museum, Acc. No. 06.1021.47.

[35] No. B 668; Hoppin, *Handbook*, II, 331.

[36] Della Seta, *Dedalo*, III, 1922–1923, pp. 207 ff.; cf. also list of references to other
publications given in *Arch. Anz.*, 1922, p. 56, note 1.

(fig. 283), which occurs in identical fashion on the paintings by Euthymides (fig. 279[37]); and the radiating folds of the chiton sleeves in the Amazon of the Athenian Treasury,[38] the Athena of the Eretria pediment[39] (fig. 281), and the draperies by Peithinos (fig. 282),[40] Sosias, and others.[41]

FIRST HALF OF FIFTH CENTURY

The first half of the fifth century is a period of great development in drapery as it is in every phase of Greek art. There is a gradual increase in naturalism, but always joined to the old decorative sense. The folds no longer fall with monotonous regularity according to an accepted scheme; they vary their direction just as they do in nature, but underlying their arrangement is the conscious composition of the artist. This combination produces singularly happy results. The mantle of Theseus in the Eretria pediment[42] (fig. 284), with its studied and yet natural arrangement, the similar mantle on the Aristogeiton in Naples[43] (fig. 573), the draperies of the Berlin seated goddess[44] (fig. 65), all show in a happy way this combination of the old decorative tendency with the new feeling for naturalism. The mourning woman on the Boston relief (fig. 477) with the beautiful interrelation of its various parts, of smooth and variegated surfaces, is another striking example. The thin texture of the chiton, the heavier one of the mantle, are successfully conveyed, the folds where they hang loose or are pulled tight are convincing, and yet the composition is by no means the fortuitous one of nature; it has the design quality of an artist with a highly decorative sense; the same definite scheme is behind it which we feel in the statues of the human figure of this period. The union of these two elements of naturalism and design produces also the "architectural" draperies of this period—those of the Delphi Charioteer[45] (fig. 285), of the Herculaneum Dancers (figs. 260, 497), of the Athena of the Olympia metope[46] (fig. 319), and of the terracotta fragment in New York[47] (fig. 286). In these the fine simplicity of

[37] Hoppin, *Handbook*, I, p. 435. [38] *Fouilles de Delphes*, IV, pl. XL.
[39] *Antike Denkmäler*, III, pl. 29.
[40] Berlin, No. 2279; Hoppin, *op. cit.*, II, p. 335.
[41] Cf. Langlotz, *Zur Zeitbestimmung der strengrotfigurigen Vasenmalerei und Plastik*, pp. 72, 73.
[42] *Antike Denkmäler*, III, pls. 27, 28. It has been variously placed at the beginning of the fifth and the end of the sixth century; it probably belongs to the last decade of the sixth, to judge by the rendering of the face.
[43] Ruesch, *Guida del Museo Nazionale di Napoli*, No. 104 (6010).
[44] *Antike Denkmäler*, III, pls. 37 ff.
[45] Homolle, *Fouilles de Delphes*, IV, pls. XLIX–L.
[46] Treu, *Olympia*, III, pl. XLIII, 12.
[47] Metropolitan Museum, *Handbook* (1930), p. 111, fig. 73.

the folds, hanging down like flutings of a column, give the whole a
feeling of grandeur and stability; but the simplicity is never monotonous, for the scheme is infinitely various; only the variety is
concealed by not being accentuated. At first sight the vertical folds
of the chiton of the Delphi Charioteer (fig. 285) or the horizontal
folds on the sleeves all look alike, but if we look closer we shall find
every one different; the under edge appears at first perfectly horizontal; but in reality it makes a distinct curve. This quality of creating an appearance of simplicity but enlivening it with an under-
current of richness and variety is one that underlies all Greek art.
It is the product of a mind with a rich imagination controlled by
taste, one that can combine simplicity with subtlety.

The vases of the period reflect the same progress in knowledge
and conception. The draperies of Makron, of the Brygos painter,
of the Pan painter show a new life, a new stir and swish in the garments, tempered by a strong stylistic quality. How expressive are
the turbulent chitons in the Maenad dance by Makron in the Berlin
Museum[48] (fig. 287), how much they help to convey the ecstasy of
the wild maidens, and yet how restrained and harmonious is the design as a whole! And in the Makron cup in the Metropolitan Museum[49] (fig. 288) how convincingly the folds of the girl's chiton follow the action of the knee and then hang loosely and quietly down;
and how much they contribute to the harmonious composition!
Again in the krater by the Pan painter in Boston[50] what a splendid
design is formed by the chlamys of Aktaion and how we feel the
lower part of Artemis' chiton waving to and fro as she steps back to
send her deadly arrow! Drapery has indeed become by now as eloquent a means of expressing the action and emotion of a scene as
the human figure. And examination shows many parallels in details
of renderings in sculpture and vase-painting; for instance, the similar designs for the mantles on the Theseus of Eretria (fig. 284)
and on the Douris vases (cf. fig. 290 on p. 98) with their widely spaced
folds stacked in two directions; or the beautiful transparent folds
of the chitons of the Ludovisi Hora[51] (fig. 289) and the Makron
hetaira (fig. 288).

The treatment of the drapery in the second half of the fifth cen-   SECOND HALF
tury is the logical sequence of that in the first half. But changes are   OF FIFTH
CENTURY

[48] Berlin Museum, No. 2290.   [49] Acc. No. 12.231.1.
[50] Furtwängler und Reichhold, *Die griechische Vasenmalerei*, pl. 115.
[51] Helbig, *Führer*,[3] II, No. 1286.

now rapid. The trend toward naturalism gains ground quickly and the design quality, though still strong, becomes less obvious. In the figures of the Parthenon frieze (*c.* 442–438) though there is a marked retention of the old severity, the new spirit begins clearly to show itself. Folds have greatly multiplied and they go in many different directions. Nevertheless we feel throughout the conscious composition of the artist in the distribution of light and shade,

Fig. 290. Detail of a kylix
Museum of Fine Arts, Boston

caused by the variety of volume in the folds. Thus in the "herald" of the slab in the Louvre (fig. 291) we have first the bare chest, then the deep folds on the left shoulder and round the waist, then the relieving flat surface of the right leg contrasting with the folds hanging down his left side. In the maidens marching in procession[52] (fig. 291) we note the same love for contrasting surfaces and the same device of putting one leg slightly forward and drawing the drapery tightly over it with only a few ridges to show the presence of the garments. This distribution of light and shade besides forming a pleasing design supplies the chief structural accents at a distance, and greatly helps the understanding of the whole.

In the Parthenon pediment figures (*c.* 437–432; cf. figs. 69, 91, 292) the development toward naturalism has made distinct strides and we note another important change. The sculptor finally has courage to hew deeply into his marble; the adherence to flat surfaces dear to the archaic artist is entirely given up, and folds, even those

[52] Smith, *Sculptures of the Parthenon*, pls. 39, 55.

of the chiton, once shown by incised wavy lines, are often an inch or
two deep; while the heavy folds of the mantles have a volume of four
inches or more. In the Iris (fig. 91) the direction of the folds conveys not only the rapid flight of the figure but the action of the wind
blowing through it. But in spite of the increased realism the feeling
for design is still strong and shows itself in the composition of the
drapery. In the reclining "Fate"[53] (fig. 292), for instance, we begin
with the bare neck and right shoulder, then comes the variegated
surface of the chiton lying on the breast, then the strong shadows of
the folds formed by the double thickness of the chiton bunched over
the belt; then again a comparative rest where the chiton lies close
over the body below the waist; then the dramatic effect of the heavy
himation with its many folds of great volume placed over the upper
part of the legs; and finally the smoother part of the himation lying more or less foldless over the knees and lower part of the legs.
The effect of the whole is suggestive of the rhythmic movement of
waves. This conscious arrangement is a translation of the confusion
of nature into an artistic composition.

Another characteristic of the drapery of this period is the increase in its transparency. The forms of the body beneath it show
through much more clearly than before, though the garment always
retains its separate entity.

We note the same qualities in the drapery of contemporary monuments—the group of watching deities of the "Hephaisteion"[54] (fig.
293) so reminiscent of the seated figures in the Parthenon pediment,
and the stele of a seated woman in New York[55] (fig. 294). We have
here the same naturalistic effect combined with conscious composition, the same pleasant interrelation of contrasting lights and
shadows, the same treatment of the drapery as a separate entity in
spite of the increased softness.

It should be noted that the edges of draperies of the second half
of the fifth century sometimes show a border of short transverse
grooves (cf. figs. 4, 356), apparently to represent the selvage of
the fabric, since this treatment occurs always on opposite, not adjoining edges.

By the last quarter of the fifth century another characteristic
style is developed—that of making the drapery, particularly the

53 Smith, *Sculptures of the Parthenon*, pl. 5.
54 Sauer, *Das sogenannte Theseion*, pl. III; Dinsmoor, *Hesperia*, Suppl. V.
55 Metropolitan Museum, *Handbook* (1930), p. 249, fig. 173.

Ionic chiton, very transparent, of minimizing its presence and letting the body appear clearly through it. It is an accentuation of a tendency which we noted as a characteristic of Greek art in general, which became more marked in the period immediately preceding this one, and which now attains its climax. It is of course possible, indeed probable, that these transparent garments are intended to reproduce very thin materials which may have come into use at this time, that they represent in fact the διαφανῆ χιτώνια referred to in Aristophanes' *Lysistrata*, l. 48, and the χιτώνια ἀμόργινα which "make women appear naked" (l. 150). Possibly they were of silk,[56] for this material is mentioned in Greek literature not long afterwards (Aristotle, *Hist. anim.* V. 19), and silk garments are often described as transparent in Roman literature. That the beautiful folds created by silk should have appealed to the Greek artist and have suggested the clinging draperies of this period would be only natural. But though temporary fashion may have influenced the rendering of drapery at this period the sculptor clearly did not merely copy nature. In the Nike adjusting her sandal (fig. 504) the legs could never in reality show so clearly through two layers of material—the chiton and the himation. As in archaic art it is not realism that is aimed at, but artistic effect.

Joined to this transparency we note another characteristic feature in the drapery of this period: the decorative use of sweeping folds—generally of the himatia—blown around the figure. The deep, broad channels creating dark shadows contrast with the smoother modelling of body and limbs and play an effective part in the design.

The combination of these two styles is characteristic of practically all the monuments of the late fifth century. The "balustrade" of the Nike temple, datable about 410, furnishes striking examples. We have already cited the Nike adjusting her sandal[57] (fig. 504), where the contrast between the practically nude body and the deep shadows of the surrounding drapery is very striking. The Nike with the bull[58] (cf. fig. 506) shows this transparency combined with turbulent, highly decorative effects. Folds of great volume running in different directions are massed between the legs and form a variegated, dramatic background. It is a beautiful combination of stateli-

[56] On this subject, cf. Richter, *A.J.A.*, XXXIII, 1929, pp. 27 ff.
[57] Casson, *Catalogue of the Acropolis Museum,* II, pp. 156 f., No. 12.
[58] *Ibid.,* p. 155, No. 11.

ness and turmoil. The Karyatids of the Erechtheion[59] (fig. 502),
dated between 421 and 413, show the same transparent drapery
where it is laid against the left leg or over the breasts; at first sight
we are not sure whether the upper part of the left leg is not bare—
a doubt which would be impossible in the Parthenon figures. Moreover, in the breasts of the Karyatids the contours are distinctly visible through the drapery while in the Parthenon only their general
shape is recognizable. The lovely but scanty fragments of the frieze
of the Erechtheion[60] (409–406) are similar in style. In the group
of the woman and child[61] (fig. 296) the folds of the drapery are practically confined to the surfaces surrounding the legs, whereas the legs
appear almost nude. The Nike of Paionios in Olympia[62] (fig. 637)
was dedicated, according to the inscription, by the Messenians and
Naupaktians to Zeus with a tithe of the spoils taken from their enemies. The campaign referred to is most easily identified as that of
Sphakteria, 425, which would place the statue round 420. It brings
out strikingly the characteristics we are analyzing. The transparency of the drapery over the portions of the body which it covers is
so great that it does not affect the forms at all. The draped right leg
is modeled as carefully as the bare left one and its contours show as
distinctly. The presence of the drapery is only recognizable by the
occasional ridges introduced to indicate the folds. By way of contrast
the drapery is shown blowing behind in deep, restless folds creating
strong shadows.

In the frieze of the Athena Nike temple—built probably about
426[63]—we have on the one hand quiet standing figures[64] (fig. 297)
in which one leg though completely draped is carefully modeled with
both contours showing—very different from the Parthenon treatment, where only the outer outline shows and the inner is lost
through the covering drapery, and very similar to the Erechtheion
Karyatids[65] (fig. 502); we have on the other hand a violent battle

[59] Smith, *Catalogue of Greek Sculpture in the British Museum*, I, No. 407;
Stevens-Caskey-Fowler-Paton, *The Erechtheum*, pls. XXXVIII, XXXIX, pp. 232 ff.
[60] Stevens, etc., *op. cit.*, pp. 239 ff., pls. XL ff.
[61] Casson, *Catalogue of the Acropolis Museum*, II, p. 181, No. 1075.
[62] Treu, *Olympia*, III, pls. XLVI–XLVIII.
[63] Anderson-Spiers-Dinsmoor, *The Architecture of Ancient Greece* (1927), p. 126.
[64] In situ in Athens; cf. Blümel, *Fries des Tempels der Athena Nike*, pls. I–III,
10–12; Carpenter, *The Sculpture of the Nike Temple Parapet*.
[65] C. Blümel in his *Fries des Tempels der Athena Nike* ignores this important
characteristic in his attempt to associate these figures more nearly with the Parthenon frieze.

scene[66] (fig. 295) in which the draperies of the contestants are blown right and left in turbulent masses of considerable volume, a device which greatly adds to the stir and tumult of the contest. The fragmentary sculptures of the Argive Heraion[67] (about 420) contain several beautiful examples of transparent, clinging drapery.

We learn from Pausanias[68] that the Phigaleia temple was built by Iktinos, the architect of the Parthenon, and dedicated to Apollo Epikourios, "the Succorer" "for the help he gave in time of plague . . . at the time of the war between the Peloponnesians and Athenians." The date has been disputed. Those who accept Pausanias' statement hold that the most probable time is during the peace of Nikias which began in 421; for we are expressly told by Thucydides[69] that the plague which devastated Athens in 430 scarcely touched the Peloponnese; moreover, it is hardly probable that an Athenian architect should have been employed to build a temple in the Peloponnese while hostilities were actually going on between the two countries. The style of the sculptures, both of the frieze (cf. figs. 298[70] and 299[71]) and the metopes (figs. 300[72] and 301[73]), points to a date about 420.[74] The drapery in particular shows the characteristics we have noted in the sculptures of this period—the peculiar transparent quality with the contours of the bodies clearly shown and only occasional ridges to indicate the presence of the garments, and the decorative splashes against the background. Moreover, some figures bear a striking similarity to other late fifth-century reliefs; for instance, the Lapith woman on figure 299 to the Nike and bull from the "balustrade" (fig. 506). Taken as a whole, however, the composition in the Phigaleia frieze is wilder, more turbulent than that in the other monuments, reflecting the wildness of the Arkadian mountains in the tumult and agitation of the draperies.

The Nereids of the Nereid monument[75] (cf. figs. 302–304) show the same characteristics we have been discussing, in an advanced

---

[66] Smith, *Catalogue of Greek Sculpture in the British Museum*, I, No. 422.
[67] Waldstein, *The Argive Heraeum*, I, pls. XXXV, XXXVII.
[68] VIII. 41. 5.   [69] II. 54.
[70] Smith, *op. cit.*, I, No. 531.   [71] *Ibid.*, No. 530.
[72] *Ibid.*, No. 512.   [73] *Ibid.*, No. 517.
[74] Attempts have been made to identify the Niobids in Rome (fig. 4) and Copenhagen (figs. 92, 118) and two figures in Paris as pedimental sculptures and akroteria, respectively, from this temple (cf. Dinsmoor, *A.J.A.*, XLIV, 1939, pp. 27 ff., and Picard, *Monuments Piot*, XXXIX, 1943, pp. 49 ff.); but the evidence is not decisive.
[75] Smith, *op. cit.*, II, No. 909.

form. The thin Ionic chiton of one is indicated by a few ridges only, and interferes little with the modeling of the body, and even the heavy, woolen peplos of the other shows the forms distinctly; as soon as the draperies are separate from the figures they become deep, restless folds, while the mantles held up behind (fig. 303) form sweeping masses. The treatment is a *tour de force* in the art of sculpture and forms the climax of this style. Stylistically, therefore, this monument is best dated at the very end of the fifth century.

The lovely seated figure on a didrachm of Terina of about 420–400[76] (fig. 310) has a chiton and mantle through which the whole contour of the leg is visible. The reliefs from Eleusis[77] and in the Louvre[78] (fig. 307), dated by their inscriptions in 420 and 410 respectively, show similar renderings. The Palatine "Nike"[79] (fig. 305), the grave reliefs of Hegeso[80] (fig. 429) and Glykylla[81] (fig. 306), the Medea relief in the Lateran[82] (fig. 308), and the "Venus Genetrix" in Paris[83] are all stylistically related to the monuments we have discussed.

The difference in the treatment of drapery between the third and the last quarter of the fifth century is apparent also in vase-painting. We need only compare the works of the Boston Phiale painter or the Achilles painter (contemporary with the sculptures of the Parthenon) with those of Meidias and Aristophanes (allied to the artists of the Nike "balustrade" and the Nereid monument) to appreciate the change. In the earlier works the drapery still has a monumental quality, and it retains its separate entity and independence; as in the beautiful Amymone by the Boston Phiale painter in the Metropolitan Museum of Art,[84] who bears a marked resemblance to the Iris of the Parthenon (fig. 91). In the later paintings the drapery clings closely to the body with multitudinous little folds clearly revealing the forms beneath it, as in the figures

---

[76] Regling, "Terina," *Sechsundsechzigstes Winckelmannsprogramm,* 1906, pp. 21, 50, pl. II, θθ.

[77] *Ath. Mitt.* XIX, 1894, pl. VII.   [78] *Ibid.,* XXXV, 1910, pl. IV, 2.

[79] Found on the Palatine and formerly in the Museum there, now in the National Museum of the Terme; Aurigemma, *Le Terme di Diocleziano e Il Museo Nazionale Romano,* p. 63, no. 159.

[80] Conze, *Attische Grabreliefs,* No. 68, pl. XXX.

[81] Smith, *Catalogue of Greek Sculpture in the British Museum,* III, No. 2231.

[82] Helbig, *Führer,*[3] II, No. 1154.

[83] Harcum, *A.J.A.,* 1927, p. 151, fig. 4 (the legends of figs. 3 and 4 should be interchanged).

[84] *A.J.A.,* XXVII, 1923, pp. 282–283, figs. 19 and 20.

of the lovely scene of women perfuming clothes by the Meidias painter in the Metropolitan Museum[85] (fig. 309).

FOURTH CENTURY The late fifth-century treatment of transparent garments lingers on through the early fourth century. The Aphrodite on the silver stater of Aphrodisias (?), Kilikia, dated about 379–374, wears a diaphanous garment[86] (fig. 311); and this is still true to some extent of the Kerkyra on the treaty relief dated 375.[87] Several of the Epidauros sculptures[88] (of about 400–375; cf. figs. 710 ff.) have the transparent fluttering draperies of former times, though the folds have now more variety of direction. The Delphian Karyatids[89] (fig. 312) with their diaphanous garments and faces in which we can note the transition from the severer fifth-century type to the softer fourth-century one (with triangular forehead) are best placed in this period of the early fourth century.[90]

By the second quarter and the middle of the fourth century a great change in the rendering of drapery has taken place. The naturalistic treatment finally wins over the former decorative one. It is now possible to mistake a sculptured garment for a real one, as was the case with the Hermes of Praxiteles (fig. 664), of which a photograph was sent to a well-known archaeologist soon after its discovery; the archaeologist admired it greatly, but asked why they had left the mantle hanging on the tree trunk when they took the photograph. The Maussollos[91] and Artemisia[92] in the British Museum (figs. 314, 313,) show the new tendency clearly. The conscious arrangement of the earlier monuments where every fold had its distinct value in a beautiful design has given place to a more complicated, more naturalistic treatment. The smooth parts no longer alternate with bunched folds in a harmonious composition; the folds run in every direction as they would in reality, with a heavy mass of material gathered round the waist. The resultant effect is both more confusing and tamer.

In the majority of the fourth-century grave stelai (cf. fig. 317) the new style is firmly established; likewise in such monuments as the Demeter of Knidos in the British Museum[93] (fig. 315), the fig-

---

85 Beazley, *A.R.V.P.*, p. 832, no 7.   86 Hill, *Select Greek Coins*, pl. XLII, 2.
87 Athens, no. 1467. *B.C.H.*, II, pl. 12.   88 Defrasse and Lechat, *Épidaure*, p. 177.
89 Homolle, *Fouilles de Delphes*, IV, pls. LX–LXII.
90 For a probable dating at about 400 B.C. on historical grounds, cf. Pomtow, *Jahrbuch*, XXXV, 1920, p. 114.
91 Smith, *Catalogue of Greek Sculpture in the British Museum*, II, No. 1000.
92 *Ibid.* No. 1001.   93 Smith, *op. cit.*, II, No. 1300.

ures on the Ephesos drums[94] (fig. 705), and the mourning women
on the Sidon sarcophagus[95] (fig. 316), all of the middle of the century, and in the Asklepios relief in Copenhagen,[96] dated by its inscription in 329. The draperies now have the right values, the mantles are heavy and cumbrous, they perform their proper function of
covering the bodies, but their artistic effect is not on the same high
level. Even in such lovely creations as the Muses on the Mantineia
base (figs. 680, 681) and the terracotta statuettes from Tanagra
(cf. fig. 256) the draperies have the characteristic fourth-century
denseness. Though they are consciously composed for artistic effect
the general impression is naturalistic and lacks the grandeur of the
earlier creations.

The progressive development in Greek drapery from the fifth to
the fourth century can be clearly visualized in a series of female
figures standing in similar attitudes and each wearing a Doric
peplos. A statue in Copenhagen[97] (figs. 320, 321) and the Athena
on the Olympia metope (fig. 319) illustrate the architectural style
of the transition period, with stiff, almost perpendicular folds, and
few diversions on the overfold. A bronze statuette in the Bibliothèque Nationale,[98] a Roman copy of a work of about 450–440
(fig. 318), retains the quiet majesty of the Olympia sculptures, with
a distinct lessening, however, of the tension. The Athena Parthenos
(figs. 599–601), the "Athena Medici"[99] (fig. 322), and a torso in
Venice[100] (fig. 323), of about 440–435, show the grandiose, Pheidian
style with considerable life and variation. More folds are now introduced in both the upper and lower parts, and the leg is placed considerably more sidewise, which takes away from the perpendicular
effect. Another torso in Venice[101] (fig. 324) illustrates the stage
contemporary with the Parthenon pediments. The drapery is becoming softer and more transparent and the leg which does not

[94] Smith, *Catalogue of Greek Sculpture in the British Museum*, II, No. 1206.
[95] Mendel, *Catalogue des sculptures du Musée à Constantinople*, No. 10.
[96] *Ny Carlsberg Glyptotek, Billedtavler*, No. 231.
[97] Arndt, *La Glyptothèque Ny Carlsberg*, pls. 7–8.
[98] Babelon and Blanchet, *Catalogue des bronzes antiques*, No. 1045.
[99] Furtwängler, *Masterpieces*, fig. 6, pp. 27 ff.; Brunn-Bruckmann, *Denkmäler*, pl. 171.
[100] Furtwängler, *Griechische Originalstatuen in Venedig* (in *Abh. d. I. Cl. d. R. Ak. d. Wiss.*, XXI, II Abth.), pl. VII, 2. Since Furtwängler's publication of this interesting series of draped female figures—all less than life-size—they have been freed from their restorations and are exhibited in the new Archaeological Museum on the Piazza S. Marco.
[101] Furtwängler, *op. cit.*, pl. VI, 2.

carry the weight is sharply bent, giving greater ease to the attitude. The style of the last quarter of the fifth century is seen in the
torso at Eleusis[102] (fig. 325), the Erechtheion Karyatids[103] (fig.
502), and the figure from the Gjölbaschi monument[104] (fig. 326).
The drapery shows a further increase in softness and variation and
has assumed a completely transparent quality in certain portions,
for instance over the breasts and the bent leg. But the old feeling
for design is still apparent. A torso in Venice[105] (fig. 327) of this
period is in the same soft, transparent style, with a lively variegation in the folds of the kolpos, which gives it the same dramatic
quality we note in the Phigaleia frieze (p. 102). A figure on the
Ephesos drum in the British Museum[106] (fig. 328) and another
statue in Venice[107] (fig. 329) illustrate the fourth-century style.
The garment has lost its former fluidity and transparency and has
become completely naturalistic. The vertical folds over the supporting leg no longer fall in uninterrupted vertical lines, as before, but
the channels show variations; the tightly drawn portion between the
vertical folds and the flexed leg has disappeared and a heavy fold
falls from the right knee—as it would in nature. In other words the
right value is now given to each portion but the former sense for
composition is impaired.

HELLENISTIC   In the succeeding Hellenistic period we have many fine render-
PERIOD   ings, but it is not easy to trace a continued development; for since
complete naturalism has now been reached it is merely a question of
introducing variations on a given theme. Moreover, art is now
largely eclectic and reverts to and combines earlier creations. Among
such adaptations of former styles we may mention as particularly
successful the splendid Victory of Samothrake (fig. 95) which shows
on the one hand the transparency of the late fifth-century style as
well as its dramatic effect of sweeping folds, on the other the concentration of heavy masses characteristic of the middle of the
fourth; but the whole further complicated by a greater variation of
direction. The Nike of Brescia[108] (fig. 330) shows the same combination of late fifth- and fourth-century styles—a transparent chiton

---

102 Herrmann in Brunn-Bruckmann, *Denkmäler,* pl. 536.
103 Stevens-Caskey-Fowler-Paton, *The Erechtheum,* pls. XXXVIII f.
104 Benndorf, *Das Heroön von Gjölbaschi-Trysa,* pl. VII.
105 Furtwängler, *Griechische Originalstatuen in Venedig,* pl. IV, 2.
106 Smith, *Catalogue of Greek Sculpture in the British Museum,* II, No. 1206.
107 Furtwängler, *op. cit.,* pl. V.
108 Dütschke, *Antike Bildwerke in Oberitalien,* IV, p. 153.

covering the upper part of the body and a dense, heavy himation
wrapped round the lower; only here the complication of the folds is
more marked. A Hellenistic torso of a woman in Boston[109] (fig. 332)
has the diaphanous garment of the late fifth century, treated, however, with greater elaboration. How closely earlier styles are sometimes adhered to can be seen by comparing the Themis of Chai-
restratos[110] (fig. 331; first half of the third century) with the
Artemisia from the Mausoleum (fig. 313). The Themis is merely a
more formalized treatment of the earlier, naturalistic rendering.

Besides these eclectic copies and adaptations we have important
new contributions. Just as in the representation of the human figure there is introduced in the Hellenistic period a love of movement
and of violent contrasts, so in the drapery we find a tendency toward
dramatic and turbulent effects. The Pergamene frieze[111] (cf. e.g.,
fig. 334) and the statue of the Gaul killing himself (fig. 108) supply us with excellent examples. The sweep and swirl of the draperies
caused by the violent motion and the strong shadows of the deep
channels between the folds make on us an impression of power and
restlessness. An interesting detail which may be observed on some of
the Pergamene figures and which appears from the fourth century
onward[112] is the horizontal and vertical stripes crossing one another,
generally referred to as "Liegefalten," the idea being that they
represent creases caused by the folding of the garment while not in
use; though perhaps a more plausible explanation is that the artist
meant to indicate a striped pattern. Characteristic of this period is
the rendering of the chiton by multitudinous folds placed close together and nowhere transparent—suggesting a considerable thickness of material. We may mention as good examples some of the figures on the Pergamene frieze (cf. fig. 335) and the Anzio Girl in
Rome[113] (fig. 336).

Another new style, prevalent during the second century, is that of
transparent drapery, not as heretofore to show the body beneath it,
but to display other drapery. It was a *tour de force*, for it implied
the showing of one set of folds beneath another, the two going in

[109] Caskey, *Catalogue of Greek and Roman Sculpture*, No. 51.
[110] National Museum, Athens, No. 231.
[111] Museen zu Berlin, *Altertümer von Pergamon*, III, 2.
[112] Cf. list of sculptures given in my *Catalogue of Bronzes in the Metropolitan Museum*, p. 150, and *A.J.A.*, XLVIII, 1944, p. 238.
[113] Helbig, *Führer*,³ II, No. 1352.

different directions, and crossing one another. The problem is ably solved in such statues as the figure from Magnesia in Constantinople,[114] the Muse in Berlin[115] (fig. 337), and the statue from the Giustiniani Collection in the Metropolitan Museum[116] (fig. 338); but the effect of the whole is in each case confusing.

A beautiful contribution of Hellenistic times is found in standing and seated portrait statues wearing himatia, such as the "Hermarchos" (fig. 241) and the seated statue signed by Zeuxis[117] (fig. 339) in the Metropolitan Museum, the bronze seated figure in the British Museum[118] (fig. 333), and the Sophokles in the Lateran (fig. 249). The mantle is arranged in comparatively few, significant folds, beautifully composed with reference to a general design and yet bringing out in an admirable manner both the chief forms of the body and the heavy quality of the material. The former sense of design and the later naturalism are here combined in happy fashion.

[114] Mendel, *Catalogue des sculptures,* No. 549.
[115] *Beschreibung der Skulpturen in Berlin,* No. 221.
[116] *Galleria Giustiniani,* I, pl. 33. Cf. also a figure restored as Cleopatra in the new Museo archeologico in Venice, Inv. No. 53; a torso from Delos, *Revue des études grecques,* 1909, p. 293; the figures from Kos published by Bieber, *Antike Plastik, Walther Amelung zum 60ten Geburtstag,* pp. 19 ff.; etc.
[117] Metropolitan Museum, *Handbook* (1930), p. 278, fig. 197.
[118] Walters, *Select Bronzes,* No. LXV.

CHAPTER VII

ANIMALS

IT has often been said that the study of the human figure formed the sole interest of the Greek sculptor and that he attempted little else. But this is not strictly true. Being a lover of form, and of form in motion, he could not but be attracted by the various animals surrounding him and attempt their portrayal. We find him indeed at work on this study throughout his career. Several great sculptors attained renown for their representations: Kalamis, for instance, for his horses;[1] Myron for his famous cow set up on the Akropolis;[2] and Strongylion for his horses and oxen;[3] furthermore, Nikias is called by Pausanias[4] "the greatest painter of animals of his time" (i.e., fourth century B.C.).

As we pass in review the animal sculpture of the Greeks we realize that it had the same course of development as that of the human figure. Beginning with conventionalization and stylization it became gradually more and more naturalistic, passing through a period in the fifth century when the blending of the two conceptions brought about some remarkably fine renderings, and finally emerging in the Hellenistic period with realistic representations comparable to our own nineteenth-century art—comparable and yet distinct; for, just as in the human figure the long period of stylization left its imprint even on the later Greek conceptions, so in the highly naturalistic animals of Hellenistic times there is always a generalization which gives them a certain grandeur and stamps them as "classical." And throughout this long history the Greek sculptor showed his wonted ability to seize the essentials, to mark each animal with its characteristic traits, and thus bring out its individual nature.

We can mention here only a few of the outstanding representations which have survived.[5]

The decorative feeling of the archaic artist is clearly apparent in Lion such works as the limestone lion from Perachora in the Boston

---

[1] Cf. p. 203. [2] Cf. p. 209.
[3] Cf. p. 244. [4] I. 29. 15.
[5] For a fuller treatment see my *Animals in Greek Sculpture*, Oxford, 1930.

Museum[6] (figs. 340, 341; second quarter of the sixth century). We find here the same rectangular conception, the strictly symmetrical scheme that we observe in the contemporary human figure. The body is represented in full profile, the head in full front, without any of the twists and turnings natural to a living animal. The mane is indicated by highly ornamental rows of flame-like locks; but there is also a distinct attempt at representing the swelling muscles of the legs and trunk as well as the ribs; so that—as always in Greek art—the stylization is grounded on nature and is not purely abstract.

Perhaps the finest Greek representations of lions we have are the reclining lion in Berlin[7] (fig. 342; second half of sixth century) and the dead lion of the Olympia metope[8] (fig. 343; about 465–460). The lion in Berlin is fortunately in a good state of preservation. We could have no better example of the happy combination of stylization and increasing naturalism current at the time. The forms of the body are correctly indicated in a generalized manner; the planes are simple, the effective stylization of the mane is retained. But there has entered into the representation a better understanding of the essential nature of the animal. We note it in the completely relaxed body with both hind legs brought over to one side and head resting on one paw, in the indication of the loose skin over the right hind leg, and more especially in the expressive face with its small, watchful eye and soft parts round the mouth. The Olympia animal is more advanced in naturalism, but retains a monumental quality. The helpless, relaxed body, one paw placed under the head, the other doubled up on the side, is wonderfully convincing. The head is modeled with more detail, but the mane is in the old conventionalized manner.

In the second half of the fifth century the lion is not nearly so popular as in the earlier art. Moreover, in these increasingly realistic renderings it becomes more apparent that the artist had no opportunity to study from life.[9] We may take as examples the lions of

---

[6] Caskey, *Catalogue of Greek and Roman Sculpture*, No. 10; Brunn-Bruckmann, *Denkmäler*, pl. 641; in the text to pls. 641 ff. Schröder gives an excellent essay on classical lions.

[7] Wiegand, *Berliner Museen*, XLVIII, 3, 1927, pp. 1 f. It is there dated in the early sixth century. But it would be an anomaly at that time, for such intimate observation of nature as evinced by the indication of the folds of skin on the hind leg cannot be paralleled before the second half of the sixth century.

[8] Treu, *Olympia*, III, pl. XXXV, 1.

[9] The lion was extinct in Greece proper in historic times. Herodotos VII. 125, 126 and Aristotle, *Historia Animalium* VI. 31 and VIII. 28 both say that lions occur in Europe only in the extreme north of Greece between the rivers Acheloos and Nestos.

the Nereid monument[10] of the late fifth century and the related example in the Metropolitan Museum[11] (figs. 344, 345). Here the pose, the slender body, the elongated skull, the short hair on the neck resemble those of a dog rather than of a lion; only in the wide-open mouth has the artist conveyed successfully the impression of a fierce animal of prey. The lion from the Mausoleum[12] (fig. 346) is a typical example of the fourth century (about 350). Again the sculptor has given it the build of a dog with straight legs placed wide apart and he has in no way conveyed that strange restlessness of a lion's body which suggests motion even when in repose, or the quality of his skin as it glides to and fro over the powerful muscles. And the detailed modeling makes us the more conscious of the misunderstanding of such salient features.

We have a wealth of beautiful representations of the horse in Greek art. Effective early examples are those from Prinias[13] (fig. 347; second half of seventh century) and on the Siphnian frieze (fig. 487; about 525 B.C.), both highly decorative. From the first part of the fifth century we may select the marble horses in the Akropolis Museum,[14] with their fine aristocratic bearing and curiously pointed muzzles (fig. 348; about 500–480); and shortly afterward the large bronze statuette in New York[15] (figs. 349, 350; about 480–470). The latter sums up in an eloquent way the achievements of the Greek sculptor at this period. He has by now practically mastered the anatomy of a horse; but this knowledge does not prevent him from seeing the form as an artistic whole—in which the important functional parts are accented but no details obtrude. And the stylizing sense inherited from the past has stood him in good stead—in the effective treatment of the bone of the nose, of the mane, of the forelock, and of the contour of the whole and of each individual part. It is a beautiful piece of design and yet there are few horses in the history of art that convey to us so vividly the essential nature of the animal—its high spirit, proud carriage, and nervous temperament. Only a lover of horses and a great artist could have created such a work.

The second half of the fifth century produced the horses of the

HORSE

---

[10] Smith, *Catalogue of Greek Sculpture in the British Museum*, II, Nos. 929, 930.
[11] Metropolitan Museum, *Bulletin*, 1910, pp. 40–41.
[12] Smith, *op. cit.*, II, Nos. 1075 ff.   [13] *Bolletino d'arte*, 1908, p. 458.
[14] Dickins, *Catalogue*, Nos. 697 and 700.
[15] Metropolitan Museum, *Bulletin*, 1923, pp. 89 ff.

Parthenon frieze (fig. 486; c. 442–438) and pediment (cf. fig. 351; c. 438–431). Naturalism has made great strides. As we study the surface of the marble we shall note infinite modulations, closely observed from nature. The complicated muscles and veins of a horse's head, its fleshy and bony parts, are carefully rendered with a wealth of light and shade; and yet there is no confusion, because the transitions are clear and gradual, so that an impression of simplicity is still obtained; the greater complexity only adds richness and variety to the quiet majesty of former times. There are few artistic enjoyments comparable to that of watching the cavalcade of riders on the southern frieze of the Parthenon, so lively and yet so clear-cut, or the horse of Selene from the eastern pediment (fig. 351), one of the grandest conceptions of a horse known.

In the fourth century comes a gradual receding to a tamer level. The horse, perhaps by Skopas, on the Mausoleum frieze (fig. 697; about 350) has still much of the fire and simplicity of its predecessors, but its companions on the same frieze (figs. 720, 721, 729) and in the chariot group[16] (cf. fig. 352) have not the former refinement. And gradually with the increasing realism the difference in the various planes is accentuated and the whole becomes more elaborate. The horses on the "Alexander sarcophagus"[17] (fig. 748; last quarter of the fourth century) and on the contemporary relief in New York[18] (fig. 353) are excellent examples of such naturalistic renderings. And this elaboration becomes more marked in the later Hellenistic period. Nevertheless the former sense of design is never completely lost sight of. It lends distinction to the bronze head in the Museo Archeologico in Florence,[19] which may be regarded as a forerunner of the fine creations of the Renaissance (e.g., the horse of Colleoni by Verrocchio).

BULL AND COW   There are many excellent renderings of the bull and the cow in a variety of attitudes both in the round and in relief. The bronze statuette from Delphi[20] (fig. 354; late archaic) shows a walking cow with finely simplified modeling, the chief bones of the legs and head well accentuated, the loose skin of the neck rendered by a series of delicately incised lines.

16 Smith, *Catalogue of Greek Sculpture in the British Museum*, II, No. 1002.
17 Mendel, *Catalogue*, No. 68.
18 Metropolitan Museum, *Handbook* (1930), pp. 273 ff.
19 Amelung, *Antiken in Florenz*, No. 270.
20 Pedrizet, *Fouilles de Delphes*, V, pl. XVI.

The high-water mark in the rendering of the bull and the cow is reached in the metope of the Zeus temple at Olympia with Herakles and the Cretan bull[21] (fig. 355; about 465–460), and a little later in the cows of the Parthenon frieze[22] (fig. 356; about 442–438) and the bronze statuette of a cow in the Cabinet des Médailles in Paris[23] (fig. 357). In the Olympia bull how successfully the turn of the head is conveyed, how decorative and yet how natural is the raised swinging tail, and above all how convincing the powerful body ready for attack! The Parthenon cows and the bronze cow are rather quieter specimens, modeled with a beautiful, restrained naturalism. The ponderous motion, the sleek body and stiff legs, the powerful bones, are faithfully rendered, and yet with the same idealizing tendency that we note in the contemporary human figures. It is this combination of advanced naturalism and simplification that must have distinguished the famous cow of Myron (cf. p. 211).

The contrast between the early simplified rendering and the later realistic one is well brought out in a comparison of the boar of the "Sikyonian" Treasury at Delphi[24] (fig. 358) and the statue in the Uffizi[25] (fig. 359). The former shows the animal as a fierce creature, its forefeet set forward, the head lowered ready for attack; only the important functional parts are indicated and the outline stands out clearly. In the Uffizi statue it is represented—with a wealth of detail—sitting in characteristic, lazy attitude.

BOAR

We have a delightful series of bronze statuettes of goats belonging to the late archaic period. The animal is shown in a variety of postures. We may mention as conspicuous examples a goat lying down with head to one side in the British Museum[26] (fig. 360) and a leaping goat in the Metropolitan Museum[27] (fig. 361). The forms of the goat—its elastic body and strong slender legs, its eager, long-nosed face, and little turned-up tail are well observed and rendered in the simplified manner of the period, while the shaggy hair of the beard and brow and along the ridge of the back is indicated by deli-

GOAT

---

21 Treu, *Olympia*, III, pl. XXXVI, 4.
22 Smith, *Sculptures of the Parthenon*, pls. 40, 88–91.
23 Babelon and Blanchet, *Catalogue des bronzes antiques de la Bibliothèque Nationale*, No. 1157.
24 Homolle, *Fouilles de Delphes*, IV, pl. III, and p. 22.
25 Amelung, *Antiken in Florenz*, No. 9.
26 Walters, *Catalogue of Bronzes in the British Museum*, No. 233.
27 Metropolitan Museum, *Bulletin*, 1921, p. 36; *Handbook* (1930), p. 76.

cately incised lines. In each case the contours form lovely curves and the composition has the decorative quality of a carefully planned design. In the bronze statuette of a standing goat in Geneva[28] (fig. 362; second half of fifth century) the hair is stylized but the modeling of the shaggy legs and of the head is naturalistic. As fourth-century examples we may cite the butting goats in Athens[29] (fig. 363) which served as finials of gravestones and which, though realistically rendered, are decoratively composed for the purpose they served.

Dog   The dog appears frequently in Greek sculpture and is observed in many characteristic postures—of expectant listening, running, attacking its prey, sniffing the ground, sleeping, licking its body, in a cat-and-dog fight, and patiently submitting to a child's caresses. The dog in the cat-and-dog fight on the statue base in Athens (fig. 283; end of sixth century) is an excellent early characterization of the eager yet hesitant way in which the dog attacks its arch enemy. The thin, agile body with the strong hind legs and finely curved, sensitive tail are well observed. A large hound standing quietly with its head uplifted as a dwarf pats it on the neck is engraved on a carnelian of late fifth-century style in the Metropolitan Museum[30] (fig. 364). Though on a small scale it is one of the finest representations we have of the period. All essentials in the beautiful, lithe body are indicated, and yet simply modeled in a large style; and the dog's mingled enjoyment and patient endurance of the caress are vividly conveyed. The seated hound of serpentine in the Conservatori Palace in Rome[31] (fig. 367) is another well-characterized rendering, probably a Roman copy of a fourth-century work. Like the fine greyhound in the Glyptothek, Munich,[32] and the famous example still in situ in the Kerameikos, Athens,[33] the original probably came from a grave monument, the dog being conceived as a guardian of the tomb. In the Barracco Museum is a dog lying down with its head turned back to lick a wound on its leg[34] (fig. 365). It is perhaps a

28 Deonna, *Catalogue des bronzes figurés antiques*, No. 105.
29 National Museum, No. 805; cf. also Nos. 781, 783, 786, 806; Conze, *Attische Grabreliefs*, pls. CCCLVII–CCCLVIII, Nos. 1685–1688.
30 Richter, *Catalogue of Engraved Gems*, No. 38. It is about one-half inch long.
31 Stuart Jones, *The Sculptures of the Palazzo dei Conservatori*, p. 145, No. 27a, pl. 96.
32 Wolters, *Führer* (1923), No. 497.
33 Collignon, *Les Statues funéraires*, pp. 240 f.
34 Barracco and Helbig, *La Collection Barracco*, pl. LVIII.

Roman copy of a Greek original described by Pliny[35] as a dedication in the temple of Juno on the Capitol. The Barracco dog is certainly extraordinarily lifelike with its lanky body and the pose and face suggestive of suffering. We have clearly here reached the naturalistic stage of the late Greek period, in which the sculptor is in full sympathy with his subject and renders it directly as he sees it.

There is a series of seated dogs in the Vatican,[36] the Uffizi[37] (fig. 366), and elsewhere,[38] evidently Roman copies of what must have been a famous original. The animal is represented with head lifted to one side, mouth open, forelegs spread apart in a momentary posture; he is in that breathless state of expectancy preceding violent action which we know so well in the dog. The transitory pose and the masterly realism with which it is conveyed place the sculptor in the Hellenistic age. The breed of these dogs is the pseudo-Molossian, the same as the dog in the Kerameikos (see above). It is differentiated from the true mastiff or the Molossian by the more pointed muzzle, mane-like hair on the neck, and bushy tail.[39]

There are many notable representations of birds in Greek sculpture. They occur both as attributes in statues and statuettes of various deities and as single representations on coins and gems. We can attempt to list here only a few distinguished examples.

BIRDS

The majestic eagle appears on the coins of Elis, Akragas, and other cities during the fifth and fourth centuries—as quietly sitting, beating its wings, or devouring its prey.[40] Its striking beauty evidently appealed to these die-engravers and they have reproduced in masterly fashion the grand curves of its neck as it bends down on its prey (fig. 368[41]) or lifts its head, the beautiful design of its wings, and its shapely head with the hooked beak and deep-set eyes (fig. 369[42]). The swans on the coins of Klazomenai are equally successful. The bird is represented walking, beating its wings, or turning its head to preen its wings (fig. 370)—all naturalistic and yet highly decorative postures in which the curves of the long neck and the lines of the wings are effectively utilized.

---

[35] *N.H.* XXXIV. 38.

[36] Amelung, *Die Skulpturen des vaticanischen Museums,* II, No. 65.

[37] Amelung, *Führer der Antiken in Florenz,* Nos. 10, 11.

[38] Cf. the list given by Amelung, *Die Skulpturen des vaticanishen Museums,* II, p. 164. All of them are extensively restored.

[39] Cf. Keller, *Die antike Tierwelt,* I, p. 112.

[40] Imhoof-Blumer and Keller, *Tier-und Pflanzenbilder,* pls. IV and V.

[41] Coin of Akragas, about 413–406 B.C.   [42] Coin of Elis, about 421–400 B.C.

On Greek gems of the later fifth century birds are favorite representations and among them are several extraordinarily fine renderings. We may select for illustration the heron standing on one leg[43] (fig. 371). The salient characteristics of the bird are brought out, while the whole is simplified into a beautiful design adapted to fill the given space.

MISCEL-
LANEOUS
ANIMALS

There are several beautiful representations of minor animals on Greek coins and gems; of these we will select the crab on the coins of Akragas of about 472–450[44] (fig. 372) with delicately modeled claws and denticles, and the bee on the fourth-century coins of Ephesos[45] (fig. 373).

[43] Beazley, *The Lewes House Collection of Ancient Gems*, pl. 5, 66.
[44] Imhoof-Blumer and Keller, *Tier- und Pflanzenbilder*, pl. VIII, 1 ff.; Hill, *Select Greek Coins*, pl. LIX, 2.
[45] *Ibid.*, pl. VII, 19 ff.

CHAPTER VIII

COMPOSITION

WE have examined the Greek sculptor's work as it appears in his single figures—his rendering of the human body, the head, the drapery, and his representation of animals. There is another important aspect of his work, the grouping of his figures in relation to one another, in other words, their composition. That the Greeks were intensely interested in design we know from their studies in proportion and interrelations.[1] It is indeed likely that a definite system of proportion, probably geometrical rather than arithmetical, underlay Greek design[2] and that it is this subtle symmetry based on an interplay of the parts to one another and to the whole which creates in us the singular satisfaction we derive from a Greek temple, an Athenian vase, and a pediment composition. Greek interest in geometric proportion is attested by the definite assertions of ancient writers.[3]

The Greeks had, moreover, extensive opportunities of practising design, so that they developed it to an extraordinary degree. Both in their architectural sculptures and in their minor arts they were confronted with problems the solution of which they attacked with wonted application. The fitting of a large number of figures into the triangular space of a pediment, the composition of groups to occupy the rectangular space of a metope, of a grave relief, or of a long

[1] Besides Polykleitos (cf. p. 245) many other ancient artists wrote books on proportion: Praeterea minus nobiles multi praecepta symmetriarum conscripserunt uti Nexaris, Theocydes, Demophilos, Pollis, Leonides, Silanion, Melampus (Melanthius), Sarnacus, Euphranor (Vitruvius VII, Preface 14). Of these the sculptor Pollis can be dated at least before 480, probably in the later part of the sixth century (Robert, *Jahrbuch*, 1915, p. 241).

[2] For such analyses, cf. J. Hambidge, *The Greek Vase* and *The Parthenon;* Caskey, *The Geometry of Greek Vases;* E. Mössel, *Die Proportion in Antike und Mittelalter;* I. Richter, *Rhythmic Form in Art,* all of whom find the "golden section" commonly employed in Greek design.

[3] Plotinus, *Ennead* I. VI. 1 (cited on p. 26); Plato, *Timaios* 31 c—a description of the "golden section" or proportion of the "whirling square" (this reference I owe to my sister, I. Richter); Plato, *Republic* VII. 529: ". . . just as we might employ diagrams which fell in our way, curiously drawn and elaborated by Daidalos or some other craftsman or painter. For, I imagine, a person acquainted with geometry, on seeing such diagrams, would think them most beautifully finished, but . . . ." This shows definitely that artists used geometrical proportion.

frieze, or the fitting of a design into the circular space of a coin or a sealstone; all these were problems of great difficulty and were satisfactorily solved only after many experiments. Since the Greeks ultimately achieved such splendid results, it will be of interest to study the road they traveled.

A large part of early Greek sculpture is architectural, that is, served to decorate the temples and "treasuries" of the period. Its composition therefore became of special importance, for it had not only to form a pleasing design in itself, but to play a part in the larger composition. Unfortunately it is impossible for us to see these sculptures in their original setting, as a part of the larger scheme. It is difficult enough in most cases to reconstruct the composition of the individual group; so battered and disjointed are the fragments. To view them upon the pediment or in the friezes of a well-preserved Greek temple—harmonizing with it and making their own contribution—has not been vouchsafed us in a single instance. We must try to bridge this gap with our imagination, supplying it first with all the evidence available.

The lines of a Greek temple are largely vertical and horizontal (cf. fig. 375). There are the horizontal steps, the vertical columns with vertical flutings, the horizontal epistyle, the vertical triglyphs, the horizontal cornice. This design in straight lines needed diversity. It was furnished by the sculptured decorations—the metopes between triglyphs; the continuous friezes; the pedimental groups crowning each end; the splendid akroteria at each angle of the pediment standing free against the sky; and the antefixes and waterspouts ranged along the cornice on the sides. The sculptures by their variety of line saved the buildings from any impression of monotony. This important function we must keep in mind in our study of their composition.

(a) Pediments

THE pediment groups presented peculiar difficulties. The chief requirements were: to place in the center a prominent figure or group, since here comes the chief accent; to fill the awkward space of the angles; and to compose figures for the intervening parts of constantly diminishing heights. And the composition as a whole had to produce the needed variety of line and create a harmonious effect. The gradual evolution from primitive renderings to the wonderful solutions of the Parthenon are fascinating to watch.

One of the earliest Greek pediments so far known is that of the temple at Corfu,[4] worked in local limestone (fig. 374; about 600–580). The great achievement here is the effective centerpiece. The Medusa stands out in all her grandeur and importance. The other figures—the little Chrysaor on the right, the Pegasos on the left, the lions on each side, and the diminutive figures right and left— are secondary as far as the impression of the whole is concerned; they are completely overshadowed by the great Gorgon. The problem of filling the angle is solved by a reclining figure (fig. 109); not one with feet in the corner and head raised, as later at Olympia and in the Parthenon; but a curious person lying in a completely horizontal position, his head in the angle, apparently quite unconnected with the rest of the group. The intervening figures consist of two panthers or lions (effective in that they keep up the scale of the Medusa and supply desirable horizontal and oblique lines) and smaller figures of a seated figure (fig. 61), attacked by an enemy of whom only the lance-head is preserved, and of a group with Zeus brandishing his thunderbolt against a giant (fig. 96). The combat groups furnish a pleasing variety of direction, while the seated figure reduces the height of the human figure without making it too diminutive; here this device is not yet adequately carried out, but it is successfully utilized later in the eastern pediment of the Parthenon. The weak points in the composition are the lack of concerted action and unity as well as the ludicrously small scale of the side figures compared with the central Gorgon and the lions.

The chief difficulty experienced by the early sculptor was evidently the adaptation of his figures to the slope of the pediment. It is not surprising therefore that he avoided compositions with only human figures. Animals and monsters were more adaptable than the human frame, and their wriggly tails and claws fitted admirably into the narrowing space; and moreover they could expand conveniently toward the middle. This scheme appears in several of the poros pediments found on the Akropolis of Athens.

In the small Hydra pediment[5] (fig. 376; about 590) Herakles is the great central figure. The Hydra with her manifold heads and curling tails occupies the whole right side, supplying an admirable variety of line and filling the space in a convenient manner. Iolaos, Herakles' companion, is ready with his chariot on the left. He had

---

[4] Βερσάκης, Πρακτικά, 1911, pp. 164 ff.; Rodenwaldt, *Korkyra* II, pls. I ff.
[5] Dickins, *Catalogue of the Acropolis Museum*, No. 1.

to be made distinctly smaller than Herakles; but he is still of acceptable size, being fairly near the center. The horses with heads down form a good lengthwise group toward the left; but they do not quite reach the angle, so the large crab which is said to have been sent by Hera to harass Herakles was provided as a filler.

Similar solutions are offered in the "Bluebeard" and Triton pediment also from the Akropolis[6] (figs. 378, 379), where a huge monster occupies each sloping side; in one case a three-headed being, in the other a fish-tailed Triton strangled by Herakles, whose body is shown in appropriate scale crouching beside it. The central group between these two sloping compositions may have been supplied by a bull attacked on each side by a lion[7] (fig. 377), in the scheme current in early archaic art;[8] while portions of still other pediments show a lioness devouring a bull,[9] Herakles and Triton,[10] and curling snakes.[11]

Fairly successful though these devices were in decorating the allotted space, they did not satisfy the Greek sculptor for long. Monsters were being rapidly ousted from Greek art, and it was desirable to develop more satisfactorily a composition with only human figures. Such a group had been tried as early as about 570–550 in the poros pediment of the Introduction of Herakles into Olympos[12] (fig. 380). Here large seated figures of Zeus and Hera occupy the center; and a little Herakles, and a still smaller figure with a fawnskin are placed further down the slope. Between Hera and Herakles must have been an Athena, escorting the hero; and on the other side of the pediment was probably an assembly of deities. The sculptor has succeeded here in providing an effective centerpiece, as well as a unified subject; but for the problem of the slopes he frankly knew no way out except the awkward diminutive figures.

Another early pediment with a unified subject appears to have been the one with the little water carrier, perhaps to be identified as representing Troilos, Polyxena, and Achilles by the well house.[13]

---

[6] Dickins, *Catalogue of the Acropolis Museum*, Nos. 35, 36; Buschor, *Ath. Mitt.*, 1922, pp. 53 ff. and 106 ff.

[7] Dickins, *op. cit.*, No. 3. Cf. note 16.

[8] Cf. the parallels on black-figured vases given by Buschor, *op. cit.*, 1922, pls. 13 and 14.

[9] Akropolis Museum, No. 4; Dickins, *op. cit.*, p. 76.

[10] Dickins, *op. cit.*, No. 2.

[11] Akropolis Museum, Nos. 39, 40; Dickins, *op. cit.*, pp. 74, 75.

[12] Cf. Dickins, *op. cit.*, p. 62.

[13] Buschor, *Ath. Mitt.*, 1922, pp. 81 ff., pl. VI; Zanotti-Bianco, *Rendiconti della Pont. Acc. rom. di Arch.*, XIX, pp. 371 ff.

In the pediment of the Siphnian Treasury (fig. 382) at Delphi[14] (about 525) the composition with human figures is more successfully carried out. The subject is the contest of Herakles and Apollo for the Delphian tripod. In the center is Athena overtowering everyone else. Apollo and Herakles, the contestants for the tripod, and Artemis, Apollo's helpmate, come next in scale. Then appear slightly smaller figures, the convenient groups of chariots and horses familiar from the Herakles and Hydra pediment; and other persons decreasing in height toward the corners, among them a crouching charioteer and a reclining man. Of the latter only a small part is preserved, but enough to show that the head is no longer resting in the corner like that of his predecessor on the Corfu pediment, but is slightly raised and placed toward the central group, foreshadowing in fact the Kladeos of Olympia and the Ilissos of the Parthenon (figs. 115, 119). To represent a figure crouching behind a chariot is likewise an important step in advance. It forecasts the use of kneeling, crouching, falling figures which could be adapted to the diminishing space without unduly reducing the scale. There is no apparent relation between the sparse subsidiary figures and the crowded central group; the sculptor has not yet learned to produce an interrelated composition. And the row of vertical standing figures in the center is somewhat monotonous in design.

The group of Athena and a giant (fig. 112), and the crouching giants[15] (fig. 385) in the Akropolis Museum (datable early in the last quarter of the sixth century) must have belonged to an important Peisistratid building.[16] The center of the pediment was occupied either by this one group of Athena and her giant, or more probably by Zeus (or Poseidon) and Athena, each with an opposing giant.[17] For there are preserved a left foot larger than Athena's (which must have belonged to an important personage placed near the center) and several other feet presumably belonging to giants. Athena's giant should be placed farther to her right than shown in the illustration, which would bring out the fine striding figure of the goddess

14 Homolle, Fouilles de Delphes, IV, pl. XVI–XVII, 1 and 1a.

15 Dickins, Catalogue of the Acropolis Museum, Nos. 631 A, B, C; Schrader, Akropolis, pp. 345ff., pls. 185 ff.

16 The building used to be identified as the peristyle added by Peisistratos to the "old temple of Athena," and the "Bluebeard" and Triton pediments were thought to have belonged to the older structure. Recently various theories have been advanced regarding this temple; cf. Schuchhardt, Ath. Mitt., 1935–1936, pp. 1 ff., and Dinsmoor, A.J.A., 1947, pp. 109 ff.

17 Perhaps in the scheme of the painting on an amphora in Brussels, cf. Six, Ath. Mitt., 1925, p. 117, pl. I.

to better advantage. The splendid crouching giants helped to fill the slopes. The composition must have been one of great power.

The pediments of the temple of Apollo at Delphi[18] (about 510) are unfortunately also very fragmentary. Enough remains of the eastern one[19] (figs. 381, 384, 386), however, to show that the center was occupied by Apollo's four-horse chariot seen in full front, flanked on either side by standing figures, and with groups of lions attacking animals in the corners (cf. fig. 384). The sculptor has avoided the strongly diminishing scale, but the many vertical lines in the middle are monotonous and the animal groups frankly a subterfuge. The western pediment is still more fragmentary; from the remains (cf. fig. 387) we can only judge that its subject was one of action—apparently a combat of gods and giants.

A marked development is seen in the pediment of the Megarian Treasury at Olympia[20] (fig. 383), with its battle of gods and giants (about 520–510). Here we have at last a unified composition. Zeus and his opponent form the middle group; then comes a striding deity on either side with a falling opponent; then a crouching deity with a fallen enemy; and in the extreme corners animals. It is a harmonious, animated composition of figures of about the same scale, knit together by unity of action. And there is no longer any monotony of lines; they flow in every direction, thus performing their function of supplying variety of movement in the composition of a Greek temple. Unfortunately the preservation is very poor. The soft limestone is so battered and broken that it was only with great difficulty that a reconstruction of the group proved possible.

The same theme of an animated contest appears in the pediments of the temple of Aphaia (figs. 388, 389) at Aigina[21] (about 500–480); for once discovered it naturally found favor, since it seemed to supply the chief desiderata—unified action, variety of direction, and an occasion for placing figures in all sorts of postures, thereby reducing their heights and not too much their scale. In both the west and east pediments the center is occupied by an Athena, slightly larger than the contestants. She no longer takes part in the struggle as she did in the Siphnian pediment; she is detached, and by her

---

18 *Fouilles de Delphes,* II, fig. 83.
19 Homolle, *Fouilles de Delphes,* IV, pls. XXXII–XXXVI.
20 Treu, *Olympia,* III, pls. II, III.
21 We follow here the reconstructions by Furtwängler, published in his *Aegina,* pls. 104–106.

quiet, stately presence dominates the scene of turmoil.[22] In the west pediment the contestants on each side are divided into two distinct groups of three (in the Megarian pediment there were two groups of two) separate and independent of each other. The reclining figure in the angle (cf. fig. 113) is being stabbed and shot at by his opponents and thus becomes part of the fighting scene. For that purpose he faces toward the center, just as did the early reclining figure in the Corfu pediment; but his head is now partly raised, and he has therefore been pushed a little away from the angle which is occupied by helmets. The chief weakness in the design is the fact that the two groups of three do not interconnect, which gives the whole a staccato appearance.

This mistake is rectified in the later, eastern pediment. Here each side is occupied by one interconnected group of four warriors, one striding, one falling, one crouching, one kneeling; and then, in the corner, a wounded warrior (cf. fig. 114), his back to the others, but turning toward them and therefore of them; his feet very neatly fitting into the angle. This interrelation of the various figures greatly helps the unity of the whole. We see it accomplished here for the first time in the history of Greek pediments.

Twenty years later comes the temple of Zeus at Olympia[23] (about 465–460). In the west pediment (figs. 391, 392) there is again a central dominating figure, calm amid the restless confusion of battle. The bodies of Centaurs, of young Lapiths, and of Lapith women intermingle in the violence of the struggle, as they seize one another by the head, by the arm, by the waist. We can make out three separate groups on each side, with two reclining women at each corner; but the figures are so closely intertwined that we have none of the staccato feeling of the western pediment of Aigina. And miraculously, in spite of the violence of action, the effect of the whole is beautifully rhythmical. As so often in Greek art, the splendor of the composition transcends the subject, makes us forget it, and fills us with pleasure in its harmonious design.

On the eastern pediment (figs. 390, 393[24]) are represented the

[22] The Athena of the Eretria pediment was so far as we can tell a similarly detached central figure. Not enough remains of the pedimental statues to allow a reconstruction of the composition. To her right probably came the Theseus and Antiope (fig. 284) mounting a chariot (cf. Furtwängler, *Aegina*, pp. 321 ff.).

[23] Treu, *Olympia*, III, pls. XVIII–XXI.

[24] The position of some of the figures is debated; cf. the articles on the subject by Winter, *Ath. Mitt.*, 1925, pp. 1 ff., and Bulle, *Jahrbuch*, LVII, 1942, pp. 199 ff.

preparations for the race of Pelops. It is a quiet, restful scene, a presiding Zeus in the center, two standing figures on each side, then chariots with crouching figures, and seated and reclining spectators in the angles (cf. figs. 115, 116). The scheme with its vertical central figures followed by horizontal chariots and crouching people is more old-fashioned than that of the western pediment; strongly reminiscent, in fact, of the Siphnian pediment, only of course less harsh, more subtly interconnected. As a design it does not reach the height of the western pediment. Curiously, though less animated it is not more restful.

In the Parthenon pediments (about 438–432) we reach the climax of Greek pedimental composition.[25] Here are no violent battles, no falling, crouching, striding warriors; and yet the scenes are full of life and action, as well as of rest and composure. The design of the west pediment[26] (figs. 394, 395) is happily preserved to us in a drawing made in 1674, a few years before its destruction. In the middle are Athena and Poseidon, moving diagonally away from the center and by their size and position dominating the scene. Then come the familiar chariot groups, but now with splendid rearing horses and with full-size charioteers. Then sitting figures in a great variety of attitudes, no longer parallel to the background, but in various oblique postures, thus leading gradually and naturally to the reclining figures at the corners (cf. fig. 119).

The middle portion of the east pediment[27] is irretrievably lost. We have not even a drawing, for it was already gone in 1674. We only know, from Pausanias,[28] that the subject was the birth of the goddess Athena. The preserved ends (fig. 396) are not dissimilar from those of the west pediment, consisting chiefly of seated and half-reclining figures, subtly interconnected by their attitudes, by a slight turn to the right or the left. The early device of the Corfu pediment of a seated figure for adaptation to the slope is here perfected. For the filling of the corners the sculptor has used a novel and bold device—Helios rising with his horses from the sea at one end, Selene disappearing into it at the other. Throughout we feel that the designer here at work had reached his full stature. After a

25 The pediment(?) which included the Niobids in Rome and Copenhagen (figs. 4, 92, 118) must have been an outstanding composition a decade or so previous to that of the Parthenon. Cf. p. 102, note 74.

26 Smith, *Sculptures of the Parthenon,* fig. 27.

27 *Ibid.,* figs. 8 and 9. 28 I. 24. 5.

century or two of continued struggle he has emerged from all preparatory stages, and, building on the results of former trials and
gropings, is able to fashion his composition into a magnificent, harmonious whole.

After the Parthenon there is no outstanding pedimental composition, at least now known. The east pediment of the Nereid monument[29] (fig. 397) is an awkward composition, reverting to the timid
solutions of archaic times: two groups in the center followed by figures of strongly diminishing heights, and animals in the corners.
What is preserved of the west pediment[30] shows a combat scene not
harmoniously interrelated. The remains of the pediments of the temples of Athena Alea at Tegea[31] (about 360; cf. p. 270) and Asklepios at Epidauros[32] (first quarter of the fourth century; cf. p.
276) are too scanty to be judged. Other small pediments of the
fourth century, for instance, those from an Attic tombstone[33] and
from the Sidon sarcophagus of Mourning Women[34] (fig. 398; middle of fourth century) show inadequately filled spaces, the corners
left vacant. The pediments of the Alexander sarcophagus[35] (cf.
figs. 399, 400; last quarter of the fourth century) revert to the old
contest scenes with crouching and striding warriors, with the innovation, however, that the central figure consists of a rider on a
rearing horse. They are able compositions, but in no way noteworthy developments of what has gone before.

(b) Metopes

A LESS complicated task than the designing of a pedimental group
was the composition of a metope, that is, the fitting of one or more
figures into a rectangular space. Here too the requirement was a
harmonious filling of the space itself, as well as the introduction of
variety in the vertical and horizontal design of a Doric temple. We
can trace an interesting development from the primitive efforts of
the seventh and early sixth centuries to the finished productions of
the Parthenon.

In the painted metopes of the temple of Thermos[36] (figs. 401,

---

29 Smith, *Catalogue of Greek Sculpture in the British Museum*, II, No. 924.
30 *Ibid.*, No. 925; Brunn-Bruckmann, *Denkmäler*, pl. 219.
31 Dugas, *Le Sanctuaire d'Aléa Athéna à Tégée*, pls. XCVI ff.
32 Defrasse and Lechat, *Épidaure*, p. 55.
33 Furtwängler, *Aegina*, p. 333, fig. 268.
34 Mendel, *Catalogue des sculptures du Musée à Constantinople*, I, No. 10.
35 *Ibid.*, I, No. 68.   36 *Antike Denkmäler*, II, pls. 50 ff.

402; perhaps about 640–620[37]) the composition is stilted and obvious. In the single figure of Perseus the legs and arms are simply spread out in the attitude of running to occupy the broad space; and the three seated goddesses fill it too compactly, without the interplay of crossing lines.

The same angularity is found in the metopes of the "Sikyonian" Treasury in Delphi[38] (about 570–550). A single animal with a subsidiary figure is a favorite motive (fig. 358). More ambitious compositions are attempted in the Dioskouroi and the sons of Aphareus[39] bringing back the cattle (fig. 404) and in the Dioskouroi with Orpheus in the Argo.[40] But there is a sameness of posture, a strict adherence to the vertical line, which has a monotonous effect. In the metopes of the temple of Assos[41] (third quarter of the sixth century), nothing intricate in the way of a composition is attempted (cf. fig. 403). We find confronting sphinxes, single centaurs, single animals; and when there is a group of two figures they are merely placed side by side, not properly interconnected. The metopes of temple C of Selinus[42] (c. 550–540) show the same tendency to accentuate the vertical line, the same lack of interrelation between the component parts. They do not form an interesting design in themselves nor do they adequately perform their function of creating diversity in the composition of a temple. The Athena, Perseus, and Medusa (fig. 405) are, for instance, simply placed side by side; so are the Herakles and the Kerkopes.[43] The only oblique direction is given in the striding legs of the heroes.

In the metopes of the Athenian Treasury[44] (about 510–500[45]) we

---

[37] Koch, *Ath. Mitt.*, 1914, pp. 237 ff.

[38] Homolle, *Fouilles de Delphes*, IV, pl. IV; Poulsen, *Delphi*, pp. 73 ff. The metopes were found in the foundations of the "Sikyonian" Treasury and therefore may have belonged to any older nearby building. Dinsmoor (*B.C.H.*, 1912, pp. 467 ff.) proposes the Syracusan Treasury.

[39] Only Idas is preserved. The names are identified by the painted inscriptions.

[40] Homolle, *op. cit.*, IV, pl. IV top.

[41] Bacon and others, *Investigations at Assos*, pp. 145, 147, 151.

[42] Benndorf, *Die Metopen von Selinunt*, pls. I–IV.   [43] *Ibid.*, pl. II.

[44] Homolle, *op. cit.*, IV, pls. XXXVIII ff.; Poulsen, *op. cit.*, pp. 158 ff.

[45] Some would place this Treasury after 490 B.C., on account of Pausanias' statement (X. 11. 5): "The Athenian Treasury (was built) with the spoils taken from the army which landed at Marathon under the command of Datis." But Pausanias was probably misled by the inscription on the platform immediately adjoining the Athenian Treasury: ᾿Αθεναῖοι τ[ο͂]ι ᾿Απόλλον[ι ἀπὸ Μέδ]ον ἀκ[ροθ]ίνια τε̑ς Μαραθ[ο͂]νι μ[άχες], "The Athenians dedicated first-fruits of Marathon to Apollo," which doubtless referred to offerings mounted on this platform (the foundation of which is indeed entirely separate from that of the Treasury). At all events potent considerations point to an earlier date for the Treasury: (1) The Treasury still has the swallow-tail clamps

at last get a more varied design. The oblique line is now boldly introduced by placing Herakles on top of the hind, which breaks up entirely the old monotonous arrangement and introduces a refreshing element of diversity and interrelation (fig. 406). It is not yet an entirely successful design, however, for it is rather top-heavy; even when the hind was whole it was too slender compared to the Herakles above. In the Herakles and Kyknos metope (fig. 124) the two figures are both placed in markedly oblique positions. They fill the space admirably and present an interesting variation. There are many other novel compositions among the metopes of this Treasury and we regret the more the fragmentary condition of most of them. In the group of Theseus and the Minotaur (fig. 407) the hero steps forward in a strongly slanting position and clutches the Minotaur, whose upper part is vertical but whose legs form oblique lines. In another metope (fig. 409) is a warrior in the same oblique attitude as Theseus, holding out a large shield, while his opponent is collapsing diagonally in front of him. The sculptor has realized the importance of crossing lines in his composition, a device used later with such splendid effect in the Parthenon. The metope with Athena and Theseus (fig. 408) shows the earlier arrangement of two figures standing side by side, but with a new spaciousness. The figures are not so close together, and the arms they extend toward each other create diversity.

The metopes of temple E at Selinus[46] (second quarter of fifth century) are among the most beautiful remains of late archaic art. We note two schemes in their design. In the group of Herakles and an Amazon (fig. 412) and in that of Athena and a giant (fig. 413) we have two strongly oblique figures, similar to the Herakles and Kyknos of the Athenian Treasury (fig. 124). In the Zeus and Hera (fig. 410) and in the Artemis and Aktaion groups (fig. 411), one figure is vertical and occupies only a small portion of the relief while the other is placed obliquely across the remaining portion. There is

while the platform has the later Z-shaped clamps; (2) the form of the capitals with the stiff echinus of the period just before 500 B.C.; (3) the fact that the marble is Parian, not Pentelic, which would have been the more likely material used after 490 B.C.; (4) the consideration of the expected return of the Persians after 490, which would prevent the erection of important monuments (cf. p. 7); (5) the style of the sculptures, which appears to be earlier than the Aigina pediments. For varying theories cf. Dinsmoor, *A.J.A.*, L, 1946, pp. 86 ff., and *Architecture of Greece*, p. 117; Picard, *Manuel*, II, pp. 24 ff.; Richter, *Archaic Greek Art Against Its Historical Background*, pp. 144 f.; Schefold, *Museum Helveticum*, III, 1946, fasc. 2, pp. 72 ff.; Kähler, *Gr. Metopenbild*, pp. 80 ff., 102 f.

[46] Benndorf, *Die Metopen von Selinunt*, pls. VII–X.

a beautiful harmony in these compositions—in the interrelation of
the two figures and in the pleasing empty spaces. In spite of the
violent movement and the agonizing subject of the Aktaion metope,
it charms and rests us by the beauty of its design. Just as in the
Lapith and Centaur contest of the western pediment of Olympia,
the rhythmical quality of the composition completely transcends the
theme.

This sense of harmony is characteristic also of the metopes of the
Olympia temple[47] (about 460). Many of them are scenes of violent
movement—Herakles fighting the Cretan bull (fig. 355), Herakles
cleaning out the Augean stables.[48] But this feeling of struggle is
largely mitigated by the interplay of lines and surfaces, and by the
restful empty spaces against which the contours of the figures stand
out effectively. Moreover, each fourth metope when in place on the
temple had a quiet design—on the east side Herakles and Atlas[49]
(fig. 414), on the west side Herakles and the Stymphalian birds.
Without question this arrangement was intentional. It was intended
for relief and variety, just as in a Greek drama there is the juxtaposition of violent scenes with quiet choruses. And it makes us feel
poignantly how much we miss in not seeing these architectural compositions in their original setting. An extract from a Greek play is
still beautiful out of its context, but it has lost much of its dramatic quality. Similarly a piece of architectural sculpture when removed from the place it occupied in the building may be lovely in
itself, but we miss the part it played in the composition of the
whole.

In the metopes of the Parthenon[50] the Greek sculptor reaches his
highest level. Horizontal, oblique, and vertical movement, beautiful
curves, and empty spaces are now used with the greatest freedom
and effectiveness; and there is infinite variety in the compositions.
Unfortunately many of the metopes are fragmentary; and just because they are so carefully composed we miss the lost portions more
acutely. A few, however, are sufficiently well preserved for an adequate appreciation of the composition. What a splendidly bold design is the Centaur rushing in triumph over the dead body of a
Lapith (fig. 416)! How beautifully the space is occupied, how well
the contours stand out, what a pleasing variety the lines must have
created in their original setting! Another Centaur and Lapith

[47] Treu, *Olympia*, III, pls. XXXV–XLV.　　　　[48] *Ibid.*, pl. XLV, 12.
[49] *Ibid.*, pl. XLV, 3.　　　　[50] Smith, *Sculptures of the Parthenon*, pls. 16 ff.

group (fig. 415) may be accurately described as follows: "The Centaur is wounded and turns to fly while he presses the wound in his back with his right hand. The Lapith restrains him, grasping the side of his head, while preparing for a sword thrust."[51] But how little we note or care about these harassing details when we look at and enjoy the relief. How much more conscious we are of the magnificent body of the Lapith standing out against the simple folds of his mantle, the fine way in which his left leg crosses the Centaur's body, the harmonious spacing of the whole. The beauty of line and of composition makes us forget the violence of the struggle, for it gives these fighting Lapiths and Centaurs a regal grandeur quite independent of their action.

Often in the Parthenon metopes the figures are not kept strictly within the rectangular frame but project over it; as in the group of the Lapith attacking a Centaur (fig. 105),[52] where the upper part of the Centaur's head covers the upper ledge. This cutting into the horizontal lines of the temple architecture was doubtless made for variation and occurs also elsewhere; for instance, on the Athenian Treasury (in the metope with Athena and Theseus), and at Olympia (in the metope with the Augean stables).

The metopes of the Hephaisteion[53] also show bold compositions (cf. fig. 417), generally not so harmonious as those of the Parthenon; but they are mostly not well enough preserved to be judged. Of the Phigaleia metopes[54] (cf. figs. 300, 301) only a few fragments are preserved, executed with rather more finish than the frieze, so we regret the more that so little is left.

This brings us to the end of our study of Greek metopes; for we have no fourth-century remains of importance. The Doric style fell more into disuse, giving place to the Ionic and Corinthian, so that metopes were no longer needed.

(c) Continuous Friezes

A STUDY of the continuous friezes of Greek temples and "treasuries" from the point of view of their composition brings out the same interesting development in the spacing and interrelation of figures which we have noted in the pediments and metopes. Only

---

[51] Smith, *Sculptures of the Parthenon*, p. 35, pl. 22, fig. 1.
[52] See also fig. 415, and Smith, *op. cit.*, pl. 19, 1.
[53] Sauer, *Das sogenannte Theseion*, pls. V and VI.
[54] Smith, *Catalogue of Greek Sculpture in the British Museum*, I, Nos. 510–519.

here our material is more scanty, for we have not so many examples
of the earlier periods well enough preserved to admit a safe judgment of their design. In the reliefs of the temple of Assos[55] (third
quarter of sixth century; cf. fig. 403) there is the same staccato
feeling, the same confusing juxtaposition of figures of completely
different scale that we noted in the early pediments (cf. fig. 374).
In the frieze of the Siphnian Treasury[56] (figs. 418, 419; c. 525)
great progress has been made in the interrelation of the figures by
the introduction of oblique lines and interlocked groups; but the effect of the whole is still somewhat harsh. The late archaic relief of
cocks and hens[57] and the procession of chariots[58] (c. 470) from
Xanthos are widely spaced compositions in which each figure stands
out effectively. In the frieze of the Ilissos temple[59] (c. 450) several
interrelated groups are successfully introduced, but there is still a
lack of harmony in the composition (fig. 420).

And this brings us to the great achievement of the Parthenon
frieze[60] (about 442–438). It was clearly conceived as a unified
whole. From the start of the action (in the southwest corner) with
the mounting of the riders, through the lively cavalcades of horsemen (fig. 486) and charioteers (along the western ends of the north
and south sides), and the slowing down of speed in the men with
sacrificial animals and vessels (at the eastern ends of these sides) and
the solemn advance of the maidens, to the magnificent climax of the
seated deities (figs. 488, 489) and the handing over of the peplos (in the center of the east side)—throughout this long composition of over five hundred feet in length the sculptor has created a
beautifully harmonious, interrelated design. And the effect is never
monotonous, for lively action and quiet poses are intermingled, producing the needed contrast in composition and interest.

The Phigaleia frieze[61] (about 420) is a more tempestuous, viva-
cious conception (figs. 298, 299), full of boldly designed groups
and flying draperies with deep shadows forming a highly decorative

---

[55] Bacon and others, *Investigations at Assos*, pp. 145 ff.
[56] Homolle, *Fouilles de Delphes*, IV, pls. VII ff.; Picard and Coste-Messelière,
Fouilles de Delphes, IV (2), pp. 72 ff. (fig. 34 shows the probable order of the slabs
after a recent study of the material); Poulsen, *Delphi*, pp. 101 ff.
[57] Pryce, *Catalogue of Sculpture in the British Museum*, I, 1, No. B 149.
[58] *Ibid.*, B 165.
[59] *Antike Denkmäler*, III, pl. 36; *Jahrbuch*, XXXI, 1916, pp. 169 ff.
[60] Smith, *Sculptures of the Parthenon*, pls. 30 ff., pp. 50 ff.
[61] Smith, *Catalogue of Greek Sculpture in the British Museum*, I, Nos. 520–542.

background. It has not the restraint and majesty of the Attic Parthenon, but its life and tumult are exhilarating.

In the friezes of the Gjölbaschi[62] and Nereid monuments[63] (late fifth century) we find an important innovation. Hitherto the Greek sculptor had confined his representation to limited groups of figures of which the beginning and end were clearly visible. In other words the many scenes of battle and contests and banquets resolve themselves into a limited number of participants, variously grouped. Even in the Parthenon frieze the impression is never conveyed that this is a section of a procession which continues beyond the actual representation. On the contrary the procession is complete in itself —it begins where the sculptor starts it and ends where he leaves it off. But that the Greeks forestalled later artists in the suggestion of continuance over and beyond the actual representation is shown in the renderings on the Gjölbaschi (figs. 421, 422) and the Nereid friezes.[64] Here in the massed formations of soldiers we obtain for the first time the sense that this is merely a section of a larger whole; just as in the reliefs of the arch of Titus we feel that this is only part of a long procession.

The friezes of the Mausoleum of Halikarnassos[65] (middle of the fourth century; cf. figs. 697–699, 720, 721, 729, 730, 735) show a less compact, more spacious composition, the contour of each figure standing out effectively against the background and the whole making a quieter impression than the closely interlocked figures of the earlier reliefs. But the interconnection of the figures is brought out not only in the crossing lines (cf. p. 174) but in the wave-like pattern which runs through the design. The same spaciousness marks the friezes of the Lysikrates monument[66] (fig. 491) and the sarcophagus of Mourning Women from Sidon[67] (fig. 316) of the middle of the fourth century. With the advent of the Hellenistic period there is a reversion to crowded compositions and closely interlocked groups, as shown in the friezes of the "Alexander sarcophagus"[68] (end of the fourth century; fig. 748) and the Pergamon altar[69]

[62] Benndorf, *Das Heroön von Gjölbaschi-Trysa;* Körte, *Jahrbuch,* XXXI, 1916, pp. 257 ff.
[63] Smith, *Catalogue of Greek Sculpture in the British Museum,* II, Nos. 850 ff.
[64] *Mon. dell'Instituto,* X, pls. XV, XVI.   [65] Smith, *op. cit.,* II, Nos. 1006 ff.
[66] *Ibid.,* I, No. 430 (description of cast); the original is in situ in Athens.
[67] Mendel, *Catalogue des sculptures du Musée à Constantinople,* I, No. 10.
[68] *Ibid.,* No. 68.
[69] Berlin, Pergamon Museum, cf. Winnefeld, Die Friese des grossen Altars, in *Altertümer von Pergamon,* III, 2.

(second century; figs. 334, 335). In the latter the relief is very high and effective use is made of strong shadows which add to the feeling of restlessness and turmoil.

(d) Grave Stelai

BESIDES these architectural sculptures there is another type of relief, like the metopes rectangular in form, which is interesting to study for the development of its composition, viz., the grave stele. We can note definite stages in its evolution.

The early grave stele is high and narrow and generally contains only one figure, which takes up the entire available field. The stele of Aristion by Aristokles[70] (about 510) is a typical example (fig. 424). Occasionally two figures are compressed into the same narrow space, as in the gravestone of a youth and his sister[71] (fig. 423) in the Metropolitan Museum (about 550–530) crowned by a handsome capital of lyre design and surmounted by a sphinx. The stele by Alxenor[72] (fig. 425) and that of a girl from the Esquiline—both of the early fifth century—are a little wider in proportion to their height, so that the sense of crowding is less marked; but even the man on the gravestone in Naples[73] (second quarter of the fifth century) still completely fills the available space. By the middle of the century the slab has become distinctly wider, so that the sculptor could afford more space around the figure and create a more harmonious composition with interesting interrelated surfaces. And naturally the contours of the figure now become more effective. It could either be placed in approximately the middle of the slab, as in the girl with the pigeons now in the Metropolitan Museum[74] (fig. 426) or to the extreme left, which gave room for the action in front, as in the stele of the girl with a casket in Berlin[75] (fig. 427), and of Philis in the Louvre.[76] In some of these examples the palmette finials which crowned the slabs are still preserved, adding greatly to the effect of the whole.

During the second half of the fifth century we have a further in-

[70] National Museum, Athens, No. 29.
[71] Richter, *Archaic Attic Gravestones*, pp. 64 ff. (The original of the head of the girl is in Berlin.) Cf. also the stele from Thespiai, National Museum, Athens, No. 82.
[72] National Museum, Athens, No. 39.
[73] Ruesch, *Guida del Museo Nazionale di Napoli*, No. 98 (6556).
[74] *Antike Denkmäler*, I, pl. 54; Metropolitan Museum, *Bulletin*, 1927, pp. 101 ff.
[75] Berlin Museum, No. 1482; *Antike Denkmäler*, I, pl. 33, 2.
[76] Prachov, *Annali dell'Instituto*, 1872, pl. L, p. 185.

crease of the width in relation to the height; and this allows room for
an additional figure and yet a retention of the restful empty spaces.
The stelai of Hegeso (fig. 429) and Glykylla (fig. 306) are masterpieces in design, harmonious groupings with an effective prominence
of the chief figures. The slabs are now regularly crowned with pediments, and engaged pillars are generally added at each side.

In the fourth century we have approximately the same proportions, but the compositions now become more crowded, there are
fewer empty spaces, the contours become less important, and we no
longer enjoy the interrelation of the figures and of the spaces in the
background (cf. fig. 317). Occasionally there are more spacious
groupings of one or two figures; but even then their interrelation
appears less carefully planned. And the depth of the relief increases. Sometimes it is so great that parts of the figures are actually in the round and the regular framework of a pediment resting
on side pillars becomes so deep as to give the appearance of a shrine
or ναΐσκος [77] (fig. 428). The strong shadows thereby created make
a pictorial rather than a sculptural effect.

And here the story ends. The anti-luxury decree of Demetrios of
Phaleron (c. 317) forbade the erection of sculptured gravestones in
Athens; and thenceforth there appear only insignificant pillars,
bowls, and slabs in the graveyards. The new law killed one of the
most beautiful forms of artistic expression in Attica. Not until the
second century B.C. did elaborate sculptured gravestones reappear.

[77] Metropolitan Museum, *Handbook* (1930), p. 257, fig. 180.

CHAPTER IX

TECHNIQUE

IN the preceding chapters we have treated Greek sculpture
solely from the artistic point of view—which forms indeed our
chief interest today. But we cannot thoroughly understand even
the artistic quality of Greek sculpture without some knowledge of
its technique; for any art is conditioned by the methods employed in
producing it.

Regarding the technical processes of Greek sculpture[1] we know
practically only what the monuments themselves can teach us,
though we get a little help from a few statements of ancient writers,
from inscriptions, and from representations of sculptors at work.
And of course a study of the methods employed in the making of
sculpture today is also helpful.

(a) Materials

THE materials used by Greek sculptors were wood, bronze, soft limestone, marble, terracotta, silver, gold, ivory, lead, wax, iron, and am- WOOD
ber. That wood was employed, especially in early archaic times, we
know by the frequent references in ancient literature to various figures in that material. Pausanias in his travels through Greece in the
second century A.D. still saw a good many of the primitive "xoana"
that owed their survival among the later products to their religious
sanctity. That wooden figures were produced later also, we know from
specific instances; e.g., in the third century at Delos[2] and in Roman
times.[3] Only a few examples are preserved today. The damp climate
of Greece has destroyed practically all.

Bronze was probably the commonest material of Greek sculpture BRONZE
and certain distinguished sculptors, like Polykleitos and Lysippos,
worked almost exclusively in that material. It is largely due to this
circumstance that so few original works by the greatest Greek artists have survived; for the intrinsic value of bronze caused it to be
melted down in later times; and this brought about the destruction

---

[1] Cf. on this subject, Daremberg and Saglio's *Dictionnaire*, s.v. *Sculptura* and
Statuaria; Blümel, *Bildhauerarbeit,* and *Bildhauer an der Arbeit;* Casson, *Technique.*
[2] *B.C.H.,* 1890, p. 502.   [3] Conteleon, *Ath. Mitt.,* 1889, p. 91.

of a large output of Greek art. A Greek bronze statue today is a
rarity, though bronze statuettes and various kinds of small reliefs
have been preserved in graves and sanctuaries in large numbers.

The earliest bronze statues were plated, that is, made of ham-
mered sheets of bronze, riveted together.[4] Bronze casting is said to
have been an invention by Rhoikos and Theodoros of Samos[5] (sixth
century B.C.) ; as a matter of fact Greek examples of even hollow casting are known from the seventh century. Statuettes are mostly cast
solid; but in full-size statues both the weight and the cost were against
such a practice, and hollow casting was resorted to. Both in solid and
in hollow casting the Greeks mostly used the so-called *cire perdue*
process, which is still employed in a modified form at the present day,
but casting from sand moulds was also practised to a limited extent.[6]
Solid casting was comparatively simple. The object to be cast was
first modeled in wax and then surrounded with a mixture of clay and
sand which formed a kind of mantle. When this was thoroughly dry,
an opening was made at an appropriate place and the whole heated
until all the wax melted away. The molten metal was then poured in,
a few ventholes having previously been made in the mantle to allow
for the escape of the air. After cooling, the mantle was broken up and
the bronze was ready for the finishing touches.

The process of hollow casting by the *cire perdue* process was apparently as follows: A core of clay or plaster was surrounded with a
layer of wax, which was modeled in the shape of the required statue
and made of the same thickness that the bronze was to be. Before the
application of the outer mantle, wax rods, to act as future gates
and vents, were probably attached to the figure, in the same way
that they are nowadays; for one of the difficulties of bronze casting
is that the metal cools quickly and therefore has to be conveyed to
the various cavities through several channels at the same time.
Moreover, in order to keep the interior core from becoming dis-
placed on the disappearance of the wax, metal rods were inserted,
which pierced through the wax, joining the core to the mantle.
When the outer mantle had been added, the whole was treated as in
solid casting, that is, it was heated in a furnace until the wax all

---

[4] Plates of bronze riveted on a wooden body are found also in Gothic sculpture,
e.g., in the funerary statue of Blanche de Champagne in the Louvre, No. 167.

[5] Pausanias VIII. 14. 8: "The first to cast statues in molten bronze were the
Samians Rhoikos, the son of Phileas, and Theodoros, the son of Telekles."

[6] Cf. Kluge and Lehmann-Hartleben, *Die Antiken Grossbronzen*, I, pp. 82 ff.

disappeared, whereupon the liquid bronze was poured in, which now occupied only the spaces left vacant by the molten wax instead of the whole interior. When the mantle was broken up there emerged the bronze, from which had to be removed the inside core, the rods which had been inserted to keep the core in place, and the gates and vents, which were now of bronze. Also, any defects of casting caused by air-bubbles and other accidents had to be repaired, generally by means of small patches (still visible on many ancient bronzes).

That bronze statues were worked in parts is shown in an attractive picture of a Greek foundry on a kylix in Berlin[7] (fig. 430); and can be noted on extant figures, for instance on the Delphi charioteer. The surface was treated to prevent the golden color of the bronze from being too glaring, but not artificially patinated as is done today.[8] Occasionally it was gilt or silvered.[9]

Local limestones were employed by Greek sculptors, especially in early times. The pediment figures of the early temples on the Akropolis were made of local Piraeus stone, the λίθος πώρινος of the ancients, and are hence often referred to as "poros" sculptures. The softness and lightness of these stones made them easy to cut and handle, and the unattractive surface could be hidden by paint. The sculptors of Cyprus used their own coarse limestone throughout their career. But elsewhere this inferior material was mostly given up in the course of time in favor of marble.

SOFT LIMESTONE

Iron was used at all periods as we know from ancient writers; but through corrosion practically nothing has survived.[9a]

IRON

The general employment of marble[10] in Greek sculpture begins in the seventh century B.C., and becomes firmly established during the sixth. At first it was the island marbles, especially the coarse-grained Naxian and the finer-grained Parian which were in demand. Early in the fifth century[11] Athens developed the quarries of her own Mount Pentelikon, and henceforth much of her sculpture is in this

MARBLE

---

7 Furtwängler and Reichhold, *Griechische Vasenmalerei*, III, pl. 135.

8 Cf. my *Catalogue of Bronzes in the Metropolitan Museum*, p. xxvii ff.

9 Cf. Pausanias X. 18. 7 and 14. 7; Pliny, *N.H.* XXXIII. 64. On gilding and silvering bronzes cf. my *Catalogue of Bronzes in the Metropolitan Museum*, p. xxvi.

9a Cf. Picard, *Manuel* I, pp. 171 f.

10 Cf. the list of marbles used by the Greeks given by G. Lafaye in Daremberg and Saglio, *Dictionnaire*, under *Marmor*, pp. 1601 ff.; also Lepsius, *Griechische Marmor-studien*, in the *Abhandlungen d. Akad. d. Wissensch. zu Berlin*, 1890. Henry S. Washington, *A.J.A.*, 1898, pp. 1 ff., has pointed out that all quarries vary, and that identical marbles are sometimes found in very different localities.

11 Pentelic marble occurs occasionally also in sixth-century monuments.

close-grained, milky white marble;[12] though the crystalline, beautifully transparent Parian was often preferred for single statues.[13] Occasionally the bluish gray marble of Mount Hymettos[14] was employed, also, and elsewhere local marbles occur; for instance the coarse Doliana variety in some of the sculptures of Tegea.[15] The quarries of Carrara and Luna of Italy were not worked till Roman times.[16] Their products are greatly inferior to those of Greece. Their untransparent denseness is singularly unattractive compared to the luminous quality of the Greek stones.

All the Greek marbles are white or whitish. Colored stones, so popular in Egypt and in imperial Rome, were not favored in Greece. Only occasionally do we find black Eleusinian stone introduced as the background of a frieze or as a color note in architecture.[17]

TERRACOTTA

Terracotta was commonly used for statuettes at all periods, but only occasionally in Greece for large statues.[18] In Italy, on the other hand, and also in Cyprus, it was a favorite material[19] (cf. figs. 79, 460). The difference is explained by the source of supplies, Greece having abundant provision of marble, Italy hardly any, at least until the opening of the Carrara quarries.[20] Greek terracotta statues were built; statuettes though occasionally modeled are usually moulded and hollow. This process was briefly as follows: A mould of clay was first made and baked to considerable hardness. Its surface was then covered with layers of moist clay until the required thickness was reached. The shrinkage of the clay in drying allowed the figure to be easily removed from the mould. The back was made separately (either in another mould, or, if summarily worked, by hand) with a

---

12 Exposure gradually turns it a golden brown by the oxidation of the iron which it contains. On these marbles, cf. Lepsius, *Griechische Marmorstudien*, pp. 11 ff.

13 The Hermes of Praxiteles is of Parian marble. This marble was called λυχνίτης or λιχνεὺς λίθος in ancient times, according to Pliny, *N.H.* XXXVI. 5, because it was worked by lamplight (λύχνος).

14 The Moschophoros is in that material.   15 Cf. p. 270.

16 Pliny, *N.H.* XXXVI. 14, 49, 135; see below, note 20.

17 E.g., in the Erechtheion, the Parthenon and the Propylaia, in the Zeus temple at Olympia, and at Eleusis.

18 On Greek terracotta statues cf. Richter, *A.J.A.*, LII, 1948, pp. 331 ff.

19 Cf. especially the terracotta sculptures in the Syracuse Museum (Orsi, *Monumenti antichi*, XXV, pls. 16, 17), those from Veii in the Villa Giulia Museum, and the warriors in New York (*M. M. Papers*, no. 6).

20 The Etruscans used Carrara marble to a slight extent (Müller, *Die Etrusker*, I, 2, p. 226), more generally that of Pisa (Strabo V. C223; Müller, *op. cit.*, I, 2, p. 227).

21 On the technique of building cf. Binns in *M. M. Papers*, no. 6.

venthole for evaporation. The two parts were carefully joined, the necessary retouching done in the more careful examples, and the whole then baked; finally the entire surface was painted (cf. p. 150). The same mould could be used again and again, but to insure the desired diversity the head and arms were often moulded separately and different moulds variously combined. The many hundred Tanagra statuettes in spite of their obvious similarity include few duplicates.

The use of such precious materials as gold and silver was naturally not common for full-size statues. Silver indeed seems only to have been employed for statuettes and small reliefs. Gold, however, in conjunction with ivory was in general use for the so-called chryselephantine statues. The Athena Parthenos and the Olympian Zeus by Pheidias are the most famous examples known, but we hear of a number of other temple statues of the kind;[22] moreover a number of gold and ivory fragments of such statues, of the archaic period, have recently been found at Delphi, and a few other ivory pieces are also known.[23] Since the technique is no longer practised today, we know little of the processes involved. The nude parts—the head, arms, and feet—were made of plates of ivory, the drapery of sheets of gold, applied probably over a wooden framework. The glitter of the gold was, at least sometimes, neutralized by the addition of painted patterns, as we know in the case of the Olympian Zeus.[24] That the effect was exceedingly beautiful and impressive is attested by the universal admiration of the two great Pheidian masterpieces. The Zeus would not have been considered to have "added something to religion" if the impression had been merely gaudy, as some critics claim.

Occasionally we hear of gilded statues, not only of bronze but of marble. The Eros of Thespiai by Praxiteles, for instance, had gilt wings.[25] Phryne is said to have dedicated a gilt[26] (or gold?[27]) statue of herself at Delphi, executed by Praxiteles. In Roman times it became a practice to gild Greek statues to cater to the taste for gaudiness.[28]

SILVER GOLD AND IVORY

---

22 Cf. pp. 229, 248, 281.
23 Cf., e.g., Albizzati, *J.H.S.*, XXXV, 1916, pp. 373 ff., pls. VIII–IX; Lethaby, *J.H.S.*, XXXVII, 1917, pp. 17–18; Amandry, *J.H.S.*, LXIV, 1944, pl. XI.
24 Strabo VIII. 353.
25 Julian. Imperat. *Orat.* II. 54B (unless the gilding was added later).
26 Pausanias X. 15. 1 (ἐπίχρυσον).
27 Athen. XIII. 591B (χρύσεον); cf. also Plutarch, *De Pyth. orac.* 15 etc.
28 Cf., e.g., Pliny, *N.H.* XXXIV. 63.

COMBINATION
OF WOOD
WITH MARBLE
AND IVORY

The so-called akrolithic[29] statues (literally "with extremities of stone") were made of wood, often gilded, with face, hands, and feet of marble;[30] and single ivory feet or hands have also been found (fig. 432) provided with holes for fastening, probably to wooden bodies. In localities where marble was scarce stucco or plaster was sometimes used to piece out the marble. This practice is commonly found in Egypt,[31] cf. also the recent finds (of the later periods) at Kalydon.[32]

STUCCO AND
PLASTER

AMBER
WAX
LEAD

Amber was in occasional use for statuettes and small reliefs, especially in Etruria; likewise wax and lead.

Only marble sculptures have survived in any large quantity up to our time; for their weight and the lack of intrinsic value of their material made them less desirable for transportation. It is only their use in limekilns that worked for their destruction. In our account of technical processes, therefore, we shall have the marble remains mostly in mind.

(b) Methods of Work

DIFFERENT
APPROACH BY
THE ANCIENT
AND LATER
ARTISTS

There is an important difference between the methods of a Greek and some modern sculptors in marble. Nowadays we might start by making a full-size model in clay on a lead armature, then make a plaster cast of this model, and finally translate the cast into marble by the process of pointing.[33] Since both the cast and the marble copy are produced by mechanical means it follows that the clay model is the only original creation of the modern artist. The Greek method was different. The making of plaster casts of statues was said to have been invented by Lysistratos, the brother of Lysippos, at the end of the fourth century B.C.[34] And for the employment of

---

[29] Pausanias IX. 4. 1.

[30] *Ibid*, 10. 2 tells of such a statue of Athena by Pheidias, and Vitruvius II 8. 11 of one by Leochares.

[31] Dickins, *Hellenistic Sculpture*, p. 22.

[32] Poulsen and Rhomaios, *Erster vorläufiger Bericht über die dänisch-griechischen Ausgrabungen von Kalydon* in *Historisk-filologiske Meddelelserudgivne af det kgl. Danske Videnskabernes Selskab,* XIV, 3, p. 67, and passim.

[33] That is, a number of points are marked on the cast, transferred to the stone block, and then drilled in to the required depth; whereupon the superfluous marble is cut away until the points are reached.

[34] *N.H.* XXXV. 153: Idem et de signis effigies exprimere invenit, crevitque res in tantum, ut nulla signa statuaeve sine argilla fierent, "He also discovered how to take casts from statues, a practice which was extended to such a degree that no figure or statue was made without a clay model." The passage has been much discussed, some authorities referring *idem* to (the previously mentioned) Boutades, on account of the next statement: "Hence it is clear that the art of clay modeling is older than that of

pointing we have ample evidence from the early first century B.C. on[35] (cf. fig. 436), when it was extensively used.[36] The thousands of Roman copies of Greek works we have today were doubtless produced in this way.

The first mention by ancient writers[37] of models for statues is that concerning Arkesilaos and Pasiteles, sculptors of the first century B.C.: "[Marcus Varro] also praises Arkesilaos . . ., for whose models [proplasmata] artists would pay more than was given for the finished works of others. . . . Varro further praises Pasiteles who said that modeling was the mother of chasing, statuary, and sculpture, and who, though he excelled in all these arts, never executed any work without first making a model."[38] Possibly the latter was the first to introduce the practice of copying a full-size model exactly.[39] At all events the specific mention of Pasiteles as never executing a work without making a model suggests that he was a pioneer in mechanical copying. It would seem therefore that the Greek sculptor during his best periods cut into his marble block free-hand. That is, while later artists created their figures by the successive addition of lumps of clay on an armature that admits of bending in any direction (fig. 434), the Greek artist worked by cutting layer after layer from his rigid block of stone. The Greek worked from the outside in,[40]

USE OF A MODEL

bronze casting." Pliny has clearly mixed up his sources somewhat. Cf. S. Reinach, *Rev. arch.*, XLI, 1902, pp. 9 ff.; Brunn, *Geschichte der gr. Künstler*, I, pp. 402 f.; also Plutarch, *De sollertia animalium*, p. 984b (discussed by S. Reinach, *Rev. arch.*, II, 1902, pp. 5 ff.), who speaks of casting a statue of Kore for Ptolemy Soter (end of fourth century B.C.). Actual plaster moulds of the Hellenistic period have been found from time to time; cf. Rubensohn, *Hellenistisches Silbergerät in antiken Gipsabgüssen* and the references there cited on pp. 3–5. The use of plaster casts doubtless facilitated the making of free copies like those found at Pergamon.

[35] Furtwängler, *Statuenkopieen im Altertum*, p. 21, note 4, gives a list of statues in which puntelli are still visible, none of them earlier than the first century B.C. Cf. also E. A. Gardner, *J.H.S.*, 1890, p. 142, note 1; and Blümel, *Griechische Bildhauerarbeit*, pls. 33, 34a, b, d, 35a, b. Blümel (pp. 30 ff.) points out that the ancient method of pointing was not nearly so thorough as it is today; only a few salient points were obtained while today three or four hundred points may be placed on one head.

[36] For the bosses on some of the Olympia sculptures and their significance cf. Blümel, *Gr. Bildhauer an der Arbeit*, p. 53.

[37] The τύποι of Timotheos, by some interpreted as models, were more probably reliefs; cf. p. 275. The horse modeled by Athena (fig. 431; cf. also Furtwängler und Reichhold, *Griechische Vasenmalerei*, pl. 162, 3) on an Athenian red-figured vase in Berlin was probably for a bronze statue.

[38] Pliny, *N.H.* XXXV. 156.

[39] Cf. Kekulé, *Die Gruppe des Künstlers Menelaos*, pp. 19 ff.; Furtwängler, *Statuenkopieen*, p. 21.

[40] This applies of course only to stone (and wood) sculpture; in bronze and terracotta statues the techniques require the reverse process.

the later artists from the inside out.[41] To this different approach is largely due the difference in conception. Greek marble sculpture, especially during the early period, is compact and unified, the mass being conditioned by the block of stone. Later sculptures having no such restrictions are often composed in a variety of directions, and so are more elastic, but also generally more confusing. For a restricted, unified depth makes for a quiet, restful impression.[42]

That the Greek sculptor did not mechanically translate clay models into stone does not of course mean that he made no use at all of preliminary models and sketches.[48] The Greek artist was essentially painstaking. He loved precision, interplay of proportion, harmonious composition. Polykleitos wrote a book on proportion and embodied his theories in a statue.[44] And other sculptors were engrossed in the same subject.[45] Even vase-painters made preliminary sketches of their designs with many corrections. How can we imagine, then, Greek sculptors taking blocks of stone and hewing into them without a carefully worked out scheme? Especially in the creative periods of the fifth and early fourth centuries B.C. such preparatory experimentation would seem essential. And if probable in the production of single statues it is even more likely in that of architectural sculpture, the great pediments and metopes and continuous friezes which together had to form a harmonious whole. In the building accounts of the Erechtheion are entries of wages paid to a number of sculptors who executed single figures in the con-

---

41 Many sculptors of today have reverted to the old method of stone-cutting; e.g., R. Laurent of New York and Eric Gill and Frank Dobson of England. Hildebrand in his *Problem der Form* recommends it to his fellow artists.

42 Cf. p. 27.

48 On this subject, cf. Johansen, *Arch. Anz.*, 1923–1924, pp. 141 ff. (he assumes life-size clay models, but does not take into account the literary evidence); and Blümel, *Griechische Bildhauerarbeit*, pp. 24 ff. (he proposes models about half life-size for the Parthenon pediments [p. 83] and large drawings for the Parthenon frieze [p. 84]). Personally I hesitate to assume large, carefully worked out models for the reason admirably stated by the English sculptor, Eric Gill, in his *Sculpture, An Essay on Stone Cutting* (1924), pp. 26 f.: "It is not desirable to make exact models in clay, because the sort of thing which can be easily and suitably constructed in clay may not be, and generally is not suitable for carving in stone. . . . Modeling is a process of addition; whereas carving is a process of subtraction. The proper modeling of clay results in a certain spareness and tenseness of form and any desired amount of 'freedom' or detachment of parts. The proper carving of stone results in a certain roundness and solidity of form with no detachment of parts. Consequently a model made to be full size of the proposed carving would be, if modeled in a manner natural to clay, more of an hindrance than a help to the carver, and would be labour, and long labour in vain. . . . The finished work is not a piece of carving but a stone imitation of a clay model." Greek sculptures all seem "thought out" in stone.

44 Cf. p. 245.   45 Cf. p. 117, note 1.

tinuous frieze.[46] In the building accounts of the Parthenon are recorded the wages paid to "the sculptors" (perhaps ten) of the pediments in the year 434–433.[47] Surely such sculptors, however able, must have worked from a design created by a single artist. That no such sketches and models have survived is natural, for they would have been executed in wax[48] or perishable clay[49] (as is customary nowadays [cf. fig. 435] and was in the Renaissance[50]), or drawn on equally perishable papyrus.

The use of a living model was certainly not the rule with Greek sculptors; at least there is little mention of it. Only occasionally in a later period is the opinion expressed that a certain woman served as a model for a particular statue; for instance, Athenaios[51] tells us that Phryne was the model for the Aphrodite of Knidos while Clement of Alexandria[52] states it was Kratine. During the earlier period when naturalism was a secondary object sculptors studied the systems evolved by previous artists rather than nature directly. Quintilian[53] states that sculptors took the Doryphoros of Polykleitos as a model; and Pliny[54] tells us how much impressed Lysippos was with an answer by Eupompos: "That artist, when asked which of his predecessors he followed, pointed to a crowd of men and replied that Nature herself and no artist was the true model"—evidently an unusual attitude before that time. On the other hand, the custom of athletes' stripping for their exercises gave the sculptor plentiful opportunities of studying the human figure; and his great interest in it is attested by the whole history of Greek sculpture and its constant development toward greater naturalism. In the Hellenistic period when the study of anatomy became absorbing, the use of the living model by artists must have become inevitable.

The tools used by the Greek sculptor[55] in the carving of his

USE OF A LIVING MODEL

TOOLS

---

[46] *I. G.* I, 324 c, d; Loewy, *Inschriften*, No. 526; Stuart Jones, *Selected Passages*, No. 159; Stevens, Paton, etc., *The Erechtheum*, p. 389. The average price paid for a single figure is 60 drachmas. We must remember that the frieze is small in scale, about two feet high. Cf. p. 101.

[47] Cf. p. 230, note 127.

[48] We know definitely that the models of rosettes for the Erechtheion were made in wax; cf. Stevens, Paton, etc., *op. cit.*, p. 395.

[49] The little terracotta reliefs, thought by Waldstein (*Essays on the Art of Pheidias*, pp. 212 ff., pls. IX, XI, XIII) to have served as models for the frieze, are clearly modern forgeries.

[50] Cf. Vasari's *Life of Garofolo* (*Sansoni, Milanesi*), VI, p. 464: "Fece modelli di terra per veder meglio l'ombre ed i lumi."

[51] Δειπνοσοφισταί XIII. 59.   [52] Προτρεπτικὸς πρὸς Ἕλληνας IV. 47.

[53] V. 12. 21.   [54] *N.H.* XXXIV. 61.

[55] Cf. on this subject Blümner, *Gewerbe und Künste*, II, p. 194 and III, p. 192;

blocks seem to have been much the same as those employed today: viz., chisels of various shapes and sizes worked by the help of a mallet (cf. figs. 439–441). The procedure of modern stone-cutters[56] is as follows: the pointed chisels (the punch or point) are first used for the trimming of the stone into the general shape of the statue, then the claw chisels (with dentated edge) for the removal of the outer layers of the stone; and as one approaches nearer and nearer to the final surface the finer ones are required—the gouge and the more delicate claw chisels; lastly, for smoothing the surface, the flat chisel, files, rasps, and soft stones.[57] A polish can be added by rubbing with sand. Greek practice was similar. Several unfinished statues in Athens and elsewhere show the marks of these tools[58] (cf. figs. 433, 436, 437) and throw interesting light on the processes employed. Apparently in the earlier periods the use of the flat chisel and the gouge was limited, while the pointed and claw chisels[59] were extensively used. From the later fifth century onward the flat chisel was employed on the nude parts for the final smoothing. A comparison between the slightly rough surfaces of the earlier marbles and the smooth texture of later sculptures will bear this out.

For the smoothing of plane surfaces the archaic Greek stone cutter used the drove[60]—a very broad flat chisel in common use also today. Later this tool seems not to have been employed, at least the striations it produces are not observable on extant post archaic sculptures.

The simple drill (*Stichbohrer*) was known from early times, as we learn from the drill holes for the attachment of earrings and other ornaments in early archaic sculptures.[61] The running drill (*laufender Bohrer*)—probably in the form of a bow-drill—must have been introduced at least as early as the second half of the fifth

---

E. A. Gardner, *J.H.S.*, 1890, p. 137, fig. 3; Dugas in Daremberg and Saglio, *Dictionnaire, Sculptura*, p. 1138; Blümel, *Griechische Bildhauerarbeit*, pp. 1 ff.

56 I had the great advantage of joining a class in stone-cutting under Mr. Robert Laurent at the Art Students' League in New York which gave me a new insight into this subject.

57 Plutarch, *Discr. adul. et amic.*, 34, 74E, refers to the smoothing and polishing of statues; cf. also Pliny, *N. H.*, XXXVI, 53 and 54.

58 E. Gardner, *J.H.S.*, 1890, pp. 129 ff.; Blümel, *Griechische Bildhauer an der Arbeit*, pp. 10 ff.

59 Marks of the claw chisel occur as early as the second quarter of the sixth century, for instance on the Akropolis kore 593, and on the head in Munich, Blümel, op. cit., figs. 20, 21.

60 On the use of the drove cf. Richter, *A.J.A.* XLVII, 1943, pp. 188 ff.

61 Homer refers to such a tool, τέρετρον and τρύπανον, in the working of wood.

century,[62] for traces of the grooves it produces are visible on monuments of that period, for instance, on the Parthenon frieze and pediment.[63] The deeply carved folds of the latter could indeed hardly have been produced without it. In earlier times a makeshift method was used, *viz.* a number of holes were bored side by side and then connected.

It is interesting to observe the treatment by the Greek sculptor of the backs and other parts of his marble[64] figures when they did not show. As a general rule he seems to have carefully finished only those portions which were visible. When a marble statue was exposed to view where it could be seen from all sides it was equally finished all around. But when a statue was seen only from the front or the side, not from behind, as in the pediment figures, the back did not generally receive the same attention (fig. 442). The tool marks were often not removed and even the modeling is sometimes only cursory; but the composition of each figure as a whole was carried out. On the other hand there are instances when the backs are beautifully worked even when they did not show, as in the Aigina and the Parthenon pediments (cf. fig. 70). Single statues when intended to be placed against the wall or where the back was not seen are likewise often unfinished behind. We may mention as examples the Hermes of Praxiteles (fig. 444), the Zeus of Mylasa,[65] and the standing youth in Boston.[66] The backs of grave stelai in the Kerameikos in Athens are likewise left quite rough (fig. 438). In reliefs the receding planes are often superficially worked, especially in the grave monuments. In other words the attitude of the Greek sculptor was the same as that of the Greek potter—he did not waste labor where it profited nobody.[67]

Nowadays a sculptor generally makes his statue out of a single   PIECING

[62] The bow-drill was known in Egypt at least as early as 1200–1000; cf. the drill caps of diorite and bone from Lisht in the Metropolitan Museum.

[63] I have been able to observe these both on the pediments (especially on the "Fates") and on the frieze (especially on the maidens and deities of the east side). Others deny the use of the running drill on the Parthenon figures; cf. Puchstein, *Arch. Anz.*, 1890, p. 110. Cf. on the use of the drill also de Villefosse in Daremberg and Saglio, *Dictionnaire*, under *Terebra;* Blümel, *Griechische Bildhauerarbeit*, p. 15, and *Griechische Bildhauer an der Arbeit*, pp. 35 ff. For the tradition that Kallimachos "was the first to bore marble," see p. 240.

[64] A bronze figure was naturally finished throughout.

[65] Caskey, *Catalogue of Sculpture*, No. 25.   [66] *Ibid.*, No. 41.

[67] The insides of amphorae and hydriai are left unturned, for they did not show; those of kylikes and kraters, which were exposed to view, are always carefully finished; on this subject, cf. my *Craft of Athenian Pottery*, p. 14.

block. The Greeks—perhaps on account of the difficulty of transportation—used smaller blocks and pieced them. The parts were
skilfully joined by means of marble tenons fitting into mortises, or
two smooth surfaces were secured with metal dowels or, when the
addition was small, merely with cement.[68] The archaic statues of the
Akropolis are almost all made in several pieces,[69] the arms and heads
often separate from the bodies, and fastened to one another by
means of large marble tenons and mortises secured with molten lead
or lime[70] (cf. figs. 270, 272) ; likewise parts of the drapery, locks of
hair, etc. And this practice is general in Greek art at all periods.[71]
Many statues show the original dowel-holes—sometimes with the
iron or bronze dowels still adhering—by which the arms, heads,
etc., were originally attached. A good example is the statue in New
York[72] signed by Zeuxis (fig. 445) in which the attached parts have
all become separated. There is a large mortise for the insertion of
the head and neck; the arms and the right foot were fastened by
iron dowels; and part of the left foot was attached with cement or
lime. Many heads which have become separated from their bodies
were worked to fit into large hollows (cf. fig. 443[73]). The top of the
head is sometimes separate from the rest, the two surfaces being
smoothed to fit and kept in place by small dowels.[74] This accounts
for such parts being often missing (cf. fig. 446).

Occasionally the piecing is not original but was done later as a repair. An excellent example of such an ancient repair is seen on the
figure from Laurion in the Metropolitan Museum[75] (figs. 448,
449) ; here the head and left arm are worked in separate pieces in a
style later than the rest of the figure; the outline of the hair of the
original archaic head can still be seen at the back (fig. 448). The
Kore No. 670 in the Akropolis Museum—of Island marble—has the
right sleeve repaired in Pentelic marble.

Occasionally the piecing is in different materials. In the Selinus

---

[68] Cf. Treu, *Jahrbuch*, 1895, p. 8.

[69] All except the statue by Antenor; cf. Lechat, *Au Musée de l'Acropole*, pp.
227 ff.

[70] Cf. Lechat, *op. cit.*, p. 228.

[71] Cf. on this subject the list of references given by Dugas in his article, *Sculptura*,
in Daremberg and Saglio, *Dictionnaire*, p. 1144.

[72] Metropolitan Museum, *Bulletin*, 1910, pp. 234–235.

[73] *Ibid.*, pp. 276–278.

[74] E.g., in the head of a girl from Priene, British Museum No. 1153, the Chios head
in Boston, etc.; cf. also the instances in the Louvre cited by Héron de Villefosse,
Monuments Piot, I, p. 72, note.

[75] *Handbook* (1930), p. 240, fig. 165.

metopes the head, hands, and feet of the female figures are of marble, the rest of coarser limestone[76] (fig. 410). In the girl from Anzio,[77] (fig. 336) and the Demeter of Knidos[78] (fig. 315) the heads are of a finer marble than the rest of the figures.

Another general practice was the addition of accessories in different materials. The eyeballs, though generally painted on a smoothed surface, were occasionally inset, probably in ivory, stone, or glass. Early examples are No. 682 of the Akropolis figures, the Antenor statue, No. 681 (fig. 273),[79] and a head from an archaic grave relief in the Metropolitan Museum[80] (fig. 447). A fragment of a head in the British Museum[81] has likewise hollow eye-sockets. In bronze heads the inset eyeballs are occasionally still in place (cf. fig. 450).[82] Sometimes the eyelashes were worked separately in little bronze plates with dentated edges[83] (figs. 454, 450). Locks of hair were occasionally made in bronze or lead (fig. 451);[84] necklaces and earrings and the ornaments of diadems, sometimes even the diadems or wreaths themselves, were added in bronze or gold.[85] In these cases they have of course generally disappeared, only the holes for their attachment remaining (cf. fig. 452); but occasionally they are still preserved.[86] The spears and swords, the reins and bridles of horses, and the sceptres were often added in metal (wholly or in part) or painted on the background of the reliefs. The holes for their attachment show their former presence. The Siphnian, Parthenon, and Mausoleum friezes, the Aigina and

ADDITION OF
ACCESSORIES
IN OTHER
MATERIALS

Fig. 454. Bronze
plate with eyelashes
for insertion in a
statue
Delphi Museum

---

76 Benndorf, *Die Metopen von Selinunt*, pp. 41 f.

77 Helbig, *Führer,*[3] II, No. 1352.

78 Smith, *Catalogue of Greek Sculpture in the British Museum*, II, No. 1300.

79 Cf. Lechat, *Au Musée de l'Acropole*, p. 242.

80 Metropolitan Museum, *Bulletin*, 1913, p. 174.

81 Smith, *op. cit.*, I, No. 328.

82 In Copenhagen. Cf. F. Poulsen, Ny Carlsberg Glyptotek, *Katalog,* No. 460a.

83 Such separate plates belonging to bronze statues have been found at Delphi (*Fouilles de Delphes*, V, p. 43, No. 87, fig. 131). The Delphi Charioteer has them still in place; so has the marble statue of Antenor (No. 681 in the Akropolis Museum).

84 Cf. Wace, *J.H.S.*, LVIII, 1938, pp. 90 ff., and Gjerstad, *Erani*, XLIII, 1945, pp. 236 ff. Cf. also Amelung, *Oest. Jahresh.*, XI, p. 179 (a head of Athena); and some of the Akropolis Maidens, Lechat, *op. cit.*, p. 236, Nos. 8 and 9 and footnote 2; and a male head in the Akropolis Museum, No. 657 (*Ath. Mitt.*, 1882, pl. IX, 1, p. 193).

85 Cf., e.g., the examples of Akropolis Maidens cited by Lechat, *op. cit.*, pp. 209, 212-213. The Agorakritos Nemesis has holes in the diadem for the attachment of figures (see p. 239).

86 E.g., in the head from Delos in the National Museum, Athens, No. 23; cf. *B.C.H.*, III, 1879, pl. VIII, 1.

Olympia sculptures, and the figures of the "Alexander sarcophagus" were so provided. The Thasos reliefs in the Louvre[87] still have bronze pegs for the additions of the kerykeion of Hermes, the wreaths of the nymphs, and the strings of the lyre of Apollo (cf. fig. 453). The cheek-pieces and other parts of helmets were often separately attached, as we learn from the Aigina sculptures.

(c) Color

SUCH accessories in various materials are conceivable only in painted sculpture. And this brings us to what is probably the greatest difference between ancient and modern statues—the use of color. Nowadays the rule is to leave the marbles, limestones, and woods we use in their original finish; only occasionally of late have we taken to painting the surface. But Greek sculpture throughout its career was painted,[88] irrespective of whether its material was limestone, terracotta, wood, or marble. If this thought comes to us at first as somewhat of a shock, let us remember that unpainted sculpture is a recent taste. The universal practice in olden times was to paint sculpture.[89] The Egyptians had done it before the Greeks, the Etruscans and Romans copied it from their predecessors, and the Gothic sculptors carried on the tradition.[90] It was only in the Renaissance when taste reverted to classical sculpture—which had in the meantime lost

[87] Rayet, *Monuments de l'art antique*, I.

[88] On this subject see especially Collignon, *La Polychromie dans la sculpture grecque*, in *Revue des Deux Mondes*, 15 fev., 1895, pp. 845–846; Girard, *La Peinture antique*, p. 282; Treu, *Sollen wir unsere Statuen bemalen?*; also *Jahrbuch*, 1889, pp. 18 ff., 1895, pp. 25 ff.; E. Robinson, *Did the Greeks Paint their Sculptures?* in the *Century Magazine*, XLIII, 1892, pp. 869 ff.; *Museum of Fine Arts, Boston, The Hermes of Praxiteles and the Venus Genetrix, Experiments in Restoring the Color of Greek Sculpture*, by Joseph Lindon Smith, described and explained by Edward Robinson (1892); Richter, *A.J.A.*, XLVIII, 1944, pp. 321 ff.; L. F. Hall, *ibid.*, pp. 334 ff. On the technical side, cf. Berger, *Die Maltechnik des Altertums* (1904), pp. 49 ff.; Laurie, *Greek and Roman Painting* (1910), pp. 104 ff., and *The Materials of the Painter's Craft* (1910); Eibner, *Entwicklung und Werkstoffe der Wandmalerei* (1926), pp. 67 ff.

[89] On the pigments used by the ancients, cf. especially A. Reinach, *Textes grecs et latins relatifs à l'histoire de la peinture ancienne*, pp. 8 ff., and Laurie, *Greek and Roman Painting*, pp. 9 ff. They knew the earth colors—the yellow and red ochres, terre verte, and probably the siennas and umber; also white earth, blue carbonate of copper, and artificial pigments. From a simple palette they proceeded to a more and more complicated one. "Painters had a very complete palette at their command, a palette which remained the same, with a few modifications right through the history of painting and up to the dawn of modern chemistry" (Laurie, *op. cit.*—judging apparently from Hellenistic and Roman paintings, not from earlier Greek).

[90] Post, *A History of European and American Sculpture from the Early Christian Period to the Present Day*, I, pp. 31 f. and 59.

its color—that unpainted figures were produced.[91] And we have inherited this taste from our more immediate past.

So much of Greek sculpture is architectural—and we know that Greek architecture was painted—that it would indeed be inconceivable that the statues and reliefs should not have conformed to the general scheme. Moreover, in the brilliant Greek light and at the height from which they were seen the differentiation of color was essential. But since comparatively few Greek sculptures have their color preserved,[92] we must examine the evidence carefully to form a proper picture.

That wooden figures were entirely painted is likely since their surfaces needed protection from the atmosphere. An inscription from Delos of the third century B.C.[93] shows that the wooden statue offered annually to Dionysos was painted.

ON WOOD

That the whole surface of limestone sculptures was painted we know sufficiently from the painted Akropolis groups (figs. 376–380) and the statues and reliefs from Cyprus.[94] The chief colors used[95] were blue and red; yellow, brown, black, and white occur in smaller washes; also green.[96] The coloring is conventional, bulls, horses, beards often appearing blue, merely for their general effect, not to imitate nature.

ON LIMESTONE

On the tufa metopes of the temple C of Selinus[97] numerous color traces could be distinguished, especially when they were first unearthed (1822–1823). Again the predominant colors were red, blue, and yellow, with occasional green, and touches of black and white.

Terracotta sculpture, like limestone, was wholly painted. Some of the archaic sculptures from the Athenaion in Syracuse give us a good idea of the brilliance of this coloring.[98] A fragment of a terra-

ON TERRACOTTA

---

[91] Though many Renaissance figures, especially those in wood and terracotta, are of course also colored.

[92] This loss is easily explained by the nature of the mediums used by the ancients (gum, glue, and white or yolk of egg). "Such mediums can all be dissolved and mixed with water, and while serving to attach the pigment do not really protect it from attack by air or moisture or prevent its easy removal" (Laurie, *Greek and Roman Painting*, p. 18). The quick disappearance of the colors after the discovery of the sculptures also indicates their temporary character.

[93] Homolle, *B.C.H.*, 1890, pp. 396, 502. Color is preserved on some wooden statuettes.

[94] Myres, *Handbook of the Cesnola Collection*, p. 131.

[95] The same palette of colors is found in Egyptian sculpture.

[96] What today appears green is sometimes blue which has turned green. On the Persian rider in the Akropolis Museum, however, we find green and blue.

[97] Benndorf, *Die Metopen von Selinunt*, pp. 42–43.

[98] Cf. Orsi, *Monumenti antichi*, XXV, 1918, pls. XVI, XVII.

cotta statue in New York[99] (fig. 460) has numerous traces of color left. The terracotta statuettes which have come down to us in such large numbers were all originally painted. They were first covered entirely with a white engobe and over this the colors were added. The garments show a variety of bright shades—blue, red, pink, yellow, brown, violet, and, rarely, green. The color of the flesh where preserved is generally reddish or pinkish,[100] of the hair auburn brown, of the lips red, of the eyes blue. Gilt and black appear for details. Unfortunately the white coating has largely flaked off and with it the colors, leaving only the drab terracotta surface. Originally the impression was colorful and gay.

ON MARBLE

Archaic Period

We can form some idea of the use of color in archaic marble statues from the Akropolis figures found in the "Persian debris."[101] Being safely hidden away not so long after their creation they have retained at least occasionally some of their colors in fair condition (figs. 270–272).[102] Only a portion of the surface is painted; that is, the color is confined to parts of the head (the hair, the eyes, the lips, and such accessories as earrings and diadems) and to the embroidered bands and ornaments of the drapery; and it is used as a solid wash on a garment generally only when a small part of it shows. The evidence available at present indicates that in archaic times women's flesh was left whitish and the flesh of men painted brownish, and that only in later times the flesh of women as well as of men was colored[102a] (see below). The clear definition of archaic sculptures with their sharply marked boundaries made the use of color doubly effective. In fact it is possible that the employment of color in its turn influenced the precision of individual forms, for instance of the lips and eyes.[103]

Besides the Akropolis figures numerous other archaic marble figures show remains of color. In the metopes of the "Sikyonian" Treasury at Delphi (cf. fig. 404) color traces are preserved on the figures but not on the background: e.g., dark red on the draperies

99 Metropolitan Museum, *Bulletin,* 1925, p. 15, fig. 3.

100 Cf., e.g., Acc. Nos. 06.1096 and 14.146 in the Metropolitan Museum.

101 After the havoc wrought by the Persians the Athenians buried the old broken statues in convenient pockets on the hill (p. 7).

102 The colors have faded somewhat since the figures were first found. The casts in the Metropolitan Museum have been colored by M. E. Gilliéron from the original sketches made by his father shortly after their discovery in 1880.

102a On this evidence cf. Richter, *A.J.A.,* XLVIII, 1944, pp. 324 ff.

103 On this point, cf. Solon, *Polychromy,* pp. 122 f., 130.

of Europa and the Dioskouroi.[104] On the standing maiden in Berlin (figs. 267–269) the color is still vivid in places—red on the chiton, yellow on the mantle, yellow on the hair, blue, red, and yellow on the meander border.[105] On a fragment of a head from Ephesos there are remains of red on the skin and black on the hair.[106] The frieze of the Siphnian Treasury in Delphi (cf. figs. 418, 419) retained much of its original color scheme when first found—blue on the background, blue, green, and red on the figures.[107] The statuette of the treasurer 144 in the Akropolis Museum, has traces of red on the flesh parts. Two sphinxes, finials of grave monuments in the Metropolitan Museum, have red, blue and black on the feathers and the hair.[108] The Naxian sphinx at Delphi was likewise gaily colored.[109] One of the statue bases in Athens (fig. 283) has a good deal of red preserved on the background. On archaic grave reliefs we often see some color (generally red) still adhering to the background or the hair.

No fifth-[110] or fourth-century statue has survived with its colors at all well preserved. But traces of paint have been observed, for instance, on the Aigina marbles (cf. figs. 388, 389),[111] on the seated goddess in. Berlin (fig. 65),[112] on the Olympia pediments and metopes (cf. figs. 390–393, 414),[113] the gravestone of Philis in the Louvre,[114] the frieze of the Hephaisteion (cf. fig. 293),[115] and the charming little votive relief from Eleusis dating from about 400[116] (fig. 461). There is no certain evidence of color having been found

Fifth Century

[104] Poulsen, *Delphi*, pp. 81, 88.   [105] Wiegand, *Berliner Museen*, 1926, 2, p. 18.
[106] Pryce, *Catalogue of Sculpture in the British Museum*, I, 1, No. B 93.
[107] Poulsen, *op. cit.*, p. 141.
[108] Richter, *Archaic Attic Gravestones*, pp. 15, 65 f.
[109] Poulsen, *op. cit.*, p. 100.
[110] Except of course the early fifth-century figures from the Akropolis like the "Boudeuse" and the Blond Boy (Nos. 686 and 689).
[111] Furtwängler, *Aegina*, pp. 300 ff., e.g., red on the whole of the mantle of Athena of the eastern pediment, blue and red on the scales of her aegis, blue on some of the helmets, red on the inside of the shields, etc.
[112] Wiegand, *Antike Denkmäler*, III, p. 46; no actual colors are preserved, but incised decorations and weathering show their former presence.
[113] Cf. Treu, *Jahrbuch*, 1895, pp. 25 ff., e.g., red on the mantle of Apollo (the whole garment was evidently painted, forming an effective background for the nude figure) and on some of the horses' tails; red on various parts of the metope figures, blue on their background.
[114] Prachov, *Annali dell'Instituto*, 1872, p. 186, e.g., a pinkish tone on the flesh, especially on the cheek.
[115] Sauer, *Das sogenannte Theseion*, p. 187: slight remnants of green, blue, and red on the garments, and blue on the background.
[116] Rodenwaldt, *Jahrbuch*, 1921, pp. 4 ff., pl. I: blue on the background, reddish brown on the hair, yellow on the veil of Demeter, red on the eyes, eyebrows, and contours of the figures.

Fourth Century

on the sculptures of the Parthenon,[117] a fact which is not surprising considering the long period during which they were exposed. On the frieze[118] and statues[119] of the Mausoleum, however, the traces of color were unmistakable; likewise on the hair and sandals of the Hermes by Praxiteles[120] (fig. 664). On a few fragments of the fourth-century sculptures of Ephesos there are remains of color including some on the skin.[121] Several fourth-century Athenian grave stelai show extensive remains of color.[122] For instance, the monument of Aristonautes[123] has red on the inside of the shield, green near the shoulder straps, and blue on the background; that of Prokleides[124] has traces of a red background and blue on the drapery. Finally the reliefs of the rock tomb at Myra in Lycia (probably fourth century) when found had their colors beautifully preserved.[125] One of these has a blue background, violet, red, and yellow draperies, and flesh-colored nude. Another has a red background, violet drapery, a yellow couch with blue and red ornaments, and again flesh-colored nude.

Hellenistic Period

Traces of color have likewise been found on Hellenistic and Roman sculpture. Of these the most important is the "Alexander sarcophagus" from Sidon in the Constantinople Museum[126] (fig. 748). On its reliefs representing battle and hunting scenes are the most varied hues of color—purple, violet, yellow, blue, and different

---

[117] Michaelis, *Der Parthenon*, pp. 124 f. (metopes), 156 f. (pediments), 226 f. (frieze).

[118] They were particularly vivid when first found. Newton (*Travels and Discoveries in the Levant*, II, p. 131) writes soon after their discovery: "The whole frieze was colored. From the examination of a number of fragments on their first disinterment I ascertained that the ground of the relief, like that of the architectural ornaments was a blue, equal in intensity to ultra-marine, the flesh a dun-red, and the drapery and armor picked out with vermilion and perhaps other colors." Cf. also Smith, *Catalogue of Greek Sculpture in the British Museum*, II, p. 97.

[119] Cf. Newton, *Halicarnassus*, II, 1, pp. 222, 232.

[120] Reddish brown on the hair and red and gilt on the sandal.

[121] In the British Museum: the lower part of the head of a youth, Inv. No. 74. 7–10.272 (gray on the flesh probably originally pink); the head of a girl, Inv. No. 1927. 2–14.1 (on the hair traces of brown, eyebrows and pupils brown, flesh pinkish). The latter is from Ephesos, but not certainly from the temple and perhaps of later date. I owe this information to F. N. Pryce.

[122] For a list of Greek stelai with color traces, cf. Brueckner in *Sachregister* of Conze, *Attische Grabreliefs*, IV, p. 142; and Rodenwaldt, *Arch. Anz.*, 1922, p. 170.

[123] Conze, *op. cit.*, pl. CCXLV, No. 1151.　　　　[124] *Ibid.*, pl. CXLI, No. 718.

[125] Fellows, *Discoveries in Lycia*, third plate after p. 198 (colored). Colored casts of these reliefs were shown in the Mausoleum Room of the British Museum (Smith, *op. cit.*, No. 954).

[126] Cf. Hamdy-Bey and Th. Reinach, *Une Nécropole royale*, text and plates (some colored); F. Winter, *Alexander-Sarkophag* (colored plates).

shades of red and brown on the garments, not merely as borders but covering the whole surface; on the bodies some parts such as the hair and the iris are picked out in color. The flesh itself is covered with a light, transparent wash, light yellow for the Greek soldiers, a darker yellow for the Persians. On other examples there are more meagre traces. The old market woman in the Metropolitan Museum (fig. 219) has some deep red preserved on her sandal-strap and bright pink on her mantle. On a head of a girl from Priene[127] in the British Museum traces of red remain in the iris of the eye, the eyebrow, and the curls. The head of Athena in Berlin (fig. 602),[128] a Roman copy of the Athena Parthenos, has yellow on the helmet, red on hair and eyebrows, dark brown on the iris. A female head in Athens,[129] a copy of a fifth-century work, still shows color on the hair and the eyes. Another head from the Esquiline in the British Museum[130] (fig. 459)—a Roman copy of a fourth-century Greek original—has copious traces of red and yellow on the hair and, what is specially interesting, pink on the skin. The statue of Augustus from Prima-porta in the Vatican has remains of a richly variegated color scheme.[131] Finally we may mention a wall-painting from Pompeii in which a woman is actually represented painting a piece of sculpture.[132]

Roman Period

In addition to painting there is another process which we hear of in antiquity, that of γάνωσις or κόσμησις. Vitruvius[133] gives the

Ganosis

---

127 Smith, *Catalogue of Greek Sculpture in the British Museum*, II, No. 1153.
128 *Antike Denkmäler*, 1886, I, pl. III.
129 National Museum, No. 177; Wolters, *Jahrbuch*, 1899, pp. 143 ff.
130 Cf. Treu, *Jahrbuch*, 1889, pp. 18 ff. and pl. I (colored).
131 Amelung, *Die Skulpturen des vaticanischen Museums*, I, No. 14: "red and pink on the tunic and the mantle; the cuirass bordered with yellow and blue fringes; red, yellow, blue, pink, and brown on the ornamental relief; brown on the tree-trunk; reddish brown on the hair."
132 Mau, *Pompeii* (1904), p. 282, fig. 133; Museo Borbonico, VII, 3. Cf. also Robinson, *Century Magazine*, XLIII, 1892, p. 883, where frescoes are mentioned with colored statues.
133 *De arch.* VII. 9. 2–4: (Minium) cum est in expolitionibus conclavium tectoriis inductum: permanet, sine vitiis, suo colore. Apertis vero, id est peristyliis aut exhedris, aut ceteris ejusdem modi locis, quo sol et luna possit splendores et radios inmittere, cum ab his locus tangitur, vitiatur; et, amissa virtute coloris, denigratur, ... At, si qui subtilior fuerit, et voluerit expolitionem miniaceam suum colorem retinere, cum paries expolitus et aridus fuerit, ceram punicam igni liquefactam paulo oleo temperatam saeta inducat; deinde postea, carbonibus in ferreo vase compositis eam ceram a proximo cum pariete calefaciundo sudare cogat, itaque ut peraequetur; deinde tunc candela linteisque puris subigat uti signa marmorea nuda curantur. Haec autem γάνωσις graece dicitur. Ita, obstans cerae punicae lorica non patitur nec lunae splendorem, nec solis radios, lambendo eripere ex his politionibus colorem.

following account of it: "Though it [red[184]] keeps its color perfectly when applied in the polished stucco finish of closed apartments, yet in open apartments, such as peristyles and exedrae or other places of the sort, where the bright rays of the sun and moon can penetrate, it is spoiled by contact with them, loses the strength of its color, and turns black. . . . But if anyone should be more particular and should wish the red finish to retain its color he must, when the wall is polished and dry, rub over it with a stiff brush Punic wax melted and mixed with a little oil; and afterwards melt the wax by warming it and the wall at close quarters with charcoal enclosed in an iron vessel; and finally smooth it off by rubbing it down with a candle and clean cloths, as nude marble statues are treated. This is termed γάνωσις in Greek. The protecting coat of Punic wax prevents the light of the moon and the rays of the sun from licking up and drawing the color out of such polished finishing." Pliny[185] gives a similar description, again mentioning Punic wax, known for its purity,[186] and ends by saying: "as one treats marble figures to make them brilliant." Elsewhere Pliny[187] gives a receipt for Punic wax. Important is Plutarch's statement[188]: "The 'ganosis' of the statue is necessary, for the red ochre[189] with which the

---

[184] *Minium*, though often translated by vermilion, is really red lead, Pb_3O_4, while vermilion is cinnabar, HgS (mercury). This information I owe to Prentice Duell. See also Baldinucci, *Vocabulario toscano dell' arte del disegno* (1681), p. 98, under *minio*, who describes it as made of lead and white lead.

[185] *N.H.* XXXIII. 122: Inlito solis atque lunae contactus inimicus. Remedium ut, parieti siccato, cera punica cum oleo liquefacta candens saetis inducatur iterumque admotis gallae carbonibus inuratur ad sudorem usque, postea candelis subigatur ac deinde linteis puris, sicut et marmora nitescunt.

[186] Pliny, *N.H.* XXI. 83. Cf. Treu, *Jahrbuch*, 1889, p. 23.

[187] *N.H.* XXI. 84: Punica fit hoc modo: ventilatur sub diu saepius cera fulva, dein fervet in aqua marina ex alto petita, addito nitro. Inde linpulis hauriunt florem. id est candidissima quaeque, transfunduntque in vas, quod exiguum frigidae habeat, et rursus marina decocunt separatim, dein vas ipsum aut aquam refrigerant. Et cum hoc ter fecere, juncea crate sub diu siccant sole lunaque. Haec enim candorem facit, sol siccat, et, ne liquefaciat, protegunt tenui linteo. "Punic wax is prepared in the following manner: the yellow (unbleached) wax is placed for a long time in the open air. Then it is boiled in sea water, obtained from the open sea, with *nitrum* added. Then the top, that is, the purest part, is skimmed off with a ladle and poured into a cool vessel. When this has been repeated three times, the wax is then dried on woven rushes in the sunlight and the moonlight. This process bleaches it. It is whiter still if it is boiled once more in the sunlight. The sun dries it without melting it and it is covered with a soft linen cloth."

[188] Quaest. Rom. 287 D: ἡ δὲ γάνωσις τοῦ ἀγάλματος ἀναγκαία, ταχὺ γὰρ ἐξανθεῖ τὸ μίλτινον ᾧ τὰ παλαιὰ τῶν ἀγαλμάτων ἔχρωζον.

[189] Τὸ μίλτινον or ἡ μίλτος should be translated by red ochre, "an earth colored by haematite (oxide of iron, Fe_2O_3)" (Duell).

ancient statues are painted soon loses its color." Eloquent is also
the derivation of γάνωσις: γανόω = to make bright, polish; γεγα-
νωμένον = lacquered. In the inventories of Delian temples of the
year 279 B.C. accounts appear for the articles used in the κόσμησις
of statues which include sponges, nitre, oil, linen, wax, and per-
fume.[140] In some cases the oil is described as ἔλαιον λευκόν, white
oil.[141] Clearly the object was to apply a colorless varnish over the
whole surface for the preservation of the surface and especially of
the colors. This is also borne out by the fact that in these same
Delian inscriptions[142] salaries are paid for the κόσμησις of a figure
in addition to those paid to the sculptor and the painter of the
statue.

Frequent applications of this oil and wax mixture were apparently necessary, for we hear of specialists known as κοσμηταί[143] who
commanded considerable salaries. It is natural therefore that no
trace of it now remains.

It has been suggested that this application "toned" the marble
sufficiently to make the addition of color to the nude parts unnecessary.[144] Practical experiments do not bear this out. An application of Punic wax does not affect the color of the white marble sufficiently to make it harmonize with the painted hair, eyes, and
mouth.[145] We have also seen that in the Mausoleum frieze, the Sidon
sarcophagus, the Myra reliefs, and a few other pieces, actual colors
on the nude parts were and sometimes are still visible,[146] and the
same is borne out by the literary evidence in which the faint flush
of the cheeks and a body color "not too white but just suffused with
red" is referred to (see below). And in the related case of terracotta statuettes, covered over their whole surface with a white engobe in imitation presumably of marble statues, the reddish or
pinkish tone applied on the white for the flesh is often preserved; as
also in the statues which appear on Roman frescoes and mosaics.[147]
Furthermore in Egyptian sculpture where the original paint is

---

140 Homolle, B.C.H., 1890, p. 498.   141 Ibid., p. 499.
142 Ibid., pp. 502–503.   143 Ibid., p. 500; 1882, p. 48.
144 Cf., e.g., Gardner, Handbook of Greek Sculpture, pp. 29 ff.
145 Richter, Metropolitan Museum Studies, I, pp. 25 ff.; A.J.A., XLVIII, 1944,
pp. 327 ff.
146 The fact that the hair and drapery have an uneven, often slightly roughened
surface while the nude parts are smooth would help to account for the better preservation of the color on the former. This variety in finish admirably suggests the difference in texture between skin and hair or drapery.
147 E. Robinson, Century Magazine, XLIII, 1898, p. 883.

often well preserved the skin is regularly colored, that of men reddish brown, that of women yellow; in Gothic sculpture the flesh is likewise painted. There seems no reason therefore not to assume a similar practice in classical Greek times. We must then interpret γάνωσις as an application over the colors for their better preservation.

The literary evidence on the subject shows that great emphasis was placed on successful coloring. Pliny[148] tells us that when Praxiteles was asked which of his statues he valued most he replied, "those to whom Nikias has put his hand. So much did he prize the *circumlitio*[149] of that artist." As Nikias was a famous painter[150] it is significant that he did not think it beneath him to paint statues. And this is borne out by an inscription from Delos of the third century B.C. which records equal sums paid to the sculptor of a statue and to its painter.[151] Furthermore Lucian[152] in his description of his ideally beautiful woman borrows not only various features from famous sculptors but apportions its painting among the most illustrious artists of antiquity. The passage is important, so we will quote it in full:

"What do you think, Polystratos? Will the figure be beautiful?"

"Yes, surely, when it has been completed to the uttermost detail: for there is still, despite your unexampled zeal, one beauty that you have left out of your statue in collecting and combining everything as you did."

"What is that?"

"Not the most unimportant, my friend, unless you will maintain that perfection of form is but little enhanced by color and appropriateness in each detail, so that just those parts will be black which should be black, and those white which should be, and the flush of life will glow upon the surface, and so forth. I fear we will stand in need of the most important features!"

"Where then can we get all that? Or shall we call in the painters of course, and particularly those who excelled in mixing their colors and in applying them judiciously? Come then, let us call in Polygnotos and Euphranor of old, and Apelles and Aëtion. Let them divide up the work, and let Euphranor color the hair as he painted Hera's; let Polygnotos do the becomingness of her brows and the faint flush of her

[148] *N.H.* XXXV. 133.
[149] *Circumlitio* = "the application of color," literally "the besmearing all around."
[150] Cf. Overbeck, *Schriftquellen*, 1811 ff.   [151] Cf. Homolle, *B.C.H.*, 1890, p. 502.
[152] Εἰκόνες 6. 27.

cheeks, just as he did Kassandra in the Lesche at Delphi, and let him also do her clothing, which shall be of the most delicate texture, so that it not only clings close where it should, but a great deal of it floats in the air. The body Apelles shall represent after the manner of his Pakate, not too white but just suffused with red; and her lips shall be done by Aëtion like Roxana's. But stay! We have Homer, the best of all painters, even in the presence of Euphranor and Apelles. Let her be throughout of a color like that which Homer gave to the thighs of Menelaos when he likened them to ivory tinged with crimson; and let him also paint the eyes and make her 'ox-eyed.' The Theban poet, too, shall lend him a hand in the work, to give her 'violet brows.' Yes, and Homer shall make her 'laughter-loving' and 'white-armed' and 'rosy-fingered,' and, in a word, shall liken her to golden Aphrodite far more fittingly than he did the daughter of Briseus."

Another important testimony is the famous passage of Plato:[153] "If we were to paint statues and someone were to come and object that we do not employ the most beautiful colors for the most beautiful parts of the body; that, for instance, we do not paint the eyes vermilion, but black, we should think that we had answered the censor very well by saying to him: 'Do not think that we ought to paint eyes so beautifully that they cease to be eyes; and what I say of this part of the body must be understood of the others likewise.'" A passage in Plutarch[154] is equally eloquent: "They (the actors in a drama) are like toilet-makers and chair-bearers of a luxurious woman; or rather like the encausters and gilders and colorers of statues (ἀγαλμάτων ἐγκαυσταὶ καὶ χρυσωταὶ καὶ βαφεῖς)."

We have abundant evidence, then, of every description—monumental, literary, and epigraphical—to show that coloring of sculptures in all materials was prevalent with Greek sculptors throughout their career. We cannot as yet trace its development stage by stage; but a comparison between the sixth-century Maidens and the fourth-century "Alexander sarcophagus" shows that progress was made in the direction of a more extensive palette, a more delicate harmony of tone, and a more naturalistic rendering; though doubtless thereby was gradually lost the highly decorative character of the archaic scheme with its greater vividness and precision. Whatever prejudices one may have against colored sculpture in theory, the fact remains that what has been actually preserved—from the

[153] *Republic* IV. 420 c.   [154] *De glor. Athen.* 6.

Akropolis Maidens to the "Alexander sarcophagus"—is so pleasing that it makes the white sculpture appear tame by comparison. And if we sense this in museums we can imagine that the contrast would be even greater in the glare of a Greek sun.

(d) Mounting

WHEN a statue was completed it had to be set in place.[155] If it was a single statue or relief it was mounted on a base, which was sometimes of an inferior material such as limestone. The shape of the base is generally rectangular or round; occasionally triangular (e.g., the Nike of Paionios), or in the shape of a column (e.g., the Naxian Sphinx at Delphi[156] and several archaic korai in Athens[157]). It was regularly provided with a dedicatory inscription (cf. fig. 724) and occasionally with the signature of the artist. Now and then it was decorated with reliefs (cf. e.g., fig. 723). The fastening was generally done by metal dowels secured with molten lead (fig. 458);[158] or the plinth of the statue was inserted into a corresponding depression in the base and fastened with molten lead (fig. 457).[159]

The early pediment figures are in relief, at first low (e.g., Corfu and Hydra pediments; figs. 374, 376) then high relief (e.g., "Bluebeard" pediment; fig. 378). The sculptures of the pediments of the Siphnian Treasury (fig. 382) and of the temple of Apollo at Delphi (figs. 381, 384, 386, 387) are partly in relief, partly in the round. The figures of the Eretria pediment were fastened with large dowels to the background (fig. 442). After that the figures stand free, e.g., in the Aigina and Olympia pediments and in the Parthenon (cf. fig. 70), and the plinths, with which they are now regularly[160] provided, are secured to the cornice with bronze clamps and leaden pegs.[161] The later pediment figures must have been carved before they were set up, since they are worked in the round. For such work, in so far as it had to be executed under cover, a temporary studio (ἐργαστήριον) near the temple was erected.[162] Certain changes had naturally often to be made after the figures were

---

[155] On the mounting of Greek studies cf. Raubitschek, *Bull. de l'Institut arch. bulgare*, XII, 1938, pp. 132 ff.

[156] Poulsen, *Delphi*, p. 98, fig. 29.   [157] Akropolis Museum, Nos. 686 and 609.

[158] *A.J.A.*, XLV, 1941, p. 159, figs. 1, 2.

[159] Cf., e.g., Nos. 609, 681, 624, 596 in the Akropolis Museum.

[160] The Epidauros figures are an exception.

[161] Furtwängler, *Aegina*, pp. 203–204, 206.

[162] We hear of such workrooms at Olympia, on the Akropolis, and at Epidauros.

placed, and this was rendered easy by the practice of piecing.[163] The metopes were presumably also worked on the ground. With the continuous friezes the method varied. In the Parthenon the slabs seem to have been carved in situ, for they are of great depth and weight, and the risk to the reliefs in mounting would have been great; moreover the figures overlap from stone to stone. In the Phigaleia temple the slabs were clearly worked separately and then erected, for each has a complete composition, and occasionally when a piece protrudes the hollow into which it fitted is carved in the adjoining stone.

Throughout great care was taken to calculate the effect of the sculptures at their proper height. The Parthenon frieze is carved in deeper relief at the top than at the bottom.[164] A comparison of the Nike of Paionios at the height she was intended for and when placed low down[165] (figs. 455, 456) gives us a realization of the importance of such a calculation. That some sculptors failed in this provision also in Greek times is brought out in the anecdote[166] of the contest of Pheidias and Alkamenes for a statue of Athena which was to be mounted on a high column; we are told that Alkamenes' statue was very delicate and greatly admired until it was set up, when the effect was entirely lost; while Pheidias' work was properly calculated to be seen at the height intended.

(e) The Status of Greek Sculptors

OUR study of the methods employed by the Greek sculptor has brought him very near to us, and has made us feel interested in his life. What do we know of the conditions under which Greek sculptors lived? Very little. They were regarded of course as hand workers, like all artists in the old days; and this circumstance made their standing low in certain parts of Greece and in the estimate of some people. In the military state of Sparta no citizen was allowed to do any manual work[167]—and so Sparta has produced few artists. In the Roman period, as we might expect, artists were also despised. Plutarch[168] gives out this sentiment: "Labor with one's own hands on lowly tasks gives witness, in the toil thus expended on useless

---

[163] Treu, *Jahrbuch*, 1895, p. 20.
[164] The depth in the Parthenon frieze is 5½ cm. top, 3½ cm. below (Dinsmoor).
[165] Cf. Treu, *Olympia*, III, p. 192, figs. 223–224.
[166] Tzetzes, *Chil.* VIII. 353 ff.   [167] Xenophon, *Lac. resp.* VII. 1-2.
[168] *Perikles* II. 1.

things, to one's own indifference to higher things. No generous
youth, from seeing the Zeus at Pisa, or the Hera at Argos, longs to
be Pheidias or Polykleitos; nor to be Anakreon or Philetas or
Archilochos out of pleasure in their poems. For it does not of necessity follow that if the work delighted you with its grace, the one who
wrought it is worthy of your esteem." The same sentiment prevailed
in England a generation or two ago when the church, the army, and
the navy were the only professions open to a gentleman. But it is a
mistake to generalize for the whole of Greece at all periods from
such sentiments; just as it would be misleading to generalize for the
modern outlook from English nineteenth-century prejudices. Solon
passed a law against idleness in accordance with which every citizen
had to declare his means of livelihood,[169] and he thereby set his seal
on respect for work of all kinds. In Athens artists, at least the
prominent ones, were certainly in high standing. Many of them belonged to the citizen class. They became intimate with the mighty.
Pheidias and Perikles were close friends.[170] The sister of Kephisodotos the Younger, the son of Praxiteles, married Phokion, a member
of a distinguished old family.[171] The same Kephisodotos filled the
functions of a trierarch,[172] which required considerable wealth.
Nikias, the painter, was accorded a public funeral.[173] Moreover, the
prices paid to sculptors were comparatively high—not a bad criterion of contemporary appreciation. Each small figure in the Erechtheion frieze cost about sixty drachmas[174] (at a time when the wage
of a skilled workman was one drachma a day[175] and the value of
silver was about seven or eight times what it is today[176]). For the
three Epidauros akroteria, all executed in one year by one man, the
payment amounted to 3,010 drachmas.[177] A little later (in the time
of the philosopher Diogenes) we hear of 3,000 drachmas being paid
for a single statue.[178] Naturally in Roman times collectors paid huge
prices—500 talents, for instance, for the colossal statue of Apollo
by Kalamis;[179] but that was mostly for "antiques." That some of the

169 Cf. Herod. II. 177; Plutarch, Solon 17. 1; cf. also 2. 3.
170 Cf. p. 224.　　　　　　　　　171 Plutarch, Phokion 19. 1.
172 Loewy, Inschriften, No. 555.　　173 Pausanias I. 29. 15.
174 Stevens-Caskey-Fowler-Paton, etc., The Erechtheum, p. 289.
175 Ibid., p. 381. The Athenian drachma was then equivalent to about 22½ cents.
176 Foucart, B.C.H., 1890, p. 593, note 1.
177 Cf. p. 275; since Epidauros used the Aiginetic drachma at this period, which
was equivalent to about 33 cents, this would amount to about $993.30.
178 Diogenes Laert. VI. 35.
179 Pliny, N.H. XXXIV. 39. It was thirty cubits in height.

artists were highly educated men we can surmise from the facts that they wrote books on symmetry and proportion,[180] and that many of them combined several artistic professions, being at one and the same time architect and sculptor,[181] or sculptor and painter,[182] or sculptor and silversmith,[183] etc., just as was customary in the Renaissance.[184] We can imagine, then, the Greek sculptor as leading a pleasurable existence; gifted as few human beings have ever been, absorbed in his work and its many problems, and honored by an appreciative public.

[180] E.g., Polykleitos and Euphranor, etc.; see pp. 246, 284.
[181] E.g., Skopas; cf. p. 268.
[182] E.g., Pythagoras, Pheidias, Euphranor, and Kallimachos.
[183] E.g., Myron; cf. p. 209.
[184] E.g., Michelangelo, who was sculptor, painter, and architect, and Brunelleschi, who was architect, sculptor, and goldsmith (Vasari, Ed. Sansoni-Milanesi, II, p. 330).

CHAPTER X

RELIEF

RELIEF stands midway, so to speak, between sculpture in the round and drawing. It partakes of the qualities of both. It resembles drawing in that it has to suggest volume on a flat or comparatively flat surface; and it resembles sculpture in the round in that it has a variety of planes. The consideration of these two properties is therefore essential in relief technique. To practise it successfully a sculptor has to have a knowledge of foreshortening and a knowledge of the treatment of planes. Together they will give him the means by which to translate form as it is in nature into artistic form, giving a general impression of nature. The latter we shall call for convenience "impressional form."[1]

Both in Egyptian and Assyrian art, reliefs formed a significant part and were produced for thousands of years; but the important problem of foreshortening was not mastered by either. The garden scene on the relief from Nineveh in the British Museum[2] (fig. 462), a product of the seventh century B.C., sums up both the achievements and the limitations of Oriental art, and shows us what knowledge the Greek sculptor inherited from his predecessors in the craft. We see at once that the important law is realized that there must be a continuous front plane with nothing obtruding unduly from it, a device which gives the whole its unified effect. This is a law governing impressional form as contrasted with natural form. In nature form is not so organized and more or less isolated shapes may protrude in all directions. It is the work of the artist to combine these into a harmonious design.

Besides the two chief planes, the front plane and the background plane, Oriental art recognized practically no others. Objects clearly meant to be in the middle and far distance, like one of the two servants fanning the king and the tree behind them, are placed in the same plane with the objects nearest the eye. The farther arms of the

---

[1] For excellent analyses of "impressional form" (*Wirkungsform*) and "natural form" (*Daseinsform*) cf. Hildebrand, *Das Problem der Form*, pp. 16 ff.

[2] Jastrow, *The Civilization of Babylonia and Assyria*, pl. LXII.

king and queen are in the same plane as the nearer arms; the table in front of the couch is level with the couch; and so on. There is consequently no feeling of space; the eye is not led from plane to plane to a distance beyond, and so the forms do not appear to have their proper depths. Furthermore, no foreshortening is used in the rendering of figures and other objects. The upper part of the king's body is shown in full front when in reality it should be in three-quarters view, for he is turning from a profile to a front position; while the head reverts to the profile—a very unnatural rendering, due to the difficulty the sculptor experienced in representing the torsion of the body. On this account the other figures are all kept in strictly profile views. In Egyptian art the same conventions hold from the time of the Old Kingdom (about 3000–2500 B.C.) to the later dynasties. Even at a late date the three-quarters view is incorrectly shown (fig. 463).[3]

The Greeks began where the Egyptians and Assyrians had left off, in relief technique as in other branches of art. But they realized, as their predecessors apparently never had, the importance of foreshortening and of the feeling for space in relief; and they set themselves to this task with wonted initiative and concentration. Within a century or two they succeeded in introducing them in their work. In the Hegeso relief of the end of the fifth century (fig. 429) there is a uniform front plane for the heads, the nearer arms, the nearer legs, and the chair; from this the eye is led to the background by several planes gradually succeeding one another; and in the farthest plane are placed the left arm of the attendant, the lid of the open chest, and part of the drapery of Hegeso. Moreover, the bodies are represented in correct three-quarters view, the farther portions in less high relief than the nearer portions. Thereby everything takes its right place, and we obtain the impression of depth and distance.

Let us see how this was accomplished; for it was only by gradual stages that the Greek artist arrived at this perfect solution.

An unfinished archaic relief from Naukratis[4] (fig. 464) and an unfinished portion of the frieze of the Nereid monument[5] (fig. 467), both in the British Museum, show us clearly how the Greek sculptor proceeded. He did not work from the background up, but from the front backward. That is, he did not—as we are apt to nowadays—

[3] Limestone relief of the Ptolemaic period in the Metropolitan Museum.

[4] Pryce, *Catalogue of Sculpture in the British Museum*, I, 1, No. B 437.

[5] Smith, *Catalogue of Greek Sculpture in the British Museum*, II, No. 908.

begin with a smooth clay background and gradually add his figures
to it, and when it was finished translate his clay creation into stone
through the intermediary of a plaster cast. He started with his marble block, smoothed it out, producing thereby his outer plane, drew
his figure on it, and then cut away the surrounding portions, thus
obtaining his background. Automatically he has created thereby his
two chief planes, and he has kept the front plane uniform. Any details of modeling added later were kept within these two planes. This
method of work, doubtless practised also by the Egyptians and
Assyrians, sufficiently explains the flatness, the unified planes,[6] and
the lack of foreshortening in early reliefs. It was much more difficult
to experiment in different planes while carving into a stone than
while adding malleable clay to a background; and it was in the nature of such work to obtain a uniform front plane. The only shadows
in these early reliefs are those cast by the contours of the figures,
which thereby are made to stand out clearly against the background
plane. The relief makes an impression of two-dimensional design.

In the relief of the dancing women from Branchidai, now in the
British Museum[7] (fig. 466; about 540), the principle of the uniform
front plane is beautifully observed, but the absence of intermediate
planes leads to confusion. The arms are all in the same plane regard-
less of their positions, and we find it difficult in consequence to apportion them to their respective figures; for we obtain no clear impression which parts are behind which. The same is true of the man
stabbing a lion on the sepulchral chest from Xanthos also in the
British Museum;[8] of the horsemen and deer from Sardes;[9] in fact,
universally of archaic Greek reliefs.

Occasionally we find intermediate planes introduced; for instance
in the Orestes relief from Sparta[10] (fig. 465; early sixth century),
where the farther arm of the man is in lower relief than the rest of
the composition; but, since there is no gradual leading down to it by
intervening planes, the effect is not convincing. The use of a series
of planes was rendered especially desirable where the relative position of the figures demanded it—for instance in the relief from the
"Sikyonian" Treasury (fig. 404) where three oxen are represented

SIXTH
CENTURY

<hr />

[6] The uniform outer plane is not always observed in other sculpture; cf. Ben-
venuto Cellini's Perseus and Andromeda in the Bargello in Florence.

[7] Pryce, *Catalogue of Sculpture in the British Museum*, I, 1, No. B 285.

[8] *Ibid.*, B 286.   [9] *Ibid.*, B 269, B 270.

[10] Tod and Wace, *Catalogue of the Sparta Museum*, p. 132, No. 1.

alongside one another. A distinct attempt is here made to place the legs, the chests and the heads of the oxen in a series of receding planes. Thereby a certain impression of depth is obtained, so that there is no question in our minds which figure is behind which. But the transition from one plane to the next is abrupt and angular; there is no graduated recession. The same is true of the relief from Sparta in the Berlin Museum[11] (fig. 468).

In the Siphnian frieze (c. 525) we find the same partial knowledge. Where one figure is definitely placed in front of another, as in the Apollo and Artemis group (fig. 418, left), the farther one is appropriately sunk; but in the fighting warrior in front the two striding legs are placed in the same plane, though one is behind the other. And the transition from one plane to the next is sudden.

This tentative use of different planes continues in works of the end of the sixth century. In the monument known as the Harpy tomb[12] the farther arms and legs are sometimes appropriately sunk, at other times they are not. For instance, the farther arm of the figure holding a pomegranate (fig. 473), on the south side, is too high, while the farther arm of the figure standing before him is properly sunk. One takes its place in relation to the other parts, the other does not. In the group of a seated figure receiving a helmet (fig. 472), on the north side, the planes of the farther arms and legs are fairly successful, except for the left leg of the warrior and the right hand of the seated figure which are too prominent. In the Aristion stele (fig. 424) the calf of the far leg protrudes unduly, while the far arm is shown correctly as in the farthest distance. It is interesting to observe in this connection how difficult the archaic artist found the placing of one foot behind the other. Since he could not get his effect by a variety of planes we often have the impression that one foot is on top of the other, and that the staff held in the hand rests on the toe of the foot (cf. fig. 470).[13] In these cases of superimposed forms the right impression is sometimes achieved by sinking the parts immediately adjoining; as is the case in the feet of the Aristion stele. This stele also shows in a convincing way how careful the Greek sculptor was to keep his outer plane uniform. The nearer arm does not stand out from the body, but is carved into the figure, so that it is on a level with the highest plane of the body. Natural form would

---

11 *Beschreibung der antiken Skulpturen,* No. 731.
12 Pryce, *op.cit.* I, 1, No. B 287; Tritsch, *J.H.S.,* LXII, 1942, pp. 39 ff.
13 Metropolitan Museum, *Handbook* (1930), p. 236; Acc. No. 12.158.

demand more volume for the arm; but from the point of view of impressional form the rendering is successful, for the arm takes its
proper place in the composition.

In the charioteer relief in Athens (fig. 275; c. 510–500) the dis-
position of the planes is beautifully managed. We obtain an impression of depth and motion from the way the eye is led farther and
farther into the background by the gradually receding planes; and
yet the number of planes is restricted so as to insure a harmonious
impression. In these later archaic reliefs the interplay of light and
shade on the surface of the figure begins to suggest a certain roundness, but the projections are so slight that they do not interfere with
the more accentuated shadows of the contours. The design is still
conceived as two-dimensional.

A device conspicuous in the Siphnian frieze, and general in Greek
reliefs of all periods, is the irregularity of the background plane.
For instance, when the inside of a shield is represented it is hollowed
out so as to penetrate deeper than the general background (fig. 418,
right). This cutting into the background plane was useful not only
for obtaining the farthest distance but also in giving life and variety
by creating deeper shadows and providing accents where needed. We
note it in the cock and hen reliefs from Xanthos, in the "Harpy
tomb" (figs. 472, 473), and in many contemporary and later works
where the grouping of the figures did not necessarily demand it—
showing clearly the artistic preference for an enlivened rather than
a uniform background.

The question of distance planes is intimately connected with the
representation of the three-quarters view,[14] for to convey this correctly the height of the relief must gradually diminish in the farther
portions. Naturally, before the Greek sculptor learned to distinguish between a middle and a far distance he was unable to represent
it convincingly; moreover, the torsion of the body involved in it was
more than his knowledge of anatomy could cope with. So the best
plan seemed to be to avoid the three-quarters view and to restrict
himself as far as possible to the profile and full front. And this is
what the early sculptor tried to do. When he did attempt the three-
quarters view he dealt with it very simply—by putting a front
upper body on a profile lower one; as in the Perseus and Medusa

[14] For the sake of convenience I am taking this to mean any view intermediate between the profile and the full front.

group on the Selinus metope (fig. 405) and in the warriors on the
Siphnian frieze (fig. 418). The difficult problem of representing
the junction was generally avoided by the wearing of a garment or
the placing of some concealing object at the critical place.

Fig. 471. Javelin-thrower, from a
psykter by Oltos
Drawing by Lindsley F. Hall
Metropolitan Museum of Art

Similar primitive render-
ings of the three-quarters
view occur in the black-figured and early red-figured
Athenian vases.[15] The upper
part of the body is always
in complete front, the lower
in profile, and garments
generally hide the junc-
ture; when a nude body is
represented there are only
a few lines to indicate the
construction (fig. 471).

At the end of the sixth
and the beginning of the
fifth century, interest in the
representation of a three-
quarters view became more
and more acute, and we
note constant attempts at
dealing with it. The same
device of a front upper
body and a profile lower one with a concealing garment at the junc-
ture is adopted in the youth holding a cat on the statue base in
Athens (fig. 283; c. 510–500). In the lance thrower on the same
base the whole body is shown in front view while one leg and the head
are in profile; the foot turned toward the spectator shows an interesting attempt at foreshortening. But the problem is squarely faced
in the ball player on this relief (fig. 469) and in the runner from
Athens (fig. 84), though in the latter the construction is curious; the
median line describes an extraordinary spiral curve. In the Alxenor
relief (fig. 425) the torsion is suggested by placing one leg in front
view, the other in profile with the toes protruding beyond the front
plane and carved on the lower moulding of the frame.

---

[15] For the development of perspective cf. Richter, *Greek Painting*[2] (1949).

During the transitional period of 480–450 the problem is further
thrashed out and the right solution gradually found. How convincingly, for instance, in the "Birth of Aphrodite" on the three-sided
relief in Rome[16] (fig. 474) the arms of the three women are shown
one behind the other, and how harmoniously one plane glides into
the next! And in the mourning woman on the companion piece in
Boston[17] (fig. 477) how gently we are led from one plane to another
until we reach the farthest distance in the wings of Eros! The three-
quarters view attempted in both women on this slab also marks a
great advance on former times. The upper portion of the body is
shown in gradually retreating depth, and the farthest portion is
distinctly flatter than the nearest part. The only archaizing trait left
is that the breasts do not take their proper place. The nearer seems
too close to the arm, the farther is not sufficiently sunk. The same is
true of the lovely stele of a youth from Sounion[18] (fig. 494; c. 470);
the farther portion is too prominent. In the Zeus of the Selinus metope (fig. 410) the three-quarters view is almost correct. The farther
part of the chest protrudes a little too much, and the same is true of
the Hera. But we are coming close to a perfect solution.

This lingering hesitancy to decrease sufficiently the depth of the
farther parts is general in the works just before the middle of the
fifth century, for instance the "Mourning Athena" (fig. 206) and
the grave relief of an athlete in the Vatican[19] (fig. 480). Even in the
Eleusinian relief[20] (fig. 481) of about 440 b.c. there are a few
traces of this archaism. The shoulder and back of the Demeter are
not convincingly foreshortened, though in other respects the relief
shows a consummate refinement in the treatment of planes. There is
now more variety in the use of shadows, which are no longer confined to outline but give the impression of modeled shapes. The
strands of the hair and the folds of the drapery are beautifully
carved in varying planes and add color and life to the scheme.
Though this use of shadows is still very discreet and the design is
still essentially two-dimensional, a feeling of depth is thereby introduced.

In the vase-paintings of the period there is the same gradual

16 Helbig, *Führer*,[3] II, No. 1286.
17 Caskey, *Catalogue of Sculpture in the Boston Museum*, No. 17.
18 National Museum, Athens, No. 3344.
19 Helbig, *op. cit.*, I, No. 246.   20 National Museum, Athens, No. 126.

progress in the knowledge of foreshortening; and the general interest in the problem is seen in the increasing use of the three-quarters
view. Achievements vary. Sometimes the rendering is just the same
as in early times, with the upper part in complete front, the lower in
profile, and no indication of the muscles where the torsion takes
place; as for instance in a satyr by the Pan painter in New York[21]
(fig. 482). At other times though the chest is still in front view the
torsion is shown in the rectus abdominis which is placed obliquely,
ending apparently on the farther hip; as in a satyr by the Brygos
painter in the Metropolitan Museum[22] (fig. 117). Gradually it was
understood that the farther side of the chest must be contracted and
the median line no longer placed in the center. A quite successful
effort is seen in the engaging boy by the Berlin painter on an oinochoë in the Metropolitan Museum[23] (fig. 484). The vases of about
475–460 show still more advanced renderings (fig. 485), almost
completely successful, with occasional lapses (cf. figs. 130, 483), just
as in the contemporary sculptures.

SECOND
HALF OF
FIFTH
CENTURY
By the second half of the fifth century complete knowledge of relief technique has been attained. The Parthenon frieze (about 442–
438) is a supreme example (figs. 488, 489). The three-quarters
view is now rendered without difficulty and becomes in fact the pre-
vailing pose. We have a uniform front plane and a number of others
leading us gradually to the background, suggesting space and distance. Moreover, the sculptor now understands thoroughly the requirements of impressional form. Thereby he is able to accomplish
astounding things. In the cavalry procession,[24] for instance, he represents as many as eight horsemen abreast in a relief of only about
two inches in depth, and the effect is convincing (fig. 486).

Let us see how he accomplished this feat. In the early frieze from
Prinias (fig. 347; c. 650–625) one horse is simply placed behind
the other and all difficulties are thereby avoided. In the metope of
the "Sikyonian" Treasury (fig. 404; c. 570–550), in order to represent several animals alongside one another a series of planes was
resorted to, one behind the other in steplike formation, and the various heads and legs were all made alike, except that the three heads in
the front plane were shown full front, whereas the others are in profile. The resultant impression was awkward and monotonous. By

21 Metropolitan Museum, *Handbook* (1930), pp. 122–123, fig. 81.
22 *Ibid.*, p. 120, fig. 78.   23 *A.J.A.*, XXX, 1926, p. 37, fig. 6.
24 Smith, *Sculptures of the Parthenon*, pls. 53 ff.

the time of the Siphnian frieze (c. 525) the sculptor has learned
that impressional form is better served not by trying to put each
animal immediately behind the next but by stringing them along.
In the chariot groups of the southern and western friezes[25] (cf. fig.
487) two horses are placed a little in front of two others, and the
crossings of the lines thereby produced give the desired effect. But
the horses which are immediately behind have the same awkward
look as the "Sikyonian" oxen; we have to count their heads or legs
to see how many there are. In the Parthenon frieze the lesson has
been completely learned. The whole fore part of every horse is represented, as well as a considerable part of every rider, and they are
placed one next to the other, occupying a considerable area. The
effect that one rider moves alongside another is attained by an ingenious variation of planes where the different shapes cut across
one another. Keeping to the important principle of a uniform front
plane, the riders' and horses' heads and much of their bodies, irrespective of the positions they occupy, are placed in the front plane; but
where one figure cuts against its neighbor—be it the leg of a rider
against a horse's body, or the front legs of a horse against the body
of an adjacent horse, or a horse's head against the next rider's body
—in these areas the recession of planes is always quite clearly
marked; often by sinking the receding surfaces considerably. This
is best seen when a single figure appears against a horse's body or
—in the procession of cattle—against a cow's body (fig. 356). Here
the figures of the men are carved on the same level as the animals
behind them, but they appear convincingly in front of them because
the animals' bodies cave in where the lines cross. There could be no
better instance of impressional form as against natural form in relief
technique.

This principle of crossing lines and the sinking of the surface of
the adjoining parts is used throughout the frieze with good effect.
In the assembly of deities[26] the impression of one god sitting behind
another instead of alongside is successfully conveyed by the simple
device of making the rails of the farther chairs oblique, and by placing the legs of the adjoining figure so that they cross the rail. Poseidon (fig. 488) evidently sits on the outside, for his chair rail is
horizontal. And that is why he is shown in profile (with his right

25 *Fouilles de Delphes*, IV, pls. IX–X.
26 Smith, *Sculptures of the Parthenon*, pls. 33, 34, 36. I have followed Mr. Smith in
his names for these deities.

arm flattened so as to be in the uniform front plane) ; while Apollo
and Artemis, who sit next to him, have oblique chair rails and the
upper parts of their bodies are in three-quarters views. The same
is true of the groups of Athena and Hephaistos and of Hera and
Zeus; not, however, of the group of Hermes, Dionysos, Demeter,
and Ares (fig. 489)—where the chair legs are horizontal and only
once a leg crosses the adjoining stool. These gods are clearly conceived as sitting next to one another in a horizontal row.

An excellent example of the effect of crossing lines can be observed in the frieze of the Gjölbaschi monument. Here we have a row
of armed soldiers in a fortress (figs. 421, 422). They are closely
massed; the height of the relief in each is about uniform, but we get
the distinct impression that one is behind the other by the crossing
lines of the shield and the depression of the farther shield where it is
cut by the rim of the nearer one. It is a clever device which only
long experience in relief work could teach.

The Phigaleia frieze is likewise able, experienced work from the
point of view of relief technique. The depth here is considerably
greater than in the Parthenon frieze, and portions of the figures are
actually modeled in the round and detached from the background
(cf. figs. 298, 299) ; while in other places, for instance when the insides of shields are represented, the carving sinks beneath the background plane (fig. 299). The drapery sometimes stands out in deep
folds (fig. 298) ; at other times it is in very low relief (fig. 299) or
is actually sunk into the background, like the mantle of the Centaur
in slab 527 (fig. 203). By this variety of planes we obtain a beautiful impression of depth and distance. The background itself is also
very uneven. It bulges in and out, sinking with the draperies and
shields, protruding with other portions, as occasion demands, so that
sometimes there is a difference of several inches in its depth; and
this variation adds to the life and movement of the whole. Effective
also is the use of crossing lines. In the scenes of combats where one
figure is locked with another, this device enables the sculptor to
show their relative positions clearly without any sense of confusion.
But in spite of the tumult, the high relief, the uneven background,
and the frequent crossing lines, the unity of the whole is preserved
by the strict adherence to the uniform front plane. Nothing ob-
trudes beyond it; even when a shield is held out from the body (e.g.,
in slabs 535 and 527) it is in the same plane with the body; and by

gradual and slow stages the eye is led to a middle and farther distance which give depth and solidity to the figures. Naturally in this treatment shadows are no longer confined to outline but accompany the movement of every figure, modeling it in the round, and helping to give it a three-dimensional aspect. It must be remembered that the frieze was intended to be seen at a considerable height and the high relief would make it more visible and effective from below.

The frieze of the Erechtheion is an interesting experiment in relief technique. The figures are worked singly without background and were fastened in situ against the frieze wall of black Eleusinian stone; in other words, it was appliqué relief. Unfortunately we cannot obtain the original effect.

The parallelism we have noted of achievements in sculpture and in vase-painting is apparent also during the second half of the fifth century. On the vases likewise the three-quarters view now presents no further difficulty and is correctly rendered throughout. For the period of the Parthenon, good examples are the Poseidon and Amymone by the painter of the Boston Phiale in the Metropolitan Museum[27] (fig. 493), and, for the end of the century, the woman on the oinochoë by the Meidias painter in the same museum[28] (fig. 309). By this new knowledge of foreshortening Greek vase-paintings gained in spaciousness, and at last convey the impression of the third dimension. Thereby they come nearer to a painting in the modern sense of the word than they ever did before. But inevitably they lose also in carrying power as design. And since pots are more appropriately ornamented with two-dimensional designs than with representational paintings, the decorative effect of the whole is impaired.

Fourth-century reliefs carry on the traditions of their predecessors, and show able handling of relief technique.

FOURTH
CENTURY

In the Mausoleum frieze of the middle of the century (cf. figs. 697–699) the figures are much less crowded than in the Parthenon and Phigaleia friezes. Each combatant stands out practically singly against the background. To accentuate the contours a deep groove runs along them. Care is taken that the figures should interconnect by crossing lines. Sometimes it is just the tail of the horse crossing the adjoining figure's head, or two feet crossing, or a foot crossing a hoof. Though slight it is enough to prevent the contestants from

27 Richtler and Hall, *Red-figured Vases in the Metr. Mus.*, pl. 122.   28 *Ibid.*, pl. 158.

being isolated. The background is quite uneven; indeed since so much of it is unoccupied, variation was necessary to prevent monotony.

How important some use of crossing lines is in the grouping of widely spaced figures can be appreciated in portions of the friezes of the Nereid monument[29] and of the Lysikrates monument,[30] where the figures are entirely unconnected (figs. 490, 491). A curious staccato effect is the result. The figures appear isolated and the sense of unified action disappears. Even a slight employment of such crossing lines in the hunting scene of the Nereid frieze[31] (fig. 492), where some of the horses' feet cross the bodies in front of them, obviates this isolation.

In the grave reliefs of the fourth century (cf. fig. 317) the problem is encountered of compressing a group of people into a comparatively small space. There is now no trace of the two-dimensional design of the earlier stelai with its strongly marked contours. The figures no longer seem attached to the background, but stand out in varying depths, modeled in light and shade. Large expanses of shadows break up the uniformity, and the silhouette no longer counts. The pictorial point of view intrudes on the purely sculptural conception.

HELLENISTIC
PERIOD

In Hellenistic reliefs the three-dimensional conception and the strong contrasts between light and shade are still further accentuated, the figures often being modeled practically in the round. Furthermore, the composition of the friezes again becomes crowded (cf. the "Alexander sarcophagus" [fig. 748] and the Pergamon frieze), adding to the restless effect of the whole.

Relief work on a rounded surface, though it appears occasionally in the sixth[32] and fifth centuries (cf. fig. 496[33]), became popular only during the fourth century and the Hellenistic period. We find it on the Ephesos drums (cf. fig. 705) and the Lysikrates monument[34] (fig. 491), and commonly on marble tomb vases (cf. fig. 495[35]). On the last the relief is often very low; the rounded surface

29 Smith, *Catalogue of Greek Sculpture in the British Museum*, II, No. 886.
30 De Cou, *Papers of the American School of Classical Studies in Athens*, VI, pp. 316 ff.
31 Smith, *op. cit.*, II, No. 888.
32 For two instances, cf. the sixth-century drums from Ephesos (figs. 265, 266) and the polos of the "Knidian" karyatid (Homolle, *Fouilles de Delphes*, IV, pl. XIX).
33 Metropolitan Museum, *Bulletin*, 1947, pp. 179 ff.
34 De Cou, *op. cit.*, VI, pp. 316 ff.
35 Metropolitan Museum, *Bulletin*, 1913, pp. 173–174.

of the vase was then a distinct advantage, for it enabled the sculptor
to obtain a feeling of depth and perspective without having to vary
the height of the relief so much. The curved surface of the vase
supplied the necessary variation, and the sculptor could keep to a
fairly uniform shallow depth.

CHAPTER XI

GREEK SCULPTURE COMPARED WITH ROMAN COPIES AND MODERN FORGERIES

WE have studied Greek sculpture from many points of view —its conception, its modeling, its composition, its technique, and the treatment of its relief. In this chapter we shall study it from still another angle—an indirect one, but one that is particularly illuminating—its relation to Roman copies and modern forgeries; for it is often by comparison with other products that the inherent qualities of a work of art are realized. Moreover, the consideration is a practical one, since in our examination of ancient sculpture we are continually confronted with these questions of origin.

(a) Roman Copies

IT is important to remember that much of what we have come to call Roman art was produced by Greek artists and other people of non-Roman origin.[1] When, therefore, we use the term Roman it is meant to signify a period rather than a nationality. The Roman Empire created an outlook that pervaded all communities and is manifest in the art produced in its wide domains.

As a consequence of the Roman conquest of Greece a multitude of Greek works of art had been transferred to Italy and had been exhibited in public places. By this direct contact the Romans had come to appreciate Greek art. By the first century B.C., the natural supply of originals through looting by the conquering generals had waned and so the public demand had to be supplied by a vast output of copies. These copies of earlier works were either made mechanically by the pointing process (cf. p. 141), in which case a Greek work was produced as exactly as possible, or, they were adaptations with slight variations.

---

[1] For recent discussions cf. Rizzo, I Romani e l'arte greca, in *L'Urbe*, X, 1947, pp. 3 ff.; Vessberg, *Studien zur Kunstgeschichte der römischen Republik*, pp. 26 ff., and passim; and my forthcoming *Three Critical Phases in the Development of Greek Sculpture*.

The direct copies have the greatest value for us today; for many a Greek work is preserved to us only in such Roman reproductions. But in trying to visualize through them the lost Greek originals we must be aware of the differences and supply in our minds what the Roman copies do not give.

DIRECT
COPIES OF
GREEK
WORKS

The most important thing a Roman copy reproduces is the composition of the original statue or group. There may be an occasional variation in detail, but a faithful copy, made by the pointing process, preserves the general scheme. From works like the Diadoumenos of Delos (fig. 650) we get a realization of the harmonious design of a Greek fifth-century original. In fact our whole knowledge of Polykleitos is based on such Roman copies. So are our understanding of the art of Myron with its important innovations in attitudes of movement, and our realization of the Athena Parthenos by Pheidias, one of the most famous works of antiquity.

The difference between such Roman reproductions and the Greek models shows itself therefore chiefly in the execution. The sculptors of Roman times, copying as they did earlier Greek creations by mechanical means, missed the imperceptible variety that gave them life. And so their modeling is mostly cold and lifeless. Instead of a delicately variegated surface with gradual, gentle transitions we have a much harder, more summary treatment. Naturally the rendering varies. Some Roman copies are much better than others; some even approximate the Greek originals so closely that it is difficult to distinguish between them; but mostly they lack the sensitiveness that characterizes Greek work. A few examples will bear this out. For such comparison we have selected copies of average execution, since they are best suited to bring out the difference.

In spite of the apparent simplicity of the drapery of the transition period of 480–450 we shall find, when we study it, a great deal of variety and feeling for the texture of the material and the continuity of the folds. For instance, in the Sterope and Hippodameia of the Olympia pediments[2] (fig. 393) and the standing Athena of one of the metopes[3] (fig. 319), the folds, though apparently alike, are as a matter of fact infinitely varied. No groove is parallel to another; the direction of each is slightly different, and one is a little wider, another a little narrower; and between the chief grooves are a number of shorter ones, all various lengths, that start at the waist but are not carried all the way down. Moreover, the construction of

[2] Treu, *Olympia*, III, pl. X.   [3] *Ibid.*, pls. XL and XLIII.

the garment is made perfectly apparent: a thick woolen tunic, belted, pulled up to form a short pouch, and worn with an overfold. The bunched folds just above the waist are convincing; we feel that there are two thicknesses of cloth, and laid above it the one thickness of the overfold. The few folds on this overfold sufficiently indicate the heaviness of the material and moreover add the necessary variety. After our enjoyment of this sensitive treatment, the contrast in the maidens from Herculaneum[4] (cf. fig. 497) or the Hestia Giustiniani[5] is immediately apparent. They are Roman copies of Greek works of about the same period as the Olympia sculptures and they reproduce their majestic compositions admirably. But how hard is the rendering of the folds! How relentless are these deep grooves running practically parallel to one another, all starting at the top and ending at the bottom, with only occasionally a little pretense at variation! The pouch looks like a second overfold, not two thicknesses of material. We have here no sense of the varied effects of nature treated in a decorative manner, as in the Olympia sculptures; rather a hard, mechanical copying of an artistic rendering inadequately understood.

And other styles of drapery are copied with the same lack of comprehension. If the mantle held by the Lapith on the Parthenon metope (fig. 415) gives us pleasure, if we enjoy the fine swing and consecutiveness of its curving folds, what do we feel before the mantle of a Roman copy with a similar composition (fig. 499)[6]? It is no longer an enjoyment to follow each fold and feel its lifelike and yet rhythmical effect. The stolid vertical folds on the sides and the hesitating curving folds in the middle have nothing in common with their prototypes except their general direction. Again, if we have any appreciation for the beauty of the drapery of the Erechtheion Kore (fig. 502), for the variegation of its "vertical" folds, for the fine curve made by the overhanging pouch, for the little pleats on the overfold, each one of which appears inevitably occasioned by the fall of the garment and yet plays a part in the artistic whole, how hard will seem by contrast the Roman rendering in the Vatican[7] (fig. 503) with its leaden, lifeless folds! An instructive comparison is the Nike adjusting her sandal from the Balustrade[8] (fig. 504)

[4] Brunn-Bruckmann, *Denkmäler*, pls. 294–295.   [5] *Ibid.*, pl. 491.
[6] Cf. also the back of the "Venus Genetrix."
[7] Amelung, *Die Skulpturen des vaticanischen Museums*, I, No. 5.
[8] Cf. p. 100.

with a copy of it on a Roman relief in Munich[9] (fig. 505). How
stilted and dull the oblique lines seem on the copy[10] compared to the
fifth-century model; how monotonously regular are the zigzag lines
along the edge of the mantle compared to the varied treatment on
the earlier figure! How much of the effect of the original is lost in
making the drapery less transparent! The same contrast is presented in the relief of the Nikai and the bull from the Nike Balustrade (fig. 506) and the Roman version of it in the Vatican[11] (fig.
507).

We can multiply such contrasts and comparisons—the fine swing
of the backward-flying drapery of the Paionios Nike (fig. 637),
splendidly decorative and yet so naturalistic that we can feel the
wind blowing against it, and the rigidity of the backward-flying
drapery on the Chiaramonti Niobid[12] in the Vatican (fig. 498);
the lifelike effect on the Parthenon "Fate"[13] (fig. 500), where with
all the amazing variety there is a steady downward trend, and the
more ribbon-like folds of the Barberini "Suppliant"[14] (fig. 501) in
the Louvre which seem to be applied on the surface; the convincing
and delicate treatment of the thin chiton with its multitudinous little
folds showing beneath the thick mantle of the Kore on the Eleusis
relief in Athens[15] (fig. 481) and the more mechanical interpretation
of this same effect on two Roman reliefs in the Metropolitan Museum
—one a direct copy,[16] the other an adaptation[17] (fig. 510).

In the rendering of the body and the head there is the same difference. We need only pass from the infinitely varied surface of the
Praxiteles Hermes (fig. 664) to such good Roman copies as the
Lansdowne Herakles (fig. 707) with its hard grooves and ridges
to realize the different degrees of sensitiveness of the two sculptors;
or from the Greek head found on the southern slope of the Akropolis[18] (fig. 508) to a copy of it in Berlin[19] (fig. 509) to see how the
melting look of the eyes, the variegated hair, the sensitive lips have
hardened. The softness of outline, the imperceptible passing of one
plane into another that constitute the chief charm of the Greek
original have disappeared. We note the same distinction when we

9 Furtwängler, *Beschreibung der Skulpturen in der Glyptothek*, No. 264.
10 It must be remembered, however, that some of the folds are restored.
11 Amelung, *Die Skulpturen des vaticanischen Museums,* II, p. 270, No. 94, pl. 7.
12 *Ibid.,* I, No. 176, pl. 44.
13 Smith, *Sculptures of the Parthenon,* pl. 5.   14 Helbig, *Führer,*3 II, No. 1820.
15 National Museum, No. 126.   16 'Εφ. 'Αρχ., 1937, pp. 20 ff.
17 *Handbook* (1930), p. 246, fig. 170.   18 National Museum, Athens, No. 182.
19 Berlin, *Beschreibung der antiken Skulpturen,* No. 610.

compare the Greek and Roman versions of the "Eubouleus" in the National Museum in Athens,[20] one of Greek workmanship (fig. 512), the other an indifferent Roman copy (fig. 511). Particularly strong is the contrast in the rendering of the hair. One is a delicate treatment in which the growth from the head is suggested, the other a hard, precise representation in which the locks appear as if laid on the skull.

We now know that the reliefs in Madrid[21] (fig. 515), Rome, and New York[22] (fig. 638) with representations of Maenads,[24] formerly thought to be adaptations of Greek works, are really direct copies of late fifth-century originals; for two of the reliefs, in Madrid and New York, are exactly alike in composition and size (see page 243). Lovely and charming though these figures are—and they are among the most beautiful works of the Roman period that are preserved to us—when we compare them with their predecessors on fifth-century vases (figs. 287 and 513) the difference becomes immediately apparent. The true zest for life so noticeable in their predecessors has somehow passed from them. Compared with the earlier figures they show all the difference between real ecstasy and its reflection. The frenzy of the Roman Maenads seems mere make-believe; they appear as if suddenly arrested, posing in attitudes of exaltation, not really " θεοῦ πνοαῖσιν ἐμμανεῖς." It is, in fact, the difference between an epoch of direct inspiration and one of imitation.

In addition to these mechanical copies we have adaptations of earlier works. For instance, the late fifth-century Maenads that have survived in direct copies also occur on the marble vases, altars, and candelabra so popular in Roman times. They are there reduced in scale and shown in different groupings, with slight variations in the attitudes, gestures, and attributes, to adapt them to their new milieu. On a krater in New York[23] (fig. 514), for instance, are a number of figures, including maenads and nymphs, which are known from other reliefs.[24] In these transformations some of the freshness of the original creations is of course lost. How charmingly natural are the folds in

ADAPTATIONS OF GREEK WORKS

---

[20] Nos. 181, 1839. Three further Roman replicas are in Athens, Nos. 2650 and 2394 in the National Museum and a small one in the Akropolis Museum; cf. Lippold, *Kopien und Umbildungen griechischer Statuen*, pp. 116 f. and 'Εφ. 'Αρχ., III, pl. 3, p. 39.

[21] R. Ricard, *Marbres du Musée de Prado*, Nos. 178 ff.

[22] Rizzo, *Thiasos;* Richter, *A.J.A.*, XL, 1936, pp. 11 ff.

[23] Richter, *J.H.S.*, XLV, 1925, pp. 201 ff.

[24] Cf. Hauser, *Die neuattischen Reliefs*, passim.

the Gjölbaschi dancer[25] (fig. 516), daintily holding up the edge of her garment, and how artificial, by comparison, the similar treatment on the Roman relief in the Vatican[26] (fig. 517) with its stiffly converging lines!

ECLECTIC
WORKS

Sometimes figures in the round belonging to different periods are combined in one group. For instance, the statue of a youth by Stephanos[27] (fig. 773), the pupil of Pasiteles, is clearly derived from a work of the transitional epoch of the second quarter of the fifth century. The same youth appears in a group in Naples[28] with a woman of late fifth-century style, and in another group in the Louvre[29] with a youth also in a later style.

A style that became very popular in Roman times is the so-called archaistic, in imitation of the Greek archaic of the sixth century, with an inevitable admixture, however, of later elements.[30] A statue of Artemis of which there are several copies[31] (figs. 518,[32] 519,[33] 520[34]) is a characteristic example. The drapery with its zigzag folds and wavy lines is in the sixth-century manner (though the treatment does not show the lifelike variety or the subtle curves of genuine Greek work); the head is in the developed style, with the eye modeled in various planes and the forms rounded instead of angular. Similar discrepancies between the rendering of the face and the drapery are evident in such works as the "Borghese Altar"[35] and the figures on a candelabrum in Rome (fig. 521).[36] Sometimes the freshness of Greek archaic art is reproduced with more sensitive understanding, as in the archaistic bronze statuette in the British Museum[37] (fig. 523), where the folds are less stiff and mechanical; it is only when we compare it with a genuine Greek work like No. 11691 in the National Museum in

25 Benndorf, *Das Heroön von Gjölbaschi-Trysa*, pl. XX.
26 Amelung, *Die Skulpturen des vaticanischen Museums*, I, No. 644.
27 In the Albani Collection; cf. Helbig, *Führer*,³ II, No. 1846.
28 Cf. Ruesch, *Guida*, No. 110
29 Cf. Brunn-Bruckmann, *Denkmäler*, pl. 307.
30 Many of these archaistic works have now been recognized as copies of earlier creations; cf. the recent article by Becatti, *Critica d'Arte*, 1941, pp. 32 ff.
31 For an identification of the original of these copies with the chryselephantine statue of Artemis Laphria by Menaichmos and Soidas, cf. Studniczka, *Röm. Mitt.*, III, pp. 277–302.
32 Ruesch, *Guida*, p. 31, No. 106, fig. 8.
33 Milani, *Il Museo archeologico di Firenze*, pl. CXLV, p. 261.
34 Dütschke, *Antike Bildwerke in Oberitalien*, V, p. 122, No. 309.
35 Froehner, *Notice de la sculpture antique du Louvre*, No. 1.
36 A recent discovery. I owe the photograph to the kindness of Mr. Pietrangeli.
37 Walters, *Select Bronzes*, pl. II.

Athens[38] (fig. 524) that we become conscious of such deficiencies as
the multitude of parallel grooves in the folds hanging from the arm,
the monotonous regularity of the zigzag lines, and the lack of feeling
for the thinness of the chiton sleeve where it emerges from the himation. It is interesting to compare the London statuette with a similar
one, also archaistic, in the Bibliothèque Nationale[39] (fig. 522). The
latter shows the same conception, but is vastly inferior in workmanship.

(b) Modern Forgeries[40]

In judging between ancient works and modern forgeries[41] we have
to deal with an entirely different problem. However different the
Greeks were from the Romans, they both had the horizon of the
classical world. But so diverse is the Greek spirit from our own
that it is rare that a modern mind can catch it sufficiently to reproduce it in a work of art. To distinguish therefore between Greek
works and modern reproductions our best method is to be thoroughly familiar with Greek art, to become steeped in its conceptions,
to appreciate the style of its modeling, to be acquainted with the
paraphernalia it employs. And then our eyes will quickly detect the
almost invariable inconsistencies in modern forgeries.

Let us take a few examples: A common device of the forger is to
copy an extant statue or design, varying it a little in the process.
For even he, or rather he of all people, realizes how hard it is for a
modern mind to create an ancient work; so he prefers to have a
starting point. Figure 526 is a head bought in Italy by an American
collector and given to the Metropolitan Museum for purposes of
study. The first things that strike us in it are the apparent correctness of the type and the flabbiness of the modeling. It is clearly in
the style of the Aiginetan marbles. In fact, a closer examination
shows that it is a copy of the fallen warrior from the east pediment
(cf. fig. 525), broken and therefore seen upright, and so not too
obviously reminiscent of its model. The heads are almost line for
line the same, except that in the copy all the sharpnesses of the

[38] Papaspiridi, *Guide du Musée National*, p. 213, fig. 41.

[39] Babelon-Blanchet, *Catalogue*, No. 265.

[40] In the following discussion of forgeries I am presenting merely my own opinions
as to the authenticity of certain "antiquities" and "in my opinion" must be understood throughout in any definite statements made.

[41] Very little has been written on this absorbing but precarious subject. The best
analysis is still Furtwängler, *Neuere Fälschungen von Antiken* (1899).

original are gone; the edge round the nose-piece is not there, the
precise ridges for the beard have become blunt, the little sharp
ridges on the eyelids and lips have disappeared, the teeth no longer
show between the lips. And then there is another variation—one
of those blunders that a forger is so apt to commit because he is
working in an unfamiliar field, and that an archaeologist can easily
detect by his familiarity with the ancient world; one of those clues,
in fact, which are independent of style, which cannot, therefore, be
called a subjective impression, and so form a tangible, incontrovert-
ible argument. In the Aigina warrior the cheek-piece of the helmet is
turned down, a large part of it has been broken away, but the hinge
and a small portion of it are still there. The forger copied it very
much as he found it, but in his general blurring process he made the
hinge and the fracture rather indistinct; and then since he did not
understand what it meant he added another (upturned) cheek-piece
on top!

The bronze head shown in figures 529 and 530 exists in several
replicas,[42] which make their appearance from time to time in the
antique market. It evidently reproduces the familiar "Sappho" type
of the fifth century. But when we compare it with the Greek originals of that period, or with Roman replicas of such originals, we are
at once struck with its flabby appearance. The mouth appears weak
and indistinct, the eyes too staring, the rendering of the whole face
lacks firmness. The Greeks and the Romans—at least from the fifth
century onward—had a thorough understanding of the human
body. In their modeling we are made to feel not only the surface
but the substance of bony structure beneath. This head has only a
surface, not a core of muscles and bones. And inevitably we find the
usual misconceptions. The forger apparently had in his mind a
female head with her hair tied up with a long ribbon, like the
"Sappho" in the Ny Carlsberg Museum[43] (figs. 527, 528). In trying to reproduce this he made a fatal variation—the ribbon becomes
a Renaissance cap at the back, and on the front portion appears a
Renaissance ornament.

The same feeble, indistinct modeling condemns the head illustrated in figure 532, clearly copied from the fine original in Athens[44]

[42] Cf. Furtwängler, *Neuere Fälschungen von Antiken,* pp. 24 f., figs. 19 and 20;
Arndt, *Einzelaufnahmen,* No. 1059 and others there mentioned. Still another replica,
obtained by a private collector in Germany, came to New York in 1910.

[43] Arndt, *La Glyptothèque Ny Carlsberg,* pl. 43.   [44] National Museum, No. 17.

(fig. 531). The sculptor could not reproduce the precision of archaic Greek art; he has succeeded only in obtaining a superficial resemblance. How greatly we appreciate the sense of structure, the lovely decorative curves in the contours of the skull and of each feature in the Greek head, after looking at this modern imitation. And again there is a helpful "give-away." In the Greek head the locks which fall over the shoulders are all long and of about the same length. The forger has represented some of his locks rightly as if continuing beyond the break, but one he has modeled as a short complete curl.

Perhaps the most difficult forgeries to detect are those in the archaistic style; for they are imitations of imitations. A helpful comparison is that between the archaistic head of Athena of the Roman period in the Metropolitan Museum[45] (fig. 533) and a modern copy of it (fig. 534). It will make us appreciate the firm modeling of the Roman head, the fine contours of its eyelids and lips, the lovely precision of the grooves of the hair and of the ornamental fillet, all features which we miss in the imitation. A modern expression of alertness has crept into the latter which stamps it as false. Incidentally the hair has been cut short and does not continue to the break as it does in the New York original.

The head illustrated in figure 536 is typical of a large output of forgeries. It is clearly copied from the Aphrodite of Melos (fig. 535); but the face has a modern, personal note totally alien to its serene prototype. It illustrates in a somewhat obvious manner how difficult it is for a man with a twentieth-century outlook to imitate works produced more than two thousand years ago. And this difference will assert itself even when an exact copy is attempted—by means of a plaster cast and the pointing process. Figure 537 is an ancient marble head in the Metropolitan Museum;[46] figure 538 is a plaster cast of this head used to produce the modern marble imitation (with similar breaks!) shown in figure 539. In spite of the mechanical process involved, which should insure accuracy, the differences are palpable—e.g., in the modeling of the eyelids, of the ear, and especially of the hair. The hair in the original seems actually to grow out of the head, while in the copy it appears to be stuck on the surface. The living quality of the original work cannot be repro-

45 Metropolitan Museum, *Bulletin*, 1913, pp. 51–52.
46 *Ibid.*, 1927, p. 143, fig. 2.

duced in a modern copy even by the pointing process insuring mechanical accuracy.

Greek drapery is not easy to imitate. The Greek sculptor had such a strong feeling for structure that his drapery is always conceived as a logical whole; we can invariably see whence each fold emerges and where it is going. This was of course difficult to attain by someone deficient in this sense and portraying a garment unfamiliar because not in contemporary use. A good instance is the would-be archaic or archaistic statue shown in figure 543.[47] The rendering of the drapery here shows several important misunderstandings. The scheme in general is correct, that is, the himation with its overfold passes from the right shoulder beneath the left arm, and below it is seen the chiton; but the structure of the two garments is not really understood. We may ask, for instance, what has caused the bunched folds of the chiton along the left upper arm—for, since there is a quasi-horizontal edge at the bottom, the garment should hang down evenly—and why is there a deep groove between the part of the himation that covers the body and the one that hangs loosely from the right forearm? (We may contrast the archaic and archaistic renderings, figs. 271–273 and 522, 523.) How stiff and clumsy, too, are the curving ridges in the lower part of the drapery, where it is pulled sidewise by the left hand, compared with the sensitive archaic renderings (cf. figs. 271, 273, 274).

The forgeries of terracotta figurines are a good field for the study of drapery. Figure 545 is a statuette in the Metropolitan Museum, exhibited in a case of forgeries in the Study Collection, for comparison with the genuine Greek examples. The girl wears a long chiton and a himation loosely draped over the lower part of her body. The chiton appears to be girt below the breasts; but we know this only because there is a horizontal dividing line. There is no continuity between the folds of the upper part of the garment and the lower, no indication of the effect created by the drawing in of a belt, no interest in pursuing a fold from its beginning to its end. Contrast this with the treatment on a Greek statuette (fig. 544). How clearly the upper portion is conceived as part and parcel of the lower, how well the effect of the belt on the material is studied! We can see what happens to each fold above and below the depression, for there is everywhere a distinct feeling for

[47] Richter, *Handbook of the Classical Collection,* 1930, p. 343.

continuity and structure. And besides this stylistic difference there is here too a tangible clue; for the forger has made an amusing mistake in the rendering of the garment. Below the mantle the chiton becomes again visible, as it so often does in the Greek statuettes. But so little did the artist understand what he was representing that he showed it with two edges, as if the woman wore two chitons, one a little shorter than the other.

Of course the mistakes are not always so obvious. Figure 547 shows a woman wearing a chiton and wrapped in her himation. There are no palpable misunderstandings, except the way the chiton is rendered at the bottom. Naturally where it falls over the feet the vertical folds are affected, and this is correctly indicated; but this oblique direction is retained also in the intervening portions where there is no reason for any interference with the vertical hang—again a lack of structural sense on the part of the maker. Even more noticeable, however, is the hesitating way in which the folds of the himation are represented. There is not the firm swing in the required directions which we find invariably in similar Greek renderings, e.g., in figure 546. We see that a groping hand is at work, feeling its way in an unfamiliar field.

The most difficult quality of all for the modern forger to imitate is the Greek simplicity and aloofness; his figures are almost invariably affected, theatrical, and self-conscious. Extreme examples are the statuettes in New York of a young lady sitting on a rock, looking at herself in a mirror, her head a little on one side (fig. 548), and of a girl stretched out on the floor, her arm resting on a footstool, in quiet contemplation (fig. 550). The Greek figures do not assume such recherché, theatrical, self-conscious postures. If they contemplate, they make no outward show of it (cf. fig. 206). If they look into their mirrors, they do so quietly and unaffectedly (cf. fig. 549). If they hold anything, they grasp it in the natural way. It is this poise, which constitutes the charm of the Greek figures, that is so difficult to imitate, and so the lack of it becomes the distinguishing element in a modern forgery.

The comparison of a modern gem engraving of Amymone[48] (fig. 552) with its ancient prototype[49] (fig. 551) brings out the same difference in conception. According to the story Amymone was sent by her father to fetch water, and was helped in her quest by Posei-

[48] Metropolitan Museum, *Catalogue of Engraved Gems*, No. 419.
[49] Furtwängler, *Antike Gemmen*, pl. XXX, 29.

don. In the ancient representation she is stooping to fill her jug with
water in a convincing, lifelike manner; in the modern rendering she
sits upright in an uncomfortable position holding the jug as if it
were a symbol like the trident. The Greek artist conceived Amymone
in appropriate action; with the modern interpreter she becomes
ineffective.

The imitation of Greek grave reliefs is particularly difficult. The
detached serenity of the Greek figures is so far removed from modern conceptions that it is almost impossible to reproduce. A relief
from one of the store rooms of the Berlin Museum[50] (fig. 553) will
bear this out. How different are the insipid expressions of the man
and woman from those of their prototypes! The scene has become a
social incident; there is no trace of the former pathos and aloofness.
And the finial on the top of the stele appears stilted, the leaves have
not the living quality of growth so conspicuous in Greek akroteria.

In another grave relief in Berlin (fig. 554), of fifth-century style,
the modern sculptor has succeeded a little better. He has at least
avoided modern sentimentality. But instead of the grace of fifth-
century work the figures have a stiff, wooden quality. The filling of
the space—with its central figure and little boy placed on each side
—immediately strikes us as unsatisfactory when we compare it with
the harmonious compositions of even cursorily worked Greek stelai.
And then there are other "give-aways." The chair, a would-be *klis-
mos*, is misunderstood and has no back.[51] The farther arm and hand
of the woman are in too high relief. A sculptor of the second half of
the fifth century, with his knowledge of the rendering of planes in relief, would have made these parts less prominent so that they should
appear to be in the far distance (cf. p. 170).

Sometimes a Greek work that is known only in Roman copies has
been reproduced on a small scale, either entire or in part; for instance,
the Ares Borghese (fig. 542) and the Mattei Amazon (fig. 541).
These forgeries are not always obvious, for the composition is directly
copied from an original work,[52] and therefore convincing, and the
fact that they are copies of known originals is not in itself a source
of suspicion, for reduced Roman replicas of famous Greek originals

---

[50] I am greatly indebted to the authorities of the Berlin Museum for letting me
have photographs of the two pieces illustrated in figs. 553, 554, both of which have
long been recognized as forgeries by them.

[51] Cf. my *Ancient Furniture*, pp. 45 ff.

[52] Compare e.g. our fig. 541 with our fig. 620, and our fig. 542 with fig. 19 in Charbonneaux, *La Sculpture grecque classique*.

of course exist. In such cases the physical condition of the marble is the most helpful criterion (see below).

Occasionally there have come into the market important forgeries of a rather different calibre from those described—not copies or adaptations, but actual creations in the ancient style. The best known examples are the striding Athena, the youth carrying a girl, and the little maiden, all by the Italian sculptor Alceo Dossena[53] (figs. 558, 559, 555, 543). Though they are on the whole remarkably successful, their modern origin can be detected by the same criteria as those applied to the other forgeries. Analysis inevitably shows occasional inconsistencies in the rendering and a different outlook in the conception. The fine simplicity and vitality of the Greek works are apparently too difficult for us moderns to attain; and even when lively action is attempted, the effect of the whole is dead. And here too we have one of those "concrete" clues which so often give away a forgery. The grooves in the hair and hands of Dossena's youth were evidently made by the running drill, which as we know (cf. pp. 144 f.) was not used by Greek sculptors until the second half of the fifth century, whereas the style of the group is late archaic.[54]

Besides the test of style there are the physical and chemical conditions of the material to help us in our examination. Ancient marbles, for instance, having been exposed to the air and the soil for long periods of time, generally show a disintegration of the surface due to attack by acids in the air and soil, an opening of the spaces between the crystals, and a certain amount of penetration of rust and other stains, whereas in a modern marble such discolorations are merely superficial. In other words, in an ancient marble we generally find a gradual transition in color or crystalline structure from the outermost layers to those underneath, due to an interaction of the soil matter and the marble (forming, for instance, calcium silicate); whereas in a modern marble a perfectly fresh layer can be exposed immediately below the surface. Furthermore, the soil matter on the surface of a forgery is generally loosely adherent, whereas the incrustation on an ancient marble can often be soaked in water for weeks without being affected. Ancient rootmarks have generally become strongly embedded in the marble; those of more recent for-

---

[53] Cf. Studniczka's article, *Neue archaische Marmorskulpturen, Falsches und Echtes,* in *Jahrbuch,* 1928, pp. 140 ff.; Richter, Metropolitan Museum, *Bulletin,* 1929, pp. 3 ff.; Ashmole, *J.H.S.,* L, 1930, pp. 99 ff.

[54] Cf. the excellent analysis by Ashmole, *op. cit.*

mation have not penetrated beneath the surface. In an ancient marble the "weathering" varies according to exposure to the elements, the sheltered parts, for instance, of pedimental figures being generally better preserved than the exposed ones; in a forgery, on the other hand, the "weathering" often covers the whole surface.

In bronzes similar conditions obtain to those in marbles. In ancient bronzes there is an opening up of the crystals and the penetration of the products of corrosion (malachite or cuprite) into the intervening spaces, whereas in modern bronzes there is no such penetration below the surface. An ancient bronze shows a lack of uniformity in the corrosion of the surface; certain areas are much more affected than others. A modern forgery is apt to have a uniform surface throughout. Furthermore, the color of ancient bronze is generally more reddish than that of modern imitations, which usually contain more of the cheaper zinc.[55]

But also in these physical analyses there are pitfalls; at least chemists and mineralogists have been known to pronounce as genuine works which later have been proved modern. And we must always remember that a forger can select an ancient piece of marble and rework it. Nevertheless the endorsement of a stylistic judgment by physical criteria is certainly helpful in doubtful cases.

If it is important to be able to detect a modern forgery, it is at least as important to recognize a Greek original. It requires the same faculty—an appreciation of the essential qualities of a Greek work of art. Since the Greeks have a tendency to confine their representations to a limited number of established types, the natural reaction in archaeological circles when something uncommon appears is to suspect it. It is unusual; therefore it cannot be right. But that is not a safe criterion. We cannot pretend to know all that was usual among the Greeks, for their output was much greater than what remains of it today; so that we must not expect to find an exact parallel for everything. A much saner method is to draw the dividing line between what is Greek in spirit and in general practice, and what is not.

One of the most interesting archaeological controversies of our time has been waged round the Boston counterpart of the "Ludovisi throne"[56] (figs. 477–479). Its authenticity has been suspected

---

[55] I am indebted to Dr. Colin G. Fink, head of the department of electro-chemistry at Columbia University, for help in the preparation of these statements.

[56] Caskey, *Catalogue*, No. 17.

by one of the best-known English archaeologists, one of the best-
known French archaeologists, and one of the best-known German
archaeologists, the first and the last attacking it in print. It is tedi-
ous to rehearse these arguments now; for though only a decade or
two old they are already out of date and the genuineness of the reliefs is now practically unquestioned. The general trend of the pro-
tests was that the expression of emotion in the faces of the figures
had no counterpart in contemporary works, the conelike shape of
the weights on the balance had no parallel, the band on the hair of
the old woman was unusual, the position of the feet strange, etc.,
etc. In many cases, such as the expression of emotion, we can quote
similar instances enough; with others it seems negligible whether we
have parallels or not. In the things that stand out—the well-knit
human bodies, the structural drapery, the harmony of the composition, the treatment of the relief—the figures are essentially Greek.
And in the paraphernalia employed there is nowhere the slightest
mistake. The most natural inference is that it is a Greek work.

The early archaic kouros in New York (fig. 18) is another important Greek work the authenticity of which was questioned when it was
first published. The arguments advanced were that it deviated from
the known archaic works in that the body leant too far forward, that
the head was too large, the neck too long, the forearms were turned
forward in an unnatural manner, that moreover the scheme of grooves
and ridges suggesting the anatomical construction of the lower legs
was peculiar and that the neckband was not tied. A close study of
these renderings showed that they deviated, it was true, from those
current in late archaic sculpture, but that they could all be paralleled
on—and were indeed typical of—early archaic figures. Especially
convincing was the discovery of several fragments of the lower legs
belonging to the Sounion group of kouroi which had the same mark-
ings as the New York kouros.[57] As these fragments were not known
when the New York kouros was purchased they could not have been
utilized by a forger.

The Standing Maiden in Berlin (figs. 267–269) also passed
through a period of suspicion. Her farouche character seemed strange
when compared with the gracious charm of the late archaic Maidens
of the Akropolis (see figs. 270–272). Now it is realized that the apparently unusual features—the compactness of the figure, the broad
forearms, the posture of the left arm, the rendering of the quasi-ver-

[57] Richter, *Kouroi,* figs. 36–40.

tical folds, the form of the necklace, the manner in which the hair is
worn in a bag, are all typical of works datable in the second quarter
of the sixth century (cf. the Akropolis Maiden 593, the Calf Bearer
[fig. 5], the relief of the Diskophoros,[58] and some of the figures on
the François vase).

There is a small piece of sculpture in the Metropolitan Museum
which is another interesting stylistic study. It is a silver pendant of
a bracelet,[59] fashioned in the form of a satyr playing the syrinx
(fig. 556), the provenance said to be South Russia. The satyr is
represented half crouching, half sitting, with the hoof of one leg
tucked under the knee of the other in a charmingly lifelike attitude;
and though only a little over one inch in height, it is modeled with
all the care and finish one might bestow on an important statue.
The curved little body, the shaggy hair on the goat's legs, every
feature of the face, all are beautifully rendered; even such a detail
as the pressing of the fingers on the pipes of the syrinx is carefully
indicated, though it can hardly be seen with the naked eye. But most
remarkable of all is the expression of the face. The satyr is evidently absorbed in the music he is making, and he is giving himself
up completely to his pleasurable sensation. It is instructive to compare it with a modern gold copy (fig. 557). The piping satyr is similar in attitude, and it is suspended also from a chain, though a much
coarser and clumsier one. But how different the conception of the two!
Where the silver Pan is unaffectedly absorbed in the music he is
making, the gold one has a sentimental expression that condemns
it immediately as non-Greek. Moreover, he is holding the syrinx to
his chin instead of to his lips, so that he could not be making any
sound. Very noticeable also is the difference between the shaggy hair
so clearly growing out of the legs of the silver satyr, sufficiently differentiated and yet headed more or less in one direction, as is the case
on living animals, and the little unattached curls going every which
way on the forgery.

When experts disagree and leading critics can be found at vari-
ance regarding the authenticity of certain works, how can such
questions be finally settled? Sometimes we are so fortunate as to be
able to discover the actual forgers. But that is rare. In many cases
the question remains open, and in these we can only say with
Gaugin: "Criticism passes, good work remains."[60]

58 Payne and Young, *Acropolis,* pl. 12.
59 Metropolitan Museum, *Bulletin,* 1922, pp. 134 f.
60 Quoted by E. Abbot on the title-page of her book, *The Great Painters.*

PART TWO
GREEK SCULPTORS

CHAPTER I

ARCHAIC PERIOD

WE have tried in the foregoing chapters to study Greek sculpture purely as an artistic manifestation. Our endeavor has been to appreciate its manifold beauty and to follow the story of its achievements by a direct consideration of the products themselves. So as not to encumber our path we have given little attention to the sculptors who produced these works—deeming their art more important than themselves. Nevertheless, a study of Greek sculpture is not complete without a realization of the personalities who helped to determine its development. To recapture in our imagination the individualities of these great men, to gauge the separate contribution of each to the history of Greek sculpture is an inspiring but also a difficult task. For to arrive at a correct appreciation we must sift carefully the evidence at hand—literary, epigraphical, and stylistic—which has become somewhat confused by many conflicting theories and doubtful attributions. In our analysis of these artists we shall endeavor to admit only such data as appear unassailable, citing where possible the original sources of our knowledge rather than the opinions of recent writers. In this way only can we build our reconstructions on a solid foundation.

We know little of the individual sculptors of the early and middle archaic periods. Ancient writers[1] give some general information about the beginnings of Greek sculpture, generally in connection with the legendary figure of Daidalos. They also mention a few sculptors by name and even assign specific works to them—for instance, Smilis of Aegina who is said to have made the wooden cult statue of Hera in Samos; Rhoikos and Theodoros of Samos (see p. 136); Melas of Chios and his descendants Mikkiades and Archermos; and Dipoinos and Skyllis of Crete and their pupils. Rarely, however, has it been possible to associate extant works with these names. A few names are known from signatures; but again only in a few instances can these signatures be connected with specific works. The inscription on the base of Kleobis and Biton (cf. fig. 17) informs us that the Argive

---

[1] Cf. Overbeck, *Schriftquellen*, nos. 74 ff., 314 ff.

(Poly)medes made them.[2] One of the seated statues from Branchidai
in the British Museum (B 273) is inscribed "Eudemos made it." Gen-
eleos signed a group of statues erected in the Heraion of Samos.[3] The
name Phaidimos is now known from three signatures—one on the base
of a kore, of which, however, only part of a sandalled foot is preserved; another on a base that may perhaps have belonged to the
stele of a youth; and a third in which he is called σοφός, skilful, but
which was found without any sculpture.[4] The names Mikkiades and
Archermos, mentioned by Pliny, appear on a base that may have
belonged to the Nike of Delos[5] (fig. 77). And so on. Scanty though
these records of individual Greek sculptors are, we can nevertheless appreciate what they collectively accomplished. They were the
leaders in that phenomenal transition from the primitive, geometrized
renderings of the eighth century to the archaic kouroi (cf. figs. 13
ff.). Diodorus (IV. 76) describes this change in picturesque language, ascribing the whole movement to Daidalos: "And in the sculptor's art he so far excelled all other men that in after times the fable
was told of him that the statues which he made were like human beings;
for they saw and walked, and, in a word, exercised every bodily function, so that his handiwork seemed to be a living being. And being the
first to give them open eyes, and parted legs, and outstretched arms,
he justly won the admiration of men: for before his time artists made
statues with closed eyes and hands hanging down and cleaving to
their sides." It is evident that the rapidity of this development was
helped by the inspiration derived from Egypt (cf. p. 51). Later,
when Greek sculpture had become more sophisticated, these early
efforts were naturally not appreciated. According to Plato,[6] for instance, sculptors of his time held "that Daidalos, were he now to be
born and to make statues such as those by which he won his fame,
would be laughed to scorn." And yet it was admitted that "a kind
of divinity rested upon his works."[7] We too when we view these early
creations have the same mingled impression of primitiveness combined with grandeur.

In the later archaic period our knowledge becomes somewhat en-

[2] Poulsen, *Delphi*, p. 95; von Premerstein, *Oest. Jahresh.*, XIII, 1910, pp. 41 ff.;
Tod, *Greek Historical Inscriptions*, pp. 4 f.

[3] Buschor, *Altsamische Standbilder*, figs. 90–101.

[4] Richter, *Archaic Attic Gravestones*, pp. 43 ff., figs. 62–65; Pezopoulos, 'Εφ. 'Αρχ.,
1937, p. 538; Karousos, 'Επιτύμβιον Χρ. Τσούντα, pp. 542 f., 572.

[5] Raubitschek, *Dedications*, p. 485; Richter, *Archaic Greek Art Against Its Historical Background*, p. 116 f.

[6] *Hipp. maj.* 282A.   [7] Pausanias II. 4. 5.

larged. We know now by name a number of sculptors who can be connected with specific works. Thus Endoios is probably the sculptor of the seated Athena in the Akropolis Museum[8] (fig. 64), for it was found at the northern slope of the Akropolis, that is, near the Erechtheion where Pausanias[9] saw a statue of Athena by Endoios; and Endoios can be dated in the period of the Akropolis statue by several inscriptions.[10] Antenor made the early group of the Tyrannicides[11] (cf. p. 199), and he signed his name on a base on which perhaps stood one of the most imposing of the Maidens in Athens[12] (fig. 273). Ageladas of Argos, the reputed teacher of Pheidias, of Myron, and of Polykleitos,[13] made a Zeus for the Messenians[14] the general composition of which appears to be reproduced on coins of Messene[15] (fig. 562). Aristokles has signed the famous stele of Aristion[16] (fig. 424) and Alxenor of Naxos one from Boetia.[17] And so on.

[8] Dickins, *Catalogue,* I, No. 625.   [9] I. 26. 4.

[10] Cf. Loewy, *Inschriften,* No. 8, and one of the statue bases found in Athens (*Arch. Anz.,* 1922, p. 59). For a recent study of Endoios cf. Raubitschek, *A.J.A.,* 1942, pp. 245 ff., and *Dedications,* pp. 491 ff.

[11] Pausanias I. 8. 5.

[12] Akropolis Museum, No. 681; Raubitschek, *A.J.A.,* XLIV, 1940, p. 58, note 2, and *Dedications,* pp. 481 ff.

[13] Suidas, Γελάδας; Tzetzes, *Chil.* VIII. 325; Schol. Aristoph., *Frogs* 504; Pliny XXXIV, 55 and 57.

[14] Pausanias IV. 33. 2.

[15] Imhoof-Blumer and Gardner, *Numismatic Commentary,* pl. P, iv and v. The date of Ageladas has given rise to much discussion.

[16] Loewy, *op. cit.,* No. 10; Richter, *Archaic Attic Gravestones,* fig. 93.

[17] Athens, National Museum, No. 39.

CHAPTER II

TRANSITIONAL PERIOD

WHEN we reach the transitional period of 480–450 a new era dawns. Greek sculpture passes from archaism to freedom and experimentation, and naturally such an epoch produced and was probably largely conditioned by great leaders. Our study of Greek sculptors as individual artistic personalities properly begins now, for only from now on have we the material on which to base it. The outstanding names of this time are Kritios (with his collaborator Nesiotes), Pythagoras, Kalamis, and Myron.

(a) Kritios

KRITIOS was probably an Athenian, for he is called Attic by Pausanias[1] and his recorded works were all produced in Athens. He signed his name with that of Nesiotes on six statue bases found on the Akropolis datable about 460 or earlier.[2] One of these inscriptions gives the name of the dedicator Epicharinos and therefore probably formed part of the work seen by Pausanias[3] and described in the words: "Among the portrait statues which stand next to the horse is that of Epicharinos, who practised the race in armor." But Kritios owes his fame, with posterity at least, to his statues of the Tyrannicides Harmodios and Aristogeiton with which he was commissioned after the original statues by Antenor had been carried off by Xerxes. The story is succinctly told by Pausanias:[4] "Not far off (in the market-place) are the statues of Harmodios and Aristogeiton, who slew Hipparchos. The one pair are the work of Kritios while the older ones were made by Antenor. When Xerxes captured Athens after the Athenians had deserted the city, he carried them away as spoils, and Antiochos afterward restored them to the Athenians." (According to Arrian[5] and Pliny[6] it was Alexander the Great who restored them to Athens, and according to Valerius Maxi-

ORIGIN

DATE

[1] VI. 3. 5.
[2] Loewy, *Inschriften*, Nos. 38–40; Raubitschek, *Dedications*, Nos. 120–123, 160, 161, pp. 513 ff.
[3] I. 23. 9.
[4] I. 8. 5.
[5] *Anabasis* III. 16. 7–8.
[6] *N.H.* XXXIV. 70.

mus[7] it was Seleukos.) The statues are referred to also by a number of other writers. They evidently enjoyed a great reputation. We know moreover the exact date in which they were set up, viz., in the archonship of Adeimantos, i.e., Olympiad 75,4 = 477 B.C.[8] They were probably of bronze, as were those by Antenor.[9] Though there is no detailed description of these statues it has been possible to identify copies of them (since groups at this period are rare and the subject is uncommon) in two advancing men which occur on a number of monuments. These consist of coins, vases, and marble reliefs[10] as well as full-size statues (cf. figs. 565 ff.), the latter of the style of the period in question. The most complete marble copies are those in the Naples Museum[11] (fig. 571[12]). Other replicas of the head of Harmodios are in the National Museum of the Terme in Rome[13] and in the Metropolitan Museum in New York[14] (figs. 565, 566); further copies of the head of Aristogeiton are the so-called Pherekydes in Madrid,[15] and two in the British Museum,[16] and in the Vatican[17] (fig. 574); there is a torso of Aristogeiton in the Boboli Gardens[18] and a recently discovered one, in the Museo Nuovo in Rome,[19] which fits the Vatican head (fig. 573).

STYLE   To appreciate the composition of this remarkable work we must remember that the Naples group has been extensively restored.[20] We shall obtain a more adequate idea of its original appearance from the copies of the group on the minor monuments, with the help of which full-size casts have been reconstructed, reproducing the original ac-

[7] II. 10 ext. 1. [8] *Marm. Par. Epoch.* I. 1. 70 ff.

[9] The lost Antenor group, formerly placed in the last decade of the sixth century, has on new evidence been dated shortly after 490; cf. Raubitschek, *Dedications,* p. 513 f.

[10] For an enumeration of these cf. Frazer, *op. cit.,* II, pp. 94 ff., and Richter, *A.J.A.,* 1928, p. 5.

[11] Ruesch, *Guida del Museo Nazionale di Napoli,* Nos. 103, 104 (6009, 6010).

[12] I am indebted to A. Maiuri, director of the Naples Museum, for permission to publish this photograph which shows the Aristogeiton as recently reconstructed—with the fourth-century head replaced by a cast of the head found in the Magazzini of the Vatican.

[13] Formerly in the Villa Mattei, cf. Arndt, *Einzelaufnahmen,* No. 115.

[14] *A.J.A.,* 1928, pp. 1 ff., figs. 1 and 2.

[15] Hübner, *Ant. Bildw. in Madrid,* p. 110, No. 176.

[16] Smith, *Catalogue,* No. 1612.

[17] Kaschnitz-Weinberg, Sculture del Magazzino del Museo Vaticano, No. 1, pls. I, II.

[18] Arndt, *op. cit.,* No. 99.

[19] Bocconi, *Collezioni Capitolini,* Supplement issued in 1948, p. 12.

[20] Of Harmodios: the plinth and tree trunk, the right leg (almost entire), the left leg from the knee down, both arms. Of Aristogeiton: the head, the left hand, small pieces of the drapery and the plinth, three toes of the left foot; the left arm wtih the drapery has been broken off and replaced.

tion (figs. 573–577). Their relative positions have given rise to much discussion;[21] but it seems clear that they stood side by side (as on the Kyzikos coin), not one behind the other. The group forms an amazingly vigorous composition, introducing a number of innovations which mark an advance over older striding figure (cf. p. 65), such as the position of the right arm in the Harmodios, with the forearm brought over the head, which imparts a new energy to the whole figure.[22] Lucian's[23] estimate of the style of the school of Kritios and Nesiotes as "closely knit and sinewy and stiff and severe in outline" is based on the conceptions of a later age. Compared with what went before them the Tyrannicides show an astonishing progress. On the strength of this work Kritios[24] must be classed as a leader in the new era. His greatness and the appreciation in which he was held are further indicated by the fact that he was the founder of a school and had several distinguished pupils.[25]

Other works have been tentatively attributed to Kritios on the strength of their general resemblance to the Tyrannicides, especially the Youth in the Akropolis Museum[26] (fig. 30). But even the latter has not quite the same clear demarcation of the muscles or the swing of the composition which characterizes both the Harmodios and the Aristogeiton. It is better to build our estimate of Kritios solely on these two well-authenticated works.

(b) Pythagoras

PYTHAGORAS was a Samian by birth, for he signs himself Πυθαγό- **ORIGIN**
ρας Σάμιος in the inscription on the base of a portrait of Euthymos the boxer;[27] and Pliny[28] and Pausanias[29] refer to him as "of Rhegion"; so that he probably was one of the emigrants who left Samos after its fall in 496 B.C. for Zankle and thereby became subject to Anaxilas of Rhegion.[30] He is said to have been the pupil of Klear-

---

[21] For recent theories cf. Schefold, *Jahrbuch*, LII, 1937, pp. 33 ff.; Buschor, *Die Tyrannenmördar*, pp. 8 ff.; Bakalakis, *Oest. Jahr.*, XXXIII, 1941, p. 26.

[22] Cf. Richter, *A.J.A.*, 1928, pp. 1–8.   [23] *Rhet. Praecept.* 9.

[24] Since Kritios is several times mentioned by ancient writers without Nesiotes he has been thought to be the more important of the two; but cf. Raubitschek, *op. cit.*, p. 514.

[25] Cf. Pausanias VI. 3. 5; Pliny XXXIV. 85; Lucian, *Rhet. Praecept.* 9; Pfuhl, *Die Schule des Kritios*, in *Jahrbuch*, 1926, p. 48.

[26] Dickins, *Catalogue*, No. 698.   [27] Loewy, *Inschriften*, No. 23.

[28] E.g., *N.H.* XXXIV. 59.   [29] E.g., VI. 18. 1.

[30] This twofold origin is probably responsible for the confusion which led Pliny (*N.H.* XXXIV. 59) and Diogenes Laertios (VIII. 46) to distinguish two sculptors, one of Samos, the other of Rhegion.

DATE　chos of Rhegion.[31] His date can be determined by the facts that he made a statue of the runner Astylos,[32] in celebration of his first victory at Olympia (488), that his statue of the boxer Euthymos was set up after the latter's third victory in 472,[33] and that there were statues by him of the wrestler Leontiskos of Messene[34] (456), of the hoplite-runner Mnaseas of Kyrene[35] (456), and of Kratisthenes of Kyrene[36] (448). So his activity appears to lie in the period during STYLE　and following the Persian wars. In his work he is said to have combined a certain advance in naturalism—Pliny[37] speaks of him as "the first to represent sinews and veins and to bestow attention on the treatment of hair"—with a new sense for harmonious composition: "He is thought to have been the first to aim at rhythm and proportion."[38] In other words he recognized and dealt with the two great needs and tendencies of his time; and his achievements brought him great fame and recognition, for he is listed with the foremost Greek sculptors by Pliny[39] and was judged to have surpassed even WORKS　Myron with a statue of a pankratiast dedicated at Delphi.[40] The subjects of his works enumerated by ancient writers include—in addition to the usual victorious athletes[41] and a four-horse chariot group of Kratisthenes the Kyrenean with himself and a Nike mounted on the car[42]—such individual creations as "a lame man at Syracuse the pain of whose wound seems to be felt by the spectator,"[43] "a magnificent bronze group at Tarentum of Europa carried away by the bull,"[44] "Apollo transfixing the serpent with his arrows,"[45] and "Eteokles and Polyneikes killing each other."[46] In his attempt at new compositions and his novel interest in emotion he was again a child of his time and doubtless a leader in this new movement.

With this somewhat general information it is not surprising that

[31] Pausanias III. 17. 6.
[32] Pliny, *N.H.* XXXIV. 59; Pausanias VI. 13. 1.
[33] Loewy, *Inschriften*, No. 23; Pausanias VI. 6. 4–6; Grenfell and Hunt, *Oxyrhynchus Papyri*, II, p. 88, col. I, lines 12 and 25.
[34] Pausanias VI. 4. 3; Grenfell and Hunt, *op. cit.*, II, p. 89, col. II, line 2.
[35] Pausanias VI. 13. 7 and 18. 1; Pliny, *N.H.* XXXIV. 59.
[36] Pausanias VI. 18. 1.　　　　　　　[37] *N.H.* XXXIV. 59.
[38] Diogenes Laert. VIII. 46.　　　　[39] *N.H.* XXXIV. 49.
[40] *N.H.* XXXIV. 59.
[41] Besides the references quoted above, cf. Pausanias VI. 7. 10 (statue of Dromeus), Pausanias VI. 6. 1 (statue of Protolaos).
[42] Pausanias VI. 18. 1.　　　　　　　[43] Pliny, *N.H.* XXXIV. 59.
[44] Varro, *L.L.* V. 31.　　　　　　　 [45] Pliny, *N.H.* XXXIV. 59.
[46] Tatian, *c. Graec.* 54.

it has not been possible to identify with certainty any of his works with extant statues. There has of course been no lack of attributions. The "Omphalos Apollo" (figs. 36, 37) has been thought to reproduce his statue of the boxer Euthymos,[47] the Valentini torso in Rome his lame Philoktetes,[48] a bronze statuette of a kithara player in the Hermitage[49] (fig. 67) his lyre-player,[50] and a group of Europa and the bull in the British Museum[51] his representation of this subject.[52] Several bronze statuettes have been attributed to him for their "rhythm and fine proportion."[53] But tempting though it be to connect some of the few statues we have of this period with one of its most prominent artists, we must admit that we are not adding to our knowledge thereby. We may make a few guesses and regard them as such; we may surmise that the influence of Pythagoras' creations was widespread and survived in many later representations: that, for instance, the wounded Philoktetes on a later fifth- or early fourth-century gem in the Louvre[54] (fig. 564) is reminiscent of the sculptor's famous statue; or that the fifth-century terracotta statuettes of Europa[55] give us some idea of the harmonious composition of his group; or again, that the Apollo killing the serpent on the coins of Kroton[56] (fig. 563) is based in a general way on Pythagoras' design. But these are all conjectures, and unfortunately do not enable us actually to realize the personality of one of the greatest and most original of Greek sculptors.

(c) Kalamis

EQUALLY tantalizing is our ignorance of Kalamis, a slightly younger contemporary of Pythagoras. We do not even know his ORIGIN origin. His works were widely scattered, but he was active also in Athens, and had there some important commissions;[57] so it is sometimes assumed that he was an Athenian. His date may be deduced DATE from the following recorded facts: He made "race horses with boys

[47] Waldstein, *J.H.S.*, I, pp. 168 f.
[48] Waldhauer, *Pythagoras of Rhegium*, pp. 73 ff., figs. 16–18.
[49] *Ibid.*, pp. 69 ff., figs. 13–15.   [50] Pliny, *N.H.* XXXIV. 59.
[51] Cf. Smith, *Catalogue*, III, pl. 1, No. 1535.   [52] Waldhauer, *op. cit.*, pp. 63 ff.
[53] Langlotz, *Fruehgriechische Bildhauerschulen*, pp. 147 ff. Another recent attribution is an akrolithic statue of Apollo found at Cirò in South Italy (cf. Della Seta, *Italia Antica* [1928], p. 157, fig. 156).
[54] Furtwängler, *Antike Gemmen*, pl. XXXI, 10; cf. also pl. XXI, 20–24.
[55] Cf. Metropolitan Museum, *Handbook* (1930), p. 142, fig. 100; the similar figure in the British Museum, No. C 184, has a head which does not belong to it.
[56] Head, *Historia num.*, p. 96, fig. 54.   [57] Cf. pp. 203, 204.

seated on them for a chariot group commemorating the Olympic victories of Hieron, tyrant of Syracuse."[58] The victory was won in 468; but since Hieron died the following year, "the debt was paid to the god by Deinomenes, the son of Hieron,"[59] that is, the group must be after 467. He was employed by Pindar (c. 522–c. 442) for a statue of Zeus Ammon at Thebes.[60] In Quintilian's[61] Canon of Sculptors he is placed between Hegesias and Myron. Pausanias states that he made a statue of Apollo[62] the Averter of Ill (Alexikakos) and that this epithet was given to the god "because he put an end to the plague which afflicted them at the time of the Peloponnesian war by means of an oracle from Delphi."[63] The great plague of the Peloponnesian war was so terrible an experience that it seems to have wiped out all memories of former visitations. We may infer therefore that Pausanias here makes this common error; for 430–429 would be an improbably late date for Kalamis. All the other evidence[64] points to 475–450 as his most flourishing period.

STYLE　　We have some valuable, though again rather general information regarding his style. Quintilian[65] and Cicero[66] both estimate his statues as less stiff and rigid than those of Kallon, Hegesias, and Kanachos, but not so supple as those of Myron. That is, his work retains only slight traces of archaism but has not yet reached the freedom of the compositions of Myron. Lucian[67] in his description of the Panthea, the ideal woman which is to combine the excellencies of all the best works of art, wants Kalamis and his Sosandra "to adorn her with reverence and supply the noble and unconscious smile of the goddess, and the simple and orderly arrangement of the drapery, except that she shall not have her head covered."[68] The refinement of his work is also brought out in the passage of Dionysios

---

[58] Pausanias VI. 12. 1.   [59] Ibid.

[60] Pausanias IX. 16. 1.   [61] XII. 10. 7.

[62] For the temple of Apollo Patroos in the Kerameikos.   [63] Pausanias I. 3. 4.

[64] Pausanias' statement (X. 19. 4) that Praxias, a pupil of Kalamis, worked on the pediments of the temple of Apollo at Delphi presumably refers to a later Kalamis; for this temple completed c. 510 was not destroyed till c. 373, and Praxias is named as son of Lysimachos in an inscription from Oropos datable a little before 338 B.C. (Loewy, Inschriften, No. 127a). On the younger Kalamis cf. Studniczka, Kalamis, pp. 5–14; Anti, 'Calamide,' Atti di R. Istituto Veneto, LXXXII, pp. 1105 ff.; Raubitschek, Dedications, p. 506.

[65] Inst. orat. XII. 10. 7: Nam duriora et Tuscanicis proxima Callon atque Hegesias, iam minus rigida Calamis, molliora adhuc supra dictis Myron fecit.

[66] Brut. 18. 70.

[67] Εἰκόνες 6. Cf. also his Dialogues of the Hetairai III. 2.

[68] ἡ Σώσανδρα δὲ καὶ Κάλαμις αἰδοῖ κοσμήσουσιν αὐτήν, καὶ τὸ μειδίαμα σεμνὸν καὶ λεληθὸς ὥσπερ τὸ ἐκείνης ἔσται, καὶ τὸ εὐσταλὲς δὲ καὶ κόσμιον τῆς ἀναβολῆς παρὰ τῆς Σωσάνδρας πλὴν ὅτι ἀκατακάλυπτος αὕτη ἔσται τὴν κεφαλήν.

of Halikarnassos[69] in which he compares "the oratory of Isokrates to the art of Polykleitos and Pheidias with its grandeur and breadth of style and sublimity, and that of Lysias to the art of Kalamis and Kallimachos with its delicacy and grace." He was a great sculptor of horses and had indeed no equal in this field.[70] Praxiteles is said to have placed a charioteer of his own on a four-horse chariot of Kalamis "lest the artist who excelled in representing horses should be thought to have failed in his treatment of the human figure.[71]

The most famous of Kalamis' works seems to have been the Sosandra referred to with so much praise by Lucian. Since Lucian[72] speaks of her as "seen by all who ascended the Akropolis," it has been suggested that she was identical with another work by Kalamis —a statue of Aphrodite dedicated by Kallias[73] which Pausanias saw at the entrance of the Akropolis.[74] A fragment of a base which was recently found in the Agora with parts of the names Kallias and Kalamis may have belonged to this dedication.[74a] Among his figures of deities were two statues of Apollo—the Apollo Alexikakos in the Kerameikos at Athens[75] and a colossal statue, thirty cubits in height, at Apollonia on the Black Sea,[76] perhaps reproduced on coins of that city[77] (fig. 560). Pausanias[78] mentions as a work of Kalamis a "Hermes carrying a ram on his shoulders" set up by the people of Tanagra. The statue commemorated the averting of a plague by the god's carrying a ram round the city wall; and a Hermes Kriophoros appears on Roman coins of that city[79] (fig. 561), evidently reproducing

WORKS

---

[69] *De Isocr.* 542 R.

[70] Pliny, *N.H.* XXXIV. 71; and Propertius III. 9 and 10.

[71] Pliny, *N.H.* XXXIV. 71. To our taste such a combination of styles would be a doubtful improvement. The suggestion that the reference is to the elder Praxiteles is open to the objection that Kalamis was at least as able a sculptor of the human figure as he.

[72] Εἰκόνες 4.

[73] Kallias was a brother-in-law of Kimon and is said to have won his wife Elpinike by paying fifty talents to free Kimon from arrest for a debt incurred by his father. It is suggested that Kallias' Aphrodite was nicknamed Sosandra (Saviour of Men, instead of Soteira, her usual epithet) as a result of this incident (cf. Benndorf, *Das Cultusbild der Athena Nike*, p. 45).

[74] Pausanias I. 23. 2.   [75] Pausanias I. 3. 4.

[74a] Raubitschek, *Dedications*, No. 136 and p. 507.

[76] Strabo VII. 319; Pliny, *N.H.* XXXIV. 39; Appian, *Illyr.* 30. A third statue of Apollo is attributed by Pliny, *N.H.* XXXVI. 36 to "Kalamis, the engraver" (*caelator*), the artist of two beautifully wrought cups (Pliny, *N.H.* XXXIV. 47), probably the same artist; cf. Richter, *A.J.A.*, XLV, 1941, p. 382.

[77] Pick, *Jahrbuch*, 1898, pls. 10, 26–28; Reisch, *Oest. Jahresh.*, IX, 1906, p. 222, fig. 64.

[78] IX. 22. 1.

[79] Imhoof-Blumer and Gardner, *Numismatic Commentary*, pl. X, Nos. XI–XII.

this composition: unfortunately the coins are too badly preserved to give us a clear idea. We also hear of a Dionysos with a Triton at Tanagra,[80] a wingless Victory at Athens,[81] and a Zeus Ammon at Thebes.[82] He was a precursor of Pheidias in the art of producing gold and ivory figures with an Asklepios at Sikyon[83] described as "beardless, holding a sceptre in one hand and in the other a cone of the cultivated pine." A statue of Alkmene set up at Delphi "showed him a master also in the art of representing human beings."[84] A Hermione,[85] bronze boys extending their right hands in prayer,[86] an Erinys,[87] horses,[88] and chariot groups[89] complete the list of his works.

Unfortunately none of these sculptures can be identified with extant statues. The "Omphalos Apollo" (figs. 36, 37) has been thought to reproduce his Apollo Alexikakos; the "Penelope" in the Vatican[90] (fig. 68) has been associated with his name; and his Hermes Kriophoros has been recognized by some authorities in a statue at Wilton House[91] and in a relief in Athens;[92] all, however, on slender evidence.[93] The horse in the Metropolitan Museum (figs. 349, 350) and the Poseidon found off Cape Artemision[94] may give us some idea of the beauty of his products in bronze; and such works as the girl with pigeons in New York (fig. 426) may help us to picture the "simplicity and orderliness" (τὸ εὐσταλὲς δὲ καὶ κόσμιον) of the drapery of the Sosandra. But so far we must be content to visualize Kalamis in a general way as a celebrated artist of the transitional period, distinguished for his grace and refinement rather than for the originality of his poses; capable, however, of producing colossal works; working in bronze and marble, as well as in gold and ivory; and a great sculptor of horses. It is a vague picture, but

[80] Pausanias IX. 20. 4. By some identified with the figure on coins of Tanagra, Imhoof-Blumer and Gardner, *Numismatic Commentary*, pl. X, Nos. VII and VIII, which, however, appears to be of a later style.

[81] Pausanias V. 26. 6.

[82] Pausanias IX. 16. 1; commissioned by Pindar, see above.

[83] Pausanias II. 10. 3.   [84] Pliny, *N.H.* XXXIV. 71.

[85] Pausanias X. 16. 4.   [86] Pausanias V. 25. 5.

[87] Schol. Aeschin. *Timarch.* 747 R.   [88] Pausanias VI. 12. 1.

[89] Pliny, *N.H.* XXXIV. 71   [90] Helbig, *Führer*,[3] I, No. 89.

[91] Michaelis, *Marbles in Great Britain*, p. 702, No. 144; Clarac, IV, 658, 1545 B.

[92] Collignon, *Histoire*, I, fig. 207.

[93] E.g., the "Omphalos Apollo" has also been attributed to Pythagoras (cf. p. 201); on the coins of Hermes Kriophoros the god is beardless, while in the marble figures he is bearded.

[94] Metropolitan Museum, *Bulletin*, 1923, pp. 89 ff.; Karouzos, Δελτ. Ἀρχ., XIII, 1933, pp. 93 f.

more definite assertions would only blot out the faint traces we have.

(d) Myron

THE greatest sculptor of the transitional period was Myron of Eleutherai, a town on the boundary of Boeotia and Attica.[95] According to Pliny[96] he was a pupil of Ageladas and a rival of Pythagoras. He made a statue of Timanthes of Kleonai[97] who won an Olympic victory in 456 B.C.[98] and two statues of Lykinos of Sparta[99] who won a chariot race about 448.[100] An inscribed base[101] placed at the entrance of the Propylaia and dating from about 446 bears the name of "Lykios of Eleutherai, the son of Myron" as the author of the statues. So that the period of Myron's activity seems to lie between 480 and 445 B.C.

Fortunately we are not dependent for our appreciation of Myron on general statements in ancient writings. It has been possible to recognize copies of two of his works in extant statues, and we can thereby obtain a clear conception of his style.

The identification of the Diskobolos we owe to Lucian's[102] description: "Surely you do not speak of the quoit-thrower who stoops in the attitude of one who is making his cast, turning round toward the hand that holds the quoit, and bending the other knee gently beneath him, like one who will rise erect as he hurls the quoit? No, for that quoit-thrower of whom you speak is one of the works of Myron." By this detailed account—so different from the brief, generalized statements in which ancient writers mostly refer to Greek sculpture—we can identify a splendid composition existing in several Roman copies as the work of Myron (fig. 578[103]). The marble statue, formerly in the possession of the Lancelotti family in Rome,[104] is the only example with the original head, turned round toward the hand with the quoit, just as Lucian describes. Other good replicas are: a statue from Tivoli in the British Museum;[105] a

95 Pliny, *N.H.* XXXIV. 57.   96 *Loc. cit.*
97 Pausanias VI. 8. 4.
98 Grenfell and Hunt, *Oxyrhynchus Papyri,* II, p. 89, col. II, line 4.
99 Pausanias VI. 2. 2.
100 Grenfell and Hunt, *op. cit.,* II, p. 90, col. II, line 34.
101 Δελτ. 'Αρχ., 1889, p. 179; Stuart Jones, *Selected Passages,* No. 147.
102 *Philopseud.* 18.
103 This illustration is taken from a composite cast of the Lancelotti head, the Vatican body, and some new restorations, especially the left arm.
104 Cf. Brunn-Bruckmann, *Denkmäler,* pl. 256.
105 Smith, *Catalogue,* I, No. 250.

statue from the same locality in the Vatican;[106] a fine torso from Castel Porziano in the National Museum of the Terme, Rome[107] (fig. 581); a torso, restored as a warrior, in the Capitoline Museum in Rome;[108] a bronze statuette with the head worked in a later style in Munich[109] (Figs. 579, 580); and representations on gems[110] (fig. 583). If we remember that the pose of the Diskobolos[111] has no antecedents, we shall realize what a courageous innovator Myron was. In his represen-

Fig. 583. Diskobolos, on an engraved gem (enlarged)

tations of a violent action he chose not the striding or crouching or falling types worked out in pedimental sculptures, as some of his contemporaries did,[112] but an entirely novel composition. And the effect of this twisted body in a momentary pose is not restless (at least if seen in full-front view as doubtless intended) but singularly harmonious. We could have no better example, in fact, of the unimportance of the actual subject in a work of art for its quieting effect, and of the significant part played by "symmetry and proportion." The criticism of Quintilian,[112a] "What can be more strained and artificial in its attitude than the famous quoit-thrower of Myron?" only applies to the actual subject; and his defense of it on the ground of its "novelty and difficulty" is not necessary. The Diskobolos is an artistic creation of the first rank, quite independent of the period in which it was produced. The harmony which we note in the composition is also apparent in the modeling. Though it is much more naturalistic than in archaic sculpture, the pattern scheme is still marked, and each group of muscles forms a decorative design interrelated with the next group. The features are beautifully modeled in

106 Helbig, *Führer*,³ I, No. 826; cf. also the fragment No. 788.

107 *Ibid.*, II, No. 1363.   108 Stuart Jones, *Catalogue*, No. 50.

109 Sieveking, in Brunn-Bruckmann, *Denkmäler*, pl. 681.

110 Furtwängler, *Antike Gemmen*, pls. XLIV, 26, 27, and LXVI, 8.

111 For some polemics regarding the details of this pose, especially the position of the left foot, cf. Schröder, *Zum Diskobol des Myron*, Strassburg, 1913; Sieveking, in Brunn-Bruckmann, *op. cit.*, text to pl. 681; and again Schröder, *Arch. Anz.*, 1920, pp. 61 ff.

112 E.g., Kritios and Nesiotes, the striding type in the Tyrannicides (p. 198); Pythagoras, the crouching type (?) in his Apollo killing the serpent (p. 201); and Kresilas, the falling type in his Volneratus deficiens (?) (p. 233).

112a *Inst. orat.* II. 13. 8.

this same severe, harmonious style, while the hair is indicated by little ringlets lying close to the skull in the fashion of earlier days.

The second identified work of Myron is the Marsyas. Pliny[113] *Marsyas* describes it: Fecit et canem et discobolum et Perseum et pristas et satyrum admirantem tibias et Minervam, "a satyr gazing in wonderment at the flutes and Athena"—unless Minervam is the object of fecit, in which case it might be a single statue, not part of a group with the Satyr. The combination of the two in one composition, however, is made likely by Pausanias'[114] mention of such a group on the Akropolis of Athens: "Here Athena is represented in the act of striking[115] the Satyr Marsyas, because he took up the flutes when the goddess wished them to be thrown aside." Groups of Athena and Marsyas answering such descriptions occur on Roman coins of Athens[116] (fig. 588), on a red-figured oinochoë in the Berlin Museum[117] (fig. 587), and on a marble vase in Athens[118] (fig. 586). From the attitudes of the figures on these representations copies in the round have been recognized. The best examples of the Marsyas are two statues in the Lateran,[119] one in fine preservation, except for the missing arms (fig. 584).[120] A bronze statuette in the British Museum[121] (fig. 592) appears to be a later version of this theme. The arms are preserved but do not correspond exactly to the attitude on the coin representations, for the right hand is brought to the head, a change which impairs the swing of the composition. A good Roman replica of the head is in the Barracco Museum[122] (fig. 585). More recently the Athena has been identified in a statue also preserved in several replicas, of which the best is in Frankfurt[123] (figs. 589–591). Another copy or adaptation is in the Boboli Gardens in Florence and copies of the head are in the Albertinum, Dresden, and in the Vati-

---

[113] *N.H.* XXXIV. 57. [114] I. 24. 1.

[115] παίουσα, perhaps "on the point of striking"; or the text may be corrupt for ἐπιοῦσα, "advancing upon," or, better, ἀπιοῦσα, "just turning round before leaving (P. Jacobsthal).

[116] Cf. Imhoof-Blumer and Gardner, *Numismatic Commentary*, pl. Z, Nos. XX, XXI.

[117] Hirschfeld, *Winckelmannsprogramm*, 1872; Furtwängler, *Beschreibung der Vasensammlung*, No. 2418.

[118] National Museum, No. 127; Heydemann, *Arch. Ztg.*, 1873, p. 96; Kekulé, *Arch. Ztg.*, 1875, pl. 8.

[119] Cf. Helbig, *Führer*³, II, No. 1179; Carpenter, *Memoirs of the American Academy in Rome*, XVIII, pl. 6, c.

[120] These used to be restored as playing the castanets; but were removed in 1925.

[121] Walters, *Select Bronzes*, pl. XVI.

[122] *Catalogue of the Barracco Museum*, pls. 37, 37a.

[123] Dragendorff, *Antike Denkmäler*, III (1909–1911), p. 8, pl. 9.

can.[124] The attitude is that of the goddess on the coins, with the left leg placed sidewise and backward and the head turned to the left. This unusual pose and the fact that the style is that of the period make the identification probable.

The Marsyas, like the Diskobolos, is a splendid composition, full of action and yet beautifully harmonious. Its rhythmical movement and sturdy modeling mark it as the conception of a great artist. The attitude of starting back (not falling) is again a novel one in Greek art though not so bold an innovation as that of the Diskobolos. In the Marsyas Myron's originality is further shown in the individualistic treatment of the lean body with its restless modeling (note, e.g., the accentuation of the muscles of the serratus magnus and the comparative absence of the "pattern scheme"), and above all in the expression of surprise in the wild face with its oblique ridges on the forehead and its shaggy hair and beard—in striking contrast to the quiet severity of the aristocratic Diskobolos. There have been attempts to combine the Marsyas and the Athena in a composition similar to that on the coins. Sieveking's reconstruction is perhaps the most satisfactory (fig. 593). The two figures with their contrasting attitudes make a harmonious design comparable to the rhythmical compositions in the vase-paintings of the period. (The right hand of Marsyas was perhaps more extended, as in fig. 587.) The Athena, as she appears at least in the Roman copies we have, may seem tame compared to the Marsyas. But if she is not so grand in conception, she has the quiet dignity befitting a goddess; and the sidewise turn of her body lends variety to the traditional pose.

Ladas

Among the other works of Myron mentioned by ancient writers our interest is aroused particularly by the statue of Ladas, a victorious runner at Olympia. A vivid description of it appears in the *Anthology:*[125] "As once thou wast, instinct with life, when thou didst fly from Thymos swift as the wind, on tiptoe, with every muscle at full strain—even so did Myron fashion thee in bronze, and stamp on thy whole frame eager yearning for the crown that Pisa gives." "He is full of hope, and on his lips is seen the breath that comes from the hollow flanks; anon the bronze will leap to seize the

[124] Arndt in *Antike Plastik, Walther Amelung zum 60ten Geburtstag*, pp. 11–12, fig. 9; Picard, *Manuel*, II, p. 240, fig. 108; Kaschnitz-Weinberg, *Sculture del Magazzino del Museo Vaticano*, No. 59, pl. xviii; Hermann, *Verzeichnis der antiken Originalwerke der Skulpturensammlung zu Dresden*, 1925, No. 48.

[125] Anth. Plan. IV. 54.

crown, and the base will hold it no longer; see how art is swifter than the wind." Here again Myron attempted a momentary pose, full of action and life; and we must regret exceedingly the apparently total loss of this work, comparable doubtless in boldness and vigor to the Diskobolos and the Marsyas.

The other works we hear of as by Myron—deities, heroes, and athletes—are unfortunately mere names to us now: a Hekate at Aigina;[126] a colossal group of Zeus, Athena, and Herakles in Samos;[127] two figures of Apollo, one at Ephesos,[128] another at Agrigentum;[129] a Dionysos at Orchomenos;[130] a statue of Herakles at Heius,[131] and one shown in the Circus Maximus in Rome;[132] a Perseus "after his exploit with Medusa" on the Akropolis at Athens;[133] an Erechtheus;[134] and a number of statues of victorious athletes.[135] But the work of Myron which made the greatest appeal in antiquity was his bronze cow which stood on the Akropolis at Athens[136] and of whose lifelike quality we have many testimonies.[137] Men and animals alike mistook her for real, the calves went up to her to be suckled, the lions to devour her. She appeared to have breath inside her (ἔμπνοος) and seemed about to bellow (μηκήσεται). We may be sure that her beauty was not due so much to the realism as to that quality of design and vigor of conception which give life and distinction to Myron's work.

Other Works

Animals

Besides the cow we hear of four bulls[138] and a dog[139] by Myron, so that he must have been greatly interested in animal sculpture. Moreover, several chased silver vases are ascribed to Myron,[140] showing the versatility of the man.[141]

---

[126] Pausanias II. 30. 2.   [127] Strabo XIV. 637b.

[128] Pliny, *N.H.* XXXIV. 58.   [129] Cicero, *In Verrem* IV. 43. 93.

[130] Pausanias IX. 30. 1; *Anth. Gr.* IV. 173. 270 (*Plan.* IV. 257).

[131] Cicero, *op. cit.,* IV. 3. 5.   [132] Pliny, *N.H.* XXXIV. 57.

[133] Pausanias I. 23. 7.

[134] Pausanias IX. 30. 1. Perhaps part of the group of Erechtheus and Eumolpos fighting each other mentioned by Pausanias I. 27. 4, as on the Akropolis.

[135] Pausanias VI. 2. 2, 8. 4, 8. 5, 13. 2.

[136] It was later removed to the Forum Pacis at Rome.

[137] Cf. Overbeck, *Schriftquellen,* 550–591. It is thought by some to be reproduced on the denarius of Augustus (Gabrici, *Studi e materiali di arch. e numismatica,* II, 1902, p. 168, fig. 20).

[138] Prop. II. 31. 7.

[139] Pliny, *N.H.* XXXIV. 57: "canem"; Benndorf emends Ladam.

[140] Martial IV. 39. 1; VI. 92; VIII. 51; Stat., *Silv.* I. 3. 50; Phaedr., *Fab.* V, prologue.

[141] It has been thought that this Myron and the *caelator Kalamis* (see p. 203, note 76) were later artists; but cf. *A.J.A.,* XLV, 1941, p. 382. It is in line with ancient—as well as Renaissance—tradition for an artist to have several fields for his activities. The

STYLE   Some critical estimates of Myron's art by ancient writers are of
interest. Pliny[142] sums up his chief characteristics: "He is thought
to have been the first to extend lifelike representation in art. He
was more versatile than Polykleitos, and more studious of symmetry.[143] Yet he too expended his care on the bodily frame, and did
not represent the emotions of the mind. His treatment too of the hair
of the head and body showed no advance on the rude attempts of
early art." Petronius refers to Myron as the one "who could almost
catch the souls of men and beasts and enchain them in bronze."[144]
He is regularly mentioned with Polykleitos, Lysippos, Praxiteles,
and Pheidias as among the most eminent sculptors of Greece.[145] His
works are considered by Cicero[146] as not yet realistic but nevertheless
beautiful, by Quintilian[147] as suppler and more advanced than those
of Kalamis. He is said to have used the Delian composition of bronze
as against the Aiginetan one employed by Polykleitos.[148]

     In other words, ancient writers agree very much with our own
estimate of Myron as a great innovator, who created lifelike yet
rhythmical renderings, slightly touched with archaisms, and whose
chief interest was the human body in a variety of beautiful postures.
He is the great representative of the period of experimentation, and
helped to determine the character of this important epoch.

ATTRIBUTIONS   Based on this definite knowledge of the works and character of
Myron there have been many attributions of extant statues as copies
of his works. Furtwängler lists nineteen such in his *Masterpieces*.[149]
The most important are the beautiful heads identified as Perseus,[150]
in the Museo Nuovo in Rome[151] and in the British Museum,[152] copies

Myron who made the drunken old woman (Pliny, *N.H.* XXXVI. 32) is described as
"qui in aere laudatur" (= the celebrated bronze caster) and is perhaps of later date.

  142 Pliny, *N.H.* XXXIV. 58: "Primus hic multiplicasse veritatem videtur, nume-
rosior in arte quam Polyclitus (et) in symmetria diligentior, et ipse tamen corporum
tenus curiosus animi sensus non expressisse, capillum quoque et pubem non emen-
datius fecisse quam rudis antiquitas instituisset."

  143 Several emendations have been suggested to prevent Pliny from saying that
Myron was more interested in symmetry than Polykleitos, the great student of pro-
portion. But that Myron's work was also beautifully rhythmical we learn from his
Diskobolos and his Marsyas.

  144 *Satyr.* 88.

  145 Cicero, *De oratore* III. 7. 26; Auctor ad Herenn. IV. 6; Lucian, *Somn.* 8; etc.

  146 *Brut.* 18. 70.   147 *Inst. orat.* XII. 10. 7.

  148 Pliny, *N.H.* XXXIV. 9. Chemical analyses have shown that there is a great
variety in the alloys of ancient bronzes, so that it is quite possible that different
compositions were favored by individual artists.

  149 Pages 165 ff.   150 Furtwängler, *Masterpieces,* pp. 197 ff.

  151 Formerly in the Antiquarium Comunale; Furtwängler, *op. cit.,* p. 198, fig. 83.

  152 Smith, *Catalogue,* III, No. 1743.

of a distinguished work of this period;[153] the Cassel Apollo;[154] the resting Herakles, of which reproductions are in the Boston and Ashmolean Museums[155] (fig. 39), and the boxer adjusting protective straps on his head (reconstructed by Amelung).[156] But we have no conclusive evidence to make any of these theories realities, and so we will not dim our clear picture of Myron with them.

In addition to these outstanding personalities there were of course other prominent sculptors. A number are mentioned by ancient writers who ascribe various works to them; for instance, Kanachos and Aristokles of Sikyon, and Kallon and Onatas of Aegina.[157] They too worked in this epoch of experimentation and doubtless their sculptures showed interest in lively action and harmonious composition. We cannot connect their names with any extant sculptures, but at least the signatures of Kallon (Kalon) and Onatas have survived on bases found on the Akropolis.[158]

[153] A Perseus is also attributed to Pythagoras.
[154] Furtwängler, *Masterpieces*, pp. 190 ff.
[155] Cf. Caskey, *Catalogue*, No. 64; Lippold, *Antike Plastik, Walther Amelung zum 60ten Geburtstag*, pp. 127 ff.; Ashmolean Museum *Guide*, p. 93.
[156] Bieber, *Jahrbuch*, XLII, 1927, pp. 153 ff. For further attributions cf. V. H. Poulsen, *Acta Arch.*, 8, 1937, pp. 136 ff.
[157] Cf. Overbeck, *Schriftquellen*, Nos. 403–428.
[158] Loewy, *Inschriften*, No. 27; Kirchner, *Imagines*, No. 16; Raubitschek, *Dedications*, Nos. 85, 236, pp. 508 f., 520 ff.

CHAPTER III

SECOND HALF OF FIFTH CENTURY B.C.

(a) Pheidias

WE know the origin of Pheidias from his own signature on the statue of Zeus at Olympia: "Pheidias, the son of Charmides, the Athenian, made me."[1] He is said to have been the pupil of Hegias[2] and Ageladas.[3] Pliny gives as his chief date the 83d Olympiad, that is 448–444 B.C.,[4] a natural period to select, since during it was begun the work on the Parthenon. He made a gold and ivory statue of Athena at Pellene in Achaia[5] before his statue of Athena Parthenos on the Akropolis of Athens, and he was commissioned with several works to celebrate the victory over the Persians,[6] showing that in the second quarter of the fifth century B.C. he was already a recognized artist. His great opportunity came soon after the middle of the fifth century when Perikles, in 449, assumed power in Athens and gave him control over his artistic undertakings.[7] The next fifteen years were a time of ceaseless activity on the little hill of the Akropolis. On the southern slope arose the Odeion founded by Perikles; the Parthenon was begun in 447–446 and in 438 the colossal temple statue of Athena by Pheidias was dedicated; by 432 the pediment sculptures were in place and the whole temple complete;[8] Mnesikles built the Propylaia in five years (437–432). Plutarch gives us a graphic description:[9] "As the buildings rose stately in size and unsurpassed in form and grace, the workmen vied with each other that the quality of

ORIGIN

DATE AND LIFE

---

[1] Pausanias V. 10. 2. [2] Dion Chrysost., *Orat.* 55. 1. 282 (as emended).
[3] Schol. Aristoph., *Frogs* 504; Tzetzes, *Chil.* VII. 929.
[4] *N.H.* XXXIV. 49. Floruit autem (Pheidias) olympiade LXXXIII, circiter CCC nostrae urbis anno.
[5] Pausanias VII. 27. 2.
[6] A bronze Athena at Athens (Pausanias I. 28. 2), a group at Delphi (Pausanias X. 10. 1), and an Athena at Plataia (Pausanias IX. 4. 1).
[7] Plutarch, *Perikles* XIII. 4: "His [Perikles'] general manager and general overseer was Pheidias, although the several works had great architects and artists besides." And XIII. 9: "Everything almost was under his [Pheidias'] charge, and all the artists and artisans, as I have said, were under his superintendence, owing to his friendship with Perikles."
[8] Cf. p. 230. [9] *Op. cit.,* XIII. 1.

their work might be enhanced by its artistic beauty. Most wonderful of all was the rapidity of construction. Each one of them, men thought, would require many successive generations to complete it, but all of them were fully completed in the heyday of a single administration." After the work on the Parthenon our evidence becomes confused. Pheidias' success was too phenomenal not to bring on him the envy of the less fortunate. In the frank words of Plutarch:[10] "And being a friend of Perikles with considerable influence over him he became an object of jealousy and acquired many enemies." But just what happened we do not know definitely, for there are contradictory accounts. Either he was put in prison shortly after 438 and died in Athens, or he went to Olympia in 438 or in 432 to execute his statue of Zeus, and either died there some ten or fifteen years later or ultimately returned to Athens to stand his trial. We will discuss this important question of chronology later.

WORKS

We have little by which to form a conception of Pheidias' great creations. Ancient writers give long descriptions of some of them in terms of the highest praise, and it has been possible thereby to identify small-scale representations of Roman date as copies of three of his chief works—the Athena Promachos, the Athena Parthenos, and the Olympian Zeus. Though they cannot make us visualize the precious gold and ivory or bronze originals several times life-size, we must try to obtain from them what help we can.

Athena Promachos or the Bronze Athena

The Bronze Athena, nowadays generally referred to as the Athena Promachos,[11] is said by Pausanias[12] to have been an offering "from the spoils of the Persians who landed at Marathon"; but the statue was probably not erected until about 456, as we learn from an inscription.[12a] She was of bronze and rose to a great height. The point of her spear and the crest of her helmet are said to have been visible even to mariners approaching from Sounion. The general attitude and imposing nature of this statue can be gathered from representations of it on Athenian coins[13] of the Roman Imperial

10 *Perikles* XXXI. 2.

11 In ancient literature she is generally called "the Bronze Athena." The epithet of Athena Promachos is directly applied to her by the Scholiast on Dem., *Androt.* 597 R, and in *I.G.*, III. 1. 638 (*c.* A.D. 410). It has made its way into modern archaeological literature, though hardly appropriate to the quiet attitude of the statue.

12 I. 28. 2.

12a Meritt, *Hesperia*, V, 1936, p. 373; Raubitschek and Stevens, *Hesperia*, XV, 1946, pp. 107 ff.

13 Imhoof-Blumer and Gardner, *Numismatic Commentary*, pl. Z, Nos. I–VII; J. P. Shear, *Hesperia*, V, 1936, pp. 285 ff. Some doubt that the statue shown in our fig. 594

period, where it appears both as a single figure (fig. 594) and as a tall statue standing on the Akropolis between the Erechtheion and the Propylaia[14] (fig. 596). In later times she seems to have been removed to the Forum of Constantine,[15] where she was finally destroyed; at least if she is to be identified with the statue described by Niketas[16] as follows: "In stature it rose to the height of about thirty feet, and was clothed in garments of the same material as the whole statue, namely of bronze. The robe reached to the feet, and was gathered up in several places. A warrior's baldric passed round her waist and clasped it tightly. Over her prominent breasts she wore a cunningly wrought garment, like an aegis, suspended from her shoulders, and representing the Gorgon's head. Her neck, which was undraped and of great length, was a sight to cause unrestrained delight. Her veins stood out prominently, and her whole frame was supple and, where the need was, well-jointed. Upon her head a crest of horsehair 'nodded fearfully from above.' Her hair was twisted in a plait and fastened at the back, while that which streamed from her forehead was a feast for the eyes: for it was not altogether concealed by the helmet, which allowed a glimpse of her tresses to be seen. Her left hand held up the folds of her dress, while the right was extended toward the south and supported her head, slightly inclined in the same direction, with the gaze of both eyes fixed on that quarter." The description tallies fairly well with the coin representations except for the action of the arms, which may have been later restorations.

The chryselephantine statues of the Athena Parthenos and the Olympian Zeus are cited as Pheidias' outstanding works.[17] Their precious material[18] and great size naturally made them conspicuous

Athena Parthenos

was the Athena Promachos; cf. Chamoux, *B.C.H.*, LXVIII–LXIX, 1944–1945, pp. 227 ff., and Langlotz, *Phidiasprobleme*, pp. 73 ff.

14 The site has been tentatively identified as one of two large leveled surfaces about thirty yards east of the Propylaia; cf. D'Ooge, *The Acropolis of Athens*, p. 299. Moreover a piece of the pedestal is preserved in a capping-course with colossal bead-and-reel and egg-and-dart mouldings (Dinsmoor, *A.J.A.*, 1921, p. 128, fig. 1; Raubitschek and Stevens, *Hesperia*, 1946, pp. 107 ff.).

15 On the other hand Arethas, the archbishop of Caesarea in the tenth century A.D., refers to the Athena in the Forum of Constantine as of gold and ivory (Schol. Aristid. *Orat.* 50). This may, of course, have been another Athena.

16 *Chron. Isaac. Ang. et Alex. F.*, p. 738 B. See on this subject the note by Stuart Jones, *Selected Passages*, 101, and E. A. Gardner, *Handbook of Greek Sculpture*, p. 281, note 2.

17 Cf., e.g., Quint., *Inst. orat.* XII. 10. 9.

18 The Athena Parthenos alone is supposed to have borne forty talents' weight of refined gold (Thuc. II. 13).

attainments, but apart from their intrinsic value they were great
artistic achievements, for Pheidias' genius appears to have embodied
in them a nobility and grandeur which left an abiding impression on
the beholder. Pausanias[19] gives a detailed description of the Athena
Parthenos: "On the middle of the helmet rests the figure of a sphinx
and on either side of the helmet griffins are represented. The statue
of Athena stands erect and wears a tunic reaching to the feet. On its
breast is represented in ivory the head of Medusa, and a Victory
about four cubits in height stands on one of its hands, while in the
other it holds a spear; at its feet rests a shield, and close to the shield
is a serpent which no doubt represents Erichthonios; on the base of
the statue the birth of Pandora is wrought in relief." Pliny[20] supplies the further information that "on the shield was wrought in relief the battle of the Amazons on the convex surface, and the combats of gods and giants on the concave side, while on the sandals
was represented those of the Lapiths and Centaurs."[21] And from
Plutarch[22] we learn that in the battle of Amazons on the shield
"Pheidias introduced a figure of himself as a bald old man lifting
up a stone in both hands, and a very fine portrait of Perikles fighting with an Amazon," his arm across his face.[23] From these descriptions several statuettes, heads, and reliefs—all of Roman date—have
been identified as copied from Pheidias' work.[24] By their combined
evidence we can reconstruct the entire figure. The so-called Varvakeion[25] Athena (figs. 599, 600) shows the sphinx and griffins on the
head, the aegis, the shield with the serpent, and the Nike. The statuettes from Monastir and in Patras[26] (fig. 603) resemble the Varvakeion statuette but are of rather better execution. The Lenormant
Athena[27] (fig. 601) gives the reliefs on the outside of the shield and
on the base. On the Strangford shield[28] (fig. 605) the relief decoration is seen in greater detail. The reliefs found in the sea at the Pi-

19 I. 24. 5.   20 N.H. XXXVI. 18.
21 According to Aristotle, De Mundo. 6. 399b, the shield contained a hidden mecha-
nism by which if the head were removed the whole statue would fall to pieces.
22 Perikles XXXI. 4.
23 This feature brought on Pheidias the charge of sacrilege, cf. p. 223.
24 Cf. the lists given by Schreiber, Die Athena Parthenos; Puchstein, Jahrbuch, V,
1890, p. 83, note 16; Robinson, A.J.A., 1911, pp. 499 ff.; Picard, Manuel, II, pp. 378 ff.
25 National Museum, Athens, No. 129.
26 Arch. Anz., 1932, cols. 89 ff.; A.B.S., III, pl. 9.
27 National Museum, Athens, No. 128.
28 Smith, Catalogue of Greek Sculpture in the British Museum, I, No. 302.

raieus[28a] give us excerpts from the Amazonomachy. The Princeton statuette[29] (fig. 604), the polychrome head in Berlin[30] (fig. 602), the Aspasios gem[31] (fig. 597), the Koul Oba medallion,[32] and the head on the coins[33] (fig. 598) show us details of the helmet and the aegis. The whole figure on the late Athenian coins[34] (fig. 595)— minute though it is—supplies two important additional points of evidence; it has the spear in the left hand and has no supporting pillar for the hand with the Victory, showing that its addition in the Varvakeion statuette may be a later feature.[35]

Our imagination has to work hard to reconstruct from these faint reflections the vision of the great temple statue about forty feet high (with its base), which the worshiper beheld when he entered the cella of the Parthenon. But from a few of them—notably the Lenormant statuette, the Berlin head, and the Aspasios gem—we may catch a faint glimmer of the majesty, the *amplitudo*,[36] which made it one of the most famous statues of the world. And the great impression it made in the artistic world may be gauged by the many adaptations, contemporary and later, especially by the fine statue from distant Pergamon[37] produced in the Hellenistic period when an entirely different taste prevailed.

The statue had a long subsequent history.[38] We hear of repairs made at different times (the first was ten years after its dedication), and a number of thefts of the precious material are recorded (e.g., in the fourth century Philourgos removed the gorgoneion from the aegis and in 296 B.C. Lachares absconded with the gold parts of the statue). In A.D. 375 it still stood inside the cella.[39] According to one report it was removed from there toward the end of the fifth century A.D.[40] There is some evidence that it perished in a fire be-

---

28a Schrader in *Corolla L. Curtius*, pp. 81 ff.; Ras, *B.C.H.*, LVIII–LIX, 1944–1945, pp. 200 ff., discusses the reconstruction of the whole composition.

29 Shear, *A.J.A.*, 1924, pp. 117 f., pls. II–IV.

30 Berlin Museen, *Beschreibung der antiken Skulpturen*, No. 76 A.

31 Furtwängler, *Antike Gemmen*, pl. XLIX, 12; removed from Vienna to Rome.

32 Kieseritzky, *Ath. Mitt.*, 1883, VIII, pp. 291 ff., pl. XV.

33 Imhoof-Blumer and Gardner, *Numismatic Commentary*, pl. Y, No. XXIII.

34 *Ibid.*, Nos. XVIII ff. Cf. also the engraved gem in New York, Richter, *Ancient Gems*, 1942, no. 48.

35 Smith, *Catalogue of Greek Sculpture in the British Museum*, I, p. 97.

36 Pliny, *N.H.* XXXVI. 18.   37 *Altertümer von Pergamon*, VII, pl. VIII.

38 Cf. Koehler, *Ath. Mitt.*, V, 1880, p. 89; Schreiber, *Athena Parthenos*, p. 628.

39 Zosimus, *Hist. nova* IV. 18.   40 Marinus, *Life of Proclus* 30.

tween A.D. 429 and 485,[41] and still another account mentions it at Constantinople[42] in the tenth century. But its ultimate fate is not definitely known.

Olympian Zeus

The greatest fruit of Pheidias' genius appears to have been the Olympian Zeus. He was even more celebrated than the Athena Parthenos. Pliny[43] says: "No one doubts that Pheidias' renown extends through all lands where the fame of his Olympian Zeus is heard"; and elsewhere refers to it as the "unrivaled statue."[44] Dion Chrysostomos[45] calls it the embodiment of peace, "the guardian of Hellas when she is of one mind and not distraught with faction," and concludes that when you stand before this statue, you forget every misfortune of our earthly life, even though you have been broken by adversities and grief and sleep shuns your eyes—so great is the splendor and beauty of the artist's creation.[46] Quintilian[47] tells us that "its beauty can be said to have added something to traditional religion, so adequate to the divine nature is the majesty of his work" (cuius pulchritudo adiecisse aliquid receptae religioni videtur; adeo maiestas operis deum aequauit). Pheidias himself when asked after what pattern he was going to fashion his Zeus is said to have[48] quoted Homer's lines: "So spake the son of Kronos and nodded his dark brow, and the ambrosial locks waved from the king's undying head; and he made Olympos quake." And this vision of the god of gods he succeeded in embodying in his Olympian Zeus, transcending all previous conceptions and creating thereby a great work of religious sculpture.

What have we by which to visualize this statue? Unfortunately little. Pausanias[49] gives a long and dry description of it and all its accessories: "The god is seated on his throne and is made of gold and ivory; on his head rests a garland which imitates sprays of olive. In his right hand he bears a Victory, also of ivory and gold, which holds a fillet and has a garland on its head; and in his left is a sceptre inlaid with every kind of metal; the bird which is perched on the sceptre is the eagle. The sandals of the god and likewise his

---

[41] Führer, *Röm. Mitt.*, 1892, pp. 158 ff.

[42] Schol. Aristid. *Orat.* 50. On the words "the ivory Athena": "It seems she is set up in the Forum of Constantine and in the Bouleuterion, or Senate as they call it" (by Arethas, archbishop of Caesarea).

[43] *N.H.* XXXVI. 18.   [44] *N.H.* XXXIV. 54.

[45] *Orat.* XII. 51 f. (period of Domitian).

[46] *Ibid.*, 51.   [47] *Inst. orat.* XII. 10. 9.

[48] Strabo VIII. 353.   [49] V. 11. 1 ff.

robe are of gold. On the robe are wrought figures and flowers; these latter are lilies. The throne is diversified with gold and precious stones and ebony and ivory and there are figures upon it painted and sculptured." And then follows a detailed account of these decorations, which covered the legs, the stretchers, the footstool, the base, and the screens, the latter painted by Panainos, Pheidias' nephew.[50] The size of the statue was about seven times life-size, occupying the full height of the temple.[51]

We must imagine this colossal figure, then, grandly conceived and carved in simple lines; gleaming with its gold and ivory, but the brightness tempered by the figures wrought in the drapery; the sceptre sparkling with precious stones; and the throne elaborately decorated—a combination of grandeur and richness. How different would be our understanding today of Greek sculpture if one of these masterpieces had survived! Instead, all that has come down to us is the little reliefs on the reverse of some of Hadrian's coins[52] showing the head (fig. 606) and the enthroned figure (fig. 607). Diminutive, late, and inadequate though they be, even they are imbued with something of the benign majesty of the original and give us a faint impression of the harmony of the composition. There is no better way to realize the astounding development of Pheidias' genius than to place side by side the coin types of the severe Athena Promachos (fig. 594), the noble Athena Parthenos (fig. 595), and the majestic Olympian Zeus (fig. 607). There can be no doubt that Pheidias was one of the chief leaders in bringing Greek sculpture to its consummation in the fifth century.

Though we have no direct copies of Pheidias' Zeus except on the coins, many later works of art reflect its influence. The marble head in Boston[53] (fig. 609), a painting from Eleusis (fig. 612),[54] and a gem in Berlin (fig. 613)[55] evidently reproduce the general style, modified to suit a later age. It is natural that the creation of a type so universally acclaimed as fitting should exercise a strong and long-felt influence.

[50] A. Reinach, *Recueil Milliet*, Nos. 162 ff. Pliny and Pausanias call him a brother of Pheidias, but the usually well-informed Strabo a nephew.
[51] Strabo VIII. 353.
[52] Imhoof-Blumer and Gardner, *Num. Comm.*, pl. P, Nos. XX–XXIII; Liegle, *Kongressbericht,* 1939, pp. 653 ff.; Seltman, *Hesperia,* XVII, 1948, pl. 28, No. 1.
[53] Caskey, *Catalogue*, No. 25.   [54] ʼΕφ. ʼΑρχ., 1888, pl. 5, p. 77.
[55] Wiegand, *Amtliche Berichte aus den kgl. Kunstsammlungen*, XXXIV, 1913, pp. 169 f., fig. 87.

The temple of Zeus was burnt down in the time of Theodosius II
in the fifth century A.D. and Pheidias' statue may have perished at
that time.[56] But according to the Byzantine historian Cedrenus[57] it
was later at Constantinople in the Palace of Lausos; and this palace
was destroyed by fire in A.D. 475.[58]

If the coins reproduce at all accurately the style of the Olympian
Zeus—and as they are of Roman date that may be assumed—they
point to a date in the second half of the fifth century. At least this is
indicated by the deep-set eyes (particularly clear in the recently discovered, well preserved coin in Berlin[60]) and the completely easy pose.
We may add that the little Nike (if it reproduces the original creation and not a later substitution) is markedly naturalistic; considerably more so than that held by the Athena Parthenos. The
slight archaism in the rendering of the hair of Zeus is not uncommon
in heads of the later fifth century.[59] But if the Zeus on stylistic
grounds suggests a date after rather than before 450, Pheidias must
have gone to Elis after his work on the Parthenos in Athens (448–
438), not before it. Since this question of chronology is still disputed
let us briefly examine the evidence.

The external evidence in favor of dating the Zeus after the
Athena Parthenos is as follows:

(1) Pausanias[61] in his description of the figures on the throne of
Zeus gives this information: "They say that the boy who is binding
his hair with a fillet is like Pantarkes in countenance, and that Pantarkes was a youth of Elis who was beloved by Pheidias. Pantarkes
won the victory in the boys' wrestling-match in the 86th Olympiad
[436 B.C.]." Pheidias is said by Clement of Alexandria to have
carved the name of Pantarkes on the finger of his Zeus.[62] Before
450 Pantarkes would have been a mere baby.

(2) Pausanias[63] tells us that the Eleans held in great honor the
descendants of Pheidias for many generations. This suggests that
Pheidias settled in Elis with his family after he was banished from
his native city, rather than that he made the Zeus early in his
career and died in Athens after completing the Athena Parthenos.

(3) Aristophanes in his Peace, 605 ff., charges Perikles with

56 Schol. Lucian, Rhetor. praecept. 10, vol. 4, p. 221, ed. Jacobitz.
57 Comp. histor. 322 B.   58 Cedren., 348 A.
59 Cf., e.g., the examples cited by Pfuhl, Jahrbuch, 1927, p. 133.
60 Cf. Liegle, op. cit., pl. 76.
61 V. 11. 3.   62 Protrept. IV. 53, p. 47, ed. Potter.
63 V. 14. 5.

having started the Peloponnesian war (which began in 432–431) to create a diversion after the "Pheidian incident":

Pheidias began the mischief, having come to grief and shame,
Perikles was next in order, fearing he might share the blame,
Dreading much your hasty temper, and your savage bulldog ways,
So before misfortune reached him, he contrived a flame to raise,
By his Megara-enactment setting all the world ablaze.

There is a long comment to this passage by a scholiast who quotes from Philochoros, a historian living in the fourth and third centuries B.C. It is so important that we must quote it at length: "Philochoros writing of the archonship of Pythodoros, 432 B.C. [corrupt for Theodoros? (438 B.C.)] says: 'The golden image of Athena was placed in the great temple. The artist, Pheidias, was thought to have been guilty of peculation in respect of the ivory used for the serpents' scales, and was put on trial. He fled to Elis, where he is said to have accepted the contract for the image of Zeus at Olympia, and, after completing it, to have been put to death by the Eleans [corrupt for Athenians?] in the archonship of Skythodoros' [corrupt for Pythodoros? (432 B.C.)]. . . . And some say that when Pheidias the sculptor was found guilty of swindling the city and banished, Perikles, alarmed because he had been associated with the making of the statue and had connived at the theft, passed the decree against the Megarians and declared war on them in order to avoid giving his accounts to the Athenians, who would be preoccupied with the war; and so he accused the Megarians of ploughing up a piece of land sacred to the two goddesses. But the suspicion regarding Perikles seems unreasonable, as the incident about Pheidias happened seven years before the beginning of the war. When Pheidias, as Philochoros says, in the archonship of Pythodoros [corrupt for Theodoros?] made the statue of Athena, he stole the gold from the serpents of the chryselephantine Athena, was detected in it, and punished by exile. And while he was in Elis he made the statue of the Olympian Zeus for the Eleans; and he was condemned by them and perished in exile." Though the names of the archons are corrupt and we cannot be sure whether Pheidias left Athens in 438 or 432, and just when he died, this does not affect the definite statement that the Zeus was made after the Athena Parthenos.

(4) Pheidias is known to have had several important commissions

in the second quarter of the fifth century, among them a chryselephantine statue at Pellene, a large group at Delphi, and the colossal bronze Athena[64] which was erected about 456.[64a] There would seem to have been little time for work on the elaborately decorated, colossal statue of the Zeus at Olympia.

(5) It would seem more natural that after the Athena Parthenos had established Pheidias' fame as a sculptor of chryselephantine statues he was summoned to Elis to execute a similar work for the most important sanctuary of Greece; rather than that such a summons should have come before his reputation was at its height.

(6) We hear of two further works which he made in Elis—an Anadoumenos in Olympia[65] and a chryselephantine statue of Aphrodite Ourania.[66] The former has been tentatively connected with the Farnese boy in the British Museum,[67] a work stylistically connected with the Parthenon sculptures, certainly not pre-Parthenon in type. Probably Pheidias made these statues at the time of or shortly after his Zeus and they represent his last works.

(7) The introduction of black Eleusinian stone on the floor in front of the statue of Zeus[68] is paralleled on the Propylaia and the Erechtheion, both post-Parthenon buildings,[69] though it is true that it occurs occasionally earlier.

(8) The expense of the statue would have been too great to have been borne only by the Eleans (cf. p. 226).

For the early dating of the Zeus there are two chief arguments:

(1) Plutarch's[70] account of the indictment of Pheidias:

"Pheidias the sculptor was contractor for the great statue, as I have said, and being admitted to the friendship of Perikles, and acquiring the greatest influence with him, made some enemies through the jealousy which he excited; others also made use of him to test the people and see what sort of a judge it would be in a case where Perikles was involved. These latter persuaded one Menon, an assistant of Pheidias, to take a suppliant's seat in the market-place and demand immunity from punishment in case he should bring information and accusation against Pheidias. The people accepted the man's proposal, and formal prosecution of Pheidias was made in the assembly. Embezzlement, indeed, was not proven, for the gold of

---

[64] Cf. p. 229.
[65] Pausanias VI. 4. 5.
[67] See p. 228.
[69] Dörpfeld, *Olympia, Ergebnisse*, II, p. 20.

[64a] Cf. p. 214.
[66] Pausanias VI. 25. 1.
[68] Pausanias V. 11. 5.
[70] *Perikles* XXXI. 2.

the statue from the very start had been so wrought upon and cast about it by Pheidias, at the wise suggestion of Perikles, that it could all be taken off and weighed, and this is what Perikles actually ordered the accusers of Pheidias to do at this time. But the reputation of his works nevertheless brought a burden of jealous hatred upon Pheidias, and especially the fact that when he wrought the battle of the Amazons on the shield of the goddess, he carved out a figure that suggested himself as a bald old man lifting on high a stone with both hands, and also inserted a very fine likeness of Perikles fighting with an Amazon. And the attitude of the hand, which holds out a spear in front of the face of Perikles, is cunningly contrived as it were with a desire to conceal the resemblance, which is, however, plain to be seen from either side. Pheidias, accordingly, was led away to prison, and died there of sickness; but some say of poison which the enemies of Perikles provided, that they might bring calumny upon him. And to Menon the informer, on motion of Glykon, the people gave immunity from taxation, and enjoined upon the generals to make provision for the man's safety." This account certainly suggests that Pheidias was indicted soon after the completion of the Athena Parthenos, that he was convicted on the flimsiest of charges (the serious one of embezzlement was evidently not proved), and that he was thereupon put in prison and died in Athens; in this case there would not have been any opportunity for going to Olympia to execute a statue there. But Plutarch is a late writer and may easily have mixed up his sources.[71] Moreover even he nowhere says that the Zeus was made before the Athena Parthenos, and such a view is a mere inference; while our other informants make definite statements to the contrary.

(2) Pausanias'[72] account regarding the temple at Olympia: "The temple and image of Zeus were made from the booty at the time when the Eleans conquered Pisa and the vassal states which revolted with her [472 B.C.]. That the image was made by Pheidias is attested by the inscription under the feet of Zeus." The temple was probably completed in 456.[73] Since the temple image is one of the most important features of a sanctuary, one would suppose that the statue of Zeus was also finished by about that time. This at least was the general practice; the Athena Parthenos was dedicated even be-

---

[71] Cf. especially Schöll, *Der Prozess des Phidias, Sitzungsberichte der phil.-phil.-u.-hist. Classe der Akademie der Wissenschaften zu München*, 1888, I, pp. 1–53.

[72] V. 10. 2.   [73] Cf. Purgold, *Arch. Ztg.*, 1882, p. 184.

fore the pediments of the temple were begun. In that case, however, we should expect the statue of Zeus to show about the same stylistic development as the other sculptural decorations of the temple—the pediments and the metopes. But we have seen that the scanty remains we have—the small-scale representations of the head and of the whole figure on Roman coins of Elis—suggest a considerably later date. Moreover, the extravagant praise of the Pheidian Zeus in Roman times—when archaic art was less appreciated—also points to a fully developed type.[75]

Moreover there are other instances of a long interval between the completion of a temple and the dedication of its cult statue; for instance the statues of the Hephaisteion were apparently not dedicated until about twenty-five years after the building was finished.[76] During this interval a statue from an earlier sanctuary probably served. Just so at Olympia another statue may have been used before Pheidias made his image, "either the primitive statue from the Heraion"[76a] or one made specially for it. If the latter was the case perhaps the seated Zeus (fig. 611) on coins of Elis of c. 471–431 B.C.[77] and the noble and severe head on coins dated c. 420[78] but clearly reproducing an earlier type[79] (fig. 610) may give an idea of it. The expense of this statue—as well as of the temple—was defrayed from the spoils taken by the Eleans when they reduced Pisa and the other dependent cities which had revolted, just as Pausanias tells us.[80] Then thirty years later the same great earthquake which caused the mutilation of the reclining figures from the angles of the western pediment and necessitated the substitution of the present figures in Pentelic marble of developed fifth-century style[81] (cf. figs. 608, 200), the same catastrophe that caused injuries to a large part of the temple,[82] also damaged this statue of Zeus. By this time the praise of the great gold and ivory statue of the Athena Parthenos was resounding throughout Greece; and Olympia determined to have a similar resplendent figure by the same master sculptor. The necessary funds must have been con-

74 Cf. pp. 219 f.

75 That the spacing of the Parthenos in the cella is preferable to that of the Zeus (Picard, *Manuel*, II, pp. 353 ff.) can be easily explained by the fact that in the Zeus Pheidias had to adapt his statue to a completed cella.

76 Cf. Dinsmoor, *Hesperia*, Supplement V, p. 156.   76a *Ibid.*

77 *British Museum Catalogue of Coins, Peloponnesos,* pl. X, 11.

78 Head, *Historia numorum,* p. 422, fig. 230.

79 Furtwängler, *Masterpieces,* pp. 217–218.   80 Pausanias V. 10. 2.

81 Though these figures have been variously dated I agree with the fifth-century assignment by Schrader, *Phidias,* pp. 106 ff., and *Jahreshefte des Österr. Arch. Inst.,* XXV, 1929, pp. 82 ff., certainly for fig. 608 and probably for fig. 200.

82 Cf. Dörpfeld, *Olympia, Ergebnisse,* II, p. 22; Dinsmoor, *A.J.A.,* 1941, pp. 399 ff.

tributed by the whole of Greece, for never could the spoils from a few neighboring cities be sufficient for a gold and ivory statue about seven times life-size. And after the statue by Pheidias was finished its splendor and its fame caused the earlier image to be forgotten.

Since therefore the two chief arguments in favor of the early dating of the Zeus are more easily disposed of than the varied evidence for the later one, the latter would seem to be the more likely. We must leave it an open question whether Pheidias left Athens in 438 or in 432, for here the accounts are too confused. If Pheidias was born in 495–490[83] he would be around sixty when he went to Olympia (and in his fifties when he depicted himself as bald-headed on the shield of the Athena Parthenos) ; and even if the date of his birth is assumed to be earlier, there is no difficulty in supposing that Pheidias as a man of sixty-five or seventy produced a great work of art. Titian worked until he was ninety-nine, Michelangelo until he was eighty-nine, and Giovanni Bellini until his eighty-fifth year.

To the question: "Which of the works of Pheidias do you praise most highly?" Lucian[84] gives the answer: "Which but the Goddess of Lemnos whereon Pheidias deigned to inscribe his name," and then proceeds to borrow certain features for his Panthea or perfect woman: "Pheidias and the Lemnian Goddess shall bestow on her the outline of her countenance, her delicate cheeks, and finely proportioned nose." Lucian does not stand alone in his admiration. Pausanias[85] is likewise carried away: "The most remarkable of the works of Pheidias, an image of Athena, called the Lemnian, after the dedicators." The statue stood on the Akropolis. The dedicators were doubtless the Athenian colonists sent to Lemnos between 451 and 448. In addition to these definite references there are others which may perhaps be applied to this statue: (1) Pliny's[86] statement that "Pheidias made an Athena of bronze of such outstanding beauty that she was called the Beautiful"; (2) a passage of Himerios[87] to the effect that Pheidias did not always represent Athena armed, but sometimes substituted beauty for the helmet; and (3) an epigram in the *Anthology* in which the statue of Athena in Athens is preferred to the Knidian Aphrodite.[88] If Lucian's and Pausanias' statements reflect a universally admitted preference, it is certainly probable

Athena
Lemnia

[83] Schrader, *Phidias*, p. 20, suggests 510–500 as the time of his birth; but Johansen, *Arch. Anz.*, 1923–1924, pp. 147 f., claims 490 b.c. as the likelier time, and that seems to me to fit the evidence better.

[84] Εἰκόνες 4.   [85] I. 28. 2.
[86] *N.H.* XXXIV. 54.   [87] *Orat.* 21. 4.
[88] *Anthol. Gr.* I. 193; cf. also IV. 168, 248.

that these references to the beautiful Athena apply to the Lemnian; and if so, we obtain from them the additional information that the statue was of bronze and did not wear a helmet.

What was this statue which could be called Pheidias' finest creation even by those who knew his two great chryselephantine figures? It must have been one which by some exquisite quality of its own made one forget its more ambitious rivals. Furtwängler's theory[89] that we possess marble copies of it in two marble statues in Dresden (cf. fig. 615) and in a head in Bologna (fig. 614) meets the evidence exceptionally well. The style corresponds in date to the Lemnian dedication (the forties of the fifth century); the sharp contours of the features, the treatment of the hair, and the hollow eyes point to a bronze original; and above all they suggest that the original was of surpassing beauty. There are indeed few heads preserved to us from antiquity of such pure and noble loveliness as the head in Bologna (Roman copy though it is) and few figures so grand in conception as this statue when we can visualize its composition holding a helmet in one hand and a lance in the other (fig. 616[90]). Our admiration goes out to her just as did Lucian's and Pausanias' of old. Moreover the points picked out by Lucian, the well-proportioned nose and the outline of the countenance with its delicate cheeks, are particularly striking here. It is its lovely oval face which adds so greatly to its attraction and distinguishes it from other "Pheidian" heads, such as the Athena Parthenos (figs. 599 ff.) and the "Athena Medici."[91] If only it were certain that by his beautiful helmetless Athena Himerios had meant the Lemnian, or even that Pliny's "bronze" Athena is the Lemnian, the case would be strong indeed. But neither of them actually says so.[92] And so we cannot regard the theory as proved.

---

[89] *Masterpieces*, pp. 4 ff.

[90] From a restored cast in Budapest (Hekler, *Pheidias*, p. 21, figs. 9, 10); in that in Strassburg (Wolters-Springer, *Kunstgeschichte*, I,[12] fig. 498) the helmet is held too high and the composition of the arms is thus less harmonious. Similar compositions appear on gems (Furtwängler, *Masterpieces*, p. 14, note 4), and on a redfigured vase in Bologna (Pellegrini, *Catalogo dei vasi delle necropoli felsinee*, p. 191, fig. 115, No. 393 [cf. our fig. 617]).

[91] Amelung tentatively sponsored her for the Athena Lemnia (*Oest. Jahresh.*, XI, pp. 195 f.), though he admitted difficulties. Though she is an imposing creation, we hesitate to think that she would have been picked out as Pheidias' masterpiece (cf. the reconstruction in *op. cit.*, p. 189, fig. 71), and the contour of her face is rather heavy than otherwise. Recent attempts to assign the Dresden and Bologna Athena to Myron (Jenkins, *J.H.S.*, 1926, II, p. XX) and to Alkamenes (Walston, *Alcamenes*, pp. 168 ff.) do not carry conviction.

[92] Furtwängler in his enthusiasm for his theory does not state this clearly, and lays himself open to attack (cf. Amelung, *op. cit.*, XI, p. 194). Amelung (*loc.*

Pliny[93] tells the following anecdote: "The most famous artists, though born at some distance of time from each other, still came into competition, since each had made a statue of an Amazon, to be dedicated in the temple of Artemis at Ephesos, when it was decided that the prize should be awarded to the one which the artists themselves who were on the spot declared to be the best. This proved to be the statue which each artist placed second to his own, namely that of Polykleitos; the statue of Pheidias was second, that of Kresilas third, Kydon's fourth, and Phradmon's fifth." Kydon is clearly a mistake due to a confusion with "Kresilas the Kydonian" (see p. 233). Whatever may be the truth of the details of this story, it suggests that four statues by the artists named stood in the temple at Ephesos perhaps as a single offering. And this is borne out by other evidence. Three distinct types occur in many replicas, indicating that they were derived from famous originals; and they are in the style of the required period, i.e., about 440, when Pheidias, Polykleitos, and Kresilas are all known to have been active; while a fourth type evidently not so popular and presumably by a lesser artist such as Phradmon also exists.[94] Furthermore a relief with an Amazon of one of the popular types has been found at Ephesos,[95] lending additional credence to the story. The question which type should be connected with what particular artist is naturally one of great interest and one that has absorbed archaeologists for some time. Furtwängler's[96] allocation of the Mattei type to Pheidias, the Berlin one to Polykleitos, and the Capitoline one to Kresilas has recently been challenged[97] and again endorsed.[98] Both on external and on stylistic evidence it still seems the most plausible.[99]

The identification of the Mattei type[100] (fig. 620) with that of Pheidias is rendered likely by its close correspondence to the repre-

cit.) even thinks that the Lemnian Athena was probably not of bronze, for Aristides (*Orat.* 50, T. III, p. 701) mentions three Athenas in Athens, "the chryselephantine, the bronze one, and, by Zeus, if you like, the Lemnian, all a paramount source of merit to the sculptor and of enjoyment to the beholder," from which he infers that the Lemnian must have been of a third material. But the "Athena Promachos" was so universally referred to as the Bronze Athena that the emphasis need not be here on the material. The Argive origin of the Dresden-Bologna Athena (Amelung, *op. cit.*) seems too problematical to be taken as serious evidence.

93 *N.H.* XXXIV. 53.   94 Cf. Furtwängler, *Masterpieces*, p. 129, fig. 52.

95 *Jahrbuch*, 1915, pl. 6.   96 *Op. cit.*, pp. 128 ff.

97 E.g., by Graef, *Jahrbuch*, XII, 1897, pp. 82 ff.; Noack, *Jahrbuch*, XXX, 1915, pp. 131 ff.; Bulle, *Der schöne Mensch*, 1922, p. 100; Anti, *Monumenti antichi*, XXVI, 1920, pp. 600 ff.; Pfuhl, *Jahrbuch*, 1926, pp. 23 f.; cf. also Johnson, *Lysippos*, p. 30, who reviews the chief arguments.

98 Bieber, *Jahrbuch*, XXXIII, 1918, pp. 49 ff.   99 See also pp. 236, 251.

100 Amelung, *Die Skulpturen des vaticanischen Museums*, II, No. 265.

sentation of a (lost) gem[101] (fig. 619) showing an Amazon grasping a lance with both hands, the right high above the head, perhaps about to swing herself on to her horse,[102] and Lucian's testimony:[103] "Which of the works of Pheidias do you praise most highly? . . . The Amazon who is leaning on her spear." The missing parts of the Mattei statue (the head and both arms) can be reconstructed from the gem engraving.

Unfortunately none of the replicas of the Mattei type have the head preserved except the supporting figure from Loukou in Athens[104] (fig. 618)—a rather generalized rendering. The head corresponds in a general way to that on the gem, and clearly goes back to a fine original. Lucian[105] wants to borrow for his perfect woman "the setting of the mouth and the neck" from the Amazon of Pheidias, so that they were evidently of special excellence. The Turin replica[106] shows that the head was slightly turned to the left (of the figure), a detail which might easily be varied in a supporting figure and in a diminutive representation on a gem.

Fragmentary though our knowledge of this statue is, we can yet appreciate a certain elasticity and splendid vigor which distinguish her from her rival sisters and give her the appearance almost of a goddess. The treatment of the soft, crinkly chiton with its many variegated folds foreshadows that of the Parthenon pediments.

Anadoumenos   Pausanias[107] saw a statue in Olympia of a "boy binding a fillet on his head" "by the great sculptor Pheidias." We have no other mention or description of it; but on stylistic grounds the Farnese Diadoumenos in the British Museum[108] (fig. 621) has been thought to be a copy of this work. It shows indeed a marked resemblance to the youths on the Parthenon frieze in the structure of the body and in a certain sublimity of conception; so that the identification is certainly possible. But we must remember that a youth binding on a fillet as a badge of victory was a popular subject, and that

---

101 Natter, *A Treatise on the Ancient Method of Engraving on Precious Stones,* London, 1754, pl. XXXI, opp. p. 48.

102 Furtwängler, *Masterpieces,* p. 137; this explanation has been doubted (cf. Amelung, *Die Skulpturen des vaticanischen Museums,* II, No. 265), but the pose calls for a specific action of this kind, cf. Langlotz, *Phidiasprobleme,* p. 59 f.

103 Εἰκόνες 4.

104 National Museum, No. 705. Cf. Amelung, *loc. cit.;* Bieber, *Jahrbuch,* fig. 15. Furtwängler (*op. cit.,* p. 138) suggested the head from Herculaneum—the pendant to the Doryphoros by Apollonios—as perhaps the type of the Pheidian Amazon. A recently discovered replica in Rome (Langlotz, *op. cit.,* pl. 32) adds weight to the identification. A reduced replica with head has been shown to be modern (cf. p. 188, fig. 541).

105 Εἰκόνες 6.   106 Furtwängler, *op. cit.,* p. 138, note 2.

107 VI. 4. 5.   108 Smith, *Catalogue,* I, No. 501.

Pheidias had many pupils, and his influence was widespread, so that the identification can be regarded only as a probable theory.

Ancient writers mention a number of other works by Pheidias: as *Other Works* early works, a group at Delphi of Athena, Apollo, Miltiades, Erechtheus, Kekrops, and other heroes—a tithe offering after Marathon,[109] a chryselephantine Athena at Pellene,[110] an Athena of gilt wood with marble face, hands, and feet at Plataia;[111] during Perikles' administration, an Aphrodite Ourania of Parian marble at Melite;[112] in his later years, an Aphrodite Ourania of gold and ivory with one foot on a tortoise at Elis,[113] a bronze Apollo,[114] a marble Hermes at Thebes,[115] a bronze Athena,[116] a marble Aphrodite[117] "of great beauty," and so on. They are mere names to us now, unfortunately.

The diversity of Pheidias' genius is attested by the fact that he worked in marble,[117a] bronze, and gold and ivory; and that he was also a painter,[118] an engraver,[119] and, in the words of Pliny, opened up new possibilities in embossed metal work (toreutice).[120]

Inevitably a considerable number of statues of the period have *ATTRIBU-* been brought into connection with the magic name of Pheidias; *TIONS* e.g., the fine Apollo from the Tiber in the National Museum in Rome (fig. 38), the Eleusis relief in Athens (fig. 481), the statuesque Zeus in Dresden, the Demeter in Cherchel, the Kore in the Villa Albani. They all have the Pheidian grandeur, but they do not really help us to visualize his style, for their connection with the master is not certain.

Is this, then, all we know of the greatest of Greek sculptors—a few reproductions on Roman coins and in Roman statues of a handful of his works? Fortunately we have other material to help us in our search. Since Pheidias was placed in charge of the artistic undertakings during Perikles' administration[121] he must have been responsible for the greatest of these—the Parthenon. Plutarch[122] tells us that under him worked many architects, artists, and artisans, but "everything was under his direct charge." It stands to reason

109 Pausanias X. 10. 1. Erected probably about 465 B.C.
110 Pausanias VII. 27. 2.   111 Pausanias IX. 4. 1; Plutarch, *Aristid.* 20.
112 Pausanias I. 14. 7.   113 Pausanias VI. 25. 1.
114 Pausanias I. 24. 8.   115 Pausanias IX. 10. 2.
116 Pliny, *N.H.* XXXIV. 54.   117 Pliny, *N.H.* XXXVI. 15.
117a Cf. Lucian, *Zeus Tragoedus*, 7.   118 Pliny, *N.H.* XXXV. 54.
119 Martial III. 35; IV. 39. 1, 4; X. 87. 15 f.; Nicephor. Gregor., *Hist.* VIII. 7; Julian. Imperat., *Epist.* 8.
120 Cf. on this subject Richter, *A.J.A.,* XLV, 1941, pp. 377 ff.
121 Plutarch, *Perikles* XIII. 4.   122 *Op. cit.,* XIII. 9.

then that though he cannot have executed the sculptures of the Parthenon himself—probably an army of workmen was employed on this great task to complete it in the phenomenally short period of its production—he nevertheless had a guiding hand in them. He must have sketched the designs, or at least initiated and revised them. At all events his genius presided over their creation and they certainly show—one and all—"the sublimity and precision" (ἔχουσά τι καὶ μεγαλεῖον καὶ ἀκριβὲς ἅμα) which we are told were the chief characteristics of his style.[123] It was indeed a mighty task. The ninety-two metopes (of which only twenty are fairly well preserved now) were executed between 447 and 443[124] at the beginning of the building; for they had to be in place before the erection of the cornice. The frieze (524 feet, 1 inch,[125] about 160 meters long) was probably carved in situ between 442 and 438.[126] The two pediments come last in date, between 439 and 432,[127] after the dedication of the temple statue in 438. Together they show us the development of sculpture in Athens during the third quarter of the fifth century. And an astounding picture it is—from the grandiose, simple metopes (figs. 415, 416) to the quiet, rhythmical frieze (figs. 291, 356, 486, 488, 489), and ending with the rich and splendid pediment figures (figs. 69–71, 91, 119, 394–396, 622). But different though they are in details of modeling and composition they are all imbued with the same spirit—that quality of Pheidias' genius which made him excel in creations of divinities.

123 Demetrius, *De Eloct.* 14.

124 The building records of the Parthenon, fragments of which are preserved, help to establish the dates of the various parts of the building; cf. Dinsmoor, *A.J.A.*, 1913, pp. 77 ff.; 1921, pp. 242 ff. The first entry is in the year 447–446.

125 Smith, *The Sculptures of the Parthenon*, p. 52.

126 We have a record in the building inscription for wood purchased in 444–443, probably for the scaffolding necessary for the erection of the frieze and the roof; and in 438 the wood from these scaffoldings is sold; see also pp. 32 f.

127 According to the building inscription, marble for this purpose was brought to the workshops in 439–438 and the work begun the following year. In 434–433 there is an entry of 16,392 drachmas given as yearly wages to the sculptors ([ἀγαλ]ματο-ποιοις) (Woodward, *B.S.A.*, 1909–1910, pp. 196–197). That Pheidias could not have executed the pediment sculptures himself is clearly indicated by the mention of sculptors instead of sculptor (probably about ten, for they receive about five times as much as the wage given to the sculptors of the Epidauros pediment and akroteria [see pp. 275 f.] when wages were about 100 per cent higher). On the other hand a design or model of the pediment figures must have preceded the beginning of their execution; and surely Pheidias would not neglect or leave entirely to others the most important feature in the decoration of the temple. Those who think that the drapery of the "Fates" is post-Pheidian in conception should remember the garments of the Pheidian Amazon (fig. 620) and of the seated figure on the metope from the north side of the Parthenon (Smith, *op. cit.*, pl. 25, 1), both immediate precursors.

Pheidias lived through a momentous epoch in Greek art. He was born toward the end of the archaic period, took part in the experiments of the transitional one, and helped to impart to Greek art the idealism which to many now is its distinctive quality.

(b) *Kresilas*

KRESILAS from Kydonia, Crete, may be ranked among Athenian sculptors, for his chief works seem to have been executed in Athens. Five bases of statues giving Kresilas as the name of the sculptor have been found, three on the Akropolis of Athens:[128] (1) Ἑρμόλυκος Διειτρέφους ἀπαρχήν. Κρησίλας ἐποίησεν, [129] "Hermolykos, the son of Dieitrephes [set it up] as a first offering. Kresilas was the sculptor." (2) Πείκον Ἀνδρο[κ]λ[έος καὶ . . . .]ικλεός ἀνεθέτεν Ἀθεναί[αι δεκάτεν Κρεσ]ίλας ἐποίε, "Peikon, the son of Androkles, and . . ., the son of . . . ikles, dedicated (it) to Athena as a tithe. Kresilas made it." Here two fragments have been tentatively combined, one of which was formerly read [Περ]ικλέους [Κρησ]ίλας ἐποίει, [130] "[A portrait] of Perikles, Kresilas was the sculptor" c. 450, and connected with the statue of Perikles (see below). (3) [τόνδε Πύρης] ἀνέθηκε Πολυμνήστου φίλο[ς υἱòς]εὐξάμενος δεκάτην Παλλάδι Τριτογενεῖ Κυδωνιήτας Κρησίλας εἰργάσσατο, [131] "This Pyres, the dear son of Polymnestos, dedicated as a tithe to Athena the Tritoborn in fulfilment of a vow. Kresilas the Kydonian made it." (4) Ἀλεξίας Λύωνος ἀνέθη[κε] τᾷ Δάματρι τᾷ [X]θονία[ι] Ἑρμιονεύς. Κρησίλας ἐποίησε Κυδωνιάτ[ας], [131a] "Alexias, the son of Lyon, of Hermione, dedicated it to the Chthonian Demeter. Kresilas of Kydonia made it" at Hermione. Probably to be connected with another inscription, with the signature of Dorotheos from Argos. (5) Κρησίλας ἐποίη . . . ἐκ Κυδωνίας, "Kresilas of Kydonia made it" at Delphi.[132] One of his statues was evidently taken to Pergamon for a base with his signature was found there.[132a] We learn from these that Kresilas was active during 450–425, though the period can of course have been more extensive.

Pliny[133] mentions as one of Kresilas' works "Perikles the Olym-

---

128 Raubitschek, *Dedications*, Nos. 132, 131, 133, and pp. 510 ff.
129 Loewy, *Inschriften*, No. 46.   130 Δελτ. ἀρχ. (old series), 1889, p. 36.
131 Loewy, *op. cit.*, No. 47; repeated in *Anth. Pal.*, XIII, 13.
131a Loewy, *op. cit.*, No. 45; Peek, *Ath. Mitt.*, LIX, 1934, pp. 45 ff., No. 8.
132 *B.C.H.*, 1899, p. 378.
132a Jacobsthal, *Ath. Mitt.*, XXXIII, 1908, p. 418, no. 60; Raubitschek, *Dedications*, p. 512.
133 *N.H.* XXXIV. 74.

pian," and describes it as worthy of his name, adding, "The marvel of this art is that it has made men of renown yet more renowned." Pausanias[134] saw a portrait of Perikles on the Akropolis. Two herms inscribed with the name of Perikles, in the British Museum[135] (fig. 624) and in the Vatican[136] (fig. 623), are clearly Roman copies of a work of about 440. Other good replicas of the head, not inscribed, are in the Barracco Museum, Rome,[137] in the Staatliche Museen, Berlin,[138] and in the Glyptothek, Munich.[139] The original was evidently a famous work by a well known sculptor and so might well have been the portrait by Kresilas extolled by Pliny. But we must remember that apparently many portraits of Perikles were erected. For instance, Plutarch[140] says that "the images of Perikles *almost all of them* wear helmets"; so we are still bound to regard the identification as tentative. However that may be, the herms in question certainly show us a fine conception of the great Athenian who guided the fortunes of his city at one of the most critical periods of her history and to whom—more than to any other single man, except to the creative artists Pheidias and Iktinos—the great achievement of the Parthenon was due. The sculptor has admirably caught the noble, somewhat haughty spirit, which was able to rise above criticism when occasion demanded it, and which combined this detachment with a devoted friendship for people like Pheidias, Anaxagoras, and Aspasia. It would not be too much to say that such a portrait added yet more renown to Perikles' fame. The portrait though generalized in the style of the fifth century is curiously individual in details. Perikles' high skull—which earned him the nickname of squill head[141]—is shown in the Naples copy where the hair shows through the eyeholes of the helmet. The little tilt of the head in the British Museum example (which is unbroken) is evidently a characteristic pose and gives it a very lifelike quality. The small oblique wrinkles at the birth of the eyebrows with the two little horizontal cuts[142] be-

[134] I. 25.1.
[135] Smith, *Catalogue*, I, No. 549.   [136] Helbig, *Führer*,³ I, No. 276.
[137] Arndt, *Katalog*, pls. 39, 39a.
[138] Kekule, Bildnis des Perikles, 61. *Winckelmannsprogramm*, p. 16; Blümel, *Katalog*, IV, K127.
[139] No. 157. Arndt-Bruckmann, *Griechische und Römische Porträts*, pls. 411–416. Cf. V. H. Poulsen, *Acta Arch.*, XI, 1940, p. 32.
[140] *Perikles* III. 2.
[141] Plutarch, *Perikles* III. 2 and XIII. 6.
[142] These do not appear in all the replicas.

neath it accentuate the serious, thoughtful character of the head, while the full, sensuous lips suggest his more emotional and artistic side.

Another famous work by Kresilas mentioned by Pliny[143] is "a   *Volneratus* man wounded and dying [volneratus deficiens] in whom the spectator can feel how little life is left." Pausanias[144] in describing the Akropolis of Athens mentions "a bronze portrait of Dieitrephes shot with arrows." Ross conjectured that the inscription from the Akropolis on the base of the Dieitrephes by Kresilas[145] belonged to the statue mentioned by Pausanias and that this was identical with Pliny's wounded man. Pausanias[146] identifies Dieitrephes with the Athenian general mentioned in Thucydides VII. 29 (414 B.C.) and VIII. 64 (411 B.C.). But these dates are too late for the character of the letters on the inscription; Furtwängler[147] therefore suggests an elder Dieitrephes, the father of Nikostratos (Thucydides III. 75; IV. 119, 129), about whom however nothing definite is known. It is quite possible of course that Kresilas made two statues—a Volneratus deficiens and a Dieitrephes shot with arrows. The base with the Dieitrephes inscription[148] is square and the upper side is only about 27½ by 29½ inches (70 × 75 cm.), showing that the statue—if that of a volneratus—was not represented fallen, but apparently in the act of falling. The boldness of such a conception would be typical of the transitional epoch (cf. figs. 136, 578) and would show that Kresilas—at least during his youth—caught the spirit of the experimental period in which he lived and attempted the momentary poses popular at the time. We may obtain some visualization of such a statue from extant representations of falling figures of that period such as the warrior ("shot with arrows") on the lekythos in the Bibliothèque Nationale in Paris[149] (fig. 129 on p. 68), the bronze statuette in Modena[150] (fig. 128), and the bronze wounded warrior in St. Germain-en-Laye[151] (figs. 127, 625; later reconstructed as a lamp support). The last bears a certain

---

[143] *N.H.* XXXIV. 74.   [144] I. 23. 3.
[145] See above (Loewy, *Inschriften,* No. 46).   [146] I. 23. 3.
[147] *Masterpieces,* p. 123.
[148] Loewy, *op. cit.,* No. 46. The two holes on the upper face of the base noted by Loewy are not deep enough to have served for the attachment of a statue and can therefore not be taken as evidence of its pose.
[149] Furtwängler, *Masterpieces,* fig. 48.
[150] Bulle, *Der schöne Mensch,* pl. 94. Here the attitude of the legs is reversed.
[151] S. Reinach, *Gazette des Beaux-Arts,* 1905, p. 203. The genuineness of the statuette has been doubted. When I examined the original (in 1927) I could see no valid reasons for such doubts.

similarity to the Capitoline Amazon (figs. 626, 627) and the Perikles (figs. 623, 624)—in the heavy eyelids, the strongly marked tear-ducts, the full lips with depressed corners, and the oval face; its identification therefore as a copy of Kresilas' *Volneratus deficiens* (suggested by S. Reinach) is certainly attractive.[152]

Amazon　　Pliny[153] mentions Kresilas as one of the sculptors who made an Amazon in competition with Pheidias, Polykleitos, and Phradmon

(cf. p. 229) and calls it *volneratus*. The Capitoline (fig. 627) and Berlin (fig. 655) types of Amazon have both been thought to reproduce Kresilas' work. The arguments in favor of assigning the Capitoline one to Kresilas[154] are its similarity to the Perikles (cf. figs. 626, 624), and the fact that the wound is here the dominant note.[155] The right arm is wrongly restored. It should be raised and leaning on a spear, as on the gem fig. 632, an attitude more suggestive of her helplessness. Even so the composition is

Fig. 632. Amazon, on a gem (from a drawing, enlarged)
Bibliothèque Nationale, Paris

heavy and lacks the rhythmical quality we associate with Polykleitos; it seems hard to believe that this figure won the prize in competition with the statues preserved in the Mattei and Lansdowne-Berlin types (cf. figs. 620, 655). The argument that the inner vastus is pronounced in the Capitoline statue, as in Polykleitos' Doryphoros and Diadoumenos, loses weight when we remember that other fifth-century statues not associated with Polykleitos have that rendering. It seems best, therefore, to assign the Capitoline type to Kresilas. The number of copies preserved of this type, especially heads, speaks for its popularity in ancient times.[156]

ATTRIBU-　　Basing his study of Kresilas on the Perikles and the Amazon
TIONS　　(both of which however we must remember are tentative assignations) Furtwängler attributed to him the originals of the Athena

<hr />

152 The identification of the 'Protesilaos' in New York and London with Kresilas' statue (cf. the references given by Raubitschek, *Dedications*, pp. 143 f., 510) seems less likely. What connection, for instance, would the waves on the London base have with Dieitrephes?

153 *N.H.* XXXIV. 75; see also XXXIV. 53.

154 Cf. Furtwängler, *Masterpieces*, pp. 128 ff.

155 Cf. the analysis by Furtwängler, *op. cit.,* p. 134. This has of course been disputed by the adherents of other theories; but see Bieber, *Jahrbuch*, 1918, p. 72.

156 Cf. list given by Michaelis, *Jahrbuch*, I, 1886, p. 17, supplemented by Furtwängler, *op. cit.,* p. 132, note 1 and Anti, *Monumenti Antichi*, XXVI, 1920, cols. 501 ff.

Veiletri,[157] the Diomede,[158] the Medusa Rondanini,[159] and the Petworth Athlete[160] (cf. fig. 195). They certainly have in common certain marked characteristics—the long, narrow eyes with heavy lids and strongly marked tear-ducts, the vertical grooves above the nose (present in the Perikles and the Diomede), the full, finely modeled lips with a slight depression at the corners, and the rendering of the hair in a series of ringlets (somewhat freer in treatment in the Petworth Athlete). The heads are all noble, severe types with a touch of melancholy (specially noticeable in the Amazon and the Petworth head) which gives them an individual cast, imparting an interesting mingling of idealism and realism.

We have tried to peer through the darkness in which the personality of Kresilas is still hidden, and have obtained a certain realization of what his style perhaps was. But it is based only on guesses, and this we must bear in mind in any future reconstructions.

(c) Alkamenes

ALKAMENES seems to have been an Athenian; for he is referred to as such by Pliny[161] and most of his important works were made in Athens; moreover, in a competition with Agorakritos, a Parian, we are told that Alkamenes won, "not by the merit of his work, but by the votes of his city, whose people supported their townsman against an alien."[162] Besides this testimony Suidas'[163] statement that he was a Lemnian and Tzetzes'[164] that he was an islander can hardly be credited.   ORIGIN

The fame of Alkamenes was widely recognized: Pliny[165] speaks of him as "an artist of the first rank, whose works are to be found in many temples at Athens," Lucian[166] borrows from him several points for his perfect woman, and he is classed with the great Pheidias and Polykleitos by Dionysios of Halikarnassos.[167] Most of the available evidence points to the second half of the fifth century as the period of his activity. He is referred to generally as the pupil,[168] occa-   DATE

---

[157] Op. cit., p. 141.   [158] Ibid., p. 146.   [159] Ibid., p. 156.
[160] Ibid., p. 161; Metropolitan Museum, Handbook (1930), p. 253, fig. 177.
[161] N.H. XXXVI. 16.   [162] Pliny, N.H. XXXVI. 17.
[163] Under 'Αλκαμένης.
[164] Chil. VIII. 340. Unless, of course, they are referring to another Alkamenes (see p. 238).
[165] N.H. XXXVI. 16.   [166] Εἰκόνες. 6.
[167] περὶ τῆς Δημοσθένους λέξεως, 50. 1108.
[168] Pliny, N.H. XXXVI. 16 and 17, and XXXIV. 72.

sionally as the rival and contemporary[169] of Pheidias, terms not mutually exclusive of one another, for a pupil, even if considerably younger than his master, may later become his rival and even be called his contemporary. We have a definite date for what must have been one of his latest works—a colossal marble relief of Athena and Herakles "dedicated after the Tyranny of the Thirty"[170] (404–403 B.C.).

WORKS
Hermes
Propylaios

A herm of a bearded head[171] found at Pergamon (fig. 628) is inscribed: "You will recognize Alkamenes' beautiful statue, the Hermes before the gates. Pergamios set it up."[172] A similar but not identical herm found at Ephesos is also attested to be the work of Alkamenes by an inscription.[173] Both are evidently Roman copies or adaptations of a work by Alkamenes, perhaps the Hermes of the Gateway (ὃν Προπύλαιον ὀνομάζουσι) which Pausanias[173a] saw at the entrance of the Akropolis, but of which he does not name the sculptor. That it was a famous production is indicated by the large number of copies we have, large and small, preserved in many museums (cf. fig. 629[174]). The style of the herm is evidently archaistic, the formal treatment of the hair and beard being conditioned by its architectonic character; for the rendering of the eyes places it in the second half of the fifth century.

Seated
Dionysos

There are representations of a seated Dionysos on Roman coins of Athens[175] (fig. 631) which appear to reproduce the temple statue by Alkamenes seen by Pausanias[176] "in the ancient precinct of Dionysos close to the theater." The stiffness of the pose—compared to the Olympian Zeus—suggests a date before rather than after the Pheidian creation. The head, however, as it appears separately on the coins (fig. 630), in which the eyes are deep-set, places it well in the second half of the fifth century.

Other Works

Ancient writers speak of a Hephaistos "in whom, though he is standing upright and clothed, lameness is slightly indicated in a manner not unpleasing to the eyes,"[177] of a Hera in a temple on the

---

169 Pliny, *N.H.* XXXIV. 49 and Tzetzes, *Chil.* VIII. 340.
170 Pausanias IX. 11. 6.
171 Now in the Constantinople Museum; cf. Mendel, *Catalogue des sculptures*, II, No. 527.
172 Εἰδήσεις ʼΑλκαμένεος περικαλλὲς ἄγαλμα Ἑρμᾶν τὸν πρὸ πυλῶν. εἵσατο Περγάμιος.
173 Praschniker, *Oest. Jahr.*, XXIX, 1934, pp. 23 ff.; Picard, *Manuel*, II, pp. 554 f.
173a I. 22. 8.   174 Metropolitan Museum, *Catalogue of Bronzes*, No. 235.
175 Imhoof-Blumer and Gardner, *Numismatic Comm.*, pl. CC, Nos. I–IV, p. 142.
176 I. 20. 3.
177 Cicero, *N.D.* I. 30.

way from Phaleron to Athens,[178] an Ares,[179] an Asklepios,[180] and an athlete.[181] According to Pausanias[182] he was the first who made "three images of Hekate attached to each other"; and such a triple image by him called Hekate on the Tower stood in Athens beside the temple of Athena Nike. His masterpiece was evidently his Aphrodite in the Gardens, in which Lucian admired especially "the cheeks and prominent parts of the face, and furthermore the hands and the symmetry of the wrists and the delicacy of the tapering fingers";[183] "Pheidias himself is said to have put the finishing touches to this work."[184] None of these works have been satisfactorily identified[185] with extant statues. The Aphrodite of the Gardens was once thought to be reproduced in the Venus Genetrix type,[186] but except for its attractiveness and its evident popularity (there are many extant replicas[187]) we have unfortunately no convincing evidence. Moreover the figure appears too "pretty" for the sculptor of the imposing herm. Among the other attributions the one most persistently made of late is the group of Prokne and Itys in the Akropolis Museum[188] which is supposed to be identical with the group mentioned by Pausanias as dedicated by one Alkamenes—a common enough name in Athens and not at all necessarily the sculptor. Moreover the Akropolis statue has not the finish of workmanship we should expect from a great master like Alkamenes.[189]

It is difficult to form a proper estimate of the style of Alkamenes   STYLE from the meagre evidence at our disposal. We may gather at least from the descriptions of his works that his favorite subjects were deities, and that these must have suited his style best. This is borne out by Quintilian's[190] remark that Polykleitos' work lacked the majesty (*pondus*) which Pheidias and Alkamenes were both able to impart to their statues. The herm and the Dionysos certainly suggest

---

[178] Pausanias I. 1. 5.   [179] Pausanias I. 8. 4.
[180] Pausanias VIII. 9. 1.   [181] Pliny, *N.H.* XXXIV. 72.   [182] II. 30. 2.
[183] Εἰκόνες 6.   [184] Pliny, *N.H.* XXXVI. 16.
[185] For a summary of attributions made and some new suggestions, cf. Schröder, *Alkamenes-Studien* in *Winckelmannsprogramm*, 1921; cf. also Schrader, *Phidias*, pp. 184 ff.; Walston, *Alcamenes*, pp. 149 ff.; Picard, *Manuel*, II, pp. 551 ff.
[186] The best replica is in the Louvre; cf. Brunn-Bruckmann, *Denkmäler*, pl. 473.
[187] Harcum, *A.J.A.*, 1927, pp. 141 ff.
[188] Casson, *Catalogue*, pp. 257–258, Nos. 1358 and 2789.
[189] It does not stand comparison, for instance, with the Parthenon pediment figures (of which casts are conveniently placed in the same room in the Akropolis Museum), though the latter were to be seen at a considerable height.
[190] *Inst. orat.* XII. 10. 8 (7).

this quality of lofty serenity. So we can visualize Alkamenes as a worthy successor of Pheidias in his great idealistic conceptions.

But there is a piece of evidence which does not fit into this picture. Pausanias[191] in his description of the pediments of Olympia says that the pediment sculptures on the western end are by Alkamenes, "a contemporary of Pheidias and second only to him in the sculptor's art." It seems unlikely that Alkamenes should have been a prominent enough sculptor in 465–460 to be commissioned with a pediment composition of one of the most important temples in Greece and still be active after 403.[192] Moreover, the little that we learn of Alkamenes' style in the herm from Pergamon and the Dionysos on the coins is not in line with that of the Olympia pediments. We shall see later (see p. 243) that Pausanias' ascription of the east pediment to Paionios is also open to grave doubts. We must therefore either reject Pausanias' statement and put it down as one of his numerous mistakes, or we must suppose that there was an elder Alkamenes belonging to the first half of the fifth century. For the latter view some support may be gained from the fact that Pliny[193] places Alkamenes with such early sculptors as Critias (Kritios), Nesiotes, and Hegias. But since they are called contemporaries of Pheidias, and a date about 448 (83d Olympiad) is assigned to them, not much comfort can be derived therefrom; especially as Pliny's table is inaccurate in so many respects.

(d) Agorakritos

PLINY[194] gives the following account of Agorakritos: "Agorakritos of Paros was also a pupil of Pheidias, who was attracted by his youthful beauty, and so is said to have allowed his name to appear on several of his own works. Both pupils, however, entered into competition with representations of Aphrodite, and Alkamenes bore the palm; Agorakritos accordingly sold his statue, as the story goes, on the condition that it should not remain at Athens, and called it Nemesis; it was set up at Rhamnous, a deme of Attica, and was preferred by Varro to all statues." By other writers[195] this statue of

---

191 V. 10. 8.

192 For the marble relief of Athena and Herakles, cf. p. 236. Schrader's attempt (*Phidias*, pp. 135 ff.) to get out of the difficulty by assigning the later angle figures to Alkamenes is of course purely hypothetical.

193 *N.H.* XXXIV. 49.   194 *N.H.* XXXVI. 17.

195 Strabo, Zenobios, Suidas, Photios, Tzetzes, Hesychios, Pomponius, and Solinus; cf. Overbeck. *Schriftquellen*, 835–843.

Nemesis is assigned to Pheidias, in spite of the fact that on a fold of the garment was the signature of Agorakritos: Ἀγοράκριτος Πάριος ἐποίησεν, "Agorakritos of Paros made it"; the popular explanation given being that Pheidias let Agorakritos do this as a special favor. But Pliny's account is very specific and the fact that Photios,[196] who repeats the popular story, says that the statue was first made for Aphrodite reinforces Pliny's testimony.[197] Probably in later times the statue was attributed to the more famous artist and the story of Pheidias' generosity to his favorite in letting him attach his name to his own works was invented to support the claim.

We obtain further details regarding this statue from Pausanias:[198] "On the head of the goddess rests a crown bearing stags and small images of Victory; in her left hand she holds an apple branch, in her right a bowl on which Ethiopians are represented." It was of Parian marble,[199] ten cubits in height,[200] and was mounted on a base decorated with reliefs.[201] For its name, Nemesis, "of all deities the most implacable enemy of insolent men," Pausanias[202] gives a different account from that by Pliny; namely, that the Persians who landed at Marathon "incurred the wrath of the goddess for thinking in their pride that Athens lay as a prize at their feet and bringing Parian marble for the erection of a trophy as though they had accomplished their end." This marble was later made into the statue of Nemesis.

These stories assume special interest since a fragment of this statue was actually found during excavations in the temple of Nemesis at Rhamnous[203] (fig. 633). It is the upper part of a marble head and could easily be identified as the work in question, for it fits the evidence exactly. It is female, colossal, of Parian marble, of the style of the second half of the fifth century, and it has traces of a stephanos with holes above—to carry the crown described by Pausanias. So we may confidently take this little fragment as coming from the hand of Pheidias' favorite pupil. Small and battered though it is, its study teaches us that Agorakritos followed closely

196 Ῥαμνουσία Νέμεσις.
197 Cf. on this subject Wilamowitz, *Antigonos von Karystos* in *Philologische Untersuchungen*, IV, 1881, pp. 10 f.
198 I. 33. 2.   199 Pausanias I. 33. 2.
200 Zenob. V. 82.   201 Pausanias I. 33. 7–8.
202 I. 33. 2.
203 Rossbach, *Ath. Mitt.*, 1890, pp. 64 ff. It is now in the British Museum, cf. Smith, *Catalogue*, I, No. 460.

in the footsteps of his great master. The flat, wavy hair, the accentuated lower eyelid, the simple modeling of the cheek are closely paralleled on the figures of the Parthenon frieze; and they produce the same general effect of serenity and grandeur. It has been suggested that we may obtain a general idea of the statue from the representations on fourth-century coins of Cyprus of a goddess holding a phiale and a branch[204] (fig. 634); but this is problematical. There have also been found a number of fragments of the relief which decorated its base,[205] including heads of women (cf. fig. 635) and youths, parts of draped bodies, and a horse's head. The execution—in very high relief, about half life-size—is charmingly delicate, though somewhat cursory, as would be natural in a decorative composition, probably designed by Agorakritos but executed by his assistants. We learn from Pausanias that the subject was Leda bringing Helen to Nemesis in the presence of Homeric heroes;[206] and we can obtain an idea of its composition by a Roman copy of four of the figures in Stockholm.[207]

There are two other works by Agorakritos mentioned by ancient writers—a bronze group of Athena Itonia and Zeus in the temple of Athena at Koroneia in Boeotia[208] and a statue of the Mother of the Gods.[209] The latter is described as seated, holding a cymbal in her hand, and with lions under her throne. We may therefore have reproductions of it in a type which occurs in a number of replicas in many variations and corresponds to this general description.[210]

From all this evidence we learn that Agorakritos was a worthy representative of the idealistic school which Pheidias had inaugurated.

(e) Kallimachos

OF Kallimachos we know the following: he made a golden lamp for the Athena Polias[211] (in the Erechtheion, which was completed in 408) and a seated image of Hera[212] for a temple at Plataia which

---

204 Six, *Numismatic Chronicle*, 3d series, vol. II, 1882, pl. V, pp. 89–102.

205 National Museum, Athens, Nos. 203–214.   206 Pausanias I. 33. 7–8.

207 Kjellberg, *Nationalmusée Arsbok*, 1923, pp. 1 ff., fig. 1. Compare the reconstruction made previous to the identification of the Stockholm relief by Pallat, *Jahrbuch*, 1894, p. 9.

208 Pausanias IX. 34. 1.

209 Pliny, *N.H.* XXVI. 17; attributed to Pheidias by Pausanias I. 3. 5, and Arrian, *Peripl. Pont. euxin.* 9.

210 von Salis, *Jahrbuch*, 1913, pp. 1 ff.   211 Pausanias I. 26. 6.

212 Pausanias IX. 2. 7.

was erected after 426. He is said to have invented the Corinthian capital,[213] and to have been the first[214] "to bore marble"[215] (λίθους πρῶτος ἐτρύπησε), that is, to employ the drill. He was known for the finicking quality of his work. Pliny[216] says of him: "Of all the artists Kallimachos is the most remarkable for the epithet applied to him. He continually subjected his own work to the severest criticism and bestowed endless labor upon it, for which reason he was called *catatexitechnus*, 'the man who enfeebles his art'; a memorable warning that even diligence must have its limit. His dancing maidens of Sparta is a work of flawless precision, but one robbed of all its charm by the excessive labor spent on it." Vitruvius[217] and Dionysios of Halikarnassos[218] both speak of the elegance and grace of his work. It is ingenuity, then, and graceful elaboration that characterize this master. The latter quality can be detected in the archaistic relief in the Capitoline Museum of Pan and the Three Graces (fig. 636) on which is the inscription, "Kallimachos made it,"[219] apparently of Roman date. The relief is clearly not an original by Kallimachos, but perhaps a later copy of one of his works[220] or merely signed by a copyist. The Spartan dancers (Pliny's *saltantes Lacaenae*) have been recognized in a number of reliefs of the Roman period, and the stylistically related dancing Maenads, of which copies exist in Madrid (cf. fig. 515), Rome, and New York (fig. 638), have also been connected with Kallimachos.[221] The almost exaggerated transparency of the garments would place their prototypes at the very end of the fifth or the beginning of the fourth century, which is the period in which Kallimachos appears to have been active; and their elaboration and elegance bear out the estimate in which Kallimachos was held. So the attribution is certainly a possible one. And it would make us agree with Pausanias'[222] statement that Kallimachos "fell short of the first rank in his art"; for his figures, charming though they are, lack the significance of the great works of this period.

[213] Vitruvius IV. 1. 10.
[214] This can hardly be correct, for both the simple drill and the running drill were in use at an earlier period, cf. p. 144.
[215] Pausanias I. 26. 7.   [216] *N.H.* XXXIV. 92.
[217] IV. 1. 10.   [218] *De Isocrate* 543R.
[219] Helbig, *Führer*,[3] I, No. 844; Loewy, *Inschriften*, No. 500.
[220] Cf. Schmidt, *Archaistische Kunst*, pp. 62–63; Brunn-Bruckmann, *Denkmäler*, pl. 654, left.
[221] Rizzo, *Thiasos;* Richter, *A.J.A.*, XL, 1936, pp. 11 ff.; Caputo, *La Danza delle Menadi.*
[222] I. 26. 6.

(f) Paionios

PAIONIOS of Mende, in Thrace, is known to us by an original work found in Olympia in 1875.[223] It is a statue of a flying Victory with an eagle beneath her, the whole mounted on a high triangular base[224] (fig. 637). On the latter is the following inscription:[225] "The Messenians and Naupaktians dedicated [it] to Olympian Zeus as a tithe of the spoil of their enemies. Paionios of Mende made the statue and was a successful competitor in the construction of the akroteria for the temple." To make our evidence complete the statue is described by Pausanias:[226] "The Dorian Messenians who formerly received Naupaktos from the Athenians dedicated at Olympia a statue on a pillar. This was the work of Paionios of Mende, and was set up from spoils taken from the enemy when the Messenians were at war with the Akarnanians and the people of Oiniadai. Such at least is my view; but the Messenians themselves assert that the statue is a memorial of the engagement in the island of Sphakteria in which they fought beside the Athenians and that they did not inscribe the name of the enemy on the monument for fear of the Spartans, while they had no fear of the Akarnanians or the people of Oiniadai." We can imagine Pausanias in the Altis puzzling over the inscriptions and wondering who the enemy referred to was! It is not likely, however, that his guess is right, for in the expedition against the Oiniadai (in 452 B.C.) the Messenians were anything but successful and had to beat a hasty retreat by night. There is no reason, therefore, to doubt the Messenian tradition that the engagement referred to was the battle of Sphakteria. This places the statue not long after 424, a date which accords well with its style; for the transparency of the drapery against the body and its sweeping folds where it is blown around the figure are characteristics of the last quarter of the fifth century.[227] Attempts made to date the statue earlier, about 450,[228] are supposed to derive support from the early style of the head, better preserved replicas of which have recently

---

223 Furtwängler, *Olympia*, III, pls. XLVI–XLVIII, text, pp. 182 f.; for the latest reconstruction by Grüttner, cf. Pomtow, *Jahrbuch*, 1922, p. 62, fig. 5.

224 Nine blocks of the base have been found. It has been estimated that originally there were twelve blocks, which would bring the total height to nearly 30 feet.

225 Loewy, *Inschriften*, No. 49.   226 V. 26. 1.   227 See pp. 99 f.

228 Amelung, *Röm. Mitt.*, IX, pp. 168 f.; but see the discussion by Furtwängler, *Olympia*, III, text, pp. 191 ff.; and recently, Pfuhl, *Jahrbuch*, 1926, p. 25.

been discovered[229]—the "Hertz head"[230] (figs. 639, 640) and the head from the Vatican Magazzini[231] (fig. 641). But the early appearance of the former is largely due to the rendering of the nose, which is restored, while a study of the eyes with the delicately modeled lower lids and of the rounded mouth point to a later date; and this is fully borne out by the Vatican head, in which the work is more delicate and variegated, thoroughly in line with later fifth-century work. The beautiful poise of the figure and the bold and yet restrained composition show us Paionios as a sculptor of individuality, strongly imbued with the great conceptions of his period.

The date of the Nike is important in our consideration of Pausanias' attribution to Paionios of the eastern pediment of the temple of Zeus at Olympia:[232] "The sculptures of the front pediment are the work of Paionios, a native of Mende in Thrace." Though the period of time which separates the pediment sculptures from the Nike is not so great as in the case of Alkamenes,[233] it is nevertheless considerable. But a more important difficulty is the difference of style. How is it possible to attribute to the same master works stylistically so far removed from each other? It is best, therefore, to suppose either that Pausanias was mistaken, or that there was an earlier Paionios. Possibly Pausanias was misled by the statement in the inscription that Paionios "made the akroteria of the temple" and confused them in his mind with the pediment. The akroteria are elsewhere described by Pausanias:[234] "A gilt kettle is set on each extremity of the roof of the temple at Olympia; and a Victory, also gilt, stands just at the middle of the gable."[235]

(g) Strongylion

PAUSANIAS describes a bronze statue of the wooden horse which he saw on the Akropolis: "The story of the horse is that it contained the bravest of the Greeks, and the bronze horse is in accordance therewith, for Menestheus and Teukros are leaning out of it, and

[229] They show some variations from the Olympia example, e.g., in the rendering of the headband.

[230] Amelung, *op. cit.*, 1894, pp. 162 f.

[231] Kaschnitz-Weinberg, *Sculture del Magazzino del Museo Vaticano*, No. 47, pp. 29 ff., pl. XV.

[232] V. 10. 6.   [233] See pp. 237 f.   [234] V. 10. 4.

[235] That this Victory was a reduced copy of the one on the triangular base is not suggested by our present knowledge of Greek sculpture. This applies also to Pom-

the sons of Theseus also."[236] Part of the marble base of this ambitious composition was found on the Akropolis in 1840 (fig. 644) with the following inscription: "Chairedemos, the son of Euangelos of Koile, dedicated it. Strongylion made it."[237] Aristophanes refers to this horse in his *Birds*[238] and cites the first five words of the inscription. The lettering of the inscription also agrees with a date in the last quarter of the fifth century.

Pausanias and Pliny mention other works by Strongylion—an Amazon "with beautiful legs" greatly admired by Nero, who carried it with him from place to place;[239] a boy to whom Brutus became so attached that it went by the name of "Bruti puer";[240] Muses on Mount Helikon;[241] and an Artemis called "the Saviour" (Σώτειρα) at Megara.[242] The latter is represented on Roman coins of Megara and Pegai[243] (fig. 643), where the goddess appears in a short chiton, running, with a torch in each hand. Sometimes the figure is mounted on a base inside a temple. A figure in such rapid motion is unusual for a temple statue and like the bronze horse bears out the originality of the artist. From Pausanias[244] we learn also that Strongylion made "oxen[238a] and horses of remarkable excellence." He was evidently, like Myron, a great animal sculptor; and he was akin to him also in his adventurous spirit.

(h) Polykleitos

ORIGIN   POLYKLEITOS calls himself "an Argive" on the base of his statue of Pythokles[245] and he is referred to as such by Plato[246] and Pausanias.[247] Pliny's[248] statement that he came from Sikyon, the successor of Argos in civic and artistic importance, is an understandable anachronism.

DATE   He is said to have been a pupil of the Argive Ageladas.[249] Plato calls

tow's theory (*Jahrbuch*, 1922, pp. 55 ff.) that the statue erected on the Messenian triangular base in Delphi was the bronze original from which the Victory in Olympia was copied. The fifth century was an age of original creations, not of replicas.

236 Pausanias I. 23. 8. On Strongylion cf. Lippold, Pauly-Wissowa, *Lexikon*, IV A, cols. 372 ff.

237 Loewy, *Inschriften*, No. 52; Stevens, *Hesperia*, V, 1936, p. 460 f.; Raubitschek, *Dedications*, No. 176 and p. 524.

238 1128.

238a For one of his bulls cf. Stevens, *Hesperia*, Supplement III, pp. 19 ff.

239 Pliny, *N.H.* XXXIV. 82.   240 *Ibid.*

241 Pausanias IX. 30. 1.   242 Pausanias I. 40. 2.

243 Imhoof-Blumer and Gardner, *Numismatic Commentary*, pl. A, Nos. I–II.

244 IX. 30. 1.   245 Loewy, *Inschriften*, No. 91.

246 *Protag.* 311 C.

247 III. 18. 7 and VI. 6. 2. See also *Anthol. Gr.* II. 185. 5.

248 *N.H.* XXXIV. 55.   249 Pliny, *N.H.* XXXIV. 55.

Polykleitos a contemporary of Pheidias[250] and represents his sons as
of an age[251] with those of Perikles. Pythokles, the young Elean, of
whom he made a statue at Olympia[252] the base of which has been found
(see above), was victorious in the pentathlon in 452 B.C.[253] The same
year an Olympic victory was won by one Ariston,[254] probably identical
with Aristion the boxer of Epidauros, whose statue Polykleitos made
at Olympia[255] and the base of which was found there.[256] The apparently later date of the inscriptions,[257] especially in the case of that of
Aristion, which led to the former assignment of the statues to the
younger Polykleitos, can be explained by the supposition that the
original ones became defaced and were later replaced. Polykleitos'
statue of Kyniskos may be assigned by its inscription to 450–440.[258]
The chryselephantine Hera of Argos must have been made shortly
after the fire which destroyed the old Heraion in the 89th Olympiad,
c. 422;[259] hence Pliny's[260] date for Polykleitos as the 90th Olympiad,
c. 420. Pausanias[261] mentions Polykleitos as making an Aphrodite
as a support of a tripod "dedicated from the spoils of the victory at
Aigospotamoi" (405). If he (and not the younger Polykleitos) was
really at work on this monument[262] it must have been one of his latest
products; and his activity then ranges from 452 or earlier to the end
of the century.

For our estimate of Polykleitos there is no original statue extant; WORKS
but several of his famous works have been recognized in Roman
copies and from them we can derive a glimpse of this great per-
sonality. Pliny[263] describes one of Polykleitos' works as "a boy of   *The Doryphoros*
manly form bearing a lance, called 'the Canon' by artists, who
draw from it the rudiments of art as from a code (so that Polykleitos is held to be the only man who has embodied art itself in a
work of art)." This together with Pliny's statements[264] that a characteristic of Polykleitos' statues is "the way they step forward with
one leg" and that Varro thought that "they are squarely built and

250 *Protag.* 311 C.   251 *Op. cit.*, 328 C.
252 Pausanias VI. 7. 10.
253 Grenfell and Hunt, *Oxyrhynchus Papyri*, II, p. 90, col. II, line 14.
254 *Ibid.*, p. 90, line 16.   255 Pausanias VI. 13. 6.
256 Loewy, *Inschriften*, No. 92.   257 Cf. *ibid.*, Nos. 91, 92.
258 *Ibid.*, No. 50.
259 Thucydides IV. 133. The new building was started immediately by Eupolemos,
cf. Pausanias II. 17. 3.
260 *N.H.* XXXIV. 49.   261 III. 18. 8.
262 Cf. Furtwängler, *Masterpieces*, p. 224.
263 *N.H.* XXXIV. 55; cf. Stuart Jones, *ad loc.*   264 *N.H.* XXXIV. 56.

seem almost to be made on a uniform pattern," have enabled archaeologists to identify a type preserved in several replicas as Polykleitos' famous statue. It is also significant that a fourth-century
Greek stele found at Argos shows a youth in the attitude of the
Doryphoros[265] (fig. 649). The best copy in the round was found in
Pompeii and is now in the Naples Museum[266] (fig. 645). A broad-
shouldered youth is represented in a walking attitude, his weight
mostly on his right leg, his left placed sidewise and backward; with
the left hand he grasps a lance, the right arm is lowered. He has a
flat, long skull with hair arranged in superimposed, flat ringlets,
following closely the contour of the skull (figs. 646, 647,[267] 648[268]).
In spite of the hardness and mechanical character of the Roman
copies, we can sense from them some of the beauty of proportion for
which the original was famous. There is a harmony of line, a poise
and relaxation in the attitude never before attained in the history
of Greek sculpture. This is largely due to the new scheme in which
the arm which hangs loosely down is on the side of the supporting
leg, while the arm which is bent and holds an attribute is on the side
of the relaxed leg; it is a reversal of the older scheme and makes for
greater harmony by distributing the muscular action between the
two sides of the body.[269] Moreover, the modeling shows a complete
understanding of the human body. Every detail is accurately rendered and even veins are indicated. In other words the long struggles in the representation of the standing human figure here find
their consummation. Henceforth this subject could be treated differently but not more perfectly. The original seems to have played
an important rôle. We are told that Lysippos regarded it as his
master,[270] and that sculptors in general took it as their model.[271] It
evidently not only marked an epoch when it was created but long
held its own as a great achievement.

That Polykleitos wrote a book on proportion and embodied his
system in this statue is of course of great interest—especially to us
today who have begun to appreciate again the value of design. It

[265] *Ath. Mitt.*, 1878, pl. XIII; in the National Museum, Athens, No. 8153.
[266] Ruesch, *Guida del Museo Nazionale di Napoli*, No. 146 (6011); for a list of the
other replicas, cf. Furtwängler, *op. cit.*, pp. 228–229; Neugebauer, *Berliner Museen*,
XLVIII, 1927, 2, pp. 1 ff.; Anti, *Mon. ant.*, XXVI, 1920, cols. 628 ff.
[267] Shear, *A.J.A.*, 1926, p. 462.
[268] Comparetti and de Petra, *La Villa ercolanese*, pl. VIII, 3.
[269] Cf. Furtwängler, *Masterpieces*, pp. 226–227.
[270] Cicero, *Brut.* 86. 296.   [271] Quintilian, *Inst. orat.* V. 12. 21.

confirms what we know from other sources, that the Greeks found
the problems of composition absorbing. Unfortunately it is difficult
to recover Polykleitos' original scheme from the Roman copies—
which might so easily be inaccurate in detail. We know only that it
was an interrelation of parts; since Galen[272] tells us that "Chrysippos holds beauty to consist in the proportions not of the elements
but of the parts, that is to say, of finger to finger and of all the
fingers to the palm and wrist, and of these to the forearm, and of
the forearm to the upper arm, and of all the parts to each other, as
they are set forth in the Canon of Polykleitos." And this interrelation cannot have been purely arithmetical, as Vitruvius proposes,
for that has been shown not to fit. It is more likely from what we
know so far of Greek design that the scheme was geometrical[273] and
that it is the subtle interrelation of volumes that gives us delight
also now.

Pliny[274] lists as another work of Polykleitos "a youth of boyish   *Diadoumenos*
form binding his hair, famous for its price, 100 talents."[275] By a
comparison with the Doryphoros it has been possible to identify a
type preserved in a number of replicas as reproducing this statue
(cf. figs. 650–652). A youth is represented raising his arm to bind
a fillet round his head. The attitude of the body, the clear demarcation of the various planes formed by the muscles, the rather shallow
pelvic curve, and the square, broad-shouldered build are the same as
in the Doryphoros. But by certain, perhaps slight, modifications a
feeling of greater freedom is produced. The raising of the arms, the
marked inclination of the head to one side, introduce more variety
in the upper part of the figure and give it added interest. Moreover, the left leg is placed more sidewise and this increases the ani-
mation of the pose. The treatment of the head also shows considerable advance. There is more variation in the modeling of the face,
the lower part is softer and the hair is more plastic. Clearly the
Diadoumenos is a later work than the Doryphoros, dating probably
from about 430, while the Doryphoros may be placed at about 450.
We are fortunate in having several good copies which can more adequately reflect the qualities of the original than was possible in the
case of the Doryphoros. The best full-size replica was found at

272 Diels, *Die Fragmente der Vorsokratiker*⁴ I, No. 28, pp. 295 f.
273 Cf. p. 117. Cf. also Lucian, Φιλοψευδής, 18.
274 *N.H.* XXXIV. 55.
275 Paid, of course, in Hellenistic or Roman times.

Delos (fig. 650) and is now in the National Museum in Athens.[276] Another excellent copy is in Madrid.[277] The statues from Vaison in the British Museum,[278] and in Turin, are not of the same calibre; but fine heads are preserved in Dresden,[279] Cassel,[280] and New York[280a] (fig. 652), a large terracotta statuette is in New York[281] (fig. 651), and there are a number of other copies.[282] The original evidently enjoyed great popularity. And small wonder. From the point of view of composition it is unquestionably one of the most rhythmical creations of antiquity, retaining the sturdiness of the earlier age but with an added harmony. That Polykleitos could advance from the Doryphoros to the Diadoumenos shows that he, like Pheidias, was capable of great development. And that he improved in composition after he had produced his great "Canon" indicates his continued interest in and feeling for design. The other quality which we hear was characteristic of Polykleitos—his high finish—can also be appreciated in the best copies of the Diadoumenos. The treatment of the curls, especially, with their wealth of detail (and in the original bronze they would be ofcourse much crisper) reminds us of Plutarch's[283] remark that "Polykleitos said that the work was most difficult when the clay came under the nail." It was evidently the last finishing touches in which Polykleitos delighted.

Hera   Polykleitos' most important work was considered to be his temple statue of Hera in the Heraion near Argos. It is described by Pausanias:[284] "The image of Hera is colossal in size, seated upon a throne: it is made of gold and ivory, and is the work of Polykleitos; on her head is a crown adorned with Graces and Seasons; in one hand she holds the fruit of the pomegranate, in the other a scepter. They say that a cuckoo is perched on the scepter." The statue is compared by writers with the gold and ivory Zeus by Pheidias. Strabo[285] considers Polykleitos' work the more beautiful in workmanship ($\tau\acute{\epsilon}\chi\nu\eta$), but second in magnificence ($\pi o\lambda v\tau\epsilon\lambda\epsilon\acute{\iota}\alpha$) and size

276 No. 1826; cf. *Monuments Piot*, III, 1896, pp. 137 f., pls. XIV–XV.
277 Ricard, *Marbres antiques*, pp. 38 f.
278 Smith, *Catalogue*, I, No. 500.
279 Furtwängler, *op. cit.*, pls. X and XII.
280 Bieber, *Katalog*, p. 10.
280a Richter, *A.J.A.*, 1935, pp. 46 ff.
281 Metropolitan Museum, *Bulletin*, 1932, pp. 250 ff.
282 Cf. Anti, *Monumenti antichi*, XXVI, 1920, cols. 632–634, and Picard, *Manuel*, II, pp. 288 ff.
283 *Quaest. Conv.* II. 3. 2.   284 II. 17. 4.
285 VIII. 372.

to the Zeus. When the Heraion was excavated in 1892 the base of
the statue was discovered,[286] and fragments of the metopes[287] and
pediment sculptures were found; but no piece of the statue appeared. Our only means of visualizing it now is by the beautiful
head of Hera which makes its appearance on the coins of Argos
(fig. 653) at about the period of the statue,[288] and by the representations of a seated goddess on Argive coins of the Roman period[289] (fig. 654) answering closely to Pausanias' description. Even
in these little reliefs we can sense the harmony of the composition.
It differs from the Zeus by Pheidias in several important features.
In the Hera there are no side-rails to the throne, the arms of the
figure are extended more sidewise, the sceptre is grasped higher,
and the legs are placed farther forward than in the Zeus. By these
changes a greater sense of freedom is obtained. All tension has disappeared and we have a rhythmical design comparable to that of
the Diadoumenos. But at the same time—compared with the creation of Pheidias—there is an impairment of dignity. We can understand Quintilian's[290] criticism—that while Polykleitos' works excelled all others in finish (*diligentia*) and grace (*decor*), they
lacked the grandeur (*pondus*) of the products of Pheidias.

In Pliny's story of the competition in statues of Amazons (see p.   *The Amazon*
229) the one by Polykleitos was placed first, while Pheidias' came
second. Of the types of Amazons preserved to us in Roman copies
we have seen that the Mattei one has on good grounds been assigned
to Pheidias (see pp. 229 f.). That leaves the Berlin and Capitoline
types to be divided between Polykleitos and Kresilas (cf. p. 236),
and of these the former appears more distinctly Polykleitan[291] (fig.
655). An Amazon is represented leaning on a pillar, her right hand
resting on her head. Beneath her left breast is a wound, but her

---

[286] Waldstein, *Argive Heraeum*.   [287] Described by Pausanias II. 17. 3.
[288] Cf. Head, *Historia numorum*, p. 438, fig. 240. The stephanos has a decoration
of palmettes and scrolls instead of the Graces and Seasons described by Pausanias—
a natural simplification when the scale was so much reduced.
[289] Imhoof-Blumer and Gardner, *Numismatic Commentary*, pl. I, Nos. XII–XV,
p. 34.
[290] *Inst. orat.* XII. 10 (7).
[291] For differing views, cf. p. 231. Those who assign the Capitoline statue to Polykleitos hold that its square build and the prominent inner vastus of the knee are characteris-
tically Polykleitan. But surely Polykleitos might attenuate the squareness in a female
statue, and the prominent inner vastus is not peculiarly Polykleitan but occurs also in
other fifth-century statues. The harmonious composition of the Berlin type—which
makes it worthy of winning the first prize in the competition—seems to me a stronger
argument.

pain is suggested merely by a certain lassitude in the pose. A comparison with the Doryphoros and the Diadoumenos brings out a close kinship—not only in the features and the hair (fig. 656) but above all in the general conception and the pose with the identical stance of the legs and the same fine curve of the body. Here too the chief interest of the sculptor was clearly to create a rhythmical scheme attained by counterpoise: the right leg and left arm balance each other as upright supporting members, the right arm and left leg as curving supports at rest. The resulting harmony is what we have learned was the distinguishing quality of Polykleitos' work, and what moreover is conspicuously absent in the rather straight design of the Capitoline Amazon which we have assigned to Kresilas (p. 236). The graceful chiton on the Berlin Amazon with its meticulous folds is also in line with what we are told of Polykleitos' love of high finish. The many replicas of this type of Amazon show how much admired it was. The specimens in Berlin[292] and New York[293] are the best preserved (in the latter, part of the marble pillar is original).[294] The bronze statuette in Florence[295] is interesting since it is in the same material as the original probably was; but it is not carefully worked and both arms are restored.

Kyniskos   It is possible that we possess a copy of Polykleitos' Kyniskos[296] in the so-called Westmacott Athlete,[297] the statue of a boy placing a wreath on his head (fig. 658). The type is preserved in many replicas, a mark of its popularity. It shows Polykleitan affinities in the pose with one leg placed backward and sidewise, in the modeling of the body with its well-developed pelvic bones, in the hair with its clinging strands. The attitude corresponds to the footmarks on the base of Kyniskos found at Olympia.[298] The inscription on this base can be dated about 450–440, and this is also the period in which the Westmacott Athlete must stylistically be placed. So that the evidence, while not at all conclusive,[299] favors the identification.

292 *Beschreibung der antiken Skulpturen*, No. 7.
293 Formerly in the Lansdowne Collection; cf. Metropolitan Museum, *Bulletin*, 1933, pp. 2 ff.
294 For a list of other copies, cf. Michaelis, *Jahrbuch*, 1886, I, pp. 14 ff.; Anti, *Mon. ant.*, XXVI, 1920, p. 602, note 3.
295 Milani, *Il Museo archeologico di Firenze*, pl. CXXXVI, 2.
296 Cf. Pausanias VI. 4. 11: "The statue of Kyniskos, the boy boxer from Mantineia, is by Polykleitos."
297 Smith, *Catalogue of Greek Sculpture in the British Museum*, III, No. 1754.
298 Loewy, *Inschriften*, No. 50, gives a facsimile.
299 There are other "Polykleitan" figures with feet placed like the Kyniskos.

Polykleitos' gifts of exquisite finish and harmonious composition naturally marked him out as a sculptor of athletes, and we know of a number of Olympic victors whom he portrayed—Aristion of Epidauros,[300] Thersilochos of Korkyra,[301] Antipatros of Miletos,[302] Pythokles of Elis,[303] and Xenokles of Mainalos,[304] mostly young boys victorious in boxing and wrestling. Though we could play at the fascinating game of connecting preserved statues with these names, such a pastime is not within our province, since the evidence for any identification is too slight. But we can form some idea of the winning grace and finish which doubtless were the chief characteristics of these statues from the Idolino in Florence (figs. 43, 44), a copy of a late fifth-century work of this type.

The other works attributed to Polykleitos by Pliny[306] are also unfortunately mere names: a man scraping himself, a nude figure hurling a javelin, two boys playing with knuckle-bones, "considered by many to be the most faultless work of sculpture," a Hermes, a Herakles, a captain putting on his armor, and a portrait of Artemon, called the Man in the Litter.[307] We also hear of two bronze Kanephoroi, "not large in size . . ., of maidenly aspect and garb, who with uplifted arms were carrying on their heads certain sacred objects according to the custom of Athenian girls,"[308] and an Aphrodite at Amyklai.[309]

Most of these works, if not all, were probably of bronze, since Polykleitos is included in Pliny's[310] chapter on *Statuaria*, "bronze sculpture," and that material doubtless suited his highly finished style the best. Also his novel compositions with extended and raised arms would be more successful in bronze, which needed no supports. But like other Greek sculptors Polykleitos must have been many-sided and eager to try his hand in different mediums. We know that his Hera at Argos was of gold and ivory, and there is no reason to

---

[300] Pausanias VI. 13. 6; Loewy, *op. cit.*, 92; Grenfell and Hunt, *The Oxyrhynchus Papyri*, II, p. 94, line 16.

[301] Pausanias VI. 13. 6.   [302] Pausanias VI. 2. 6.

[303] Pausanias VI. 7. 10; Loewy, *op. cit.*, 91; Grenfell and Hunt, *op. cit.*, II, p. 90, line 14.

[304] Pausanias VI. 9. 2; Loewy, *op. cit.*, 90.

[305] For a replica of the head cf. Kaschnitz-Weinberg, *Sculture del Magazzino del Vaticano*, no. 60, pl. XIX.

[306] *N.H.* XXXIV. 55.

[307] An engineer employed by Perikles at the siege of Samos, 440 B.C.; being lame he was carried about in a litter.

[308] Cicero, *In Verrem* IV. 3. 5, and Symmachos, *Epist.* I. 23.

[309] Pausanias III. 18. 7.   [310] Pliny, *N.H.* XXXIV. 55.

doubt his authorship of the Zeus Meilichios at Argos[311] and the group of Apollo, Leto, and Artemis on Mount Lykone[312] purely because they were of marble.[313] We are also told by Pliny that he contributed to the development of embossed metalwork[314] (see p. 231).

STYLE While Pheidias consummated the idealistic trend in Greek sculpture and became its chief exponent, Polykleitos perfected the athletic conception—manly, harmonious, reverent. He did not rise to the same heights of conception as Pheidias, but he attained perfection in the humbler task he had set himself. In the words of Quintilian, "he made the human form more beautiful than it is but he failed to convey the majesty (*auctoritatem*) of the gods."[315] And his virile creations had an abiding influence on the art of his country.

(i) Followers of Polykleitos

OF Polykleitos' immediate followers we know little.[316] A few names have been handed down, such as Patrokles[317] and his sons Naukydes,[318] Daidalos,[319] and the younger Polykleitos.[320] Pliny and Pausanias[321] list some of their works. The subjects of most of them appear to have been figures of athletes, as we should expect from followers of Polykleitos; but we also hear occasionally of statues of deities and of larger groups, for instance, the bronze monument of gods and Spartan heroes dedicated by the Spartans after Aigospotamoi (404 B.C.). No identifications with extant statues or reliefs are, however, possible; except the little Hebe standing beside Polykleitos' Hera, which appears on Argive coins[322] of the second century A.D. (fig. 657). According to Pausanias[323] this statue was of ivory and gold and was the work of Naukydes. She is an attractive little figure in a belted chiton, with right arm lowered, the left ex-

---

[311] Pausanias II. 20. 1.   [312] Pausanias II. 24. 5.
[313] Cf. Stuart Jones, *Selected Passages*, notes on 165, 166.
[314] *N.H.* XXXIV. 56. Richter, *A.J.A.*, XLV, 1941, pp. 377 ff.
[315] *Inst. orat.* XII. 10. 7.
[316] For a full discussion of the available evidence, cf. Johnson, *Lysippos*, pp. 4 ff.
[317] Pliny, *N.H.* XXXIV. 50. 91; Pausanias X. 9. 10.
[318] Loewy, *Inschriften*, Nos. 86, 87; Naukydes must have been the eldest, for he made two statues of Cheimon (Pausanias VI. 9. 3), who won a victory in 448 B.C. (Grenfell and Hunt, *The Oxyrhynchus Papyri*, II, 95, 28).
[319] Loewy, *op. cit.*, No. 88.
[320] Pausanias II. 22. 7 and VI. 6. 2. For a good discussion of the troublesome question as to which works should be ascribed to the younger Polykleitos instead of his more famous predecessor, cf. Johnson, *op. cit.*, pp. 22 ff.
[321] Cf. Overbeck, *Schriftquellen*, 986 ff.
[322] Imhoof-Blumer and Gardner, *Numismatic Commentary*, pl. I, No. XV, p. 34.
[323] II. 17. 5.

tended toward the Hera. The quiet lines of the drapery are in keeping with the simple pose. She is evidently conceived as a subsidiary figure so as not to detract from the interest of the chief composition.

To form some idea of the larger groups of this school we may study the sculptural remains of the Heraion of Argos (fragments of the metopes and the pediments[324]). Here we find figures, often in violent action, in which the types of faces (cf. fig. 165) and the rendering of the drapery show marked Attic influence. Evidently not even the self-contained Peloponnesians could remain untouched by the achievements of Pheidias and his followers.

The wealth of artistic talent in Greece at this period can be gauged by the large number of distinguished artists whom we know only by name or perhaps by the mention of some of their works.[325] That, for instance, one Telephanes of Phokis should have been put on a footing of equality with Polykleitos, Myron, and Pythagoras,[326] and that we know nothing further of him except that his Larisa, his portrait of Spintharos and his Apollo evoked admiration,[327] make us realize the extent of our loss.[328]

[324] Cf. Waldstein, *Argive Heraeum,* I, pls. XXX ff.; Eichler, *Oest. Jahresh.,* 1919, pp. 15 ff.

[325] Cf. Overbeck, *op. cit.,* 844–850 (Kolotes), 853–869 (Thrasymedes, Theokosmos, Praxias, Androsthenes, Lykios, Styppax), 897–928 (Demetrios, Pyrrhos, Sokrates the philosopher, Nikeratos, Pyromachos, Deinomenes, Kleiton), 1020–1041 (Apellas, Nikodamos, Kleoitas and Aristokles, Kallikles, Sostratos, Patrokles).

[326] Pliny, *N.H.* XXXIV. 68.

[327] *Ibid.*

[328] It is also significant that most of the sculptors who worked on the frieze of the Erechtheion and whose names are cited in the building inscription are not known to us from any other source (cf. Caskey in Paton and others, *The Erechtheum,* p. 415).

CHAPTER IV

FOURTH CENTURY B.C.

(a) Kephisodotos

WITH Kephisodotos we pass to the next great period in the history of Greek art, the fourth century B.C. There were two sculptors by the name of Kephisodotos, both Athenians, one placed by Pliny[1] in the 102d Olympiad or 372 B.C., the other in the 121st Olympiad or 296 B.C. Since the latter was a son of Praxiteles, it is possible that the older one was Praxiteles' father or perhaps his elder brother; for the same name runs in families in alternate or, more rarely, in successive generations. It is the elder Kephisodotos that here concerns us. Pliny's date is borne out by Plutarch's[2] statement that he was the brother-in-law of Phokion (402–317).

ORIGIN AND DATE

Kephisodotos is known to us by copies of one of his works, "Peace bearing the child Wealth in her arms," which he is said to have made for the Athenians.[3] This group stood on the Areopagos[4] and was erected probably soon after Timotheos' victory over the Spartans (375), when we know that a cult of Eirene was introduced at Athens.[5] It has been identified with groups corresponding to Pausanias' description which appear on Roman coins of Athens[6] (fig. 661) and in several marble replicas. Of the latter the best preserved is in Munich[7] (fig. 659); another replica, headless and armless but of good workmanship, is in New York[8] (fig. 660); two others, considerably restored, in the Museo Torlonia;[9] and children from two

WORKS
Eirene

---

[1] *N.H.* XXXIV. 50. [2] *Phokion* 19.

[3] Pausanias IX. 16. 1. Cf. Rizzo, *Prassitele*, pp. 4 ff.

[4] Pausanias I. 8. 2.

[5] Cornelius Nepos, *Timotheos* 2. 2: "So great was the joy of the Athenians at this victory that they first made public altars to Eirene and ordained a feast for the goddess." Plutarch, *Kimon* 13. 487, speaks of honors to Eirene in celebration of the treaty initiated by *Kallias*, 371 B.C. It should be remembered, however, that Aristophanes, *Peace* 1020, speaks of an altar to Peace as early as 421 B.C.

[6] Imhoof-Blumer and Gardner, *Numismatic Commentary*, pl. DD, Nos. IX–X.

[7] Furtwängler, *Beschreibung der Glyptothek*, No. 219. The right arm is modern, the child's head is ancient but does not belong to the statue.

[8] Metropolitan Museum, *Handbook* (1930), pp. 264–265.

[9] *Museo Torlonia di sculture antiche*, Nos. 240, 290, pls. LXI, LXXIII.

other replicas, both with heads unbroken, are in Athens[10] and Dresden[11] (figs. 662, 663). The relief on the coins gives the complete composition. A woman wearing a voluminous Doric chiton is standing, sceptre in hand, holding a child and a cornucopia. The conception of Wealth in the arms of Peace is in line with the more analytical temper of the fourth century as compared with the fifth. The intimate personal relation between the woman and the child, suggested by the inclination of her head toward him, the tender expression in her face, and the playful attitude of the child, are likewise signs of the new age. Kephisodotos is indeed the true precursor of Praxiteles. We need only compare Praxiteles' Hermes (fig. 664) with this group of Eirene to note how much the later sculptor learned from his predecessor. And it is not only in a new intimacy and gentleness that Kephisodotos heralds a new style, but also in the rendering of the drapery. This has been generally interpreted as a reversion to an earlier treatment;[12] and in the general scheme it certainly is so. But its resemblance to fifth-century models is only superficial. In the development of the rendering of drapery which we have sketched above (cf. p. 105) the Eirene takes its natural place in the fourth century. For, though the garment is massive and the folds have a general downward tendency, there is not the real simplicity of the middle of the fifth century; the folds are more complicated and there is more variety in direction. Nor is there the transparency of the later fifth-century drapery, but rather the denseness and naturalism characteristic of the fourth. We may rather compare the rendering with that on a figure of the Ephesos drum (fig. 328) dated c. 355–330 and especially with those of Korkyra (375–4 B.C.) and of Athens (362–1).[13]

Other Works   Besides the Eirene we are told that Kephisodotos made "a remarkable statue of Athena in the harbor of Athens, and an altar in the temple of Zeus the Saviour,"[14] a group of Muses,[15] a Hermes

---

[10] National Museum, No. 175. The marble is supposedly Italian and the antiquity of the figure has therefore been doubted.

[11] Herrmann, *Antike Originalbildwerke zu Dresden* (1925), No. 107.

[12] Furtwängler (*Masterpieces*, p. 296) would even assign political reasons for it, but later he recognized its essentially fourth-century quality; cf. his *Originalstatuen in Venedig*, p. 308.

[13] Cf. Binnebössel, *Studien zu den attischen Urkundenreliefs*, Nos. 34, 37. Compare also the torsos in Venice (Furtwängler, *Originalstatuen in Venedig*, pl. V [our fig. 329] and pl. VII, 3).

[14] Pliny, *N.H.* XXXIV. 74.   [15] Pausanias IX. 30. 1.

caring for the infant Dionysos,[16] and an orator with uplifted arm.[17] Of these we know nothing further, except perhaps of the Hermes which has been tentatively identified with representations on coins and with statues in Madrid, Rome, and Athens.[17a] We can recognize him as a worthy precursor of Praxiteles, suggesting in many ways the chief directions in which fourth-century sculpture was to travel, without as yet achieving the consummate grace of the later productions.

(b) Praxiteles

ON a rectangular base from Leuktra which once supported a portrait statue is the inscription, "Praxiteles the Athenian made it."[18] Its date is about 330 B.C. Pliny[19] assigns Praxiteles to the 104th Olympiad (364). These are the only definite dates we have except the doubtful statement of Vitruvius[20] that Praxiteles was employed on the Mausoleum (soon after 351) and of Strabo[21] that he made an altar for the temple of Artemis at Ephesos after the fire of 356. His career perhaps extended from about 370 to 330.

ORIGIN AND DATE

With Praxiteles we are in the happy position of being able to judge his style by an original statue. On May 8, 1877, there was found in the Heraion at Olympia a marble Hermes[22] (figs. 170, 444, 664, 665), which was immediately identified as a work by Praxiteles from the casual but precious words of Pausanias:[23] "In later times other offerings were dedicated in the Heraion. Amongst these was a Hermes of marble bearing the infant Dionysos, the work of Praxiteles." This is the only original statue by a known Greek sculptor of the first rank which has survived.[24] It was by no means Praxiteles' masterpiece; except for Pausanias, ancient writers pass it over in silence. But to us it is a revelation. In beauty and finish of modeling it so far surpasses the Roman copies by which we mostly have to form our conceptions of Greek artists that it supplies us with a new standard, and helps us to transform in our imagination the other works which have survived only in inferior replicas. The condition

WORKS
Hermes

---

16 Pliny, *N.H.* XXXIV. 87. 17 Pliny, *loc. cit.*

17a Cf. Rizzo, *Prassitele,* pp. 7 ff.

18 For signatures by Praxiteles cf. Loewy, *Inschriften,* Nos. 76, 76a, 488–489. Another one has recently been found on the Agora (*Hesperia,* 1937, p. 341; 1938, pp. 329 f.).

19 *N.H.* XXXIV. 50. 20 VII. *Praef.* 13.

21 XIV. 641. 22 Treu, *Olympia,* III, pls. XLIX–LIII.

23 V. 17. 3.

24 Carpenter, Casson, Blümel and others have thought that the Hermes was a Roman copy. For views pro and contra cf. *A.J.A.,* XXXV, 1931, pp. 249 ff.

is fortunately good. Only the right forearm and the two legs below the knee are missing (one sandaled foot is preserved [fig. 667]); and both arms of the child.

The composition of the Hermes is foreshadowed by the Eirene and perhaps the Hermes of Kephisodotos (pp. 258, 259); but it is softened and made more gracious. Young Hermes in an easy, relaxed attitude turns to the child Dionysos whom he supports on his left arm; the child is stretching out its arm for the bunch of grapes he held in his right hand. Though the hand in the Olympia statue is missing, this feature is supplied by adaptations on Pompeian paintings (cf., e.g., the example from the Casa del Naviglio, Pompeii; fig. 666).[25] The intimate note in the conception, the relaxed attitude of the figure with its lovely curve, the gentle, dreamy expression of the face, the infinitely variegated and yet not sharply contrasted modeling, all help to create an impression of sensuous loveliness; and we delight in its exquisite appeal. Nevertheless we feel that the horizon has changed. We are in a more personal, less lofty atmosphere; what we have gained in grace we have lost in majesty. And this is a sign of the times. Just as Myron and Pheidias and Polykleitos represented the fifth-century outlook and embodied its conceptions, so Praxiteles reflects the fourth-century spirit and creates an art characteristic of it. For every artist, however great his creative genius, is inevitably a child of his age. The greatest work he can produce must be a spiritualization, so to speak, of the concepts and feelings of his time. And so the art of Praxiteles with its tenderness and charm sums up for us at its best the new outlook in Greece, in which the old impersonal views have given place to a more individualistic, analytical relation.

Aphrodite of Knidos
The most famous work of Praxiteles was the Aphrodite of Knidos.[26] Pliny[27] gives an eloquent account of her popularity: "The Aphrodite, to see which many have sailed to Knidos, is the finest statue not only by Praxiteles but in the whole world. He had made and was offering for sale two figures of Aphrodite, one whose form was draped, and which was therefore preferred by the people of Kos, to whom the choice of either figure was offered at the same price, as the more chaste and severe, while the other which they re-

---

25 There are no exact replicas of the Hermes, but adaptations are not uncommon; cf. Pottier in *Festschrift für O. Benndorf*, 1898, pp. 81 ff.; Rizzo, *Prassitele*, pp. 72 f.

26 Cf. Overbeck, *Schriftquellen*, 1228 ff. The *Anthology* is full of verses singing her praises; cf. Overbeck, *op. cit.*, 1236 ff.

27 *N.H.* XXXVI. 20.

jected was bought by the Knidians, and became immeasurably more celebrated. King Nikomedes[28] wished to buy it from the Knidians, and offered to discharge the whole debt[29] of the city, which was enormous; but they preferred to undergo the worst, and justly so, for by that statue Praxiteles made Knidos famous. The shrine which contains it is quite open, so that the image, made, as is believed, under the direct inspiration of the goddess, can be seen from all sides; and from all sides it is equally admired. There are in Knidos other statues by artists of the first rank . . . and there is no greater testimony to the Aphrodite of Praxiteles than the fact that amongst all these it is the only one thought worthy of mention." Lucian was evidently a great admirer of the statue. He calls it the most beautiful of Praxiteles' works[30] and borrows its head for his Panthea:[31] "The hair and forehead and the finely penciled eyebrows he will allow her to keep as Praxiteles made them, and in the melting gaze of the eyes with their bright and joyous expression he will also preserve the spirit of Praxiteles." He further describes her as nude, with one hand held in front of her, and as standing in the midst of her shrine "with a smile playing gently over her parted lips."[32] The material was Parian marble.[33] Phryne and Kratine are said to have served as models (by Athenaios[34] and Clement of Alexandria,[35] respectively). Fortunately we are not dependent on mere descriptions of this celebrated statue; from reproductions of her on Roman coins of Knidos[36] (fig. 672) it has been possible to identify a number of Roman copies.[37] The best known are in the Vatican (figs. 668, 670), Brussels[39] (fig. 669) and Munich.[40]

[28] Nikomedes of Bithynia, 278–250 B.C.

[29] Due to the forced contribution levied by Sulla in 84 B.C.

[30] Εἰκόνες 4.　　　　[31] Ibid., 6.　　　　[32] Ἔρωτες, 13.

[33] Ibid.　　　　[34] XIII. 590 f.　　　　[35] Protrept. 53.

[36] Gardner, Types of Greek Coins, pl. XV, 21.

[37] For a list of full-sized copies, cf. Furtwängler, Masterpieces, p. 322, note 3; Michaelis, J.H.S., 1887, pp. 332 ff. Rizzo, Prassitele, pp. 48 ff. Rizzo distinguishes two types—one, a direct copy of the Knidian Aphrodite (preserved, for instance, in a statue in the Museo delle Terme and in one of the statues in the Vatican), the other perhaps a variant by a later artist (preserved in the well-known statue in the Vatican and the heads from Tralles and in Toulouse). The second is differentiated from the first by its slenderer body, the fringe on the drapery, and the larger size of the hydria. The fact, however, that the original was presumably not available in a direct cast might account for variations in the copies.

[38] Helbig, Führer,[3] I, No. 310; Kaschnitz-Weinberg, Sculture del Magazzino del Museo Vaticano, Nos. 256, 257.

[39] Recently supplied with its missing head discovered in Copenhagen; cf. Blinkenberg, Illustrated London News, Jan. 21, 1928, p. 83.

[40] Furtwängler, Beschreibung der Glyptothek, No. 258.

[41] Rizzo, op. cit., pls. 87 f.　　　　[42] Ibid., pls. 85 f.

The goddess is seen standing in an exquisitely graceful pose, one hand held in front of her, the other grasping her drapery, which she is letting fall on a water jar. The nude body and the variegated folds of the drapery create an effective contrast, just as they do in the Hermes. The attitude is evidently studied from all sides, for it is equally charming from every view, having been intended as we know for an open shrine. The best replicas of the head are those in the Kaufmann Collection (fig. 671), and in Toulouse. Roman copies though they be, we can appreciate in them the points specially admired by Lucian—the soft, wavy hair with the triangular forehead, and the melting gaze of the eyes. If to this gentle, harmonious creation we can supply in our imagination the beauty and finish of the modeling of the Hermes, we may understand the great attraction of the original.

The Aphrodite of Knidos made a deep impression on contemporary art, and its influence was felt for many generations. A nude Aphrodite henceforth becomes a favorite subject and more often than not something in the pose and expression harks back to the great prototype. Just as the Pheidian Zeus created for all subsequent time the Greek conception of the chief of the gods, so the Praxitelean Aphrodite was henceforth used consciously or unconsciously as a model for the goddess of Love.

Apollo
Sauroktonos

Another work of Praxiteles has been definitely identified in extant copies from a specific description of it by Pliny:[44] "[Praxiteles] also represented Apollo as a boy with an arrow watching a lizard as it creeps up with intent to slay it close at hand; this is known as the σαυροκτόνος or Lizard-Slayer." Since it is listed with the bronze works of Praxiteles, the original must have been of that material. Reproductions of it occur on coins of Nikopolis (fig. 673) and Philippopolis[45] and in several Roman replicas,[46] the most notable of which are the marble statues in the Louvre[47] and the Vatican[48] (fig. 676)

43 *Antike Denkmäler,* I, pl. 41, p. 30.

44 *N.H.* XXXIV. 70. Cf. also Martial XIV. 172.

45 Pick, *Die antiken Münzen Nordgriechenlands,* I, 1, p. 362, No. 1288, pl. XIV, 34; Rizzo, *op. cit.,* pl. 62.

46 For a list of replicas, cf. Overbeck, *Griech. Kunstmythologie,* V, pp. 235 f.; Klein, *Praxiteles,* pp. 104 ff.; Rizzo, *op. cit.,* pp. 39 ff.

47 Klein, *op. cit.,* p. 109, fig. 14.

48 Amelung, *Die Skulpturen des vaticanischen Museums,* II, No. 264. The restorations include the left side of the face, the right eye, the right forearm, the right leg from the middle of the thigh, the left leg from the knee down, part of the trunk with the upper part of the lizard, the plinth.

and a bronze statuette in the Villa Albani[49] (fig. 675). The young Apollo is engaged in one of the sports of the boys of that time—and one that has survived to this day in southern Europe—but the action is merely a motive for a singularly graceful pose in which the sinuous "Praxitelean curve" is beautifully utilized. We could not have a lovelier conception of a dreamy young boy in a completely relaxed attitude. But how far we have traveled from the Apollo on the Olympia pediment (cf. fig. 392) ! The gods have descended from high Olympos and have become charming, serene human beings.

The god Eros with his youthful, feminine charm would naturally be a subject which would appeal to Praxiteles, and we hear of several such statues by him. Two became world-famous—the Eros of Thespiai and that of Parion in Mysia. The former was considered by Praxiteles himself as one of his masterpieces;[50] he gave it to Phryne who dedicated it in her native town.[51] No copies of it have been definitely identified[52] though some have thought that it may survive in a fragmentary, headless statue from the Palatine in the Louvre and in a torso in the Museum of Parma. It is true that in the stance and the position of the arms they resemble the Satyr pouring wine (figs. 682–684), which we know was an approximately contemporary work; but the absence of the head makes an attribution difficult. Of the Eros of Parion,[53] we gain a faint picture by the little reproductions of it on Roman coins of Parion[54] (fig. 674). He is standing in an easy attitude, his wings spread out, his mantle hanging from his left shoulder, his head turned to his left, his long hair gathered in a knot, a small herm at his side. The curve of the body is similar to that of the Sauroktonos, the weight also on the right leg; only the action of the arms is different. This conception of Eros as a charming boy impressed itself on the imagination of the people and became the starting point of the numerous representations of him in fourth-century and Hellenistic art. An Eros similar to the Sauroktonos, but with lowered right arm— of which replicas are in New York and Naples—may go back to another Eros by Praxiteles.[54a]

Eros of Thespiai

Eros of Parion

[49] Helbig, *Führer*³ II, 1852.
[50] Pausanias I. 20. 2.
[51] It became the chief attraction of that city (Cicero, *In Verr.* IV. 2.4; 60.35; Strabo IX. 410). Cf. Overbeck, *Schriftquellen*, 1249 ff.
[52] Cf. Rizzo, *op. cit.*, pp. 20 ff.
[53] Pliny, *N.H.* XXXVI. 23.
[54] Imhoof-Blumer, *Monnaies grecques*, p. 256.
[54a] Cf. Rizzo, *op. cit.*, pls. 65–67.

Artemis of
Antikyra

Pausanias[55] mentions an Artemis in a temple at Antikyra "the work of Praxiteles; it holds a torch in the right hand and a quiver hangs from the shoulder; beside it on the left is a dog; and it is taller than the tallest woman." Figures of Artemis exactly answering this description—with torch, quiver, and dog—occur on coins of Antikyra[56] (fig. 677). The goddess is stepping lightly forward, an attractive, dainty figure in her short chiton as she sets out ready for the chase. The great goddess Artemis too has been transformed into a charming girl. Whether the statue was by the famous Praxiteles or by a later artist is uncertain; but that the figure resembles Hellenistic representations is seen by the close resemblance to it of the Artemis of Versailles in the Louvre.[57] The conception and pose are similar; only the attitude of the arms has been changed.

Leto and
Chloris

Still another work by Praxiteles is known to us from coin types. Pausanias[58] describes it as follows: "[At Argos] the temple of Leto is not far from the trophy; the image is the work of Praxiteles, and the figure of the maiden standing by the goddess they call Chloris, . . . the daughter of Niobe." A group of a woman and a little maiden clearly copied from this work occurs on Roman coins of Argos[59] (fig. 678). Leto is clothed in an ample chiton, her right hand raised to her shoulder, the left extended over Chloris. It is a quiet composition with much of the stateliness of the preceding period still apparent; so we may surmise that this was an early work of the artist.

Eubouleus

An inscription on a headless herm in the Vatican reads "Eubouleus, by Praxiteles."[60] A bust of a youth from Eleusis (fig. 512) has been identified as Eubouleus from a dedicatory inscription to Eubouleus from the same locality. As it resembles the Hermes of Olympia and is an original work of the fourth century, it may even have been carved by Praxiteles himself. That it was a famous work is suggested by the fact that Roman copies exist (cf. fig. 511).

Mantineia
Base

When Pausanias[61] was at Mantineia he saw there a temple of Leto and her children. He tells us that "Praxiteles made their statues in the third generation after Alkamenes. On the base which

[55] X. 37. 1.
[56] Imhoof-Blumer and Gardner, *Numismatic Comm.*, pl. Y, No. XVII, pp. 124 f.
[57] Brunn-Bruckmann, *Denkmäler*, pl. 420.　　　　　　　　[58] II. 21. 8.
[59] Imhoof-Blumer and Gardner, *op. cit.*, pl. K, Nos. XXXVI–XXXVIII, p. 38.
[60] Cf. Rizzo, *op. cit.*, p. 104.
[61] VIII. 9. 1.

supports them are represented the Muses[62] and Marsyas playing the flute." Three slabs from this base were found at Mantineia in 1887 and are now in the National Museum in Athens[63] (figs. 679–681). On one is a stately Apollo with his Phrygian slave and Marsyas vigorously playing the flutes; on each of the others are three Muses, charming examples of fourth-century draped figures. It is clear that the Tanagra statuettes of the period were inspired from just such lovely creations. Since the base supported three statues—Leto, Apollo, and Artemis—at least two reliefs must have occupied the long side. The remaining three Muses were therefore probably carved on another plaque now lost. Pausanias does not say that the base was the work of Praxiteles, only the statues. To insure a harmonious ensemble he may well have designed the composition, and the dainty charm of the figures is in line with the spirit of his work. Compared, however, with the Hermes, the execution is perfunctory, and there is no need of assuming that Praxiteles actually carried out the work.

Pliny[64] and Tatian[65] mention an Aphrodite *pseliumene*, "with a bracelet," by Praxiteles. Perhaps it is reproduced in a bronze statuette in London (fig. 49).

Aphrodite Pseliumene

Pausanias[66] states that the cult statue in the sanctuary of Artemis Brauronia on the Akropolis of Athens was the work of Praxiteles. Mention is made of this marble statue for the first time in an inscription dated 346–345 B.C. The Artemis of Gabii in the Louvre (fig. 686) has been tentatively identified as a copy of Praxiteles' work, for the figure evidently reproduces a masterpiece of Praxiteles; moreover she is represented as fastening her garment, and we know that garments and other objects of adornment were offered to Artemis Brauronia as an ancient rite.

Artemis Brauronia

Pausanias[66a] tells us of a satyr that stood in the Street of Tripods "of which Praxiteles is said to have been extremely proud" and of which the following story was current: "They say that once when Phryne asked for the most beautiful of his works, he lover-like promised to give her it, but would not tell which he thought the most beautiful. So a servant of Phryne ran in declaring that Praxiteles' stu-

Satyr

62 Pausanias' text reads Μοῦσα, clearly a mistake for Μοῦσαι.
63 Nos. 215–217. Rizzo, *op. cit.*, pp. 86 ff.
64 XXXIV. 69.
65 Contra Graecos. 56, p. 122.
66 I. 23. 7. Cf. Rizzo, *op. cit.*, pp. 63 ff.
66a I. 20. 1.

dio had caught fire, and that most, but not all, of his works had
perished. Praxiteles at once ran for the door, protesting that all his
labor was lost if the flames had reached the Satyr and Eros. But
Phryne bade him stay and be of good cheer, telling him that he had
suffered no loss, but had only been entrapped into saying which were
the most beautiful of his works." This statue, Pausanias continues,
was represented in the act of offering a cup. It is possible that the
Satyr pouring wine, of which many copies are preserved (cf. figs.
682–684), the best perhaps in Dresden and Palermo, reproduces
Praxiteles' statue.[67] It has his gentleness and restraint, the composition and style are Praxitelean of an early period, before he reached
his maturity, and this would presumably be the time of the anecdote
of Phryne. Pliny[67a] speaks of a statue by Praxiteles as "the celebrated
Satyr, called by the Greeks 'the world-famed' [περιβόητον]" and lists
it among the bronze works of the artist. A satyr in a relaxed, "Praxitelean" pose represented leaning against a pillar occurs in so many
replicas[68] that it clearly goes back to a famous original. One of the best
copies is in the Torlonia Museum, another is in the Capitoline Museum
(fig. 51), and a fragment of exceptionally good workmanship is in
the Louvre. The conjecture is tempting that we have here a reproduction of Praxiteles' work.[69] But there is no specific description of
Praxiteles' Satyr to help us, so the identification is not certain. If the
original was by Praxiteles it was probably one of his later works; for
the picturesque composition, the almost exaggerated curve of the
body, with the foot of the flexed leg placed behind that of the supporting leg, and the personal element in the conception—a mingling of
human and animal qualities—are different from the earlier, serene,
and detached Praxitelean creations. This very picturesqueness, which
heralds the Hellenistic period, made the statue an appropriate garden
figure and accounts for its immense popularity in Roman times.

The other works attributed to Praxiteles by ancient writers[71] in-

[67] Cf. Rizzo, op. cit., pp. 17 ff.; Picard, Manuel, III, pp. 415 ff.

[67a] N.H. XXXIV. 69.

[68] They are listed by Benndorf u. Schoene, Die Bildwerke des lateranischen Museums, p. 91, and Furtwängler, Masterpieces, p. 329, note 5.

[69] That Praxiteles' περιβόητος may have been part of a group (Pliny, N.H. XXXIV.
69) is not an argument against the identification, for evidently only the Satyr became
so famous and must therefore have been a composition complete in itself.

[70] Furtwängler, op. cit., pp. 310 ff., figs. 131–132; a list of replicas is given by
Schreiber, Villa Ludovisi, p. 93, revised by Furtwängler, op. cit., p. 310, note 2.

[71] Cf. Overbeck, Schriftquellen, 1193 ff.

clude many deities, nymphs, maenads, and karyatids, a gilded portrait of Phryne at Delphi, and such subjects as Persuasion and Consolation,[72] a Weeping Matron, and a Rejoicing Harlot,[73] in which the more analytical temper of the period and the tendency to represent human emotions would find scope. Athletes or warriors—the stock subject of the former period—are rare. And naturally so. An artist who "with consummate art informed his marble figures with the passions of the soul"[74] would select for himself subtler themes than victorious athletes.

Pliny[75] in his account of Praxiteles makes the statement: "His works may be seen in Athens in the Kerameikos." May this be interpreted to mean that Praxiteles had many orders for tombstones for the cemetery in the Kerameikos? Perhaps. We know definitely of one memorial he made of a soldier standing by his horse.[76] And certainly a reflection of his style is apparent in many of the gentle farewell scenes of the Athenian stelai.

The genius of Praxiteles may be compared with that of Raphael. STYLE Their works are imbued with a serene and sober grace, and appeal by their very radiance and loveliness. The majesty of Pheidias and Masaccio have indeed gone, but the grandeur of the old conceptions is still evident in the purity and restraint of the new creations. Though we have few works which can be directly associated with Praxiteles, his influence on contemporary art was so great that we see his spirit reflected in many other works. Such charming creations as the Leconfield Aphrodite, [77] and the Aphrodite of Arles[78] (fig. 685) must owe their inspiration directly to his work; and works like the Marathon Boy[79] (figs. 46–48) and the Aberdeen Herakles,[80] being original fourth-century works, show us the high standard of workmanship attained in products of this style. Moreover Praxiteles' influence was long felt. The head from Chios in Boston[81] (fig. 174) bears his imprint, and the so-called Alexandrian style stems directly from him.

[72] Pausanias I. 43. 6.
[74] Diod., *Fragm.* XXVI.
[76] Pausanias I. 2. 3.
[77] Rizzo, *op. cit.*, pl. 110.
[78] Rizzo, *op. cit.*, pp. 24 ff. There are replicas, for instance in Rome and Athens.
[79] Rizzo, *op. cit.*, pl. 69.
[80] Furtwängler, *op. cit.*, pl. XVIII, pp. 346 f., thinks it an original by Praxiteles.
[81] Caskey, *Catalogue*, No. 29.

[73] Pliny, *N.H.* XXXIV. 70.
[75] *N.H.* XXXVI. 20.

(c) The Elder and the Younger Praxiteles

THERE appears to have been an elder Praxiteles; for certain works attributed to a sculptor by that name must be dated in the fifth century B.C. Pausanias[82] refers to statues of Demeter and her daughter and Iacchos standing by the Dipylon Gate of Athens "and on the wall is an inscription in the Attic alphabet stating that they are the work of Praxiteles." The Attic alphabet was superseded by the Ionic one in 403. Pausanias also assigns to Praxiteles a group of Rhea and Kronos "at the entrance of the temple of Hera at Plataia"[83] which was erected in 427–426, and "pediment sculptures made for the Thebans representing most of the Twelve Labours of Herakles."[84] Such subjects appear unusual for the fourth-century Praxiteles. If there was this elder Praxiteles it may be he who supplied the chariot for Kalamis' group (cf. p. 203).

It has been claimed that there was a younger Praxiteles, a nephew of the famous sculptor, and that some of the works assigned to the latter by ancient writers were by this later artist, e.g. the Artemis of Antikyra (fig. 677). A signature of a second-century Praxiteles was found at Pergamon[85] (cf. p. 298). The name is not uncommon.

(d) The Sons of Praxiteles

Two sons of Praxiteles, Kephisodotos and Timarchos, gained some eminence as sculptors. Pliny[86] says that Kephisodotos was "the heir of his father's talent" and that "much praise has been bestowed on his famous group of interlaced figures at Pergamon where the pressure of the fingers seems to be exerted on flesh rather than marble." We also hear of a number of other works by him and Timarchos, chiefly deities and portraits.[87] A statue of a seated Zeus at Megalopolis[88] may be reproduced on badly preserved Roman coins of Megalopolis.[89] Several statue bases with their names have been found, dating from the late fourth and early third century,[90] one of these of a portrait of Menander (342–291) in the theatre in Athens.[91] The busts generally identified as Menander,[92] may repro-

---

82 I. 2. 4.

83 IX. 2. 7.   84 IX. 11. 6.

85 Loewy, Inschriften, pp. 115 f.   86 N.H. XXXVI. 24.

87 Overbeck, Schriftquellen, 1331 ff.; Bieber, Jahrbuch, 1923–1924, pp. 264 f.

88 Pausanias VIII. 30. 10.

89 Imhoof-Blumer and Gardner, Numismatic Commentary, pl. V, No. I.

90 Loewy, Inschriften, Nos. 108–112.   91 Ibid., No. 108; Pausanias I. 21. 1.

92 Bernoulli, Griechische Ikonographie, II, p. 113. Others suggest Vergil.

duce this work.[93] But the safest way to visualize the style of these two sculptors is by the fragments from the sculptures which decorated the altar of Kos,[94] said by Herondas[95] to be by the sons of Praxiteles. They consist of a girl's head (figs. 687, 688), the lower half of a draped female figure (fig. 689), a fragment of a girl's head, the hand of a child, and the foot of a woman. They teach us that the sons carried on their father's traditions and created charming, delicate works, the immediate precursors of the somewhat effeminate renderings of the Hellenistic age.

(e) Skopas

THE other great sculptor of this period was Skopas of Paros.[96] Pliny[97] couples him with Polykleitos as having worked (*floruit*) in the 90th Olympiad (420 B.C.), but this must be a mistake; for we know that he worked on the Mausoleum of Halikarnassos soon after 351, on the new temple of Athena Alea at Tegea some time after the destruction of the old building in 394,[98] and on the temple of Artemis at Ephesos which was begun immediately after the fire which burnt down the older structure in 356, but was not yet completed in 334.[99] His activity therefore falls, like that of Praxiteles, wholly within the fourth century. Moreover, elsewhere Pliny[100] himself mentions Skopas as a rival of Praxiteles and of Kephisodotos the Younger (the son of Praxiteles); and the names of Praxiteles and Skopas are often coupled by other writers.[101]

With Skopas we are in the lamentable position of having no work

ORIGIN AND DATE

WORKS

[93] One of the best replicas is in Boston, Caskey, *Catalogue*, No. 86.

[94] Herzog, *Oest. Jahresh.*, VI, 1903, pp. 218 ff.; Bieber, *Jahrbuch*, 1923–1924, pp. 242 ff., figs. 1–3, pls. VI, VII, 1.

[95] *Mimes* IV. 1 ff.

[96] Cf. Bieber in Thieme-Becker, *Künstlerlexikon*, XXX, pp. 477 ff. He was perhaps the son of Aristandros of Paros, who worked on the memorial of Aigospotamoi (405 B.C.).

[97] *N.H.* XXXIV. 49.

[98] The new building was probably not begun until after 386 B.C., which marks the end of the Corinthian war, during which Tegea was allied to Sparta. For a dating to c. 370–355 B.C., cf. p. 268.

[99] "Besides, Artemidoros says that Alexander promised to defray the expense of its (the Artemision's) restoration, both what had been and what would be incurred, on condition that the work should be attributed to him in an inscription, but the Ephesians refused to accede to this" (Strabo XIV. 1. 22).

[100] *N.H.* XXXVI. 25.

[101] Cf., e.g., Martial IV. 39. 1; *Carm. Priap.* 9. 2; Apollinaris, *Sidon. Carm.* XXIII. 503.

which can be safely attributed to him, and so our whole study of his style must be based on conjecture. There are preserved, however, fragments of sculptures of the buildings on which we know he was engaged, and since stylistically these bear some resemblance to one another we have to build our structure on this uncertain foundation.

Sculptures of the Temple of Athena Alea

Pausanias'[102] account of the temple of Athena Alea is long, but not explicit regarding the authorship of the sculptures: "The old temple of Athena Alea at Tegea was built by Aleos; in later times the Tegeans caused a large and remarkable temple to be erected to the goddess. The previous building was suddenly attacked by fire and destroyed in the archonship of Diophantos at Athens and the second year of the 96th Olympiad (395). The temple which is standing at the present day is far superior to the other temples in the Peloponnese in size and magnificence. . . . I was told that the architect was Skopas of Paros, who was the sculptor of many statues in different parts of Greece proper and also in Ionia and Karia. In the front pediment is represented the chase of the Kalydonian boar . . . [then follow the names of the participants, including Atalante, Meleager, Theseus, etc.]. The sculptures of the back pediment represent the battle of Telephos against Achilles in the plain of the Kaïkos. The ancient image of Athena Alea and the tusks of the Kalydonian boar were carried off by the Roman Emperor Augustus. . . . The image . . . stands in Rome . . . made wholly of ivory, the work of Endoios. . . . The present image at Tegea was brought from the township of Manthyrenses. . . . On one side of her stands Asklepios, on the other Hygieia, made of Pentelic marble, works of Skopas the Parian." From this description we know only that Skopas was the architect of the temple and that he made the two statues which stood on each side of the temple image of Athena Alea; not that he worked on the pediment figures, though it is quite possible that he did so. The fragments of these pediments[103] which have been preserved show an individuality of style which presupposes a distinguished artist. The most important are several battered male heads[104] (cf. figs. 690–693), part of a boar,[105] and a female draped body[106] (fig. 696). In the male heads particularly, the

102 VIII. 45. 4; 46. 1.
103 Dugas, *Le Sanctuaire d'Aléa Athéna à Tégée,* pls. XCVI–CXII.
104 *Ibid.,* pls. XCIX–CII.   105 *Ibid.,* pl. CVIII, A 3.
106 *Ibid.,* pls. XCVI ff., pp. 80 ff. Some have doubted that this figure belonged to the pediments (cf. Thiersch, *Jahrbuch,* 1913, pp. 270–271), but without convincing

square form, the deep-sunk eyes, and the marked projection of the
lower part of the forehead are suggestive of force and emotion. We
may surmise that they belong to the group of the hunt of the Kalydonian boar, and that their expressions are evoked by the stress of
battle. The drapery of the Atalante, though not so soft and transparent as that of the Epidauros figures, has not yet the denseness
and realistic quality of the works of the middle of the fourth century, such as the Maussollos and the Artemisia (figs. 313, 314) and
the figures of the Ephesian drum (figs. 328, 705). We may, therefore, place the Tegea sculptures midway between the two, that is,
about 370–355.[107]

We know both from Pliny and Vitruvius[108] that Skopas worked on *The*
the sculptures of the Mausoleum. Pliny[109] gives an explicit account: *Mausoleum*
"The rivals and contemporaries of Skopas were Bryaxis, Timotheos,
and Leochares, who must be treated in a group since they were
jointly employed on the sculptures of the Mausoleum. This building is the tomb erected by Artemisia, his widow, for Maussollos,
prince of Karia, who died in the second year of the 107th Olympiad
[351]. That this work is among the Seven Wonders is due mainly
to the above-named artists. . . . The sculptures on the east side are
by Skopas, those of the north by Bryaxis, those of the south by

reasons. The head, however, once thought to belong to the Atalante, was not part
of the temple sculptures; cf. Dugas, *Le Sanctuaire d'Aléa Athéna à Tégée*, pls.
CXIII ff., pp. 117 ff.

[107] Such a time agrees well with the recent dating of the temple on architectural
grounds: "scarcely before 370–360 B.C." (Schede, *Antikes Traufleisten*, p. 46); about
370 B.C. (Reisch, *Oest. Jahresh.*, 1906, p. 215, note 41); about 365 B.C. (Weickert,
Das lesbische Kymation, p. 71). Dugas' 360–330 B.C. (*op. cit.*, p. 128) would seem
somewhat late.

A stele was found at Tegea in the court of a private house near the temple of
Athena Alea inscribed

ΙΕΥ≶
ΑΔΑ   ΙΔΡΙΕΥ≶

(*I.G.*, V, 2, 89; Foucart, *Mon. Piot*, XVIII, 1910, p. 146; *J.H.S.*, XXXVI, 1916, p. 65;
now in the British Museum.) Ada and Idreus were the sister and brother of
Maussollos and Artemisia and began their reign in 351 B.C.; Idreus died in 344. The
stele is therefore dated 351–344 B.C. The occurrence of these names at Tegea presupposes relations between Tegea and Karia, perhaps to be accounted for by the fact
that Skopas was at work in both places and took workmen from one to the other.
But since the name of the dedicator of the stele is missing we cannot know whether
he was a Karian who perhaps went with Skopas to work on the Tegean temple after
the Mausoleum, or a Tegean who had accompanied Skopas to Karia after the Tegean
work was finished and then returned to his native home. Therefore this stele cannot
help us in dating the Tegea temple either before or after the Mausoleum, even if we
connect the incident with Skopas, which is of course a mere supposition. Cf. also the
statue base found at Delphi with the names Ada and Idreus (*B.C.H.*, 1899, p. 384,
No. 631).

[108] VII. *Praef.* 13.   [109] *N.H.* XXXVI. 30.

Timotheos, and those of the west by Leochares. The Queen died before the building was complete;[110] but the artists did not abandon the work until it was finished, considering that it would redound to their own glory, and be a standing proof of their genius; and to this day they vie with one another in their handiwork. They were joined by a fifth artist. For above the colonnade is a pyramid equal to the lower structure in height, with a flight of twenty-four steps tapering to a point. On the apex stands a four-horse chariot in marble, the work of Pythis. This addition completes the building, which rises to a height of one hundred and forty feet." The chief sculptural remains of this Mausoleum are now in the British Museum.[111] They consist of three friezes, the chariot group of Maussollos and Artemisia (figs. 313, 314), and statues of lions and other figures, among them a fine equestrian statue. Of the widest frieze, representing the battle of the Greeks and Amazons, there are extant seventeen slabs; they are in more or less good preservation and rank among the most important examples we have of fourth-century sculpture. Is it possible to assign any portion of it to Skopas? The majority of the slabs were found not on the Mausoleum site but in the neighboring castle of Saint Peter, built by the Knights of Saint John in the fifteenth century largely out of the Mausoleum stones; therefore all trace of where they belonged on the building has been lost. But during Sir Charles Newton's excavations four slabs (Nos. 1013–1016) were found "lying in a row along the eastern margin";[112] that is, on the side of the building said to have been decorated by Skopas. Three[113] slabs of these form a continuous composition and stand out among all the rest by their extraordinarily fine quality (figs. 697–699). The impetuous force of each figure, the delicate workmanship, and the rhythmical composition indicate the hand of a master sculptor. The bold poses—the Amazon sitting backward on her galloping horse, the collapsing Amazon, the crouching warrior—and the harmonious composition indicate the hand of a great artist. The assignment of these sculptures to Skopas is therefore tempting and has been quite generally made.[114] And

110 Two years after the death of Maussollos.

111 Smith, *Catalogue of Greek Sculpture in the British Museum*, II, Nos. 1000 ff.

112 Newton, *Halicarnassus*, II, 1, p. 100.

113 The fourth slab is different in style and since it is a single fragment it may well have been transported from another portion of the building.

114 Cf. Wolters and Sieveking, *Jahrbuch*, XXIV, 1909, pp. 171 ff.; also the fragment 1025. Pfuhl, *Jahrbuch*, 1928, p. 47, would add slab 1022; not, I think, convinc-

stylistically they bear out what have been provisionally supposed
to be the characteristics of Skopas' style—originality, force, and
emotion, conveyed not only in the attitudes but in the somewhat
deep-set eyes and mobile mouths. Moreover since the style of some
of the charioteers of one of the smaller friezes[115] is markedly similar (cf. fig. 700), these too have been ascribed to Skopas.

The connection of Skopas with the extant sculptures of the temple of Artemis at Ephesos is very problematical. Our only information on the subject is supplied by Pliny.[116] "The length of the whole
temple is four hundred and twenty-five feet and the breadth two
hundred and twenty-five feet.[117] It contains one hundred and twenty-
seven columns, each furnished by a king and sixty feet in height; of
these thirty-six are decorated with reliefs, one by Skopas."[118] Only
three of the thirty-six decorated columns have survived in any degree of preservation and it is of course not likely that among them
should be the work of Skopas. There are nevertheless certain considerations which enable us at least tentatively to associate the best-
preserved column with Skopas. The reliefs of this drum[119] (fig.
705), generally interpreted as Alkestis being led to the upper world
by Hermes,[120] stand out as the finest of the extant remains, so superior in artistic quality that this may well be due to their execution
by a great artist. Moreover, the Thanatos and the Hermes with their
deep-set eyes and expressive faces resemble in style the figures on
the slabs of the Mausoleum frieze attributed to Skopas (cf. figs.
702, 703); and the modeling of the nude male bodies with its soft
transitions and yet clear demarcation of the salient muscles is not
unlike. We may compare especially the Ephesos Hermes with the
Mausoleum warrior who has fallen on one knee (fig. 701); even the
rendering of the hair with its curling, disordered strands is re-

*Temple of
Artemis at
Ephesos*

ingly, for Sieveking's objections hold: the action there is more tempestuous than in
1013–1015 and the draperies are differently utilized in the compositional scheme.
Moreover, Pfuhl's chief evidence for the assignment—that slab 1922 has an unoccupied field at the top similar to those of 1013–1015—seems hardly conclusive. Such
empty spaces are conditioned by the action of the figures and appear also on other
slabs; on that score 1006, for instance, might become a candidate as a work by
Skopas.

115 Smith, *Catalogue of Greek Sculpture in the British Museum*, II, No. 1036.
116 *N.H.* XXXIV. 95.
117 It ranked as one of the seven wonders of the world.
118 Some skeptical authorities would emend *una a Scopa* to read *imo scapo*, "on
the lowest drum"; but it is the reading of the best ms.
119 Smith, *op. cit.*, II, No. 1206.
120 For other interpretations, cf. Smith, *op. cit.*

markably similar. At all events the attribution of this drum to Skopas is within the range of possibilities.

Other Works

Apart from these architectural sculptures there is little that we can assign to Skopas with any confidence. Pausanias[121] saw in the precinct of Aphrodite at Elis "a bronze figure of the goddess seated

Aphrodite Pandemos

on a bronze goat . . . called Aphrodite Pandemos" and states that

it was the work of Skopas. On Roman coins of Elis[122] occurs a fine figure answering this description, but unfortunately very badly preserved (fig. 704). From this creation by Skopas are probably derived works like the beautiful mirror relief in the Louvre[123] and the sardonyx cameo in Naples.[124] Strabo[125] mentions a temple of Apollo Smintheus at Chryse (Alexandria Troas) "and the symbol which preserves the derivation of his name, i.e., the mouse, lies at the foot of the

Apollo Smintheus

Fig. 704. Aphrodite Pandemos, on a coin
(from a drawing, enlarged)
British Museum, London

statue; they are the work of Skopas of Paros." Eustathius[126] refers to the same sanctuary and adds "the symbol that lies at the foot of the statue, the mouse, is the work of Skopas." It used to be thought that Skopas made both cult image and mouse and that this statue was reproduced on coins of Chryse (fig. 695).[126a] It has now been persuasively argued that only the mouse was by Skopas and that it was added to an older image.[127]

Pliny[128] lists as one of Skopas' works "the Apollo of the Palatine"[129] and Propertius[130] gives rhetorical descriptions of two (?) fig-

121 VI. 25. 1.
122 Imhoof-Blumer and Gardner, *Numismatic Comm.*, pl. P, No. XXIV, pp. 72–73.
123 Collignon, *Monuments Piot*, 1894, pp. 144 f., pl. XX.
124 Furtwängler, *A.G.*, pl. LVII, 22.   125 XIII. 604.
126 *Ad. Il.* 30. 16.
126a The theory was first advanced by Furtwängler, Roscher's *Lexicon*, I. 466. The difficulty is that a raven appears on these coins, not a mouse.
127 Cf. Grace, *J.H.S.*, LII, 1932, pp. 228 ff.
128 *N.H.* XXXVI. 25.   129 Taken there from Rhamnous.   130 II. 31.

ures: "Fairer than Phoebus himself seems to me this marble figure as it sings its song to the silent lyre. . . . The Pythian god himself is standing between his mother and his sister,[181] making music, clothed in a long garment." A group of Apollo, Leto, and Artemis which occurs on a marble base in Sorrento[182] has been thought to reproduce the second work seen by Propertius; and several statues of Apollo playing the lyre have inevitably been associated with Skopas' work[133] (cf., e.g., fig. 706[184]). They can only be somewhat free imitations; for they differ in the positions of the legs and the arrangement of the folds. It is specially tempting to see at least the influence of a statue by Skopas in the inspired lyre player which occurs on coins of Nero (fig. 694). The beautiful, swaying attitude and forward movement are just what we should expect in Skopas' creations; but the pose does not correspond with the Apollo of the Sorrento base, and we know nothing further regarding the other Skopaic Apollo.

Pliny[185] enumerates several works concerning which it was uncertain whether Skopas or Praxiteles made them: "a group of Niobe's children meeting their death"; "a Janus" (probably a double-faced bust of Hermes) ; "Eros holding a thunderbolt," said to be in the likeness of Alkibiades. It has been thought that we have copies of "Niobe's children" in the statues of Niobe and her sons and daughters in the Uffizi[136] and elsewhere. From what we know of the two sculptors Skopas would be the more likely author of the originals, at least if we ascribe to him the Tegea heads. 'The Florence statues, particularly the Niobe, with the rather square head and deep-set eyes, are more in accord with the Tegea heads than with the radiant Hermes and Knidian Aphrodite. But of course a vague attribution in Roman times to two outstanding Greek sculptors may be due merely to a desire for big names. Moreover the attitudes, with head, trunk, and limbs in contrasting planes, are in the scheme introduced by Lysippos, and some of the heads resemble that of the Apoxyomenos. The originals could therefore hardly date before the late fourth century.

[181] The Leto and Artemis were by the younger Kephisodotos and Timotheos, respectively. On the group cf. Rizzo, *La base di Augusto*, pp. 51 ff.

[132] Cf. Wolters-Springer, *Handbuch*,[12] fig. 617; Picard, *Manuel*, III, fig. 140.

[133] The closest is a torso from Todi; cf. Picard, *op. cit.*, fig. 274.

[184] Deonna, *Catalogue des sculptures antiques au Musée d'art et d'histoire en Genève*, No. 61.

[135] *N.H.* XXXVI. 28.

[136] Amelung, *Führer durch die Antiken*, Nos. 175 ff.; Picard, *Manuel*, III, pp. 750 ff.

This sums up what we actually know of Skopas' work; and we must admit it is little indeed. Ancient writers of course mention many other statues and groups by him,[137] made for shrines both in Greece and in Asia Minor. And there have naturally been numerous attempts to recognize in extant statues copies of such works. Thus the Ares Ludovisi[138] has been associated with the "colossal seated figure of Ares" ascribed to Skopas by Pliny;[139] the Maenad in Dresden[140] (fig. 709) with the frenzied Maenad mentioned by Kallistratos;[141] the Herakles of the Lansdowne Collection[142] (fig. 707) with the statue seen by Pausanias[143] in Sikyon; the Apollo with a goose, preserved in many replicas, with the Pothos mentioned by Pausanias.[144] Moreover, many fine figures and heads with deep-set eyes and swelling foreheads—such as the Meleagers in the Fogg Museum in Cambridge, Mass., and in the Villa Medici[145] (fig. 708), and the head from a relief in New York (fig. 171)—have been set down as "Skopasian" works. But these are only guesses based on general stylistic considerations.

Faint though our picture is we nevertheless feel in Skopas the contact of a great personality, and one that apparently had a deep influence on the history of Greek art. For just as Praxiteles' subtle, graceful figures were imitated by many later generations, so some of Skopas' vehement creations opened the way for the emotional sculpture of the Hellenistic age.

(f) Timotheos

DATE   TIMOTHEOS took part in two great monuments of the fourth cen-
WORKS   tury of which remains are extant—the temple of Asklepios at Epidauros[146] (first quarter of the fourth century B.C.) and the Mau-

---

[137] Cf. Overbeck, *Schriftquellen*, 1151 ff.; a Hekate at Argos, an Asklepios and Hygieia, a Herakles at Sikyon, two Eumenides in Attica (of Parian marble and "not of terrifying aspect," i.e., in the beautifying style of the period), an Apollo at Rhamnous, a Hestia, Kanephoroi, a herm of Hermes, a Maenad, Eros, Himeros, and Pothos at Megara, Athena Pronaia at Thebes, Artemis Eukleia, Aphrodite and Pothos in Samothrake, Leto and Ortygia in Ephesos, Ares and Aphrodite both at Pergamon, a large group of Poseidon, Thetis, Achilles, Nereids, and Tritons in Bithynia; a Dionysos and an Athena at Knidos.

[138] Furtwängler, *Masterpieces*, p. 304; Collignon, *Histoire*, II, fig. 124, p. 247.

[139] *N.H.* XXXVI. 25.

[140] Neugebauer, *Studien über Skopas*, pls. III and IV, pp. 62 ff.

[141] Stat. 2; cf. also *Anthol. Gr.* III. 57. 3 and I. 74. 75.

[142] Wolters-Springer, *Handbuch*,[12] fig. 611, p. 329.   [143] II. 10. 1.

[144] I. 43. 6. Cf. Picard, *Manuel*, III, pp. 653 ff.

[145] Chase, *Greek and Roman Sculptures in American Collections*, figs. 97 and 101; Furtwängler, *op. cit.*, p. 304, note 3.

[146] Cf. Cavvadias, *Fouilles d'Épidaure;* and Defrasse and Lechat, *Épidaure*. The sculptures are now in the National Museum in Athens, Nos. 136–174.

soleum of Halikarnassos[147] (about 350, cf. pp. 271 f.). On the first
he must have worked during his youth, on the other in his later years.
His share in the sculptures at Epidauros is attested by the building
inscription recording the various contracts,[148] in which his name appears
with those of several collaborators. The lines referring to
Timotheos read: (line 36) Τιμόθεος ἕλετο[149] τύπος[150] ἐργάσα[σ]θα
καὶ παρέχεν[151] ⊟ ⊟ ⊟ ⊟ ⊟ ⊟ ⊟ ⊟ ἔγγυος Πυθοκλῆς, "Timotheos
contracted to make and furnish 'typoi' for 900 drachmas; his security
was Pythokles"; (line 90) Τιμόθεος ἐλ[ετο ἀκρω]τ[ήρ]ια ἐπὶ
τὸν ἄτε[ρ]ον αἰετὸν [X] X ⊟ ⊟ = = ἔγγυος Πυθ[οκλῆς], "Timotheos
contracted to furnish akroteria on one of the pediments for 2240
drachmas; his security was Pythokles."

The akroteria for the other pediment were contracted for by one
Theo . . . (Theotimos or more probably Theon): (line 97)
Θέω[. . . ἕλετο ἀκρωτήρια ἐπὶ] τὸν ἄτερον αἰετὸν XX ⊟ ⊟ [⊟]
[=] =, ἔγγυος Θεοξενίδα[ς], "Theon contracted to furnish akroteria
for the other pediment for 2340 (or 2420) drachmas. His security
was Theoxenidas."

The meaning of the word τύποι in line 36 is important. It used to
be interpreted by archaeologists[152] as signifying models, and so
Timotheos was supposed to have furnished the original models of
the pediments of the temple or possibly of the whole sculptural decoration,
and to have thus been the chief sculptor of the temple. But
though the word τύπος occurs in Plato in the figurative sense of
"the original type" or pattern, when the word is used in connection
with sculpture its meaning is regularly slab or relief.[153] In fact
τύπος never occurs in extant literature with the meaning of concrete
model in the field of art. The legitimate word for model in this connection
is παράδειγμα[154] and it occurs in that sense in this very

147 Smith, *Catalogue of Greek Sculpture in the British Museum*, II, pp. 65 ff.
148 Cf. Cavvadias, *Fouilles d'Épidaure*, No. 241, pp. 78 ff.; *I.G.*, IV (Argolid), No.
1484.
149 For εἵλετο.   150 For τύπους.   151 For παρέχειν.
152 First by Foucart, *B.C.H.*, XIV, 1890, 589 ff., and then generally accepted until
questioned by Ebert, *Die Fachausdrücke des griechischen Bauhandwerks*, I (*Würzburger Dissertation*, 1910), p. 34; and by Vallois, *B.C.H.*, XXXVI, 1912, pp. 219 ff.
For recent views, cf. Lippold, *Jahrbuch*, 1925, pp. 206 ff., and Neugebauer, *Jahrbuch*, 1926, pp. 82 ff. (both for τύπος = model), and Richter, *A.J.A.*, 1927, pp. 80 ff.,
and von Blumenthal, *Hermes*, LXIII, 1928, pp. 391–414 (both for τύπος = relief).
153 Cf. the many references cited by Lippold, *op. cit.*; also Richter and v. Blumenthal, *loc. cit.*
154 Lippold, *op. cit.*, claims that παράδειγμα is merely a model or pattern to serve for
a series of copies, as would be the case with waterspouts, architectural ornaments, etc.
But it is used by Herodotos V. 62 for the model of a temple. Cf. Richter, *loc. cit.*

inscription (line 303): Ἑκτορίδᾳ παρδείχματος λεοντο[κ]εφαλᾶν ἐνκαύσιος —:::, "To Hektoridas for the painting of a model of the lion heads, sixteen drachmas." The view that τύποι are reliefs, not models, is reinforced by the fact that recent researches have shown that the pediment sculptures can be adequately accounted for in the building inscription. If as Ebert[155] and Vallois[156] ingeniously propose we take κερκίς to mean half a gable (and this seems justified since the word is applied to various wedge-shaped objects[157]) and connect line 89: [Ἑ]κτορί[δ]ας ἕλετο κερκίδα τοῦ αἰετοῦ ἐργάσασθαι X ⊟ ⊟ ⊟ ⊟ ⊟ —, "Hektoridas contracted to work one wing of the pediment for 1610 drachmas" with line 111 (an entry made in the following year) Ἑκτορίδ[ᾳ] ἐναιετίων τᾶς ἀτέρας κερκιδος X ⊟ ⊟ ⊟ ⊟, "To Hektoridas for the other wing of the pediment sculptures 1400 drachmas" we obtain a total disbursement to this sculptor for one whole pediment—worked and paid for in two successive years—of 3010 drachmas. And this is the identical sum paid to the sculptor of the other pediment (whose name is lost): line 98 [τῷ δεῖνι ἐναι] ε[τ]ίων ἐ[ς] τὸν ἄτερον αἰετὸν [X]XX—, ἔνγυος Θεοξενί[δας], "To . . . for the sculptures of the other pediment 3010 drachmas. His security was Theoxenidas." The argument therefore, which has been advanced, that the sums paid for the pediment are insufficient and that consequently we must fill up a gap in the inscription and ascribe these pediments to several names—who worked under the supervision of and from the models of Timotheos[158]—falls to the ground. If three splendid akroteria carefully finished on every side cost 2240 drachmas, 3010 drachmas is not too little for a compact pediment group which was seen only from one side and need therefore not be worked throughout. As a matter of fact the execution of the pediment figures (cf. figs. 716–719[159]) is perfunctory compared to that of the akroteria (figs. 710–713), and the finest of the extant fragments of these pediment sculptures (fig. 716[160]) is so carelessly

155 *Die Fachausdrücke des griech. Bauhandwerks,* I (*Würzburger Diss.,* 1910), p. 34.

156 *B.C.H.,* 1912, pp. 226 ff. Vallois does not refer to Ebert's publication, so that he must have made the discovery independently.

157 E.g., the rod used in weaving which had a triangular end, cf. Blümer, *Gewerbe und Künste,* I, p. 146, fig. 18; a wedge-shaped division of the seats in a theater (Alex., Γυναικοκ., 1).

158 Cf., e.g., Wolters and Sieveking, *Jahrbuch,* 1909, p. 188.

159 National Museum, Athens, Nos. 136, 138, 146 (146 not certainly from the pediments).

160 *Ibid.,* No. 136.

worked at the back that the left leg does not even properly connect with the body (fig. 717), a rare feature in Greek art.

To sum up: as the sculptors of the Epidauros temple we have Hektoridas and an artist whose name is lost, for the two pediments; Timotheos and Theo . . ., for the two sets of akroteria; Timotheos, for reliefs of unknown purpose (see below). Timotheos then emerges as one of the four sculptors at work on the temple, and not necessarily the most important of them, since he receives less pay for his akroteria than Theo . . . did for his!

Three, perhaps four, of the six akroteria of the temple have survived. They consist of two Nereids (or Aurai) on horseback[161] (figs. 710, 711; Nos. 156, 157), a Nike holding a bird[162] (fig. 713), and the upper part of another Nike[163] (fig. 712). The two Nereids were found close to the western end of the temple,[164] so that their association with the western pediment is assured. The Nike with the bird was found built into a wall between the temple and the rotunda of Polykleitos,[165] that is, not far from the western end; she may therefore have been the central akroterion of the west pediment, though that is not certain. The upper part of a Nike with wings came to light northeast of the temple[166] (near a base which Kavvadias erroneously thought belonged to it). Its identification as an akroterion of the temple is due to Furtwängler.[167] In style these four figures are markedly similar. They have in common the delicate, transparent drapery with sharply cut, finely worked folds, very different from the more coarsely worked and denser drapery of the pediment figures. So whether Timotheos was the sculptor of the Nereids and the Nike with the bird from the west pediment or of the fragment of a Nike probably from the east pediment, his style was apparently characterized by this transparent rendering of drapery —which connects him with late fifth-century accomplishments.

We stated that besides the akroteria Timotheos made certain reliefs for which he received 900 drachmas (p. 277). Now there were found on the temple site two reliefs representing the seated Asklepios[168] (figs. 714, 715), of the same delicate workmanship as the

---

161 National Museum, Athens, Nos. 156, 157.   162 No. 155.
163 No. 162.
164 Kavvadias, *Fouilles d'Epidaure*, p. 21: "tout près du côté occidental du temple."
165 *Ibid.*, p. 20.   166 *Ibid.*, p. 118, fig. 19.
167 *Sitzungsberichte Münch. Akad. phil.-hist. Kl.*, 1908, p. 445.
168 National Museum, Athens, Nos. 173, 174.

akroteria and with similar transparent drapery. They cannot be sculptured metopes as Svoronos[169] once thought, for the measurements do not after all correspond,[170] and the composition of the reliefs with the legs protruding from the background is inappropriate for a metope; moreover, the use of the word τύπος for metope has no parallel. What purpose they actually served we do not know, but their affinity with the style of the akroteria as against that of the pediment figures makes it at least possible that they were the work of Timotheos.

Mausoleum   Timotheos is mentioned by Pliny[171] as one of the sculptors of the Mausoleum of Halikarnassos, along with Skopas, Bryaxis, and Leochares. We have seen that in the case of Skopas it has been possible to assign to him—with much probability—certain portions of the friezes (cf. p. 272). Is this feasible also with Timotheos? The attempt has been made. Wolters and Sieveking[172] see his hand in the slabs Nos. 1006, 1007, 1008, 1010, 1011, 1012, 1016, 1017 (cf. figs. 720–722)—for they have similar, somewhat stereotyped figures not always successfully composed, as well as the same type of stocky, muscular horse, with short, thick head, conspicuous folds on the neck, and a tail very broad at the root. The characteristics, however, are not so clearly marked as in the case of Skopas; and even if we admit that these slabs form a homogeneous group, we have no evidence by which we can assign it to Timotheos. We know only that he was at work on the south side, but only one of the slabs was found on the temple site (No. 1016) and that was on the east. In style they are certainly different from the akroteria of Epidauros.

Other Works   We hear also of single statues by Timotheos—an Artemis[173] later shown in the temple of Apollo on the Palatine, an Asklepios[174] in Troezen, athletes, etc.[175] But no trace of them has survived. The safest criterion by which to judge the style of Timotheos is therefore the akroteria of the Epidauros temple. For either the three fine figures (figs. 710, 711, 713) or one not dissimilar fragment (fig. 712) should be by his hand. Several statues have accordingly been as-

---

169 *Das Athener Nationalmuseum*, I, pp. 152 f.
170 Neugebauer, *Jahrbuch*, 1926, pp. 83 f.   171 *N.H.* XXXVI. 30.
172 Cf. *Jahrbuch*, 1909, pp. 181, 185. Pfuhl, *Jahrbuch*, 1928, pp. 46 f., would assign only 1006, 1010, 1016, 1017.
173 Pliny, *N.H.* XXXVI. 32.   174 Pausanias II. 32. 4.
175 Pliny, *N.H.* XXXIV. 91.

cribed to Timotheos on account of their general stylistic resemblance to the Epidauros akroteria,[176] the most important being the Leda in the Villa Albani[177] and a female torso in Copenhagen.[178] But we must remember in such assignments that Timotheos' associate, Theo . . ., had evidently a markedly similar style.

(g) Bryaxis

ORIGIN AND DATE

BRYAXIS, an Athenian,[179] was as we have seen (p. 271) at work on the Mausoleum about 350 B.C. An inscription on a sculptured base with the name of Bryaxis as the sculptor may be dated about the middle of the fourth century. We know furthermore[180] that he made a portrait of Seleukos (Nikator) who became king of Syria in 312; but the portrait could well have been done before Seleukos became king, for Bryaxis would have been rather old in 312, if he was an eminent sculptor in 350.

WORKS
Sculptured
Base

The signed sculptured base referred to is our chief landmark for the study of Bryaxis. It is a square block found in Athens in 1891, evidently intended for the support of a statue. It is decorated on three sides with a horseman approaching a tripod[181] (fig. 723), and on the fourth is an inscription recording that Demainetos, Demeas, and Demosthenes—a father and two sons—were victorious in horse races, and that Bryaxis made the monument (fig. 724). The base was presumably by the same sculptor as the monument. Precious as this original monument is, the reliefs of the horsemen are so sketchy that they can give us only a limited picture of Bryaxis. We obtain from them the impression of an able but rather conventional person of delicate perception and with a fine sense of composition, for the spacing of the horsemen with the tripods is very pleasing.

In the vicinity of this base (that is, fifty meters from it) was found the statue of a Nike[182] (figs. 725, 726) which has been quite generally identified as the statue originally erected on it. But the execution is too summary for a single commemorative statue, more

---

176 Cf. Amelung, *Ausonia*, III, 1908, pp. 91 ff.; Arndt, Brunn-Bruckmann, *Denkmäler griechischer und römischer Skulptur*, text to pl. 648.
177 Brunn-Bruckmann, *Denkmäler griechischer und römischer Skulptur*, pl. 648.
178 *Ibid.*, pl. 665.   179 Clement of Alexandria, *Protrept.* IV. 47.
180 From Pliny, *N.H.* XXXIV. 73.
181 National Museum, Athens, No. 1733; cf. Kavvadias, 'Εφ. 'Αρχ., 1893, pls. 6–7, pp. 39 ff.; Svoronos, *Das Athener Nationalmuseum*, I, pls. XXVI, XXVII, pp. 163 ff.
182 National Museum, Athens, No. 1732; Svoronos, *op. cit.*, pl. XXVII; Kavvadias, *loc. cit.*, pls. 4, 5.

adapted to a decorative figure placed at a great height like an akroterion;[183] and the oblique direction of its forward movement does not compose well with the rectangular base.[184] Furthermore the style of the drapery, with its finely composed, sharply cut folds and the low girding, is that of the later fifth rather than that of the middle of the fourth century (p. 104). We may compare especially such dated monuments as a figure from the Erechtheion[185] (fig. 728), for the folds on the lower part; a fragment from the Rhamnous reliefs[186] (fig. 727), for the folds of the upper part; the Nereids in the British Museum[187] (cf. fig. 304); and the Medici Athena in the Louvre (fig. 322), for the folds immediately above and below the girdle; and contrast the more diversified, more naturalistic renderings of the fourth century, such as the torso in Venice[188] and the figures on the Sidon (fig. 316) and Mantineia reliefs (figs. 679–681). The tunics of the horsemen on the base, on the other hand, are in the familiar fourth-century style, comparable to that of the Mausoleum frieze.

Mausoleum
Is it possible to use the reliefs on the base as a criterion by which to recognize part of the Mausoleum frieze as the work of Bryaxis? The attempt has been made,[189] based chiefly on a comparison of the types of horses. The thick-set build, with muscular body, triangular neck (wide at the base and narrow at the head), short head, and tail consisting of continuous long hairs, which appears on the inscribed base, occurs again on the slabs Nos. 1009, 1019 (figs. 729, 730) of the Mausoleum frieze; and these have accordingly been attributed to Bryaxis. If the assignment is correct, and it is at least ingenious, we have here works of a very different character from the

[183] Presumably of the "Hephaisteion" from which it rolled down the hill to the place where it was found (northeast of the Theseion station). This suggestion was first made by Studniczka as long ago as 1907 in his monograph on Kalamis, p. 51, and should have received greater credence.

[184] This is the case even if we imagine an intermediate column (cf. Kavvadias, Εφ. ᾿Αρχ., pl. facing p. 47). In the Paionios Nike this problem was ably solved by a triangular pyramidal base.

[185] Stevens, Paton, etc., *The Erechtheum*, pl. XLIV, 77; text, p. 269, fig. 165.

[186] Svoronos, *Das Athener Nationalmuseum*, I, pl. XLI, B209.

[187] Svoronos in his publication himself sees this resemblance but uses it only to identify the figure as a Nereid.

[188] Furtwängler, *Originalstatuen in Venedig*, pl. VII, 1, and his excellent analysis on p. 312.

[189] Cf. Wolters and Sieveking, *Jahrbuch*, 1909, p. 184. Pfuhl, *Jahrbuch*, 1928, pp. 48 f. assigns to Bryaxis slabs 1019, 1020, 1021, 1018, which are given by Wolters and Sieveking to Leochares (see p. 283, note 207).

quiet horsemen of Athens—impetuous fighting scenes with galloping and rearing horses, rapidly advancing figures and fallen bodies, the medley of the battle, boldly and yet harmoniously composed. The spirit of the two products is different indeed, but they have in common a fine feeling for design.

The rhetorician Libanios[190] describes in glowing terms a statue of Apollo by Bryaxis at Daphne near Antioch: "Imagination brings before my eyes that form, the bowl, the lyre, the tunic reaching to the feet, the delicacy of the neck in the marble, the girdle about the bosom, which holds the golden tunic together, so that some parts fit closely and others hang loose. He seemed as one that sang." We know from Cedren[191] that the statue was by Bryaxis; and it appears to be represented on coins of Antiochos Epiphanes[192] (figs. 731, 732). It is a dignified composition harking back to earlier prototypes; quite what we might expect from the able, somewhat conservative artist of the Athens base.

Apollo Kitharoidos

Of other works by Bryaxis mentioned by ancient writers[193] we know only the names. We hear of statues of various deities, including five colossal figures in Rhodes,[194] a Serapis,[195] a Pasiphae,[196] and the portrait of Seleukos mentioned above. All these, except the Serapis[196a] and an Asklepios and Hygieia, were made for Asia Minor.

Other Works

(h) Thrasymedes

THE sculptor of the statue which stood inside the temple of Asklepios at Epidauros was Thrasymedes of Paros. Pausanias[197] gives a detailed description of it: "[At Epidauros] the image of Asklepios is smaller by one half than the Olympian Zeus at Athens, and is made of ivory and gold; the inscription states that it is the work of Thrasymedes the son of Arignotos of Paros. The god is seated upon a throne and holds a staff in one hand, while he extends the other above the serpent's head. A dog is also represented lying at his feet. On the throne are represented in relief the exploits of Ar-

---

[190] *Orat.* 61.   [191] *Hist. Comp.* 306 B.
[192] Babelon, *Les Rois de Syrie*, p. 71, pl. XII, 12.
[193] Cf. Overbeck, *Schriftquellen*, 1316 ff.   [194] Pliny, *N.H.* XXXIV. 42.
[195] Clement of Alexandria, *Protrept.* IV. 48.
[196] Tatian, *Contra Graecos.* 54. 117 (ed. Worth).
[196a] The Serapis has been quite generally identified with the well known type known in several replicas (cf. e.g., Helbig, *Führer*[3], Nos. 237, 298); but this identification has recently been challenged, cf. Adriani, *Atti della Accademia Nazionale dei Lincei*, CCCXLV, 1948, pp. 438 ff.
[197] II. 27. 2.

give heroes, viz., the contest of Bellerophon with the Chimaira, and Perseus, who has decapitated Medusa." A seated Asklepios with staff, serpent, and dog which appears on the coinage of Epidauros (fig. 733) doubtless reproduces this temple statue.[198] It is a dignified figure in early fourth-century style, a not unworthy successor of the chryselephantine statues by Pheidias and Polykleitos. Even from the small coin reliefs we get the impression of the magnanimity and gentleness of the great god of healing. The statue was probably made after the temple was completed; at least it is not mentioned in the building inscription (cf. p. 277); but it cannot be much later, for the transparent drapery (which we noted also in the akroteria of the temple, cf. p. 279) still harks back to late fifth-century models. So we may date the original about 375 B.C.

The temple statue was not the only work which Thrasymedes made for the temple of Asklepios. The building inscription (line 45) tells us that he "contracted to execute the roof above and the inner doorway, as well as that between the columns, for 9800 drachmas. His securities were Pythokles, Theopheides, and Agemon." In line 65 of the same inscription we learn that 3070 drachmas worth of ivory were furnished for this door, and the gold nails mentioned in line 65 were doubtless for the same purpose. Thrasymedes' knowledge in working ivory and other precious materials must have given him these commissions. A dedicatory inscription to Apollo and Asklepios with a signature of Thrasymedes was found near the stadium.[198a]

(i) Leochares

ORIGIN AND DATE

PLINY[199] places Leochares along with Kephisodotos in the 102d Olympiad (c. 372 B.C.). Plato[200] in a letter dated c. 366 B.C. refers to Leochares as "an excellent young craftsman." As many as seven inscriptions with Leochares as the name of the sculptor have been found in Athens,[201] and these are all datable in the middle and second half of the fourth century. Pausanias[202] tells us that he made

WORKS chryselephantine statues of Philip of Macedon and his family (his parents, his wife, and his son, Alexander the Great) for the Philippeion at Olympia, and he collaborated with Lysippos in a lion hunt of Alexander (Alexander was born in 355). We also know from

198 Cf. Imhoof-Blumer and Gardner, *Numismatic Comm.*, pl. L, Nos. III–V.
198a Cavvadias, 'Εφ.'Αρχ., 1885, p. 50; *I.G.*, IV. 2. 198.
199 *N.H.* XXXIV. 50.   200 *Epistles* XIII (perhaps spurious).
201 Loewy, *Inschriften*, Nos. 77–83.   202 V. 20. 9.

Plutarch that he made a bronze portrait of Isokrates[203] (436–338).
Like most Greek artists of this period he obtained important commissions in Asia Minor, where large artistic undertakings were now
more frequent than in Greece proper. Thus he was one of the four
sculptors of the Mausoleum of Halikarnassos (soon after 351), the
western side of which was assigned to him for decoration. His chief
period of activity therefore seems to have been the middle and the
third quarter of the fourth century. Though his origin is nowhere
directly stated, the fact that so many inscriptions with his name
were found in Athens suggests that he was an Athenian, at all events
active in Athens during a considerable period.

Since part of the sculptural decoration of the Mausoleum of *The*
Halikarnassos has survived, the question naturally comes up *Mausoleum*
whether it is possible to assign any of it to Leochares. Sieveking *Frieze*
and Wolters[204] in their attempt to apportion the largest frieze between the four sculptors[205] have assigned to Leochares the slabs
1020, 1021, and 1018 (cf. fig. 735). These reliefs show a highly
individual style—markedly long figures in strongly oblique postures, constantly crossing one another, and restless, waving drapery.
They are certainly by one hand, and it is tempting to think it was
that of Leochares; for after Skopas he seems to have been the most
distinguished of the four sculptors[206] and these slabs are next to
those assigned to Skopas the ablest and most original work.[207]

Pliny[208] describes one of Leochares' works as follows: "Leochares *Other Works*
represented the eagle which feels what a treasure it is stealing in
Ganymede, and to whom it is bearing him, and using its talons
gently, though the boy's garment protects him." A group of Ganymede and the eagle extant in various replicas, of which the best is
in the Vatican[209] (fig. 737), has naturally been associated with Leochares' work; for the subject is rare in Greek sculpture, and the
group corresponds in a general way to Pliny's rather vague descrip-

---

[203] *Isocr.* 27.

[204] *Jahrbuch*, 1909, pp. 171 ff. [205] Cf. pp. 270, 278, 280.

[206] Vitruvius II. 8. 11 speaks of "nobili manu Leocharis," which is the equivalent
of famous.

[207] Pfuhl, *Jahrbuch*, 1928, pp. 48 f., would assign these same slabs to Bryaxis and
Nos. 1007–1009, 1011, 1012 to Leochares; but the stormy movement of 1020, 1021,
1018 has nothing in common with the horseman on the base, our only criterion for
Bryaxis' style (cf. p. 279).

[208] *N.H.* XXXIV. 79.

[209] Helbig, *Führer*,[3] I, No. 386. The restorations include the head and wings of
the eagle; the right forearm, left arm, and both legs from the knee down of Ganymede, and the upper part of the dog.

tion; that is, the eagle's claws are laid on Ganymede's garment. But
the group appears considerably later in date, since its picturesque
character places the original well in the Hellenistic period, and it
has nothing in common with the Mausoleum reliefs. Perhaps we may
obtain a better suggestion of Leochares' work in the beautiful bronze
mirror relief in Berlin (fig. 734), which is at least a fourth-century
original (here too the claws of the eagle are placed over the boy's
garment); though, as Furtwängler[210] pointed out, the composition
probably goes back to a famous painting, for it is not conceived as
a piece of sculpture in the round.

We hear of several other works by Leochares,[211] such as a "famous
Zeus the Thunderer," afterwards on the Capitol, "a work of un-
equalled excellence"; a colossal statue of Ares[212] of wood with marble
head, hands, and feet ($\dot{a}\kappa\rho\dot{o}\lambda\iota\theta o\nu$)—though by some this work was
ascribed to Timotheos; a series of portraits executed together with
the sculptor Sthennis;[213] etc. But of none of these have replicas been
satisfactorily identified. Because of a certain resemblance to the
Ganymede the original of the Apollo Belvedere (fig. 736) has been
ascribed to Leochares.[214] With such uncertain evidence we must admit that Leochares still remains a shadowy figure.

(j) Euphranor, Silanion, and others

Of the other sculptors who worked in Athens during this period
Euphranor was perhaps the most important. Pliny[215] gives a list of his
works, places him in the 104th Olympiad (364 B.C.), and tells us that
he "far outshone his rivals." He was a painter as well as a sculptor and
wrote books on symmetry and color. Except for his Apollo Patroos,
found in the Agora, no extant sculptures can be certainly associated
with him[216] to form a picture of his style. Silanion is said to have
made a portrait of Plato dedicated by Mithridates,[217] which has been
identified with a type preserved in many replicas. Even more indefi-
nite are Sthennis, who worked with Leochares on a portrait group;[218]

210 Collection Sabouroff, II, pl. 147.   211 Cf. Overbeck, Schriftquellen, 1303 ff.
212 Vitruvius II. 8. 11.   213 Loewy, Inschriften, No. 83.
214 Cf. Furtwängler, Masterpieces, p. 408.
215 N.H. XXXIV. 77; XXXV. 128.
216 Pausanias I. 3. 3. National Museum, Athens, 3573. On this and other attributions cf. Picard, Manuel, II, p. 358, fig. 385.
217 Diog. Laert. III. 25; Pacsanias VI. 4. 5. Cf. R. Boehringer, Platon, Bildnisse
und Nachweise. Mithridates died in 363 B.C.
218 Cf. p. 283.

and Demetrios,[219] another portrait sculptor, placed in the first half of
the fourth century by two inscriptions found on the Akropolis.[220]

(k) Lysippos

LYSIPPOS of Sikyon was the last great original sculptor of Greece. ORIGIN AND
Pliny places him in the 113th Olympiad (328 B.C.), a natural date DATE
to select, for we know that he was especially active during Alexander
the Great's reign (336–323). An inscription at Olympia[221] records
that one Troilos was victorious with horses, and Pausanias[222] states
that these victories were gained in the 102d Olympiad (372–368)
and that Lysippos made the statue. The statue need not have been
erected immediately after the victory, and the character of the inscription suggests that it was not set up till considerably later.[223]
Pliny[224] tells us that Lysippos made numerous portraits of Alexander beginning with his boyhood (Alexander was born in 355).
An inscription on a block found at Thebes associates Lysippos with
a statue of Koreidas, winner in the pankration for boys in the
Pythian games, datable about 342 or later.[225] Two statue bases
found at Corinth and inscribed Λύσιππος ἐπόησε can be roughly
dated about 325.[226] And still another statue base from Thermos
bears his signature together with a later dedicatory inscription.[227]
Athenaios[228] mentions Lysippos as a friend of Kassandros when he
founded Kassandreia in the 116th Olympiad (316). A lost inscription mentioned as early as the fifteenth century[229] reads Σέλευκος
βασιλεύς Λύσιππος ἐποίει. (Seleukos assumed the royal title in
312.) All these dates concur in placing Lysippos' activity in the
second half of the fourth century. Pausanias[230] says that he made a
statue at Olympia of Poulydamas victorious in the pankration in
the 93d Olympiad (408); if this information is correct, the statue
must have been much later than the event it celebrated.

Lysippos, we are told, was extraordinarily prolific, more so than WORKS
any other artist.[231] The number of his works is said to have been

---

[219] Cf. Pliny, *N.H.* XXXIV. 76, and Lucian, *Philops.* 18.
[220] Loewy, *op. cit.,* Nos. 62, 63.
[221] Loewy, *Inschriften,* No. 94.   [222] VI. I. 4.
[223] The evidence is summarized by Johnson, *Lysippos,* pp. 60 ff.
[224] *N.H.* XXXIV. 63.   [225] Cf. Johnson, *op. cit.,* pp. 62 ff.
[226] Powell, *A.J.A.,* 1903, pp. 29–32.
[227] Sotiriades, 'Αρχ. Δελτ., I, 1915, pp. 55 ff.; Johnson, *op. cit.,* p. 64.
[228] XI. 784.   [229] Loewy, *op. cit.,* No. 487.
[230] VI. 5. 1.   [231] Pliny, *N.H.* XXXIV. 61.

fifteen hundred,[232] "all of such artistic value that each would have
sufficed by itself to make him famous. The number became known
after his death, when his heir broke open his strongbox, since it had
been his custom to set aside a piece of gold from the price of each
statue." Unfortunately not a single one of these many sculptures
has been preserved, and—what is more amazing—we have not even a
perfectly certain reproduction of one, though a few can be so identified with considerable probability.

Youth One of Lysippos' most famous works was "a youth scraping him-
Scraping self which M. Agrippa dedicated in front of his baths."[233] Its great
Himself beauty is attested by the anecdote that the Emperor Tiberius conceived a "wonderful passion" for it and removed it to his private
chamber but had to restore it to its former location on account of
the displeasure of the Roman populace. A reproduction of this
statue has long been recognized in the Apoxyomenos in the Vatican[234] (figs. 739, 742, 743), for it seemed to bear out in a striking
way the characteristics of Lysippos summed up by Pliny:[235] "He is
said to have done much to advance the art of sculpture in bronze by
his careful treatment of the hair, and by making the head smaller
and the body more slender and firmly knit [corpora graciliora sic-
cioraque] than earlier sculptors, thus imparting to his figures an
appearance of greater height. There is no Latin name for the 'canon
of proportions' [symmetria] which he carefully observed, exchang-
ing the squarely-built figure of the older artists for a new and
untried system. He was in the habit of saying that they had represented men as they were, while he represented them as they appeared to the eye." The Vatican Apoxyomenos with its slim body,
long legs, small head, and carefully modeled hair certainly corresponds, in a general way at least, to Pliny's description. It is
obviously a conscious departure from the squarely built figures of
Polykleitos and is drier, more firmly knit than the soft Praxitelean
statues. So the identification seems probable. Unfortunately we can
obtain no real conception of the beauty of the original from this
obviously inferior marble copy. We miss altogether the "extreme
delicacy of the work even in the smallest details," which we are
told[236] was Lysippos' "most individual feature." And the lifelike

---

232 Pliny, *N.H.* XXXIV. 37.
233 Pliny, *N.H.* XXXIV. 62.
235 *N.H.* XXXIV. 65.

234 Helbig, *Führer,*[3] I, No. 23.
236 Pliny, *N.H.* XXXIV. 65.

quality which the original doubtless had is lost. All we can get is a
general picture of Lysippos' scheme of proportions.

During the excavations at Delphi there was brought to light a   *The Agias*
series of statues dedicated *c.* 344–334 by one Daochos, of Thessaly,
representing earlier members of his family.[237] The inscriptions on
the base of the dedication give the names of the individuals and their
accomplishments. One of the statues is of Agias (figs. 738, 740,
741), winner in the pankration in the middle of the fifth century B.C.
It is the best preserved and finest of the set and has the further interest that a copy of its dedicatory inscription has been found
in Thessaly (one portion in Pharsalos, the native town of Agias)—
in which Lysippos is mentioned as the sculptor.[238] The Thessalian
statue has not survived, so that we do not know what it was like. It
was presumably of bronze, for that was the favorite material of
Lysippos. Tempting though it be to regard the Agias as a marble
copy executed by Lysippos' assistants with the help of the original
mould of the bronze statue, this is only an hypothesis. As a matter of
fact exact copies were not usual in this period. Moreover the Apoxyomenos corresponds more closely to the little we know definitely of
Lysippos' style (his new scheme of proportions with a slimmer body
and with trunk, head, and limbs placed in slightly contrasting planes,
as well as his carefully worked hair) than the Agias, who is distinctly
squarer and more frontal and whose hair shows less care in execution.
And that the Agias is the finer statue of the two is merely owing to
the fact that it happens to be a Greek original, while the Apoxyomenos
is not. The differences between the two, however, are not so great as
some authorities have tried to make out. In the Agias the eyes are
more deeply set and look upward, giving the whole a much more vivid
expression. But in other respects the two heads have much in common.
The structure of the forehead is similar, and so are the small, delicately modeled mouth and firm chin. It is not inconceivable that the
two go back to the same sculptor at different stages in his career—the
Agias an earlier work, the Apoxyomenos produced toward the end
of his life.

The original of the colossal statue of Herakles Farnese in Na-   *Herakles*
ples,[238a] signed by Glykon as copyist[238b] (fig. 749), must have been an

237 Cf. Poulsen, *Delphi*, pp. 265 ff.; *Fouilles de Delphes*, IV, pls. LXIII ff.
238 Preuner, *Ein delphisches Weihgeschenk*, pp. 20, 24.
238a Ruesch, *Guide*, No. 280; Johnson, *Lysippos*, pp. 197 ff.
238b Loewy, *Inschriften gr. Bildhauer*, No. 345.

important work, to judge by the number of extant copies. One of these, in the Palazzo Pitti in Florence, has an inscription giving the name of Lysippos as artist.[238c] If the inscription is ancient and gives the correct information, the original work may have been the statue mentioned by ancient writers as having stood in the market place of Sikyon. The smaller replica in the Uffizi, Florence,[238d] in which the muscles are less prominent than in the Farnese Herakles, may reproduce the original more faithfully.

Epitrapezios Martial[239] gives us an unusually detailed description of what must have been a very engaging work by Lysippos—a statuette of Herakles less than a foot in height, used as a table decoration and therefore called Herakles Epitrapezios: "He who sits here tempering the hardness of the rock with the outstretched lion's skin, a mighty god imprisoned in the tiny bronze, and gazes with upturned eyes at the stars which once he bore, whose left hand is hot with the club, and his right with the wine-cup, enjoys no upstart fame, nor is his fame that of a Roman chisel. 'Tis a famous work and offering of Lysippos which thou seest." Statius[240] likewise gives it extravagant praise: "In how small a space what illusion of great size. What skill of hand, what deft craftsman's cunning to fashion equally well ornaments of a table and to conceive in his mind the great colossi. . . . The mild face, as though rejoicing from the heart, invites to the feast; this hand grasps his brother's drowsy cup, the other is mindful of his club; a rough seat supports him, a rock covered with the Nemean lion's skin." It is said to have belonged successively to Alexander, Hannibal, Sulla, and Novius Vindex.[241] There are numerous statuettes of Herakles, Roman reproductions, corresponding more or less to Martial's description,[242] since the hero rests on a rock on which is a lion's skin, and holds a club in his left hand (fig. 751[243]). The right hand is preserved only in a bronze figure in the Naples Museum[243a] and on a coin of Amastris of the time of Caracalla (fig. 750) which shows the same composition. It has been argued that the style is a good deal later than that of Lysippos, being indeed highly realistic in the developed Hellenistic manner. But we know too

238c Amelung, *Führer durch die Antiken in Florenz*, No. 186; Loewy, *op. cit.*, No. 506.

238d Amelung, *op. cit.*, No. 40.

239 IX. 44. 240 *Silv.* IV. 6. 241 Statius, *Silv.* IV. 6.

242 Cf. Weizsäcker, *Jahrbuch*, 1889, pp. 109 f., and Johnson, *Lysippos*, pp. 100 ff.

243 Smith, *Catalogue of Greek Sculpture in the British Museum*, III, No. 1725.

243a R. Paribeni, *Notizie degli Scavi*, 1902, pp. 572 ff.

little of the tendencies of Lysippos to be dogmatic on this subject. We must rather try to reconstruct his style from the few monuments which can be associated with him and from the testimony of ancient authors. We know that Lysippos prided himself on his realism. For instance, Pliny[244] tells the following story: "Duris asserts that Lysippos of Sikyon had no master, but originally worked as a bronze-caster, and was inspired to attempt higher things by an answer of Eupompos. That artist, when asked which of his predecessors he followed pointed to a crowd of men, and replied that Nature herself and no artist was the true model." And Propertius[245] says that "the glory of Lysippos is to make his statues full of life." Moreover Niketas'[246] description of Lysippos' colossal bronze Herakles at Tarentum certainly suggests a realistic rendering: "His breast and shoulders were broad, his hair thick, his buttocks fat, and his arms brawny." The swelling muscles of the seated Herakles are therefore not contrary to but in line with Lysippian conceptions, so that these statuettes may well be late, poor reproductions of Lysippos' highly prized little Herakles Epitrapezios.

Poulydamas

Pausanias[247] tells us that Lysippos made a statue of Poulydamas at Olympia and that some of his remarkable feats (which he enumerates) are represented on the base. A portion of this pedestal with the reliefs referred to has been found and is now in the museum at Olympia[248] (cf. fig. 752). The reliefs represent Poulydamas in combat with a lion, seated on a dead lion, and lifting a man in the air before the Persian king. Did Lysippos execute the base as well as the statue and have we here an original work by his hand? The question would be more important if the reliefs were better preserved; but they are sadly mutilated and at best are only slight works, so that they help little in our estimate of Lysippos' style, except to bear out the evidence of the Apoxyomenos regarding his slim proportions.

Zeus

A bronze Zeus, the work of Lysippos, is described by Pausanias[249] as standing in the market-place at Sikyon. On a bronze coin of Sikyon of the time of Caracalla is a long-legged Zeus standing in a pose not unlike that of the Apoxyomenos, only reversed; at least the curve described by the body is similar; so that the figure on the coin might well represent the Lysippian statue. Unfortunately it too is

244 *N.H.* XXXIV. 61.
245 III. 7. 9.   246 *Chon. de Sign. Constant.* 5.   247 VI. 5. 1 ff.
248 Treu, *Olympia*, III, pl. LV, 1–3, pp. 209 ff.   249 II. 9. 6.

badly preserved, and can teach us little beyond Lysippos' preference for a slender build.

Portrait of Alexander

Lysippos was a successful portraitist. In fact Alexander the Great would let no one else portray him in bronze. So, at least, Plutarch[250] tells us: "When Lysippos first made a portrait of Alexander with his countenance uplifted to heaven, just as Alexander was wont to gaze with his neck gently inclined to one side, someone wrote the following not inappropriate epigram: 'The man of bronze is as one that looks on Zeus and will address him thus: "O Zeus, I place earth beneath my feet, do thou rule Olympos."' For this reason Alexander gave orders that Lysippos only should make portraits of him, since Lysippos only, as it would seem, truly revealed his nature in bronze, and portrayed his courage in visible form, while others in their anxiety to reproduce the bend of the neck and the melting look of the eyes failed to preserve his masculine and leonine aspect." We know from Pliny's[251] statement that Lysippos made numerous portraits of Alexander, and it is of course natural to look among the several extant heads for copies of some of these. But we must remember that so popular a figure as Alexander was doubtless often portrayed even after Lysippos' death; for instance, by Lysippos' own son, Euthykrates.[252] The head in the British Museum[253] (fig. 745) shows perhaps best the "melting gaze and the leonine aspect." The "Azara bust"[254] (fig. 744) has certain stylistic affinities with the Apoxyomenos. The bust from the Guimet Museum[255] (fig. 746) is a particularly fine conception and of excellent workmanship; though its identity with Alexander has been doubted.[256] But closest perhaps to a Lysippian original are the heads on the coins[257] (fig. 747), which though small in scale have at least the advantage of being practically contemporary Greek work.

Portrait of Seleukos

Since we know from an inscription (see p. 287) that Lysippos made a portrait of king Seleukos, and a bronze bust in Naples[258] has been identified with Seleukos Nikator (356–281) by comparison with the coin types, it has been suggested that this bust is a copy of

---

[250] *Alex.* II. 2. Cf. also Pliny, *N.H.* VII. 125: "[Alex.] edixit ne quis ipsum alius quam Apelles pingeret quam Pyrgoteles scalperet quam Lysippos ex aere duceret."
[251] *N.H.* XXXIV. 63; see pp. 284–285.   [252] Pliny, *N.H.* XXXIV. 66.
[253] Smith, *Catalogue*, III, 1857; Bieber, *Portraits of Alexander*, fig. 46.
[254] Bernoulli, *Darstellungen Alexanders des Grossen*, pl. I, p. 21. Much restored.
[255] Reinach, *Gazette des Beaux-Arts*, 1902, p. 158.
[256] Bernoulli, *op. cit.*, p. 87.   [257] Head, *Historia numorum*, p. 242, fig. 172.
[258] Ruesch, *Guida del Museo Nazionale di Napoli*, p. 221, No. 890.

the work by Lysippos.[259] But as we know that portraits of Seleukos were also made by other sculptors, including Bryaxis (cf. p. 281) and Aristodemos, we have not enough evidence for a definite assignment.

Another field in which Lysippos evidently distinguished himself *Large* was that of large dedicatory groups of figures in violent action. For *Compositions* instance Plutarch[260] tells us that "Krateros erected a memorial of a hunt at Delphi. He caused figures of bronze to be made, representing the lion, the dogs, the king in combat with the lion, and himself coming to the rescue; some of these were made by Lysippos, the rest by Leochares." Again Arrian:[261] "Of the Macedonians there fell about twenty-five of the king's guard in the first onslaught. Bronze portraits of these stood at Dion, made by Lysippos by order of Alexander." And Pliny[262] lists among Lysippos' works "Alexander's hunt," "four-horse chariots of several kinds," and a "troop of Alexander's horse in which he introduced portraits of his friends which displayed a marvelous likeness." None of these bold creations in which Lysippos showed himself as a great composer, a portraitist, and an animal sculptor have of course been preserved; but we may form perhaps some conception of their general effect by the splendid battle scenes and lion hunt on the "Alexander sarcophagus" at Constantinople[263] (fig. 748), dated in the late fourth century.

Many other works of Lysippos are known to us either by the mere *Other Works* mention or by lengthy descriptions of ancient writers.[264] These include deities (among them a colossal Zeus over forty cubits in height, at Tarentum), heroes, athletes, and portraits (among them Sokrates[264a]), and animals (e.g., a slain lion and a free horse). We may quote as an unusual composition an allegorical statue of "Kairos" (Occasion) charmingly described in the *Anthology:*[265] "Who and whence was thy sculptor? From Sikyon. His name? Lysippos. And who art thou? Occasion, the all-subduer. Why dost thou tread on tiptoe? I am ever running. Why hast thou wings two-natured on thy feet? I fleet on the wings of the wind. Why dost thou bear a razor in thy right hand? To show men that I am keener than the

---

[259] Wolters, *Röm. Mitt.*, IV, 1889, pp. 39 f.; cf. also Johnson, *Lysippos,* p. 230.
[260] *Alex.* 40.   [261] *Anab.* I. 16. 7.
[262] *N.H.* XXXIV. 64.   [263] Mendel, *Catalogue des sculptures,* No. 68.
[264] Cf. Overbeck, *Schriftquellen,* 1451 ff., and Johnson, *Lysippos,* pp. 274 ff.
[264a] Diog. Laert. II. 43. Commonly identified with a head preserved in a number of replicas (cf. Laurenzi, *Ritratti greci,* pl. XV, No. 39).
[265] *Anthol. Palat. Append.* II. 49. 13 (66).

keenest edge. And thy hair, why grows it in front? For him that meets me to seize, by Zeus. And why is the back of thy head bald? Because none may clutch me from behind, howsoe'er he desire it, when once my winged feet have darted past him. Why did the sculptor fashion thee? For thy sake, stranger, and set me up for a warning in the entry." But neither this nor any of the other works has been satisfactorily identified among the store at our disposal.

ATTRIBUTIONS
On the other hand, there have been numerous attributions to Lysippos of extant statues based on our slim knowledge of his style; for instance, the Herculaneum Hermes[266] (fig. 72), the praying boy in Berlin[267] (fig. 54), the Eros with the bow,[268] the Satyr and infant Dionysos,[268a] and the athlete fixing his sandal.[269] They are all possible ascriptions, for the affinities with the Apoxyomenos are undeniable; but they are not material on which we can build with certainty.

Using only the actual evidence before us we obtain a picture of a highly original sculptor who by his new system of proportions, his realism, and the grandiose scale of his compositions initiated a new age. He put the finishing touch to the naturalism of the fourth century. Praxiteles and Skopas besides their qualities of grace and emotion had inherited much of the grandeur of the preceding century. Lysippos consciously went to nature as the prime master and thus began a school with a new outlook, which was carried on and developed during the Hellenistic age and from which much of the later sculpture was derived. During the three succeeding centuries the path was followed which he pointed out—of lifelike realism and of manifold subjects. However, in spite of this larger scope and variety and the perfect correctness in modeling, the effect is much tamer than in the earlier products; showing again that it is not realism, however lifelike and vigorous, but other qualities, of which the most important is a feeling for design, which make for truly great sculpture.

(l) The School of Lysippos

LYSISTRATOS
LYSIPPOS had many relatives and pupils who followed in his footsteps and some of them attained independent fame. Of his brother Lysistratos Pliny[270] tells us that he was "the first artist who took plaster casts of the human face from the original and introduced the

---

266 Comparetti and di Petra, *La Villa ercolanese*, pl. XIII, 2.
267 Berliner Museen, *Beschreib. der ant. Skulpt.*, No. 2.
268 Johnson, *Lysippos*, pp. 104 ff.   268a *Ibid.*, pp. 185 f.
269 Cf. F. Poulsen, *Ny Carlsberg Glyptotek*, no. 273a.   270 *N.H.* XXXV. 153.

practice of working over a wax model taken from the plaster. He also instituted the practice of rendering portraits with lifelike precision, while previous artists had striven to make them as beautiful as possible. He also discovered how to take casts of statues."[271] Naturally such inventions all tended in the direction of realism, which was indeed the taste and requirement of the age.

Pausanias[272] tells us that "Eutychides of Sikyon, a pupil of Lysippos, made a statue of Fortune for the Syrians who live on the Orontes, at whose hands it receives great honor"; and John Malalas[273] gives the additional information that the figure was seated "above the river Orontes." By the help of these descriptions and the figures of the Tyche of Antioch which appear on Syrian coins of Tigranes[274] (fig. 755) it has been possible to recognize copies of the group in the marble statue in the Vatican[275] (fig. 753) and in several bronze and silver statuettes in various museums (fig. 754[276]). A woman is represented seated on a rock, her foot resting on the shoulder of a youth, who is seen emerging from the ground. It is a dignified conception of a city goddess, pictorially treated, in the taste of this late period. Eutychides also made a figure of the river Eurotas "more liquid than water."[277]

Chares achieved fame by his bronze statue at Rhodes, one of the seven wonders of the world. There are many references to it in antiquity,[278] and Pliny[279] gives us a graphic account: "The greatest marvel of all, however, was the colossal figure of the Sun at Rhodes, made by Chares of Lindos, a pupil of Lysippos. This figure was seventy cubits in height and after standing fifty-six years was overthrown by an earthquake; but even as it lies prostrate it is a marvel. Few men can embrace its thumb, its fingers are larger than most statues, there are huge yawning caverns where the limbs have been broken, and within them may be seen great masses of rock, by whose weight the artist gave it a firm footing when he erected it. The story runs that twelve years were occupied in its construction, for which the artist received 1,300 talents." Since the earthquake took place about 224 B.C., the date of the erection of the Colossus is about 280.

EUTYCHIDES

CHARES

271 Cf. p. 140.   272 VI. 2. 6.   273 *Chronogr.* XI. 276.
274 *British Museum Catalogue of Coins,* XIV, pl. XXVII, 6.
275 Helbig, *Führer,*³ I, No. 862.
276 Cf. Metropolitan Museum, *Catalogue of Bronzes,* No. 259, and the references there cited; Brunn-Bruckmann, *Denkmäler,* pl. 610 (in Budapest).
277 Pliny, *N.H.* XXXIV. 78 and *Anth. Pal.* IX. 709.
278 Cf. Overbeck, *Schriftquellen,* 1539–1554.   279 *N.H.* XXXIV. 41.

CHAPTER V

THIRD TO FIRST CENTURY B.C.

ACCORDING to Pliny,[1] there were no outstanding Greek sculptors after the 121st Olympiad, i.e. after 296–293 B.C.: "A period of stagnation followed and again a revival in the 156th Olympiad (156–153 B.C.), the age of Antaios, Kallistratos, Polykles of Athens, Kallixenos, Pythokles, Pythias, and Timokles, artists of merit, but still far below those already mentioned." Of none of these late artists do we know much more than the name. There are, however, a few famous pieces of late Greek sculpture the authors of which we happen to know from inscriptions or the specific descriptions by Roman writers.

Third and Second Centuries B.C.

Polyeuktos of Athens was known for his portrait of Demosthenes, of which the following anecdote is told[2]: "[Demosthenes] asked for a tablet and wrote the elegiac couplet, which the Athenians afterwards inscribed upon his portrait. It runs as follows: 'Hadst thou, Demosthenes, had might as strong as thy resolve, the war-god of Macedon had never ruled the Greeks.' The portrait stands near the enclosure and the altar of the twelve gods, and is the work of Polyeuktos." Plutarch[3] moreover tells us that the statue had "clasped hands." A fine statue preserved in several copies (cf. fig. 757) has now been proved to be a reproduction of Polyeuktos' original. The hands are missing in the Vatican copy;[4] but they are preserved in another (otherwise very fragmentary) replica found in the gardens of the Palazzo Barberini,[5] and are there folded. The hands of a marble replica in the Ny Carlsberg Glyptotek in Copenhagen,[6] represented as holding a roll, formerly thought to be ancient, have

POLYEUKTOS

---

[1] *N.H.* XXXIV. 52: "cessavit deinde ars, ac rursus Olympiade CLVI revixit." Many explanations of this statement have been given, none certain.

[2] Pseudo-Plutarch, *Vit. X Or.* 847A. Against Crome's suggestion that Polyeuktos may be a mistake for Polykles (Arch. Anz. 1942, cols. 47 f.) cf. Dinsmoor, *Archons of Athens*, 1931, pp. 90 ff., 123 ff., and Pritchett and Meritt, *Chronology of Hellenistic Athens*, pp. 27 ff.

[3] *Demosthenes* 31.   [4] Helbig, *Führer*,[3] I, no. 22.

[5] Hartwig, *Jahrbuch*, 1903, pp. 25 f.; Loewy, *Belvedere*, 1928, Heft 64, pp. 79–81.

[6] Formerly in Knole; Michaelis, *Ancient Marbles in Great Britain*, pp. 417 f.

been shown to be modern restorations.[7] Thus the very item in Plutarch's description which formerly stood in the way of the identification has now made it a certain one. It can be dated about 280 B.C., forty years after Demosthenes' death in 322,[8] and shows us a splendid characterization of this great, morose Athenian.

DOIDALSES OF BITHYNIA

A statue of Aphrodite washing herself by Doidalses (formerly read Daedalus) is mentioned by Pliny,[9] and a cult statue of Zeus Stratios in Nikomedeia (founded in 264 B.C.) is assigned to the same sculptor by Arrian.[10] The former has been recognized in a crouching Aphrodite preserved in many copies (cf. figs. 135, 764), the latter in a Zeus that appears on Bithynian coins from Prusias I (238?–183 B.C.) to Nikodemos III. We may therefore date Doidalses in the third century B.C.[11]

SCULPTORS ACTIVE IN PERGAMON

The great activity at Pergamon during the reigns of Attalos I (241–197 B.C.) and Eumenes II (196–159 B.C.) is referred to by Pliny[12] as follows: "The battles of Attalos and Eumenes with the Gauls were represented by a group of artists—Isigonos, Phyromachos, Stratonikos, and Antigonos." On the pedestals of Attalos' monument, found at Pergamon, several names of sculptors are preserved: [Isig or Antig]onos, Xenokrates, Myron, and Praxiteles.[13] Phyromachos, Stratonikos, and Antigonos are known from other sources.[14] The famous Dying Gaul, the Gaul killing himself and his wife (fig. 108), the head of a dying Persian (fig. 178) and other marble sculptures have been recognized as copies of the bronze statues that formed part of Attalos' dedication. We have not enough evidence, however, for assigning any of these sculptures to the specific artists whose names happen to have survived.

Ampelius[15] refers to a great altar of marble at Pergamon, 40 ft. in height, with colossal sculptures representing the battle of the giant; but he does not mention the sculptor's or sculptors' names. Faint traces of some artists' signatures, however, remain alongside

[7] A cast of the folded hands has now been added, cf. F. Poulsen, *Ny Carlsberg Glyptotek, Antike Skulpturer*, No. 436a, and our fig. 757.

[8] In the archonship of Gorgias, cf. Pseudo-Plutarch, *Vit. X Or.* 847D.

[9] XXXV. 35.   [10] In Eustath., *ad Dionys. Perieg.* 793.

[11] On Doidalses cf. Robert in Pauly-Wissowa, *Lexikon*, XII, 1266.

[12] XXXIV. 84. Attalos II (159–138 B.C.) would seem to be too late, for it is not likely that the reliefs from Eumenes' altar (see below) preceded the statues of the Gauls.

[13] Loewy, *Inschriften*, No. 154.

[14] Cf. Overbeck, *Schriftquellen*, Nos. 1998–2005.

[15] *Lib. Mem.* VIII. 14.

some of the figures on this altar, which was discovered during the German excavations of 1878 and subsequent years: e.g. [Pa]lamneus, [Pel]oreus, Molodr . . ., [Men]ekratous. It has been computed that there were about forty signatures, the frieze having evidently been divided up into small portions. Presumably, one leading sculptor made the design; but his name is not known.[16]

According to Pliny,[17] the Athenian Nikeratos made, among other things, a group of Asklepios and Hygeia, and one of Alkibiades with his mother Demarate. Tatian[18] mentions portraits by him of Glaukippe and Telesilla. The inscriptional evidence connects him with Pergamon and Delos.[19] A base inscribed with his signature, found at Delos, was once thought to belong to a statue of a warrior; but the dimensions were found not to fit.[20] Though we have no extant work that can be attributed to Nikeratos, his Pergamene connection makes it likely that he was active around 200 B.C., and that his works were in the style of the Attalid dedications.[21]   NIKERATOS

We have heterogeneous evidence regarding a sculptor or sculptors named Boethos. Pliny[22] tells us that "though Boethos is more famous for his work in silver, he is the artist of the boy strangling a goose with all his might." The group has been recognized in the boy strangling a goose preserved in several copies—in Munich (fig. 762), the Capitoline Museum, the Louvre,[23] and elsewhere. The original has been thought by some[24] to be referred to in Herondas' *Mimes* (IV.31): Πρὸς Μοιρέων, τὴν χηναλώπεκ' ὡς τὸ παιδίον πνίγει, and therefore datable in the early third century B.C.; but the goose in the copies is too large to be a fox goose. Other authorities,[25] therefore, have identi-   BOETHOS

---

16 Cf. Schuchhardt, *Die Meister des grossen Frieses von Pergamon* (1925). Thimme, The Masters of the Pergamon gigantomachy, *A.J.A.*, L, 1946, pp. 345 ff.

17 *N.H.*, XXXIV. 80 and 88.

18 *Contra Graecos*, 53, p. 115, and 52, p. 114 (ed. Worth).

19 Loewy, *Inschriften,* Nos. 118, 147, 496; Fraenkel, *Inschriften von Pergamon*, No. 132.

20 Athens, National Museum, No. 247.

21 Cf. on Nikeratos, Lippold in Pauly-Wissowa, *Lexikon*, XVII, s.v. Nikeratos, and Bieber, in Thieme-Becker, *Künstlerlexikon*, XXV, s.v. Nikeratos.

22 *N.H.*, XXXIV. 84: Boethi quamquam argento melioris infans vi summa anserem strangulat. The reading *vi summa* is uncertain, for the word after infans is mutilated; *amplexando, ex aere, sex annis, sex anno, eximia, eximie* have been suggested as alternative readings.

23 Furtwängler, *Beschreibung der Glyptothek*, No. 268; Helbig, *Führer,*[3] I, No. 867; *Catalogue sommaire des marbres antiques*, No. 40, p. 3.

24 Picard, *Rev. arch.*, 1947, pp. 217 ff.

25 Cf. Herzog, *Oest. Jahrsh.* VI, 1903, pp. 215 ff., and his edition of Herondas' *Mimes*, p. 201 f., pl. IX.

fied Herondas' group with one also preserved in a number of copies, in which the bird is small and is pressed upon by the child with its hand. A bronze *Agon* (fig. 766), leaning perhaps on a herm of Dionysos (fig. 763), which is inscribed Βοηθὸς Καλχηδόνιος ἐποίει, "Boethos of Chalkedon made it," was found in the sea near Mahdia in Tunis.[26] Pausanias[27] states that Boethos made a gilt figure of a nude seated boy and that he came from Karchedon (probably = Chalkedon). A statue of Asklepios as a child is ascribed to Boethos in two epigrams.[28] Moreover, a Boethos was famous for his embossed metalware[29] and we hear of *lecti Boethiaci*.[30] There are two inscribed bases, one from Lindos, bearing the name of Boethos, son of Athanaion of Kalchadon, which can be dated about 155–150 B.C.,[31] and one from Delos of a statue of Antiochos IV (175–164 B.C.), signed by Boethos, son of Athanaion.[32] Lastly Boethos' signature appears on a cameo engraved with the representation of an emaciated Philoktetes in Hellenistic style.[33]

To judge by this evidence, it is quite possible that the same Boethos, active in the first half of the second century B.C., made all these works, for Pliny expressly says that he was a sculptor as well as a metal worker and the mention of him immediately after the Pergamene artists suggests that he belonged to the second century B.C. On the other hand, there is no valid reason why there should not have been two or more artists by that name.[34]

The famous group in the Vatican[35] of Laokoon and his sons attacked by two mighty serpents (fig. 768) is described by Pliny[36] as follows: "The Laokoon which stands in the house of the Emperor Titus, a work to be preferred to all that the arts of painting and sculpture have produced. Out of one block of stone the consummate artists Hagesander, Polydorus, and Athenodorus of Rhodes fashioned Lao-

26 Merlin and Poinssot, *Monuments Piot,* XVII, 1909, pp. 42 ff.
27 V. 17. 4.
28 *Anthol. Palat. Append.* 55, 56; Loewy, *Inschriften,* No. 535.
29 Pliny, *N.H.,* XXX, 155.   30 Porphyry, *ad. Hor. ep.,* I. 5. 1.
31 Kinch, *Bull. de l'Acad. de Copenhague,* 1904, p. 74; Hiller von Gaertringen, *Arch. Anz.,* 1904, pp. 212–213.
32 Loewy, *Inschriften,* No. 210.
33 Furtwängler, *Antike Gemmen,* pl. LVII, 3.
34 On Boethos cf. especially Robert, in Pauly-Wissowa, *Lexikon,* s.v. Boethos; Neugebauer, VI, *Internationales Kongressbericht,* 1939, pp. 421 f.
35 Amelung, *Die Sculpturen des vaticanischen Museums,* p. 181, Cortile del Belvedere, No. 74.
36 *N.H.* XXXVI. 37. The group is really constructed of six blocks, but the joints are so carefully concealed that even Michelangelo detected only three.

koon, his sons, and snakes marvelously entwined about them." The group was discovered in A.D. 1506 and has ever since evoked admiration. Michelangelo considered it the greatest work of sculpture ever produced, and Lessing made it the theme for a treatise on the principles of art. Though we to-day with our enlarged knowledge of Greek sculpture would hardly concur with these opinions, we must admit that it is a magnificent creation, superbly modelled. Those who object to the "insufficient restraint" in the expression of physical suffering should compare the Renaissance copy by Bandinelli. Its exaggeration makes one appreciate the essential reserve of the classical work. For our right appreciation of the original composition we must remember that the right arms of Laokoon and of the smaller son are restored. The original arm of Laokoon has now been identified in a strongly flexed right arm that had been supposed to belong to a smaller replica. It adds greatly to the effectiveness of the composition (cf. fig. 769).[37]

The date currently assigned to the group is 50 or even 25 B.C., on the evidence that the name of a sculptor Athanodoros—son or brother of a Hagesandros—occurs in inscriptions datable in that period.[38] But since both these names are common in Rhodes from the fourth century B.C. on,[39] there is no cogent reason why the group should not be dated in the second century B.C., at the time of or somewhat later than the Pergamene Altar, to which it is stylistically related.[40]

The Farnese Bull in Naples[41] (fig. 767), a group representing the punishment of Dirke by Amphion and Zethos, was found in A.D. 1456 in the Baths of Caracalla. It has been identified with a group mentioned by Pliny:[42] "Asinius Pollio . . . resolved that his gallery should be an object of general interest. In it stand . . . Zethos, Amphion, Dirke, the bull, the rope—all made of one block of marble and

---

[37] Cf. Vergara Caffarelli, Note sul restauro del Laocoonte, in *Archeologia classica* I, 1949, pl. XVII. Cf. also Treu's reconstruction in the Albertinum, Dresden, *Die Antike* IX, 1933, p. 57, fig. 1; Bieber, *Laocoon*, pl. I.

[38] Cf. Loewy, *Inschriften*, Nos. 479, 480, 203, 446, 302, 506; Dittenberg, *Sylloge*³, 1917, no. 765; Blinkenberg, *Röm. Mitt.* XLII, 1927, pp. 177 ff.; Blinkenberg and Kinch, Exploration archéologique de Rhodes, 3° rapport (Fondation Carlsberg), in *Oversigt over det kgl. Danske Videnskabernes Selskabs Forhandlinger*, 1905, no. 2, pp. 55 ff.; Blinkenberg, *Lindos*, II, Inscriptions, 1, 1941, cols. 29–32.

[39] Cf. e.g. Jacopi, *Clara Rhodos*, II, 1932, pp. 176, 178, 181, 205.

[40] I hope to discuss this question at greater length in my forthcoming book *Three Critical Phases in the Development of Greek Sculpture.*

[41] Ruesch, *Guida del Museo Nazionale di Napoli*, No. 260.

[42] *N.H.* XXXVI. 34.

transported from Rhodes, the work of Apollonios and Tauriskos [of Tralles]." To appreciate the appearance of the original bronze work, of which the Naples marble group is a Roman copy, we must deduct in our imagination the figure of Antiope standing at the back and some of the subsidiary figures evidently added by the copyist. The group then becomes a compact, pyramidal composition, a technical *tour de force*, more worthy of our admiration.

On the mainland of Greece and especially in Athens a so-called classicizing style was current during the second century B.C. It is in reality a harking back to former creations, both of the "classical" period of the fifth and fourth centuries B.C. and of the Hellenistic age. The names of several artists, handed down to us by ancient writers and known from inscriptions, can be connected with extant works.

We have the following account by Pausanias[43] of the sculptures of the temple at Lykosoura, fragments of which were found in 1889:[44] "The sanctuary of Despoina is four stades distant from Akakesion. The images of the goddesses themselves, Despoina and Demeter, and the throne whereon they are seated, and the footstool beneath their feet, are all of one block. . . . Each of the images is about equal in size to that of the Great Mother at Athens; they also are the work of Damophon. Demeter bears a torch in her right hand, while she has laid the left on Despoina; Despoina bears a scepter and 'cista,' as it is called, in her lap; with one hand—the right—she holds the 'cista.' On each side of the throne is a figure; beside Demeter stands Artemis, clad in a deer-skin, with a quiver on her shoulder; in one hand she holds a torch, in the other two snakes; beside Artemis lies a bitch, like those used in hunting. Close to the image of Despoina stands Anytos, attired as a warrior in full armor; the attendants of the temple say that Despoina was reared by Anytos, and that he is of the number of the Titans, as they are called. The legends of the Kouretes, who are represented beneath the images, and of the Korybantes, who are wrought in relief on the base, I omit, although I know them." The extant fragments consist of the heads of Demeter (figs. 759, 760), Artemis (fig. 758), and Anytos (fig. 757), and a richly decorated piece of garment.[45] They clearly reflect various styles—the Demeter and Artemis classical ones,

43 VIII. 37. 1.

44 Kavvadias, *Fouilles de Lycosoura;* Dickins, *B.S.A.,* XII, pp. 109 ff.; National Museum, Athens, Nos. 1734–1737.

45 Athens, National Museum, nos. 1734–1737; Papaspiridi, *Guide,* pp. 67 f.

the Anytos Hellenistic. The date of Damophon is now established by inscriptions for the first half of the second century B.C.[46] Damophon is mentioned by Pausanias as the sculptor of other works and called the "only Messenian sculptor of repute"; he also is said to have repaired Pheidias' Zeus at Olympia.[47]

Signatures of the Athenian sculptor Euboulides[48] occur on several bases found in Athens, sometimes as coworker of Eucheir, at other times as the son of Eucheir.[49] These inscriptions can be dated in the third and the second century B.C. respectively. The two names are also mentioned by ancient writers. According to Pliny,[50] Euboulides won fame with the statue of a man digitis computans, "counting on his fingers," and Cicero[51] mentions the statue of a seated Chrysippos in the Kerameikos porrecta manu, "with extended hand." It seems probable that these two descriptions apply to the same statue, especially as Sidonius Apollinaris[52] refers to Chrysippos as digitis propter numerorum indicia constrictis, "with fingers pressed to indicate numbers." It seems also likely that we may have copies of this statue preserved in a headless seated figure in the Louvre and in a number of heads and busts (cf. fig. 232);[53] for a head of this type appears on coins of Soloi,[54] the native city of Chrysippos, and a headless herm in Athens inscribed with the name Chrysippos[55] has drapery similar to that preserved on some of the heads and busts.

Pausanias[56] mentions statues of Athena, Zeus, Memory, the Muses, and Apollo, "the work and offering of Euboulides" as being "in the house of Poulytion." Fragments of statues including a head of Athena (fig. 765)—an adaptation of the Athena Velletri—and a fragmentary female figure, perhaps a Nike,[57] as well as an inscription [Εὐβουλίδης Εὐ]χειρος Κρωπίδης ἐποιησεν, ". . ., the son of Eu-

---

[46] Dickins, B.S.A., XII, pp. 109 ff.; XIII, pl. XII; and XVII, pp. 80 ff. and Hellenistic Sculpture, p. 60.

[47] Pausanias IV. 31. 6, 7, 10; VII. 23. 5–7; VIII. 31. 1–3; IV. 31. 6.

[48] On Euboulides cf. Robert, Pauly-Wissowa, Lexikon, VI, s.v. Eubulides, cols. 871 ff.; Collignon, Histoire de la sculpture grecque, pp. 619 ff.; Laurenzi, Ritratti greci, p. 80.

[49] Loewy, Inschriften, Nos. 223 ff.

[50] XXXIV. 88.   [51] De fin., I. 11. 39.

[52] Epist. IX. 9. 14.

[53] Schefold Bildnisse, p. 125, no. 3; Laurenzi, Ritratti greci, p. 121 f., no. 76, pls. XXX, XLVIII.

[54] Laurenzi, op. cit., pl. XXXII, no. 76.

[55] von Prott, Ath. Mitt., XXVII, 1902, pp. 297 ff.; Richter, A.J.A., XXIX, 1925, pp. 5 f.

[56] I. 215.

[57] Athens, National Museum, Nos. 233, 234.

cheir of Kropia made it," datable around 130 B.C., have been found in
the locality mentioned by Pausanias.[58]

From this evidence it has been computed that there were two sculptors named Euboulides, one who made the statue of Chrysippos
around 200 B.C., and another, perhaps his grandson, who lived after
the middle of the second century and made the group of statues found
in Athens.

POLYKLES AND TIMARCHIDES

Another family of sculptors active in Athens during the second
century B.C., in which the names Polykles and Timarchides recur, is
known from inscriptions and ancient writers.[59] The only definite attribution to a preserved work that can be made is that of the statue of
a Roman magistrate named Gaios Ophellios found at Delos (fig. 767),
the pedestal of which bears the signature "Dionysios, the son of Timarchides, and Timarchides, the son of Polykles, Athenians, made it."[60]
The head, which was evidently a portrait, is lost, but the figure is an
adaptation of the Hermes of Praxiteles.[61] We learn from Pausanias[62]
that Timokles and Timarchides of Athens made a copy of the shield
of Pheidias' Athena Parthenos for a cult statue of Athena at Elateia.

First Century B.C.

Whereas it seems that in the second century B.C. only free copies of
former Greek creations were made,[63] the first century B.C. marks the
introduction of mechanical copies, that is, copies made by the pointing
process (cf. pp. 141, 177). In these the Greek original was reproduced as exactly as possible. Perhaps this invention—to which we owe
much of our knowledge of Greek sculpture—was made by Pasiteles
and carried on by Arkesilaos. At least we have some rather confused
statements by Greek writers that suggest it (cf. p. 141).

PASITELES AND HIS SCHOOL

Pliny mentions Pasiteles a number of times.[64] He says that Pasiteles
was a contemporary of Pompey (106–48 B.C.), that he came from
Magna Graecia to Rome, that he wrote five books on celebrated works
of art, and that "he never executed a work without first making a
model of it." He also mentions several of Pasiteles' statues, including
a chryselephantine Zeus for the temple of Metellus, and a lion mod-

---

58 Loewy, *Inschriften*, No. 228.
59 Overbeck, *Schriftquellen*, Nos. 2208–2213; Loewy, *op. cit.*, No. 242.
60 Homolle, *B.C.H.*, V, 1881, p. 390, pl. XII; Michalowski, *Délos*, XIII, p. 21, fig. 13.
61 Collignon, *Histoire*, II, p. 625.   62 X. 34. 7.
63 Cf., besides those just mentioned, the copies found at Pergamon (Winter, *Altertümer von Pergamon*, VII, Nos. 23, 24, pp. 25 ff.) and Kalydon (Dyggve, F. Poulsen,
and Rhomaios, *Das Heroon von Kalydon*, p. 363, figs. 79, 80, a Herakles of the Farnese
type; and p. 369, figs. 91–93 a Meleager of Skopaic type).
64 *N.H.* XXXIII. 130, 156; XXXV. 156; XXXVI, 35, 39, 40.

elled from life. It would seem, therefore, that Pasiteles was an able sculptor with the antiquarian interests current in his time, that he studied from life, but that he also worked from models (from casts of earlier statues?). None of his works have so far been recognized, but we know products of his school. A statue of a youth in the Villa Albani[65] is signed by Stephanos, pupil of Pasiteles (fig. 773), and a group of a youth and a woman in the National Museum in Rome[66] is signed by Menelaos, pupil of Stephanos (fig. 775). Groups in a similar style are in Naples[67] and the Louvre.[68] Since the same youth recurs in several of these groups and its style is that of about 460 B.C., it is evident that Pasiteles' pupils practised the art of copying that had become current in their time.

Arkesilaos can be dated in the first half and the middle of the first century B.C., for Pliny[69] says that he was a friend of Lucius Lucullus (c. 110–56 B.C.) and that Lucullus ordered from him a statue of Felicitas for a million sesterces, which, however, was never finished since both died before its completion; also that he made an unfinished cult statue for the temple of Venus Genetrix in the Forum of Caesar dedicated in 46 B.C. A figure represented on coins of Sabina, the wife of Hadrian, which is inscribed Venus Genetrix[70] and which is copied from a late fifth-century statue preserved in marble copies, had been thought to reproduce Arkesilaos' statue. But the same inscription appears on Roman coins with different statues; so the identification is uncertain. We also learn from Pliny that Arkesilaos made "a lioness with Erotes playing around her"[71] and "centaurs carrying nymphs";[72] furthermore that he considered modelling the mother of embossed work as well as of sculpture in bronze and marble, and that artists would pay more for Arkesilaos' models (proplasmata) than for the finished products of others; also that he made a plaster model (exemplar e gypso) of a krater for which he was paid as much as one

---

65 Helbig, *Führer*³, No. 1846.   66 Ibid. No. 1314.

67 Ruesch, *Guida*, No. 110.

68 Collignon, *Histoire de la Sculpture Grecque*, II, p. 663, fig. 347.

69 Pliny XXXV. 155 and 156. On the conflict of dates cf. Ferri, *Plinio il Vecchio*, p. 212.

70 Mattingly, *Coins of the Roman Empire in the British Museum*, Nos. 944–949, and passim; Collignon, *Histoire de la sculpture grecque*, II, pp. 287 ff. and the references there cited.

71 XXXVI. 41.

72 XXXVI. 33. The name is here spelled Arkesilas, but presumably the same artist is intended.

talent.[73] We may perhaps surmise from this heterogeneous evidence that Arkesilaos was primarily a copyist and that he made sculptures of various styles from plaster casts by the pointing process.

THE COPYISTS:
A) ANTIOCHOS
DIOGENES,
APOLLONIOS
SON OF
ARCHIAS,
GLYKON,
APOLLONIOS
SON OF
NESTOR,
AGASIAS

The mechanical copying, initiated perhaps by Pasiteles and Arkesilaos, was continued for about three centuries. The Greek artists who made these copies for Roman patrons throughout the Empire occasionally signed their works, so we know some of their names. Antiochos, for instance, signed a copy of Pheidias' Athena Parthenos (fig. 774),[74] Diogenes a copy of the Herakles Epitrapezios by Lysippos,[75] Apollonios, the son of Archias, a bust taken from Polykleitos' Doryphoros (fig. 648), and Glykon the Farnese Herakles (fig. 749), a copy of a Lysippian work. Apollonios, son of Nestor, who signed both the Belvedere Torso in the Vatican (fig. 771)[76] and the bronze Boxer in Rome (fig. 770),[77] and Agasias, son of Dositheos, who signed the Borghese warrior in the Louvre (fig. 107),[78] were presumably also copyists, for these statues are in the exuberant style of the second century B.C., whereas the signatures date from the first century.

Besides straight copies we have many adaptations of former creations, in which elements—generally in relief and in a reduced scale—are taken from different sources and periods and combined to form new ensembles. We know the names of several of these often tasteful adapters, for they too occasionally signed their works—Sosibios, who inscribed his name on a marble altar in the Louvre,[79] Salpion, whose name appears on a marble krater in Naples,[80] and Pontios, who signed a marble rhyton in the Conservatori Museum in Rome.[81] All three call themselves Athenians.

We also know some of the names of the Greek artists who made the Roman portraits, for here again a few signatures have survived. The names of Kleomenes, Philathenaios, Hegesias, Dionysios, Sosikles, Zenon, Zenas, Antonianos are preserved on portraits of Romans ranging from the first century B.C. to the second century A.D.[82] Other Greek

---

73 XXXV. 155 and 156.

74 Loewy, *Inschriften*, No. 342; Helbig, *Führer*³, No. 1304.

75 Loewy, *op. cit.*, No. 361; Smith, *Catalogue of Greek Sculpture in the British Museum*, III, No. 1726.

76 Loewy, *op. cit.*, No. 343; Helbig, *op. cit.*, No. 124. For what seems to be a copy on a Roman coin of Lakedaimon cf. fig. 756 and Rossbach, *Arch. Anz.* 1920, col. 57.

77 Carpenter, *Memoirs of the American Academy in Rome*, VI, 1927, pp. 133 ff.

78 Loewy, *op. cit.*, No. 292.   79 Loewy, *op. cit.*, No. 340.   80 Loewy, op. cit., No. 338.

81 Loewy, op. cit., No. 339; Helbig, Führer³, No. 950; Stuart Jones, Catalogue of Sculptures II, 1926, p. 169, No. 25.

82 Loewy, *op. cit.*, No. 344; Treu, *Olympia*, III, pp. 244, 256, pls. LX, 1, LXIII;

artists signed portraits of Romans on engraved gems—Agathange-
los, for instance, Epitynchanos, Herophilos, Apollonios, Euodos.[83]
These realistic Roman portraits are the direct descendants of the late
Hellenistic products; only the sitters are now no longer Greek philosophers, poets, and intellectuals, but practical men of affairs—offi-
cials, generals, and emperors; so the physiognomies are different.

With these last names of Greeks who worked for Romans throughout the Roman Empire our history of Greek sculpture closes. Whatever we may think of the quality of the copyists' work and their lack
of originality, we owe to them, as we have said, much of our knowledge
of Greek sculpture; for the greater part of it has been preserved only
in their copies and adaptations. Moreover, by their portraits and the
Roman historical reliefs—which were doubtless also primarily made
by them—they initiated Roman art with new subjects and new spatial
concepts. A new era was inaugurated.[84]

Ugolini, *Rendiconti della Pontifica Accademia Romana di Archeologia*, XI, 1935,
p. 92; Loewy, *op. cit.*, Nos. 366, 383a and b; Squarciapino, *La Scuola di Afrodisia*,
pp. 29 ff.

[83] Furtwängler, *Jahrbuch*, III, 1888, pp. 123 ff., 329, 305, 319, and *Antike Gemmen*, Vol. II, pl. XLVII, 40, XLVII, 8, vol. III, p. 319, fig. 162; Richter, *Collection
Latomus* II, 1949, Hommages à J. Bidez et F. Cumont, p. 296, fig. 5.

[84] Some of the new theories set forth in this chapter will be further developed and
documented in my forthcoming book *Three Critical Phases in the Development of Greek
Sculpture* (Dumbarton Oaks Lectures, 1949).

BIBLIOGRAPHY

This bibliography is only a selection of the outstanding books on Greek sculpture. Though emphasis is laid on the newer publications, older works that have not been superseded are included.

Adriani, A. *Sculture monumentali del Museo greco-romano di Alessandria.* 1946.

—— *Testimonianze e Momenti di Scultura alessandrina.* 1948.

Amelung, W. *Führer durch die Antiken in Florenz.* 1897.

—— *Die Sculpturen des vaticanischen Museums.* 1903–1908 (later continued by G. Lippold).

Arndt, P. *La Glyptothèque Ny-Carlsberg.* 1912.

Arndt, P., Amelung, W., and Lippold, G. *Photographische Einzelaufnahmen antiker Sculpturen.* From 1893 (in progress).

Ashmole, B. *A Catalogue of the Ancient Marbles at Ince Blundell Hall.* 1929.

—— *Late Archaic and Early Classical Greek Sculpture in Sicily and South Italy.* 1934.

Aurigemma, S. *Le Terme di Diocleziano e Il Museo Nazionale Romano.* 1946.

Bacon, F. H. and others. *Investigations at Assos.* 1902–1921.

Bakalakis, G. *Ellenika Amphiglypha.* 1946.

Beazley, J. D. *The Lewes House Collection of Ancient Gems.* 1920.

Beazley, J. D., and Ashmole, B. *Greek Sculpture and Painting to the End of the Hellenistic Period.* 1932.

Benndorf, F. A. O. *Die Metopen von Selinunt.* 1873.

—— *Das Heroon von Gjölbaschi-Trysa.* 1891, 1893, 1895.

Bernoulli, J. J. *Aphrodite.* 1873.

—— *Griechische Ikonographie mit Ausschluss Alexanders und der Diadochen.* 1901.

Bieber, M. *Die antiken Skulpturen und Bronzen des kgl. Museum Fridericianum in Cassel.* 1915.

—— *Die Denkmäler zum Theaterwesen im Altertum.* 1920.

—— *Griechische Kleidung.* 1928.

—— *Entwicklungsgeschichte der griechischen Tracht.* 1934.

—— *The History of the Greek and Roman Theatre.* 1939.

—— *The Portraits of Alexander the Great,* 1949. (*Proceedings of the American Philosophical Society,* vol. 93, pp. 373 ff.).

Binnebössel, R. D. *Studien zu den attischen Urkundenreliefs.* 1932.

Blinckenberg, C. S. *Knidia.* 1933.

Bloesch, H. *Antike Kunst in der Schweiz.* 1943.

Blümel, C. *Staatliche Museen zu Berlin, Katalog der Sammlung antiker Skulptur,* vols. II, part 1, II, IV, V. 1928–1940.

—— *Griechische Bildhauerarbeit.* 1927.

—— *Tierplastik.* 1937.

—— *Griechische Bildhauer an der Arbeit.* Third edition, 1943.

—— *Hermes eines Praxiteles.* 1948.

Blümner, H. *Technologie und Terminologie der Gewerbe und Künste bei Griechen und Römern,* vol. III. 1884.

Bocconi, S. *The Capitoline Collections.* 1948.

Boehringer, R. *Platon, Bildnisse und Nachweise.* 1935.

Brunn, H. *Geschichte der griechischen Künstler.* 1853–59.

Brunn, H., and Arndt, P. *Griechische und römische Porträts.* From 1891 (in progress).

Brunn, H., Bruckmann, F., Arndt, P., and Lippold, G. *Denkmäler griechischer und römischer Sculptur.* From 1888 (in progress).

Buffalo, Albright Art Gallery, an exhibition in. *Master Bronzes,* by various authors. 1937.

Bulle, H. *Der schöne Mensch,* I: Im Altertum. Third edition, 1922.

Burlington Fine Arts Club, *Exhibition of Ancient Greek Art.* 1904.

Buschor, E. *Altsamische Standbilder.* 1934.

—— *Die Plastik der Griechen.* 1936.

—— *Bildnisstufen.* 1947.

—— *Pferde des Pheidias.* 1948.

—— *Phidias der Mensch.* 1948.

—— *Das Hellenistische Bildnis.* 1949.

Buschor, E., and Hamann, R. *Die Skulpturen des Zeustempels zu Olympia.* 1924.

Calza, R. *Museo Ostiense.* 1947.

Caputo, G. *Lo scultore del grande bassorilievo con la danza delle Menade in Tolemaide di Cirenaica.* 1948.

Carpenter, R. *The Sculptures of the Nike Temple Parapet.* 1929.

—— "Observations on Familiar Statuary in Rome," in *Memoirs of the American Academy in Rome,* XVIII. 1941.

Caskey, L. D. *Catalogue of Greek and Roman Sculpture in the Museum of Fine Arts (Boston).* 1925.

Casson, S. *Catalogue of the Acropolis Museum,* II. 1921.

—— *The Technique of Early Greek Sculpture.* 1933.

Charbonneaux, J. *La sculpture grecque au Musée du Louvre.* n.d.

—— *La sculpture grecque archaïque.* 1938.

—— *La sculpture grecque classique.* 1944–45.

Chase, G. H. *Greek and Roman Sculpture in American Collections.* 1924.

Collignon, M. *Histoire de la sculpture grecque.* 1892–97.

—— *Les statues funéraires dans l'art grec.* 1911.

Conze, A.C.L. *Die attischen Grabreliefs.* 1893–1922.

Curtius, L. *Die klassische Kunst Griechenlands.* 1938.

Dawkins, R. M., and others. *The Sanctuary of Artemis Orthia at Sparta.* 1929.

Déonna, W. *Les "Apollons Archaïques."* 1909.

—— *Les statues de terre cuite dans l'antiquité.* 1908.

—— *Dédale.* 1930-31.

—— *Du miracle grec au miracle chrétien.* 1945.

Dickins, G. *Catalogue of the Acropolis Museum,* I. 1912.

Diepolder, H. *Die attischen Grabreliefs des fünften und vierten Jahrhunderts v. Chr.* 1931.

Dinsmoor, W. B. *The Architecture of Ancient Greece. An Account of Its Historical Development.* 1950.

Dugas, C., and others. *Le sanctuaire d'Aléa Athéna à Tégée au IVᵉ siècle.* 1924.

Dunbabin, T. J. *The Western Greeks. The History of Sicily and South Italy from the Foundation of the Greek Colonies to 480* B.C. 1948.

Dyggve, E. *Das Laphrion. Der Tempelbezirk von Kalydon.* 1948.

Dyggve, E., Poulsen, F., and Rhomaios, K. *Das Heroon von Kalydon.* 1934.

Edgar, C. C. *Catalogue du Musée de Caire, vol. 13, Greek Sculpture.* 1903.

Encyclopédie photographique de l'art, vols. II and III. 1935–38.

Ferri, S. *Plinio il Vecchio, Storia delle Arti antiche.* 1946.

Filow, B. D. *Die archaische Nekropole von Trebenischte am Ochrida-See.* 1927.

—— *Die Grabhügelnekropole bei Duvanlij in Südbulgarien.* 1934.

Friedländer, P. *Epigrammata. Greek Inscriptions in verse from the beginnings to the Persian Wars.* 1948.

Fröber, J. *Die Komposition der archaischen und frühklassischen Metopenbilder.* 1933.

Frazer, J. G. *Pausanias's Description of Greece.* 1913.

Furtwängler, A. *Olympia,* IV: *Die Bronzen.* 1890.

—— *Masterpieces of Greek Sculpture,* edited by E. Sellers. 1895.

—— *Über Statuenkopieen im Altertum.* 1896.

—— *Die antiken Gemmen.* 1900.

—— *Beschreibung der Glyptothek.* Second edition, 1910.

Furtwängler, A., and others. *Aegina.* 1906.

García y Bellido, A. *Los hallazgos griegos de Espana.* 1936.

Grace, F. R. *Archaic Sculpture in Boeotia.* 1939.

Grinnell, I. H. *Greek Temples.* 1943.

Hampe, R., and Jantzen, U. *I. Bericht über die Ausgrabungen in Olympia.* 1937.

Hauser, F. *Die neuattischen Reliefs.* 1889.

Head, B. V. *Historia numorum.* Ed. 2, 1911.

Heberdey, R. *Altattische Porosskulptur.* 1919.

Hekler, A. *Die Bildniskunst der Griechen und Römer.* 1912.

Helbig, K. F. W. *Führer durch die öffentlichen Sammlungen klassischer Altertümer in Rom,* I–II. Third revised edition by W. Amelung, 1912–13.

Hildebrand, A. *Das Problem der Form.* 1918.

Hill, D. K. *Catalogue of Classical Bronze Sculpture in the Walters Art Gallery.* 1949.

Hill, G. F. *Select Greek Coins.* 1927.

Homolle, T., editor. *Fouilles de Delphes,* IV: *Monuments figurés;* continued by Picard, C., and La Coste-Messelière, P. de. 1909–1931.

Horn, R. *Stehende weibliche Gewandstatuen in der hellenistischen Plastik.* 1931.

Imhoof-Blumer, F., and Gardner, P. *Numismatic Commentary on Pausanias.* 1885–1887.

Jacobsthal, P. *Die melischen Reliefs.* 1931.

Jantzen, U. *Bronzewerkstätten in Grossgriechenland und Sizilien.* 1938.

Jenkins, R. J. H. *Dedalica.* 1936.

Jex-Blake, K., and Sellers, E. *Pliny the Elder. Chapters on the History of Art.* 1896.

Johnson, F. R. *Lysippos.* 1927.

Jones, H. S. *Select Passages from Ancient Writers Illustrative of the History of Greek Sculpture.* 1895.

Jones, H. S., editor. *A Catalogue of the Sculptures of the Museo Capitolino.* 1912.

—— *A Catalogue of the Sculptures of the Palazzo dei Conservatori.* 1926.

Kähler, H. *Das Griechische Metopenbild.* 1949.

—— Der grosse Fries von Pergamon. 1949.

Karo, G. *An Attic Cemetery.* 1943.

—— *Greek Personality in Archaic Sculpture.* 1948.

Karouzos, C. *To Mouseio tes Thebas.* 1936.

Kaschnitz-Weinberg, G. *Sculture del Magazzino del Museo Vaticano.* 1936.

Kastriotes, P. *Glypta tou Ethnikou Mouseiou.* 1908.

Katterfeld, E. *Die Griechischen Metopenbilder, Archäologische Unter-suchungen.* 1911.

Kekule von Stradonitz, R., editor. *Die Antiken Terra-kotten.* 1880–1903.

Kenner, H. *Der Fries des Tempels von Bassae-Phigalia,* 1946.

Kjellberg, E. *Studien zu den attischen Reliefs des V. Jahrhunderts v. Chr.* 1926.

Kleiner, G. *Tanagrafiguren.* 1942.

Kluge, K., and Lehmann-Hartleben, K. *Die antiken Grossbronzen.* 1927.

Klumbach, H. *Tarentiner Grabkunst.* 1937.

Kunze, E. *Kretische Bronzereliefs.* 1931.

—— *Neue Meisterwerke griechischer Kunst aus Olympia.* 1948.

Kunze, E., and Schleif, H. *II. and III. Bericht über die Ausgrabungen in Olympia.* 1938, 1939.

La Coste-Messelière, P. de. *Au Musée de Delphes.* 1936.

—— *Delphes.* 1943.

Lamb, W. *Greek and Roman Bronzes.* 1929.

Langlotz, E. *Zur Zeitbestimmung der strengrotfigurigen Vasenmalerei und der gleichzeitigen Plastik.* 1920.

—— *Frühgriechische Bildhauerschulen.* 1927.

—— *Phidiasprobleme.* 1947.

Langlotz, E., and Schuchhardt, W. H. *Archaische Plastik auf der Ak-ropolis.* 1941.

Lapalus, E. *Le fronton sculpté en Grèce des origines à la fin du IVe siècle.* 1947.

Laurenzi, L. *Ritratti greci.* 1941.

Lawrence, A. W. *Later Greek Sculpture.* 1927.

—— *Classical Sculpture.* 1929.

Lippold, G. *Kopien und Umbildungen griechischer Statuen.* 1923.

Loewy, E. *Inschriften griechischer Bildhauer.* 1885.

—— *La Scultura greca.* 1911.

Markman, S. D. *The Horse in Greek Art.* 1943.

Michaelis, A. *Ancient Marbles in Great Britain.* 1882.

Mendel, G. *Catalogue des sculptures aux Musées impériaux ottomans.* 1912–14.

Michalowski, C. "Les Portraits hellénistiques et romains," *Exploration archéologique de Délos,* fasc. XIII, 1932.

Müller, V. *Frühe Plastik in Griechenland und Vorderasien.* 1929.

Neugebauer, K. A. *Antike Bronzestatuetten.* 1921.

Overbeck, J. A. *Die antiken Schriftquellen zur Geschichte der bildenden Künste bei den Griechen.* 1868.

Papaspiridi, S. *Guide du Musée National* (Athens). 1927.

Paton, J. M., editor. *The Erechtheum.* 1927.

Payne, H. G. *Necrocorinthia.* 1931.

Payne, H., and Young, G. M. *Archaic Sculpture from the Acropolis.* 1936.

Payne, H., and others. *Perachora.* From 1940 (in progress).

Pfuhl, E. *Die Anfänge der griechischen Bildniskunst.* 1927.

Picard, C. *Manuel d'archéologie grecque. La sculpture.* From 1935 (in progress).

Poulsen, F. *Delphi.* 1920.

—— *Greek and Roman Portraits in English Country Houses.* Translated by G. C. Richards. 1923.

—— *Den tidlig graeske Kunst.* 1940.

—— *Katalog over antike Skulpturer, Ny Carlsberg Glyptotek.* 1940 (with *Billedtavler*).

Poulsen, V., Nygard-Nilssen, A., and Gauffin, A. *Skulpturboken, Europeisk Skulptur.* 1947.

Pryce, F. N. *Catalogue of Sculpture in the British Museum,* I, part i: Prehellenic and Early Greek. 1928.

Raubitschek, A. *Dedications from the Athenian Akropolis. A Catalogue of the Inscriptions of the sixth and fifth centuries* B.C. Edited with the collaboration of L. H. Jeffery. 1949.

Reinach, S. *Receuil de têtes antiques.* 1903.

—— *Répertoire de reliefs grecs et romains.* 1909–12.

—— *Répertoire de la statuaire grecque et romaine.* 1897–1931.

Regling, K. L. *Die antike Münze als Kunstwerk.* 1924.

Richer, P. *Le Nu dans l'art,* II: *L'Art grec.* 1926.

Richter, G. M. A. *Animals in Greek Sculpture.* 1930.

—— *Archaic Attic Gravestones.* 1944.

—— *Archaic Greek Art Against its Historical Background.* 1949.

Richter, G. M. A., with the co-operation of Irma A. Richter. *Kouroi, a Study of the development of the Greek kouros.* Two hundred and eight photographs by Gerard M. Young. 1942.

Ridder, A. de, and Déonna, W. *L'Art en Grèce.* 1924.

Rizzo, G. E. *Prassitele.* 1932.

—— *Thiasos.* 1934.

—— *Monete greche della Sicilia.* 1945–1946.

Robertson, D. S. *Greek and Roman Architecture.* Second edition, 1946.

Robinson, D. M., editor. *Excavations at Olynthus.* From 1929 (in progress).

Rodenwaldt, G. *Das Relief bei den Griechen.* 1923.

—— *Die Kunst der Antike.* 1938.

—— *Altdorische Bildwerke in Korfu.* 1938.

—— *Korkyra*, II. 1939–40.

Rodenwaldt, G., and Hege, W. *Olympia*. 1936.

Rostovtzeff, M. I. *The Social and Economic History of the Hellenistic World*. 1941.

Ruesch, A., and others. *Guida illustrata del Museo Nazionale di Napoli.* n.d.

Salis, A. von. *Die Kunst der Griechen*. 1919.

Schede, M. *Meisterwerke der türkischen Museen zu Konstantinopel.* 1928.

Schefold, K. *Die Bildnisse der antiken Dichter, Redner, und Denker.* 1943.

Shoe, L. T. *Profiles of Greek mouldings*. 1936.

Schmidt, E. *Archaistische Kunst in Griechenland und Rom*. 1922.

Schuchhardt, W.-H. *Archaische Giebelkompositionen*. 1940.

Schrader, H., with Langlotz, E., and Schuchhardt, W.-H. *Die archaischen Marmorbildwerke der Akropolis*. 1939.

Seltman, C. T. *Athens, its History and Coinage before the Persian Invasion*. 1924.

—— *Approach to Greek Art*. 1948.

Sieveking, J. *Die Bronzen der Sammlung Loeb*. 1913.

Sieveking, J., and Weickert, C. *Fünfzig Meisterwerke der Glyptothek.* 1928.

Smith, A. H. *Catalogue of Greek Sculpture in the British Museum.* 1892–1904.

—— *Sculptures of the Parthenon*. 1910.

Springer, A. H. *Handbuch der Kunstgeschichte, I: Die Kunst des Altertums*. Twelfth edition revised by P. Wolters, 1923.

Süsserott, H. K. *Griechische Plastik des vierten Jahrhunderts vor Christus*. 1938.

Svoronos, J. N. *Das athener Nationalmuseum*. 1908–13.

Tod, M. N., and Wace, A. J. B. *Catalogue of the Sparta Museum*. 1906.

Treu, G. *Olympia, III: Die Bildwerke*. 1897.

Van Buren, E. D. *Archaic Fictile Revetments in Sicily and Magna Graecia*. 1923.

Wace, A. J. B. *An Approach to Greek Sculpture*. 1935.

Waldhauer, O. *Die antiken Skulpturen der Ermitage*. 1928–1936.

Walters, H. B. *Select Bronzes*. 1915.

Webster, T. B. L. *Greek Art and Literature 530–400* B.C. 1939.

Weickert, C. *Griechische Plastik*. 1946.

Wiegand, T., and others. *Die archaische Poros-Architektur der Akropolis*. 1904.

Wuilleumier, P. *Tarente*. 1939.

Zancani Montuoro, P. *Tabelle fittile locresi* (*in preparation*).
Zancani Montuoro, P., and Zanotti-Bianco, U. *Lo Santuario di Hera Argeia a Silaris* (*in press*).
Zschietzschmann, W. *Die hellenistische und römische Kunst.* 1939.
Zürchner, W. *Griechische Klappspiegel.* 1942.

Periodicals and Series

Acta archaeologica. Copenhagen, from 1930.
American Journal of Archaeology. Concord (New Hampshire) and elsewhere, from 1885.
Annali dell' Instituto di corrispondenza archeologica. Rome, 1829–85.
Annual of the British School at Athens. London, from 1894.
Annuario della Regia Scuola archeologica di Atene e delle missioni italiane in Oriente. Bergamo, from 1914.
Antike, Die. Berlin, from 1925.
Antike Denkmäler. Berlin, 1886–1931.
Archaeologisch-epigraphische Mittheilungen aus Oesterreich-Ungarn. Vienna, 1877–97.
Archäologischer Anzeiger, see *Jahrbuch.*
Archäologische Zeitung. Berlin, 1843–85.
Archeologia classica. Rome, from 1949.
Arkhaiologikon Deltion. Athens, from 1915.
Le arti. Florence, from 1938.
Athenische Mitteilungen des Deutschen Archäologischen Instituts. Athens, from 1876.
Ausonia. Rome, 1906–21.
Berliner Museen; Bericht aus den preussischen Kunstsammlungen: Beiblatt zum Jahrbuch der preussischen Kunstsammlungen. Berlin, from 1880.
Bollettino d'arte. Milan and Rome, 1907–38; 1948–
British Museum Quarterly. London, from 1926.
Bulletin de correspondance hellénique. Paris, from 1877.
Bulletin des Musées de France. Paris, from 1929. (Superseded by Musées de France).
Bulletin of the Metropolitan Museum of Art. New York, from 1905.
Bulletin of the Museum of Fine Arts, Boston. Boston, from 1903.
Bullettino della Commissione archeologica comunale di Roma. Rome, from 1872.
Bullettino dell' Instituto di corrispondenza archeologica. Rome, 1829–85.
Clara Rhodos. Rhodes, from 1928.

Compte-rendu de la Commission impériale archéologique. St. Petersburg, 1860–83.

La Critica d'arte. Florence, 1935–38.

Dedalo. Milan, 1920–33.

Emporium, Rivista mensile d'arte . . . Bergamo, from 1895.

Ephemeris arkhaiologike. Athens, from 1883.

Fondation Eugène Piot. Monuments et mémoires. Paris, from 1894.

Gnomon. Berlin, from 1925.

Hesperia. Cambridge (Mass.), from 1932.

Imperial Archaeological Commission, Report (in Russian). St. Petersburg, 1889–1906. (Superseded by the *State Academy for the History of Material Culture*).

Jahrbuch des Deutschen Archäologischen Instituts. Berlin, from 1886; with the *Beiblatt, Archäologischer Anzeiger.* Berlin, from 1889.

Jahreshefte des Oesterreichischen Archäologischen Instituts. Vienna, 1898–1940 (renamed *Wiener Jahreshefte* in 1940).

Journal of Hellenic Studies. London, from 1881.

Journal of Roman Studies. London, from 1911.

Journal of the Walters Art Gallery. Baltimore, from 1938.

Le Musée, Revue d'art antique. Paris, 1904–09.

Liverpool Annals of Archaeology and Anthropology. Liverpool, from 1908.

Mélanges d'archéologie et d'histoire publiés par l'École française de Rome. Rome, from 1881.

Memoirs of the American Academy in Rome. Rome, from 1917.

Memorie della Pontificia Accademia romana di archeologia. Rome, from 1923.

Metropolitan Museum Studies. New York, 1928–36.

Monumenti antichi pubblicati per cura della reale Accademia dei Lincei. Milan, from 1889.

Monumenti inediti pubblicati dall' Instituto di corrispondenza archeologica. Rome and elsewhere, 1829–91.

Monuments et mémoires, see *Fondation Eugène Piot.*

Monuments grecs publiés par l'Association pour l'encouragement des études grecques en France. Paris, 1872–1897.

Musées de France, from 1948 (Supersedes *Bulletin des Musées de France*).

Münchener Jahrbuch der bildenden Kunst. Munich, from 1906.

The Museum Journal. Philadelphia, 1910–33.

Notizie degli scavi di antichità. Rome, from 1876.

Oxford Monographs on Classical Archaeology, edited by J. D. Beazley and P. Jacobsthal. Oxford, from 1947.

Papers of the British School at Rome. London, from 1902.

Philologische Wochenschrift. Berlin and Leipzig, from 1881.

Praktika tes Athenais archailogikes hetaireias. Athens, 1837–50, 1857–1922, 1826–39 (in Greek).

Programm zum Winckelmannsfeste der archaeologischen Gesellschaft zu Berlin. Berlin, from 1840.

Programm zum Winckelmannsfeste der archaeologischen Gesellschaft zu Halle. Halle, 1876–1931.

Rendiconti della Pontificia Accademia romana d'archeologia. Rome, from 1923.

Revue archéologique. Paris, from 1844.

Revue des études anciennes. Bordeaux, from 1898.

Revue des études grecques. Paris, from 1888.

Römische Mitteilungen des Deutschen Archäologischen Instituts. Rome, from 1886.

State Academy for the History of Material Culture, Bulletin (in Russian). Moscow and Leningrad, from 1921. (Supersedes the *Imperial Archaeological Commission*).

State Museum of Fine Arts, Monuments (in Russian). Moscow, 1912–26.

Studi e materiali. Florence, 1899–1905.

Symbolae osloenses. Oslo, from 1922.

University of California Publications in Classical Archaeology. Berkeley and Los Angeles, from 1929.

Wiener Jahreshefte. Vienna, from 1940. (Supersedes *Jahreshefte des Oesterreichischen archäologischen Instituts*).

Wiener Vorlegeblätter. Vienna, 1869–91.

Lexicons, Encyclopedias, Etc.

Cary, M. and others, editors, *The Oxford Classical Dictionary.* Oxford, 1949.

Daremberg, C., Saglio, E. and others, editors. *Dictionnaire des antiquités grecques et romaines.* Paris, 1877–1919.

Enciclopedia italiana, 1929–1937. Appendix, 1938–1948.

Lübke, F. *Reallexikon des klassischen Altertums,* Eighth edition by J. Geffcken and E. Ziebarth, Leipzig, 1914.

Miller, W. *Daedalus and Thespis,* I–III. New York, 1929–32.

Roscher, W. H. *Ausführliches Lexikon der griechischen und römischen Mythologie.* Leipzig, 1884–1937.

Thieme, U. and Becker, F. *Allgemeines Lexikon der bildenden Künstler von der Antike bis zur Gegenwart.* Leipzig, from 1907.

Wissowa, G., Kroll, W., and Witte, K. *Paulys Real-Encyclopädie der classischen Altertumswissenschaft.* Stuttgart, 1894–

INDEX TO THE TEXT

Italic numbers indicate the most important references; n. stands for footnote.
For museums see names of cities.

ILLUSTRATIONS

Fig. 1. Bronze head of Beethoven, by Bourdelle
Metropolitan Museum of Art
(Cf. p. 21)

Fig. 2. Head of Kladeos, from the temple
of Zeus at Olympia
Olympia Museum
(Cf. p. 21)

Fig. 3. Birth of Athena, from a hydria
Bibliothèque Nationale, Paris
(Cf. p. 31)

Fig. 4. Niobid
Museo Nazionale delle Terme, Rome
(Cf. p. 27)

Fig. 5. Calf-bearer (cf. p. 27)
Akropolis Museum, Athens

Fig. 6. Back of Fig. 5 (from a cast)

Fig. 7. Falling Gladiator, by William Rimmer
Metropolitan Museum of Art
(Cf. p. 27)

Fig. 8. Head of Acheloos
on a coin of Gela
E. T. Newell Collection, New York
(Cf. p. 32)

Fig. 9. Horse in a meadow
on a coin of Larisa
E. T. Newell Collection, New York
(Cf. p. 32)

Fig. 10. Zeus of Aetna
on a coin of Katane
Bibliothèque Royale, Brussels
(Cf. pp. 32, 40)

Fig. 11. Theseus and the Minotaur
from a red-figured plate
The Louvre, Paris
(Cf. p. 32)

Fig. 12. Odysseus and Nausikaa, from a red-figured pyxis
Museum of Fine Arts, Boston
(Cf. p. 32)

Fig. 13. Bronze group of man and centaur
Metropolitan Museum of Art
(Cf. p. 51)

Fig. 14. Bronze statuette
from Dreros
Candia Museum, Crete
(Cf. p. 52)

Fig. 15. "Apollo," from Greece
probably from Boeotia
British Museum, London
(Cf. p. 53)

346

Fig. 21. Kouros, from Anavysos
National Museum, Athens
(Cf. p. 54)

Fig. 20. Kouros, from Attica
National Museum, Athens
(Cf. p. 53)

Fig. 19. Kouros, from Melos
(Cf. pp. 23, 53)

Fig. 22. Kouros, from Tenea
The Glyptothek, Munich
(Cf. p. 53)

Fig. 23. Kouros, from Attica
The Glyptothek, Munich
(Cf. p. 54)

Fig. 24. Bronze statuette of
"Apollo"
Metropolitan Museum of Art
(Cf. p. 54)

Fig. 25. Back view of Fig. 24

Fig. 26. Side view of Fig. 24

Fig. 27. Bronze statuette of
a dancing girl
Metropolitan Museum of Art
(Cf. p. 54)

Fig. 29. Back view of the Strangford kouros
(from a cast)
British Museum, London
(Cf. p. 54)

Fig. 28. Kouros, from Boeotia
National Museum, Athens
(Cf. p. 54)

Fig. 35. Back view of Fig. 33

Fig. 34. Side view of Fig. 33

Fig. 33. Bronze statuette of a youth
Metropolitan Museum of Art
(Cf. p. 55)

354

Fig. 36. "Omphalos Apollo"

Fig. 37. Back view of Fig. 36

Fig. 38. "Apollo," from the Tiber

355

Fig. 41. Bronze statuette of a girl
Museum für antike Kleinkunst, Munich
(Cf. p. 57)

Fig. 40. Bronze statuette of a youth
Metropolitan Museum of Art
(Cf. p. 57)

Fig. 39. Statuette of Herakles
Museum of Fine Arts, Boston
(Cf. pp. 55, 213)

Fig. 42. Bronze statuette of a youth
The Louvre, Paris
(Cf. p. 57)

Fig. 43. Bronze statue, the Idolino
Museo Archeologico, Florence
(Cf. pp. 57, 253)

Fig. 44. Back view of Fig. 43

Fig. 46. Bronze statue of a youth found in the Bay of Marathon
National Museum, Athens
(Cf. p. 58)

Fig. 48. Back view of Fig. 46

Fig. 47. Side view of Fig. 46

Fig. 50. Aphrodite, from Kyrene

Fig. 49. Bronze statuette of Aphrodite

Fig. 51. Satyr

Capitoline Museum, Rome

(Cf. pp. 58, 266)

Fig. 52. Bronze statuette of Alexander

The Louvre, Paris

(Cf. p. 59)

Fig. 53. Hermaphrodite

Museum of Istanbul (Constantinople)

(Cf. p. 59)

Fig. 54. Bronze statue of a praying boy

Staatliche Museen, Berlin

(Cf. pp. 59, 292)

Fig. 56. Bronze statuette of a Satyr

Fig. 55. Poseidon
National Museum, Athens

Fig. 57. Bronze statue of a "Hellenistic Prince"
Museo Nazionale delle Terme, Rome
(Cf. p. 60)

Fig. 60. Side view of Fig. 58

Fig. 59. Back view of Fig. 58

Fig. 58. Bronze statuette of a negro musician

Fig. 61. Seated figure, from the western pediment
of the Corfu temple
Corfu Museum
(Cf. pp. 60, 119)

Photograph by W. F. Mansell
Fig. 62. Figure from Branchidai
British Museum, London
(Cf. p. 60)

Fig. 63. Terracotta statuette
Metropolitan Museum of Art
(Cf. p. 60)

Fig. 64. Athena, perhaps by Endoios
Akropolis Museum, Athens
(Cf. pp. 60, 197)

Fig. 65. Seated goddess
Staatliche Museen, Berlin
(Cf. pp. 61, 96)

Fig. 66. Athena, from a
metope of the temple
of Zeus at Olympia

The Louvre, Paris

(Cf. p. 61)

Fig. 67. Bronze statuette of
a lyre-player

The Hermitage, Leningrad

(Cf. pp. 61, 203)

Fig. 68. "Penelope" (cf. pp. 61, 80, 206)

The Vatican, Rome

Fig. 69. "Demeter and Persephone," from the eastern pediment of the Parthenon
British Museum, London
(Cf. pp. 61, 98, 232)

Fig. 70. Back view of Fig. 69
(Cf. pp. 61, 145)

Fig. 71. One of the "Fates"
from the eastern pediment of the Parthenon
British Museum, London
(Cf. pp. 61, 232)

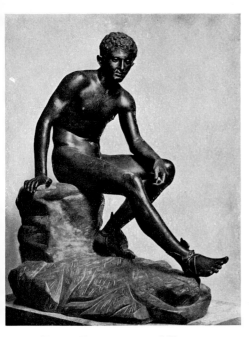

Fig. 72. Bronze statue of Hermes
Museo Nazionale, Naples
(Cf. pp. 61, 294)

Fig. 73. Terracotta statuette
Metropolitan Museum of Art
(Cf. p. 61)

Fig. 74. Drunken woman
The Glyptothek, Munich
(Cf. pp. 62, 82)

Fig. 75. Boy extracting a thorn
British Museum, London
(Cf. pp. 62, 82)

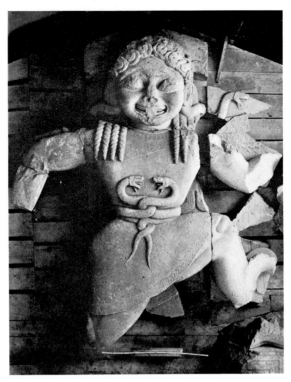

Fig. 76. Gorgon, from the western pediment at Corfu
Corfu Museum
(Cf. p. 62)

Fig. 77. Nike, from Delos
National Museum, Athens
(Cf. p. 62)

Fig. 78. Fig. 77 reconstructed (from a cast)
(Cf. p. 62)

Fig. 79. Gorgon, terracotta relief
Syracuse Museum
(Cf. p. 62)

Fig. 80. Bronze statuette of Nike
National Museum, Athens
(Cf. p. 62)

Fig. 81. Bronze statuette of a runner
Metropolitan Museum of Art
(Cf. p. 62)

Fig. 82. Back view of Fig. 81

Fig. 83. Bronze statuette of Nike
British Museum, London
(Cf. pp. 62, 95)

Fig. 84. Relief of a warrior
National Museum, Athens
(Cf. pp. 62, 168)

Fig. 85. Bronze statuette of a youth running
National Museum, Athens
(Cf. p. 63)

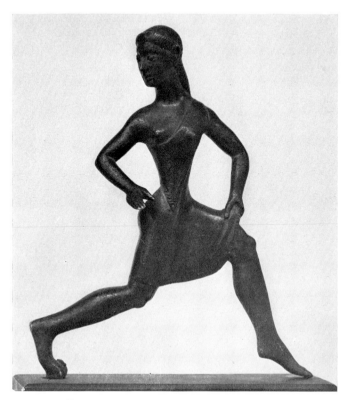

Fig. 86. Bronze statuette of a girl running
British Museum, London
(Cf. p. 63)

Fig. 87. Statuette of a running maiden

Eleusis Museum

(Cf. p. 63)

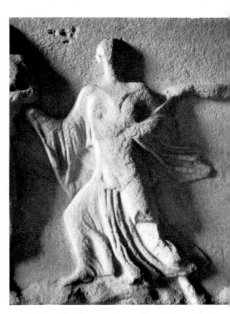

Fig. 88. Figure from the frieze of the Ilissos temple

Staatliche Museen, Berlin

(Cf. p. 63)

Fig. 89. Figure from Marmaria

Delphi Museum

(Cf. p. 63)

Fig. 90. Leto

Palazzo dei Conservatori, Rome

(Cf. p. 63)

Fig. 91. "Iris," from the eastern pediment of the Parthenon
British Museum, London
(Cf. pp. 63, 99)

Fig. 92. Niobid

Glyptotek Ny Carlsberg, Copenhagen

(Cf. p. 63)

Fig. 93. Running figure

Museum der Bildenden Künste, Budapest

(Cf. p. 64)

Fig. 94. Bronze statuette of an Eros

J. Pierpont Morgan Collection

(Cf. p. 64)

Fig. 95. Nike of Samothrake
The Louvre, Paris
(Cf. pp. 64, 106)

Fig. 96. Zeus and a giant, from the western
pediment at Corfu (cf. pp. 64, 68, 119)

Corfu Museum

Fig. 97. Warriors, from the frieze of the Siphnian Treasury (cf. p. 65)

Delphi Museum

Fig. 99. Bronze statuette of Herakles
Metropolitan Museum of Art
(Cf. p. 65)

Fig. 100. Bronze statuette of a warrior
Staatliche Museen, Berlin
(Cf. p. 65)

Fig. 101. Bronze statuette of Zeus
Staatliche Museen, Berlin
(Cf. p. 65)

Fig. 102. Bronze statue of Zeus or Poseidon
National Museum, Athens
(Cf. p. 65)

Fig. 103. Striding warrior, from the eastern pediment at Aigina
The Glyptothek, Munich
(Cf. p. 65)

Fig. 104. Warrior, from Sparta
National Museum, Athens
(Cf. p. 65)

Fig. 105. Centaur and Lapith. Metope of the Parthenon
British Museum, London
(Cf. pp. 66, 129)

Fig. 106. Herakles, from the Phigaleia frieze
British Museum, London
(Cf. p. 66)

384

Fig. 108. Gaul and his wife

Fig. 107. The Borghese Warrior

Fig. 109. Reclining figure, from the western pediment at Corfu
Corfu Museum
(Cf. pp. 66, 119)

Fig. 110. Reclining figure
Samos Museum
(Cf. p. 67)

Fig. 111. Sarcophagus, said to be from Golgoi, Cyprus
Metropolitan Museum of Art
(Cf. p. 67)

Fig. 112. Giant, from a pediment of the "Hekatompedon"
Akropolis Museum, Athens
(Cf. pp. 67, 121)

Fig. 113. Warrior, from the western pediment at Aigina (from a cast)
The Glyptothek, Munich
(Cf. p. 67)

Fig. 114. Warrior, from the eastern pediment at Aigina (from a cast)
The Glyptothek, Munich
(Cf. p. 67)

Fig. 115. "Kladeos," from the eastern pediment at Olympia
Olympia Museum
(Cf. p. 67)

Fig. 116. "Alpheios," from the eastern pediment at Olympia
Olympia Museum
(Cf. p. 67)

Fig. 117. Satyr, by the Brygos Painter, on a kantharos
Metropolitan Museum of Art
(Cf. p. 67)

Fig. 118. Niobid
Glyptotek Ny Carlsberg, Copenhagen
(Cf. p. 68)

Fig. 119. "Ilissos," from the western pediment of the Parthenon

British Museum, London

(Cf. p. 68)

Photograph by W. F. Mansell

Fig. 120. Dead Gaul
Museo Archeologico, Venice
(Cf. p. 68)

Fig. 121. Bronze statue of a sleeping Eros
Metropolitan Museum of Art
(Cf. p. 68)

Photograph by D. Anderson, Rome

Fig. 122. Sleeping Satyr
The Lateran, Rome
(Cf. p. 68)

Fig. 124. Herakles and Kyknos, metope of the Athenian Treasury

Delphi Museum

(Cf. p. 68)

Fig. 123. Falling warrior, from the frieze of the Siphnian Treasury (from a cast)

Delphi Museum

(Cf. p. 68)

Fig. 125. Bronze statuette of Ajax
Museo Archeologico, Florence
(Cf. p. 69)

Fig. 126. Back view of Fig. 125

Fig. 127. Bronze statuette of a warrior
Musée Saint Germain-en-Laye
(Cf. pp. 69, 236)

Fig. 128. Bronze statuette of a falling warrior
Museo Civico, Modena
(Cf. p. 69)

393

Fig. 130. Tityos, from a red-figured krater
Metropolitan Museum of Art
(Cf. p. 69)

Fig. 131. Centaur and Lapith. Metope
of the Parthenon
British Museum, London
(Cf. p. 69)

Fig. 132. Bronze statuette of drunken Herakles
Metropolitan Museum of Art
(Cf. p. 69)

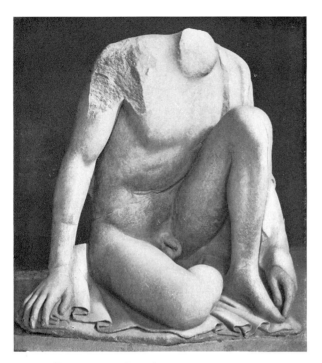

Fig. 133. Crouching figure, from the eastern
pediment at Olympia
Olympia Museum
(Cf. pp. 70, 123–124)

Fig. 134. Crouching figure, from the easter
pediment at Olympia
Olympia Museum
(Cf. pp. 70, 123–124)

Fig. 135. Crouching Aphrodite
Ostia Museum
(Cf. pp. 69, 298)

Fig. 136. Bronze statuette of a youth
finishing a jump (?)
Metropolitan Museum of Art
(Cf. p. 70)

Fig. 137. Head, from the Dipylon (cf. p. 71)

National Museum, Athens

Fig. 138. Head of Hera, probably from the
Heraion at Olympia (cf. p. 71)

Olympia Museum

139. Head of a Maiden, from Attica (cf. p. 71)

Staatliche Museen, Berlin

Fig. 140. Profile view of Fig. 139

Fig. 141. Head of Chrysaor, from the western
pediment at Corfu
Corfu Museum
(Cf. p. 71)

Fig. 142. Head of the Delphi Youth (from a c
Delphi Museum
(Cf. p. 71)

Fig. 143. Head of a Maiden
No. 679, Akropolis Museum, Athens
(Cf. p. 72)

Fig. 144. Head of a Maiden (from a cast)
No. 680, Akropolis Museum, Athens
(Cf. p. 73)

Fig. 145. Back of the head of the
Delphi Youth (from a cast)
Delphi Museum
(Cf. p. 73)

Fig. 146. Detail of the Sounion
kouros (from a cast)
National Museum, Athens
(Cf. p. 73)

Fig. 147. Head of the kouros
from Tenea (from a cast)
The Glyptothek, Munich
(Cf. p. 73)

Fig. 148. Head of a kouros
from near Sounion
Metropolitan Museum of Art
(Cf. p. 73)

Fig. 149. Head of a kouros
*William Rockhill Nelson Collection,
Kansas City*
(Cf. p. 73)

Fig. 150. Head of a Maiden
(from a cast)
No. 680, Akropolis Museum, Athens
(Cf. p. 73)

Fig. 151. Head of the kouros from Attica
The Glyptothek, Munich
(Cf. p. 73)

Fig. 152. Head of the "Apollo"
from Sounion (from a cast)
National Museum, Athens
(Cf. p. 73)

Fig. 153. Head of Chrysaor, from the
western pediment at Corfu
Corfu Museum
(Cf. p. 73)

Fig. 154. "Rampin head"
The Louvre, Paris
(Cf. p. 73)

Fig. 155. Head of a kouros from Thera
National Museum, Athens
(Cf. p. 73)

Fig. 156. Head of a man
Staatliche Museen, Berlin
(Cf. p. 74)

Fig. 157. Terracotta head of a woman
antefix from a temple at Metaurum
Metropolitan Museum of Art
(Cf. p. 73)

Fig. 158. Head of a youth
Metropolitan Museum of Art
(Cf. p. 74)

Fig. 159. Head of "La Boudeuse" (from a
No. 686, Akropolis Museum, Athens
(Cf. p. 74)

Fig. 160. Demareteion. From an electrotype of
a coin of Syracuse
British Museum, London
(Cf. p. 74)

Fig. 161. Head of a seated goddess
Staatliche Museen, Berlin
(Cf. p. 74)

Fig. 163. Head of Apollo, from the western pediment at Olympia
Olympia Museum
(Cf. p. 74)

Fig. 162. Head of the bronze statue of a charioteer
Delphi Museum
(Cf. p. 74)

Photograph by Cappellari

Fig. 166. Head of a youth (cf. p. 74)

Museo Bresciano, Brescia

Fig. 165. Head from the Argive
Heraion (cf. p. 75)

National Museum, Athens

Fig. 164. Head of a youth
(from a cast) (cf. p. 74)

Barracco Museum, Rome

Photograph by Cappellari

Fig. 171. Head from a relief
Metropolitan Museum of Art
(Cf. p. 75)

Fig. 170. Head of the Hermes by Praxiteles
Olympia Museum
(Cf. p. 75)

Fig. 173. Three-quarters view of Fig. 172

Fig. 172. Head of the bronze statue of a youth, found in the Bay of Marathon
National Museum   Athens

Fig. 175. The "Bartlett head"
Museum of Fine Arts, Boston
(Cf. p. 76)

Fig. 174. Head, from Chios
Museum of Fine Arts, Boston
(Cf. pp. 76, 267)

Fig. 176. Head of Alexander, from the
"Alexander sarcophagus"

Musées d'Antiquités de Stamboul (Constantinople)
(Cf. p. 76)

Fig. 177. Head of a giant, from the frieze
great altar at Pergamon

Pergamon Museum, Berlin
(Cf. p. 76)

Photograph by D. Anderson, Rome

Fig. 178. Head of a Gaul

Museo Nazionale delle Terme, Rome
(Cf. pp. 14, 76)

Fig. 179. Head of Zeus, on a cameo

Museo Archeologico, Venice
(Cf. p. 76)

Fig. 180. Head of Medusa
Akropolis Museum, Athens
(Cf. p. 77)

Fig. 181. Head of a giant, from a metope
of temple F at Selinus (cf. p. 77)
Museo Nazionale, Palermo

Fig. 182. Death of Aigisthos, relief (cf. p. 77)
Glyptotek Ny Carlsberg, Copenhagen

Fig. 184. Head of a mourning woman, from a relief

Fig. 183. Head of a rejoicing woman, from a relief

Fig. 185. Head of Aphrodite(?), from a relief
Museo Nazionale delle Terme, Rome
(Cf. p. 77)

Fig. 186. Head of a dying warrior, from the
eastern pediment at Aigina
The Glyptothek, Munich
(Cf. p. 78)

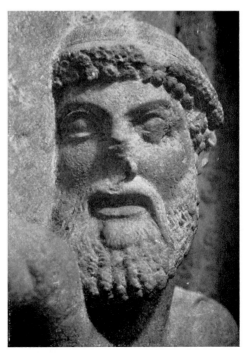

Fig. 187. Head of Zeus, from a metope of
temple E at Selinus
Museo Nazionale, Palermo
(Cf. p. 77)

410

Fig. 190. Head of Marsyas
(from a cast)
British Museum, London
(Cf. p. 78)

Fig. 193. Head of an old warrior
from a krater

Fig. 189. Head of an old woman
from a relief
Museum of Fine Arts, Boston
(Cf. p. 78)

Fig. 192. Head of a Centaur, from a
Parthenon metope (from a cast)

Fig. 188. Head of a Centaur, from the
western pediment at Olympia
Olympia Museum
(Cf. p. 78)

Fig. 191. Head of a Lapith, from the
western pediment at Olympia
Olympia Museum

Fig. 194. Head of a statue of the type of the "Cassel Apollo"
Palazzo Vecchio, Florence
(Cf. p. 79)

Fig. 195. Head of an athlete (cf. p. 79)
Metropolitan Museum of Art

Fig. 196. Head of the Niobid (cf. p. 79)
Museo Nazionale delle Terme, Rome

Fig. 197. Head of a collapsing Greek, from the
Phigaleia frieze

British Museum, London

(Cf. p. 79)

Fig. 198. Head of a dying Amazon, from the
Phigaleia frieze

British Museum, London

(Cf. p. 79)

Fig. 199. Head of a Centaur, from the
Phigaleia frieze

British Museum, London

(Cf. p. 79)

Fig. 200. Head of a woman, from the western
pediment at Olympia

Olympia Museum

(Cf. pp. 79, 224)

Fig. 201. Entreating Amazon, from the
Phigaleia frieze
British Museum, London
(Cf. pp. 80, 172)

Fig. 202. Amazon defending herself, fr
the Phigaleia frieze
British Museum, London
(Cf. pp. 80, 172)

Fig. 203. Fallen Centaur, from the
Phigaleia frieze
British Museum, London
(Cf. pp. 80, 172)

Fig. 204. Dying Amazon, from the
Phigaleia frieze
British Museum, London
(Cf. p. 80)

Fig. 206. "Mourning Athena"
Akropolis Museum, Athens
(Cf. p. 80)

Fig. 205. Detail of a stele of a girl with pigeons
Metropolitan Museum of Art
(Cf. p. 80)

Fig. 207. Head of a girl (cf. p. 81)

Henry Goldman Collection, New York

Fig. 208. Head of an athlete

Metropolitan Museum of Art
(Cf. p. 81)

Fig. 209. Head of an Amazon, from the
Mausoleum frieze (cf. p. 81)

British Museum, London

Fig. 210. Upper part of a stele
Staatliche Museen, Berlin
(Cf. p. 80)

g. 211. Bronze statuette of a mourning woman
Staatliche Museen, Berlin
(Cf. p. 80)

Fig. 212. Mourning woman, from Attica
Staatliche Museen, Berlin
(Cf. p. 80)

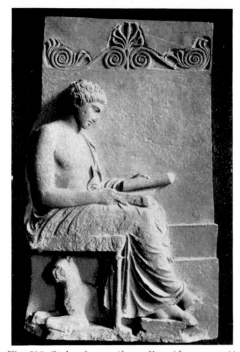

Fig. 213. Stele of a youth reading (from a cast)
Grottaferrata
(Cf. p. 81)

Fig. 214. Girl spinning, stele of My
Staatliche Museen, Berlin
(Cf. p. 82)

Fig. 215. Stele of Dexileos
Kerameikos, Athens
(Cf. p. 81)

Fig. 216. Weeping siren
Museum of Fine Arts, Boston
(Cf. p. 82)

Fig. 217. Stele of Plangon
National Museum, Athens
(Cf. p. 82)

Fig. 219. Old market woman

Fig. 218. Sleeping Satyr

Fig. 220. Terracotta statuette of a negro boy
Ashmolean Museum, Oxford
(Cf. p. 82)

Fig. 221. Terracotta statuette of a flying Eros
Metropolitan Museum of Art
(Cf. p. 82)

Fig. 222. Terracotta statuette
of an old nurse
Metropolitan Museum of Art
(Cf. p. 82)

Fig. 223. Bronze caricature
Metropolitan Museum of Art
(Cf. p. 82)

Photograph by D. Anderson, Rome

Fig. 224. Head of a dying Persian (cf. p. 82)

Museo Nazionale delle Terme, Rome

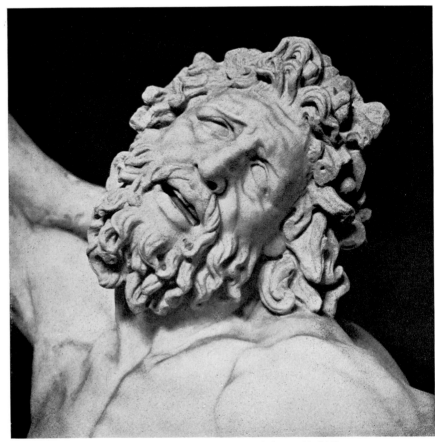

Fig. 225. Head of the Laokoon (cf. pp. 82, 300)

The Vatican, Rome

Fig. 226. Portrait of a man
on gem signed by Dexamenos
(from an impression, enlarged)
Museum of Fine Arts, Boston
(Cf. p. 83)

Fig. 227. Bronze head of Sokrates
The Glyptothek, Munich
(Cf. p. 83)

Fig. 228. Head of "Maussollos"
British Museum, London
(Cf. p. 83)

Fig. 229. Head of Euripides (from a cast)
The Vatican, Rome
(Cf. p. 84)

Fig. 230. Head of bronze portrait statuette
Metropolitan Museum of Art
(Cf. p. 84)

Fig. 231. Side view of Fig. 230
(Cf. p. 84)

Fig. 232. Head of Chrysippos
Metropolitan Museum of Art
(Cf. p. 84)

Fig. 233. Portrait head
Lord Melchett's Collection, London
(Cf. p. 84)

Fig. 234. Portrait of Demetrios, king of
Baktria, from a coin

E. T. Newell Collection, New York

Fig. 235. Portrait of Philetairos, ruler of
Pergamon, from a coin

E. T. Newell Collection, New York

Fig. 236. Portrait of Eukratides, king of Baktria and India, from a coin

E. T. Newell Collection, New York

Fig. 237. Portrait of Antiochos I
Soter, king of Syria, from a coin

E. T. Newell Collection, New York

Fig. 238. Portrait of Seleukos I, king
of Syria, from a coin

E. T. Newell Collection, New York

Enlarged *c.* 1:2
(Cf. p. 84)

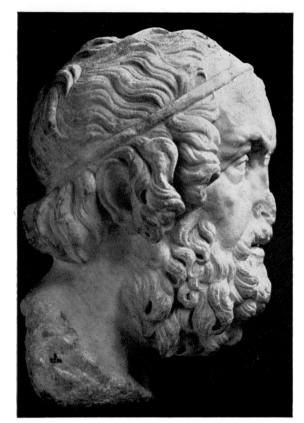

Fig. 239. Head of Homer
Museum of Fine Arts, Boston
(Cf. p. 84)

Fig. 240. Bronze portrait head
National Museum, Athens
(Cf. p. 84)

Fig. 242. Statue of Poseidippos
The Vatican, Rome
(Cf. p. 85)

Fig. 241. Bronze portrait statuette
Metropolitan Museum of Art
(Cf. p. 85)

428

Fig. 245. Theseus, from a kylix

The Louvre, Paris

(Cf. p. 88)

Fig. 246. Euphorbos carrying the infant
Oidipous, from an amphora

Bibliothèque Nationale, Paris

(Cf. p. 88)

Fig. 247. Detail of the Parthenon frieze
(from a cast)

In situ in Athens

(Cf. p. 88)

Fig. 248. Boy holding himation, from a kylix

Staatliche Museen, Berlin

(Cf. p. 88)

Fig. 249. Sophokles
The Lateran, Rome
(Cf. pp. 84, 89)

Fig. 250. Living model wearing
himation
(Cf. pp. 89, 93)

251. Youth wearing a chlamys, from a Greek vase
(Cf. pp. 89, 90)

Fig. 252. Living model wearing a chlamys
(Cf. p. 90)

Fig. 254. Detail of a kylix
British Museum, London
(Cf. p. 90)

Fig. 255. Bronze mirror support
Museum of Fine Arts, Boston
(Cf. p. 90)

Fig. 256. Terracotta statuette
Metropolitan Museum of Art
(Cf. p. 91)

Fig. 257. Back of the Hestia
Giustiniani (from a cast)
Museo Torlonia, Rome
(Cf. p. 91)

Fig. 258. Grave relief of Myttion
Broom Hall, Dunfermline, Scotland
(Cf. p. 91)

Fig. 259. Amazon, from an oinochoë
Metropolitan Museum of Art
(Cf. p. 91)

Fig. 260. Bronze statue of a
dancing girl
Museo Nazionale, Naples
(Cf. p. 92)

Fig. 261. Living model wearing a
Doric chiton
(Cf. p. 92)

Fig. 262. Female statue, formerly in
Auxerre

The Louvre, Paris

(Cf. p. 93)

Fig. 263. Statue dedicated by
Nikandre at Delos

National Museum, Athens

(Cf. p. 93)

Fig. 264. Chares, from Branchidai
(from a cast)

British Museum, London

(Cf. p. 93)

Fig. 266. Another view of Fig. 265

Fig. 265. Sculptures from the bases of columns from
the temple of Artemis at Ephesos
British Museum, London
(Cf. pp. 36, 93)

Fig. 266. Back view of Fig. 267

Fig. 268. Side view of Fig. 267

Fig. 267. Maiden from Attica

Fig. 270. Maiden (from a colored cast)
No. 679, Akropolis Museum, Athens
(Cf. pp. 94, 146)

Fig. 271. Maiden (from a colored cast)
No. 680, Akropolis Museum, Athens
(Cf. p. 94)

Fig. 272. Maiden (from a colored cast)
No. 674, Akropolis Museum, Athens
(Cf. pp. 94, 146)

Fig. 274. Back of a maiden, from Paros
Metropolitan Museum of Art

Fig. 273. Maiden, perhaps by
Antenor
Akropolis Museum, Athens

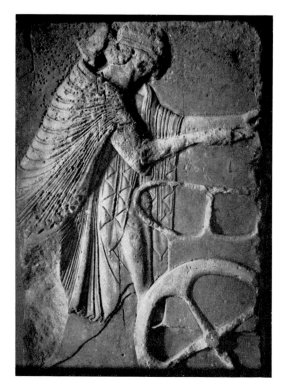

Fig. 275. Relief of a charioteer
Akropolis Museum, Athens
(Cf. pp. 94, 95, 167)

Fig. 276. Relief of Hermes
Akropolis Museum, Athens
(Cf. p. 94)

Fig. 277. Detail of an amphora
Metropolitan Museum of Art
(Cf. p. 95)

Fig. 278. Detail of an oinochoë
Metropolitan Museum of Art
(Cf. p. 95)

Fig. 279. Detail of an amphora
Museum für antike Kleinkunst, Munich
(Cf. p. 96)

Fig. 280. Scene from an alabastron
British Museum, London
(Cf. p. 95)

Fig. 281. Athena, from Eretria
Chalkis Museum
(Cf. p. 96)

Fig. 282. Peleus and Thetis, from a kylix
Staatliche Museen, Berlin
(Cf. p. 96)

Fig. 283. Relief from a statue base found in Athens
National Museum, Athens
(Cf. pp. 95, 114)

Fig. 286. Large terracotta statuette

Fig. 285. Bronze statue of a charioteer

Fig. 287. Maenads, on a kylix
Staatliche Museen, Berlin
(Cf. p. 97)

Fig. 288. Detail of a kylix
Metropolitan Museum of Art
(Cf. p. 97)

Fig. 289. Detail from a relief
Musco Nazionale delle Terme, Rome
(Cf. p. 97)

Photograph by Archives Photographiques, Paris

Fig. 291. Maidens marching in procession, from the Parthenon frieze (cf. pp. 98, 130)

The Louvre, Paris

Photograph by W. F. Mansell

Fig. 292. Two of the "Fates," from the eastern pediment of the Parthenon (cf. pp. 98 f.)

British Museum, London

Fig. 293. Seated deities, from the frieze of the Hephaisteion (from a cast)

In situ

(Cf. p. 99)

Fig. 294. Stele of a woman

Metropolitan Museum of Art

(Cf. p. 99)

Fig. 295. Battle of the Greeks and Persians, from the frieze of the temple of Athena Nike (cf. p. 102)

British Museum, London

Fig. 296. Group from the frieze of the
Erechtheion (cf. p. 101)

Akropolis Museum, Athens

Fig. 297. Standing deities from the frieze of the temple of Athena Nike
(from a cast) (cf. p. 101)

In situ

Fig. 298. Contest of Greeks and Amazons, from the Phigaleia frieze
British Museum, London
(Cf. pp. 102, 172)

Fig. 299. Contest of Centaurs and Lapiths, from the frieze shown in Fig. 298
British Museum, London

ig. 300. Metope of the Phigaleia temple
British Museum, London
(Cf. p. 102)

Fig. 301. Metope of the Phigaleia temple
British Museum, London
(Cf. p. 102)

Photograph by W. F. Mansell

Fig. 302. Nereid from the Nereid monument

British Museum, London

(Cf. p. 102)

Fig. 303. Back view of Fig. 302

Photograph by W. F. Mansell

Fig. 304. Nereid from the Nereid monument

British Museum, London

(Cf. p. 102)

Fig. 305. "Nike" found on the Palatine

National Museum, Rome

(Cf. p. 103)

Fig. 306. Stele of Glykylla
British Museum, London
(Cf. pp. 103, 133)

Fig. 307. "Record" relief
The Louvre, Paris
(Cf. p. 103)

Fig. 308. Medea and the daughters of Pelias
The Lateran, Rome
(Cf. p. 103)

Fig. 309. Scene from an oinochoë
Metropolitan Museum of Art
(Cf. pp. 91, 104)

Fig. 310. Nymph, from a coin of Terina
(from a cast, enlarged)

Private Collection, Switzerland

(Cf. p. 103)

Fig. 311. Aphrodite, from a silver coin of
Aphrodisias(?) (from a cast, enlarged)

British Museum, London

(Cf. p. 104)

Fig. 312. Dancing women from the Delphian column

Delphi Museum

(Cf. p. 104)

Fig. 315. Demeter, from Knidos (cf. pp. 104, 147)

British Museum, London

Fig. 314. Maussollos, from the
Mausoleum at Halikarnassos (cf. p. 104)

British Museum, London

(Cf. p. 104)

Fig. 313. Artemisia, from the Mausoleum
at Halikarnassos (cf. p. 104)

British Museum, London

Fig. 316. Sarcophagus of Mourning Women, from Sidon (cf. pp. 105, 131)

Musées d'Antiquités de Stamboul (Constantinople)

Fig. 317. Stele of Lysistrate (cf. p. 104)

Metropolitan Museum of Art

Fig. 318. Bronze statuette of a woman
Bibliothèque Nationale, Paris
(Cf. p. 105)

Fig. 319. Athena, from a metope of the
temple of Zeus at Olympia (cf. p. 105)
Olympia Museum

Fig. 320. Draped woman (cf. p. 105)
Glyptotek Ny Carlsberg, Copenhagen

Fig. 321. Back view of Fig. 320

Fig. 322. "Athena Medici"
The Louvre, Paris
(Cf. pp. 105, 228)

Fig. 323. Athena
Museo Archeologico, Venice
(Cf. p. 105)

Fig. 324. Draped woman
Museo Archeologico, Venice
(Cf. p. 105)

Fig. 325. Draped woman
Eleusis Museum
(Cf. p. 106)

Fig. 326. Detail from the frieze of the
Heroön at Gjölbaschi (from a cast)
Kunsthistorisches Museum, Vienna
(Cf. p. 106)

Fig. 327. Draped woman
Museo Archeologico, Venice
(Cf. p. 106)

Fig. 328. Detail from the Ephesos drum
British Museum, London
(Cf. p. 106)

Fig. 329. Draped woman
Museo Archeologico, Venice
(Cf. p. 106)

Fig. 332. Torso of a draped woman

Museum of Fine Arts, Boston

(Cf. p. 107)

Fig. 333. Bronze portrait statue

British Museum, London

(Cf. p. 108)

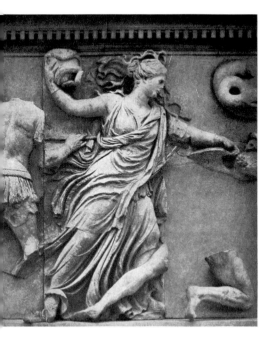

Fig. 334. Nyx, from the frieze of the great altar
of Pergamon

Pergamon Museum, Berlin

(Cf. pp. 107, 132)

Fig. 335. Eos, from the same frieze
as Fig. 334 (from a cast)

Pergamon Museum, Berlin

(Cf. pp. 107, 132)

Fig. 338. Draped woman, from the Giustiniani
Collection (cf. p. 108)

Fig. 337. Polyhymnia
Staatliche Museen, Berlin

Fig. 336. Girl from Anzio
Museo Nazionale delle Terme, Rome

Fig. 339. Statue signed by Zeuxis
Metropolitan Museum of Art
(Cf. p. 108)

Fig. 340. Limestone lion, from Perachora
Museum of Fine Arts, Boston
(Cf. p. 109)

Fig. 341. Back view of Fig. 340

Fig. 342. Lion
Staatliche Museen, Berlin
(Cf. p. 110)

Fig. 343. Lion, from a metope of the temple of Zeus at Olympia
The Louvre, Paris
(Cf. p. 110)

Fig. 344. Lion, from Rome
Metropolitan Museum of Art
(Cf. p. 111)

Fig. 345. Detail of Fig. 344

Fig. 346. Lion, from the Mausoleum at
Halikarnassos
British Museum, London
(Cf. p. 111)

Fig. 347. Frieze of horsemen, from Prinias
Candia Museum, Crete
(Cf. pp. 111, 170)

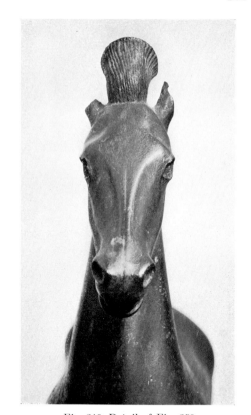

Fig. 348. Horse (from a cast) (cf. p. 111)

Akropolis Museum, Athens

Fig. 349. Detail of Fig. 350

Fig. 350. Large bronze statuette of a horse (cf. pp. 111, 206)

Metropolitan Museum of Art

Fig. 351. Head of the horse of Selene, from the eastern
pediment of the Parthenon

British Museum, London

(Cf. p. 112)

Fig. 352. Horse, from the chariot gro
of the Mausoleum at Halikarnasso

British Museum, London

(Cf. p. 112)

Fig. 353. Relief of a horseman (cf. p. 112)

Metropolitan Museum of Art

Fig. 354. Bronze statuette of a cow, from Delphi

Delphi Museum

(Cf. p. 112)

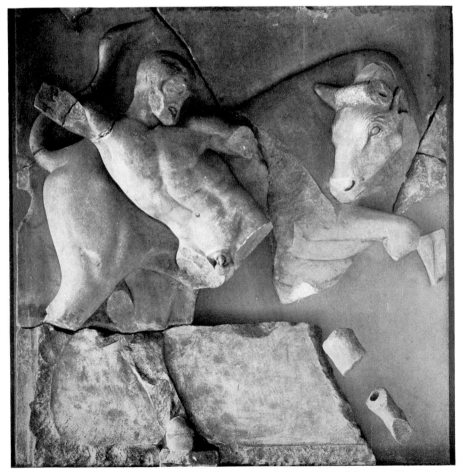

Fig. 355. Herakles and the Cretan bull. Metope of the temple of Zeus at Olympia

The Louvre, Paris

(Cf. p. 113)

Fig. 356. Cow, from the Parthenon frieze (cf. pp. 113, 171)
Akropolis Museum, Athens

Fig. 357. Bronze statuette of a cow (cf. p. 113)
Bibliothèque Nationale, Paris

Fig. 358. Boar. Metope of the "Sikyonian" Treasury at Delphi
Delphi Museum
(Cf. pp. 113, 126)

Fig. 359. Boar
Uffizi Gallery, Florence
(Cf. p. 113)

Fig. 361. Bronze statuette of a goat (cf. p. 113)

Metropolitan Museum of Art

Fig. 360. Bronze statuette of a goat (cf. p. 113)

British Museum, London

364. Dwarf with hound, on an
aved gem (from an impression)
Metropolitan Museum of Art
(Cf. p. 114)

Fig. 365. Dog
Barracco Museum, Rome
(Cf. p. 114)

Fig. 366. "Mastiff"
Uffizi Gallery, Florence
(Cf. p. 115)

Fig. 367. Hound, of serpentine
Palazzo dei Conservatori, Rome
(Cf. p. 114)

Fig. 368. Eagle devouring a hare
from a coin of Akragas
Metropolitan Museum of Art
(Cf. p. 115)

Fig. 369. Head of an eagle, from a coin of El
Metropolitan Museum of Art
(Cf. p. 115)

Fig. 370. Swan preening its wings
from a coin of Klazomenai (from a cast)
British Museum, London
(Cf. p. 115)

Fig. 371. Heron, on an engraved gem
(from an impression)
Museum of Fine Arts, Boston
(Cf. p. 116)

Fig. 372. Crab, from a coin of Akragas
(from a cast)
British Museum, London
(Cf. p. 116)

Fig. 373. Bee, from a coin of Ephesos
(from a cast)
Museum of Fine Arts, Boston
(Cf. p. 116)

Enlarged 1:2

Fig. 374. The western pediment of the temple of Artemis at Corfu
Corfu Museum
(Cf. p. 119)

Fig. 375. The Hephaisteion in Athens
(Cf. p. 118)

470

Fig. 376. Limestone pediment, contest of Herakles and the Hydra (from a water-color)

Akropolis Museum, Athens

(Cf. p. 119)

Fig. 378. Three-headed monster, from a limestone pediment (from a water-color)

Akropolis Museum, Athens

(Cf. p. 120)

Fig. 379. Herakles and Triton, from a limestone pediment (from a water-color)

Akropolis Museum, Athens

(Cf. p. 120)

Fig. 380. Introduction of Herakles to Olympos, from a limestone pediment (from a water-color)
Akropolis Museum, Athens
(Cf. p. 120)

Fig. 381. Eastern pediment of the temple of Apollo at Delphi
Delphi Museum
(Cf. p. 122)

Fig. 382. Apollo and Herakles contesting for the tripod, from a pediment of the Siphnian Treasury

Delphi Museum

(Cf. pp. 64, 121)

Fig. 383. Contest of gods and giants, limestone pediment of the Megarian Treasury

Olympia Museum

(Cf. p. 122)

Fig. 384. Lion devouring a hind, from the eastern pediment of the
temple at Delphi (cf. p. 122)
Delphi Museum

Fig. 385. Giant, from the pediment of the "Hekatompedon"
Akropolis Museum, Athens
(Cf. p. 121)

Fig. 386. Female figure, from the
eastern pediment of the temple
at Delphi (cf. p. 122)
Delphi Museum

Fig. 387. Athena, from the western
pediment of the temple at Delphi
Delphi Museum
(Cf. p. 122)

Fig. 388. Western pediment of the temple of Aphaia at Aigina, reconstruction by A. Furtwängler (cf. p. 122)

The Glyptothek, Munich

Fig. 389. Eastern pediment of the temple of Aphaia at Aigina, reconstruction by A. Furtwängler (cf. p. 122)

476

Fig. 390. Eastern pediment of the temple of Zeus at Olympia, reconstruction by Studniczka

(Cf. p. 123)

Fig. 391. Western pediment of the temple of Zeus at Olympia, reconstruction by Treu

(Cf. p. 123)

Fig. 392. Middle portion of the western pediment at Olympia, reconstruction by Treu
(Cf. pp. 55, 123)

Fig. 393. Middle portion of the eastern pediment at Olympia, reconstruction by Wernicke
(Cf. pp. 123, 178)

Fig. 394. Left portion of the western pediment of the Parthenon (as drawn in 1674)

(Cf. p. 124)

Fig. 396. Left and right ends of the eastern pediment of the Parthenon (as drawn in 1674)

(Cf. p. 124)

Fig. 397. Pediment of the Nereid monument
British Museum, London
(Cf. p. 125)

Fig. 398. Pediment of the sarcophagus of Mourning Women, from Sidon
Istanbul Museum
(Cf. p. 125)

Fig. 399. Pediment of the "Alexander sarcophagus"
Istanbul Museum
(Cf. p. 125)

Fig. 400. Pediment of the "Alexander sarcophagus"
Istanbul Museum
(Cf. p. 125)

Fig. 401. Seated goddesses, from a metope of the temple
at Thermos (from a water-color)
National Museum, Athens
(Cf. p. 125)

Fig. 402. Perseus, from a metope of the templ
Thermos (from a water-color)
National Museum, Athens
(Cf. p. 125)

Fig. 403. Reconstruction of the east side of the temple at Assos
(Cf. pp. 126, 130)

Fig. 404. Dioskouroi and the sons of Alphareos, from the "Sikyonian" Treasury at Delphi

Delphi Museum

(Cf. pp. 126, 165)

Fig. 405. Perseus cutting off the head of Medusa, from a metope of
temple C at Selinus

Museo Nazionale, Palermo

(Cf. pp. 126, 167–168)

Fig. 406. Herakles and the Kerynean hind, from a
metope of the Athenian Treasury at Delphi
Delphi Museum
(Cf. p. 127)

Fig. 407. Theseus and the Minotaur, from a metope
of the Athenian Treasury
Delphi Museum
(Cf. pp. 94, 127)

Fig. 408. Athena and Theseus, from a metope of the
Athenian Treasury

Delphi Museum

(Cf. pp. 94, 127)

Fig. 409. Contest of warriors, from a metope of the
Athenian Treasury

Delphi Museum

(Cf. p. 127)

486

Fig. 411. Artemis and Aktaion, from a metope of temple E at Selinus

Fig. 410. Zeus and Hera, from a metope of temple E at Selinus

Fig. 413. Athena and a giant, from a metope of temple E at Selinus
Museo Nazionale, Palermo
(Cf. pp. 68, 127)

Fig. 412. Herakles and an Amazon, from a metope of temple E at Selinus
Museo Nazionale, Palermo
(Cf. pp. 65, 127)

488

Fig. 414. Herakles and Atlas, from a metope of the
temple of Zeus at Olympia (cf. p. 128)
Olympia Museum

Fig. 415. Lapith and Centaur, from a Parthenon metope (cf. p. 128)
British Museum, London

416. Centaur and Lapith, from a Parthenon
metope

British Museum, London

(Cf. p. 128)

Fig. 417. Theseus and Kerkyon, from a metope
of the Hephaisteion

In situ

(Cf. p. 129)

Fig. 418. Battle of the gods and giants, from the frieze of the Siphnian Treasury

Delphi Museum

(Cf. pp. 130, 166)

Fig. 419. Seated deities, from the frieze of the Siphnian Treasury at Delphi
Delphi Museum
(Cf. p. 130)

Fig. 420. Portion of the frieze of the Ilissos temple (cf. p. 130)
Staatliche Museen, Berlin

Fig. 421. Warriors from the frieze of the Heroön
at Gjölbaschi (cf. p. 131)
Kunsthistorisches Museum, Vienna

Fig. 422. Warriors from the same frieze as Fig. 4
(Cf. pp. 131, 172)

Fig. 424. Stele of Aristion by
Aristokles (cf. pp. 132, 166)
National Museum, Athens

Fig. 425. Stele from Orchomenos
by Alxenor (cf. pp. 132, 168)
National Museum, Athens

Fig. 423. Shaft of a stele of a
brother and sister
Metropolitan Museum of Art
(Cf. p. 132)

Fig. 426. Stele of a girl with pigeons
Metropolitan Museum of Art
(Cf. pp. 132, 206)

Fig. 428. Stele of Sostrate (cf. p. 133)

Metropolitan Museum of Art

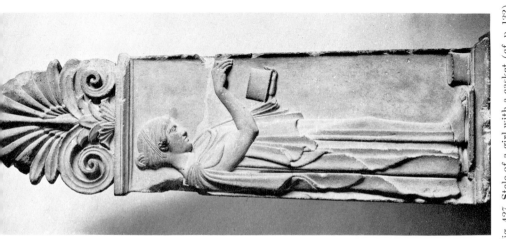

Fig. 427. Stele of a girl with a casket (cf. p. 132)

Staatliche Museen, Berlin

Fig. 429. Stele of Hegeso, from the Kerameikos
National Museum, Athens
(Cf. pp. 133, 164)

Fig. 430. Bronze foundry, from a kylix
Staatliche Museen, Berlin
(Cf. p. 137)

Fig. 431. Athena modeling a horse, from an oinochoë
Staatliche Museen, Berlin
(Cf. p. 141 note)

Fig. 432. Ivory hand from Delphi
Museum of Delphi
(Cf. p. 140)

Fig. 433. Ancient unfinished head
Private collection in New York
(Cf. p. 144)

Fig. 434. Modern armature
(Cf. p. 141)

Fig. 435. Modern unfinished head, with clay model
(Cf. p. 143)

436. Dionysos and a Satyr. Unfinished group
National Museum, Athens
(Cf. p. 144)

Fig. 437. Unfinished statue of a woman
National Museum, Athens
(Cf. p. 144)

Fig. 438. Backs of stelai (cf. p. 145)
The Kerameikos, Athens

Fig. 439. Mallet and chisel, from votive relief

Metropolitan Museum of Art

(Cf. p. 144)

Fig. 440. Modern mallet and chisel

(Cf. p. 144)

Fig. 441. Modern tools: claw chisels, punches or points, flat chisels, and drove

(Cf. p. 144)

442. Back of the Athena, from the temple of
llo at Eretria (from a cast) (cf. pp. 145, 158)
Chalkis Museum

Fig. 443. Head of a girl
Metropolitan Museum of Art
(Cf. p. 146)

Fig. 444. Back of the Hermes by Praxiteles
(from a cast) (cf. pp. 145, 259)
Olympia Museum

Fig. 445. Statue signed by Zeuxis
Metropolitan Museum of Art
(Cf. p. 146)

Fig. 446. Head of a girl (cf. p. 146)
Museum of Fine Arts, Boston

Fig. 447. Head, from a stele (cf. p. 147
Metropolitan Museum of Art

Fig. 448. Girl, from Laurion (cf. p. 146)
Metropolitan Museum of Art

Fig. 449. Side view of Fig. 448
Metropolitan Museum of Art

Fig. 450. Bronze head

Glyptotek Ny Carlsberg, Copenhagen

(Cf. p. 147)

Fig. 451. The Chatsworth head

In the collection of the Duke of Devonshire

(Cf. p. 147)

Fig. 452. Head of a youth

Akropolis Museum, Athens

(Cf. p. 147)

Fig. 453. Hermes and a Nymph, from a relief

The Louvre, Paris

(Cf. pp. 39, 148)

Fig. 455. Reconstruction of the Paionios Nike at
Olympia (photographed at the original angle)
Olympia Museum
(Cf. pp. 159, 244)

Fig. 456. Same reconstruction photographe[d]
level with ground

Fig. 457. Base and plinth from Sounion of a statue
National Museum, Athens
(Cf. p. 158)

Fig. 458. Plinth set into the capital of a st[ele]
Metropolitan Museum of Art
(Cf. p. 158)

Fig. 459. Head, from the Esquiline
British Museum, London
(Cf. p. 153)

Fig. 460. Fragment of a terracotta head
Metropolitan Museum of Art
(Cf. p. 150)

Fig. 461. Votive relief
Eleusis Museum
(Cf. p. 151)

Fig. 462. Ashurbanipal and his queen feasting in a garden. Limestone relief from Nineveh

British Museum, London

(Cf. p. 163)

Fig. 463. Egyptian sculptor's model

Metropolitan Museum of Art

(Cf. p. 164)

Fig. 464. Warrior, relief from Naukratis
British Museum, London
(Cf. p. 164)

Fig. 465. Orestes and Elektra(?), relief
Sparta Museum
(Cf. p. 165)

Fig. 466. Women dancing, relief
British Museum, London
(Cf. p. 165)

Fig. 467. Unfinished portion of the "Fourth
Frieze" of the Nereid monument
British Museum, London
(Cf. p. 164)

Fig. 468. "Ancestor Relief," from Sparta
Staatliche Museen, Berlin
(Cf. p. 166)

Fig. 469. Ball player, from a
statue base
National Museum, Athens
(Cf. p. 168)

Fig. 470. Detail of a grave stele
Metropolitan Museum of Art
(Cf. p. 166)

Fig. 472. Relief, deity(?) receiving a helmet, from the "Harpy tomb" (cf. p. 166)

British Museum, London

Fig. 473. Deity(?) receiving a dove, from the "Harpy tomb" (cf. p. 166)

British Museum, London

Figs. 474–476. Three-sided relief, Birth of Aphrodite(?)

Museo Nazionale delle Terme, Rome

(Cf. p. 169)

Figs. 477–479. Three-sided relief, subject uncertain

Museum of Fine Arts, Boston

(Cf. pp. 80, 169, 190)

Fig. 481. Demeter, Persephone, and Triptolemos, relief from Eleusis

National Museum, Athens

(Cf. pp. 169, 180, 231)

Photograph by D. Anderson, Rome

Fig. 480. Grave stele of an athlete (cf. p. 169)

The Vatican, Rome

Fig. 482. Satyr, from a krater by the
Pan painter (from a drawing)
Metropolitan Museum of Art
(Cf. p. 170)

Fig. 483. Centaur and Lapith, from a volute krater
Metropolitan Museum of Art
(Cf. p. 170)

Fig. 484. Youth, from an oinochoë by the Berlin
painter (from a drawing)
Metropolitan Museum of Art
(Cf. p. 170)

Fig. 485. Satyr, from a skyphos by the Penthesileia
painter
Metropolitan Museum of Art
(Cf. p. 170)

Photograph by W. F. Mansell

Fig. 486. Procession of horsemen, from the Parthenon frieze

British Museum, London

(Cf. pp. 170, 232)

Fig. 487. Athena mounting a chariot, from the Siphnian Treasury

Delphi Museum

(Cf. p. 171)

Fig. 488. Poseidon, Apollo, and Artemis, from the Parthenon frieze
Akropolis Museum, Athens
(Cf. pp. 170, 171, 232)

hotograph by W. F. Mansell

Fig. 489. Hermes, Dionysos, Demeter, and Ares, from the Parthenon frieze
British Museum, London
(Cf. pp. 170, 172, 232)

Fig. 490. Procession of tributaries, from the Nereid monument
British Museum, London
(Cf. p. 174)

Fig. 491. Frieze from the Lysikrates monument
In situ at Athens
(Cf. pp. 131, 174)

Fig. 492. Hunting scene, from the Nereid monument
British Museum, London
(Cf. p. 174)

Fig. 493. Poseidon pursuing Amymone
from a lekythos
Metropolitan Museum of Art
(Cf. p. 173)

Fig. 494. Grave stele of an athlete, from Sounion
National Museum, Athens
(Cf. p. 169)

Fig. 495. Farewell scene, from a grave lekythos
Metropolitan Museum of Art
(Cf. p. 174)

Fig. 496. Relief from a grave lekythos
Metropolitan Museum of Art
(Cf. p. 174)

Fig. 497. Bronze statue of a dancer
from Herculaneum
Museo Nazionale, Naples
(Cf. pp. 96, 179)

g. 498. The "Chiaramonti" Niobid
The Vatican, Rome
(Cf. p. 180)

Fig. 499. Back view of the Eirene
The Glyptothek, Munich
(Cf. p. 179)

Fig. 500. Detail of one of the "Fates," from the
eastern pediment of the Parthenon (from a cast)
British Museum, London
(Cf. p. 180)

Fig. 501. "Barberini Suppliant" (from a cast)
The Louvre, Paris
(Cf. p. 180)

Fig. 502. Karyatid, from the Erechtheion
British Museum, London
(Cf. pp. 101, 106, 179)

Fig. 503. Roman copy of the Erechtheion
karyatid (cf. p. 179)
The Vatican, Rome

Fig. 504. Nike, from the "Balustrade" of the
Athena Nike temple (cf. pp. 100, 179)
Akropolis Museum, Athens

Fig. 505. Detail from a Roman relief
The Glyptothek, Munich
(Cf. p. 180)

Fig. 506. Nike, from the "Balustrade" of the
Athena Nike temple (cf. pp. 100, 180)
Akropolis Museum, Athens

Fig. 507. A sacrifice of a bull, detail from a Roman relief
The Vatican, Rome
(Cf. p. 180)

Fig. 508. Head of Ariadne(?), from the
Akropolis (cf. p. 180)

National Museum, Athens

Fig. 509. Roman copy of Fig. 508

Staatliche Museen, Berlin

(Cf. p. 180)

Fig. 510. Demeter and Persephone, Roman version of Fig. 481 (cf. p. 180)

Metropolitan Museum of Art

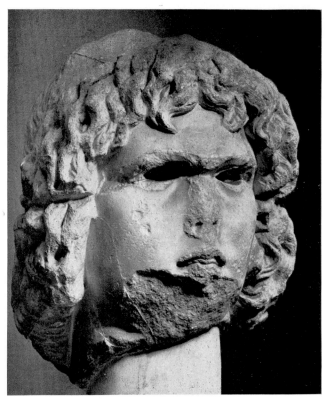

Fig. 511. Roman copy of Fig. 512 (from a cast) (cf. p. 181)
National Museum, Athens

Fig. 512. Head of Eubouleus (cf. pp. 181, 264)
National Museum, Athens

Fig. 513. Maenads, from a pyxis

National Museum, Athens

(Cf. p. 181)

Fig. 514. Maenads, from a marble vase

Metropolitan Museum of Art

(Cf. p. 181)

Fig. 515. Maenad
The Prado, Madrid
(Cf. p. 181)

Fig. 516. Dancers from the frieze of the Heroön
at Gjölbaschi
Kunsthistorisches Museum, Vienna
(Cf. p. 182)

Fig. 517. Nymphs or Graces
The Vatican, Rome
(Cf. p. 182)

Fig. 520. Archaistic Artemis

Fig. 519. Archaistic Artemis

Fig. 518. Archaistic Artemis

Fig. 521. Artemis, Archaistic
relief

Antiquarium Comunale, Rome

(Cf. p. 182)

Fig. 522. Archaistic bronze
statuette

Bibliothèque Nationale, Paris

(Cf. p. 183)

Fig. 523. Archaistic bronze statuette

British Museum, London

(Cf. p. 182)

Fig. 524. Archaistic bronze statuette

National Museum, Athens

(Cf. p. 183)

528

Fig. 526. Modern forgery copied from Fig. 525
Metropolitan Museum of Art
(Cf. p. 183)

Fig. 525. Head of a fallen warrior, from the eastern
pediment at Aigina
The Glyptothek, Munich
(Cf. pp. 77, 183)

Figs. 527 and 528. Marble head of "Sappho"
Roman copy of a Greek original
Glyptotek Ny Carlsberg, Copenhagen
(Cf. p. 184)

Figs. 529 and 530. Modern forgery in the style of Figs. 527 and 528
(Cf. p. 184)

Fig. 530. Melon-f... ...o... ...ia. From Ephesos.

Fig. 531. Archaic head of a maiden.

Fig. 533. Archaistic head of Athena
Metropolitan Museum of Art
(Cf. p. 185)

Fig. 534. Modern forgery copied from Fig. 533
(Cf. p. 185)

Fig. 535. Head of the Aphrodite of Melos
The Louvre, Paris
(Cf. p. 185)

Fig. 536. Modern forgery in the style of Fig. 535
(Cf. p. 185)

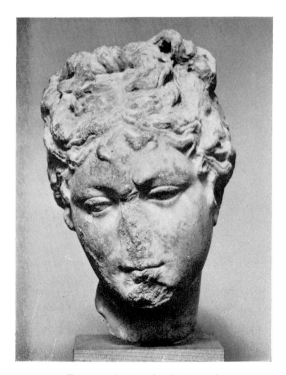

Fig. 537. Ancient head of a girl
Metropolitan Museum of Art
(Cf. p. 185)

Fig. 538. Plaster cast of Fig. 537, showing pu
for reproduction
(Cf. p. 185)

Fig. 539. Modern forgery copied from Fig. 537
with the help of the plaster cast Fig. 538
(Cf. p. 185)

Fig. 540. Modern forgery. Side view of Fig.

Fig. 543. Modern forgery of an
archaic maiden by Dossena
(Cf. p. 186)

Fig. 542. Modern forgery after the
Ares Borghese
(Cf. p. 188)

Fig. 541. Modern forgery after the
Mattei Amazon
(Cf. p. 188)

Fig. 544. Greek terracotta statuette of Nike
Metropolitan Museum of Art
(Cf. p. 186)

Fig. 545. Modern forgery of a Greek
terracotta statuette
Metropolitan Museum of Art
(Cf. p. 186)

Fig. 546. Greek terracotta statuette
of a girl
Metropolitan Museum of Art
(Cf. p. 187)

Fig. 547. Modern forgery of a Greek
terracotta statuette
Metropolitan Museum of Art
(Cf. p. 187)

Fig. 548. Modern forgery of a Greek
terracotta statuette (cf. p. 187)

Metropolitan Museum of Art

Fig. 549. Greek stele of a girl with mirror

Museum of Fine Arts, Boston
(Cf. p. 187)

Fig. 550. Modern forgery of a Greek terracotta statuette (cf. p. 187)

Metropolitan Museum of Art

Fig. 551. Amymone, Greek
engraved sardonyx

Staatliche Museen, Berlin
(Cf. p. 187)

Fig. 552. Amymone, modern
engraved carnelian

Metropolitan Museum of Art
(Cf. p. 187)

Fig. 555. Modern forgery by Dossena (cf. p. 189)

Fig. 556. Greek silver bracelet with satyr pendant
Metropolitan Museum, New York
(Cf. p. 192)

Fig. 557. Modern copy in gold of the bracelet of
Fig. 556 (cf. p. 192)

539

Fig. 560. Apollo, perhaps by
Kalamis, on a coin of Apollonia
(enlarged)
Staatliche Museen, Berlin
(Cf. p. 205)

Fig. 561. Hermes Kriophoros
perhaps by Kalamis, on a
Roman coin of Tanagra
(from a cast, enlarged)
British Museum, London
(Cf. p. 205)

Fig. 562. Zeus, perhaps by Ageladas
on a coin of Messene, enlarged
British Museum, London
(Cf. p. 196)

Fig. 563. Apollo killing the serpent, on a coin
of Kroton (from a cast, enlarged)
Staatliche Museen, Berlin
(Cf. p. 203)

Fig. 564. Philoktetes, on
an engraved agate
(from an impression, enlarged)
The Louvre, Paris
(Cf. p. 203)

Fig. 565. Marble head of Harmodios

Metropolitan Museum of Art

(Cf. p. 200)

Fig. 566. Side view of Fig. 565

Fig. 567. Tyrannicide group
on a coin of Kyzikos, enlarged

E. T. Newell Collection, New York

(Cf. p. 200)

Fig. 568. Tyrannicide group
on a coin of Athens, enlarged

British Museum, London

(Cf. p. 200)

Fig. 569. Tyrannicide group
on a fragment of a
lamp-feeder

In the Metropolitan Museum, New York

(Cf. p. 200)

Fig. 570. Tyrannicide group
shield device on a Panathenaic vase

British Museum, London

(Cf. p. 200)

Fig. 571. Group of the Tyrannicides
Museo Nazionale, Naples
(Cf. p. 200)

Fig. 572. Harmodios
Museo Nazionale, Naples
(Cf. p. 200)

Fig. 573. Aristogeiton, Museo Nuovo, Rome,
with the cast of the head in the Vatican,
Rome (from a cast in the Museo
dei Gessi, Rome)
(Cf. p. 200)

Fig. 574. Head of Aristogeiton (from a cast)
The Vatican, Rome
(Cf. p. 200)

542

Figs. 575–577. Reconstructed cast of Harmodios
Metropolitan Museum of Art
(Cf. pp. 65, 200)

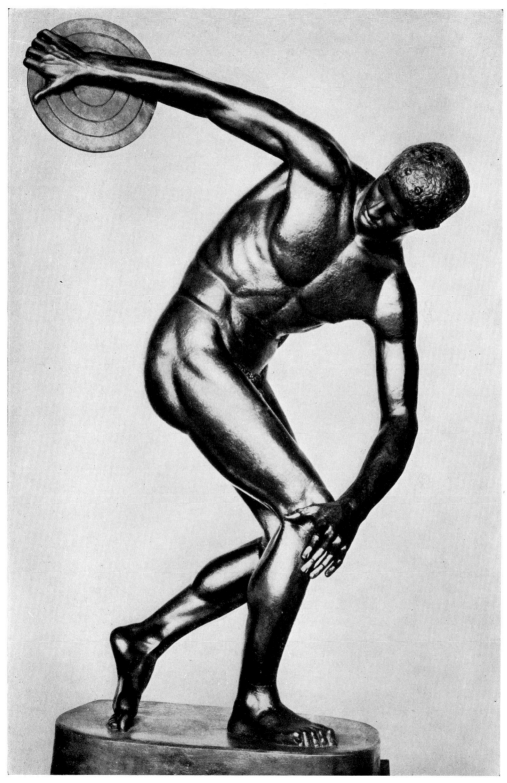

Fig. 578. Diskobolos (from a composite cast)
(Cf. pp. 70, 207)

Fig. 579. Bronze statuette of a diskobolos
Museum für antike Kleinkunst, Munich
(Cf. p. 208)

Fig. 580. Back view of Fig. 579

Photograph by D. Anderson, Rome

Fig. 581. Diskobolos, from Castel Porziano
Museo Nazionale delle Terme, Rome
(Cf. p. 208)

Fig. 582. Head of Diskobolos (from a cast)
(cf. Fig. 578)
From the Lancellotti Palace, Rome
(Cf. p. 207)

Fig. 584. Marsyas, Roman copy of a work by Myron

The Lateran, Rome

(Cf. pp. 70, 209)

Fig. 585. Head of Marsyas

Barracco Museum, Rome

(Cf. p. 209)

Fig. 586. Athena and Marsyas, detail of a marble
vase from Athens

National Museum, Athens

(Cf. p. 209)

Fig. 587. Athena and Marsyas, from
red-figured oinochoë

Staatliche Museen, Berlin

(Cf. p. 209)

Fig. 588. Athena and Marsyas, on a coin
of Athens (from a cast, enlarged)

Numismatic Museum, Athens

(Cf. p. 209)

Figs. 589 and 590. Head of Fig. 591 (from a cast)

Städtliche Skulpturensammlung, Frankfurt

(Cf. p. 209)

Fig. 591. Statue of Athena

Städtliche Skulpturensammlung, Frankfurt

(Cf. p. 209)

Photograph by W. F. Mansell

Fig. 592. Bronze statuette of Marsyas

British Museum, London

(Cf. p. 209)

Fig. 593. Athena and Marsyas, reconstruction of Myron's group, by Sieveking
(Cf. p. 210)

Fig. 594. "Athena Promachos," on a
Roman coin of Athens (from a
cast, enlarged)

British Museum, London
(Cf. p. 217)

Fig. 595. Athena Parthenos, on a
Roman coin of Athens (from a
cast, enlarged)

British Museum, London
(Cf. p. 219)

Fig. 596. "Athena Pro-
machos" on the Akropo-
lis, on a Roman coin of
Athens (from a cast)

British Museum, London
(Cf. p. 217)

Fig. 597. Head of Athena
Parthenos, on an engraved
gem by Aspasios
(from an impression)

Museo Nazionale delle Terme, Rome
(Cf. p. 219)

Fig. 598. Head of Athena Parthenos
on a coin of Athens

E. T. Newell Collection, New York
(Cf. p. 219)

Fig. 601. "Lenormant statuette" of the

Figs. 599 and 600. "Varvakeion statuette" of the Athena Parthenos

Fig. 602. Head of Athena Parthenos
Staatliche Museen, Berlin
(Cf. pp. 153, 219)

Fig. 603. Statuette of Athena Parthenos
(from a cast)
Patras Museum
(Cf. p. 218)

Fig. 604. Upper part of a statuette
of the Athena Parthenos
Princeton University Museum, Princeton
(Cf. p. 219)

Fig. 605. The "Strangford Shield"
British Museum, London
(Cf. p. 218)

Fig. 606. Head of Zeus, on a Roman coin of Elis
(from a cast, enlarged)
Bibliothèque Nationale, Paris
(Cf. p. 221)

Fig. 607. Statue of Zeus, on a Roman coin of Elis
(from a cast, enlarged)
Museo Archeologico, Florence
(Cf. p. 221)

Fig. 608. Head of a reclining figure
from the temple of Zeus at Olympia
Olympia Museum
(Cf. p. 226)

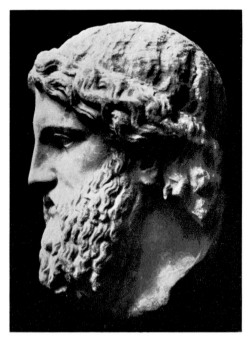

Fig. 609. Head of Zeus
Museum of Fine Arts, Boston
(Cf. p. 221)

Fig. 610. Head of Zeus
on a coin of Elis
(from a cast)
British Museum, London
(Cf. p. 226)

Fig. 611. Zeus seated, on
a coin of Elis
(from a cast)
British Museum, London
(Cf. p. 226)

Fig. 612. Zeus, Roman fresco from Eleusis
(Cf. p. 221)

Fig. 613. Head of Zeus, on a gem
(from an impression)
Staatliche Museen, Berlin
(Cf. p. 221)

Fig. 614. Head of Athena
Museo Civico, Bologna
(Cf. pp. 79, 228)

Fig. 615. Statue of Athena

The Albertinum, Dresden

(Cf. p. 228)

Fig. 616. Reconstruction of the "Lemnian Athena

From a cast in the Museum der Bildenden Künste, Budap

(Cf. p. 228)

Fig. 617. Athena, on a red-figured kylix

Museo Civico, Bologna

(Cf. p. 228, note)

Fig. 618. Head of an Amazon
National Museum, Athens
(Cf. p. 230)

Fig. 619. Amazon, on a gem (from a drawing)
(Cf. p. 230)

Fig. 620. Mattei Amazon
The Vatican, Rome
(Cf. p. 229)

Fig. 621. Farnese Diadoumenos
British Museum, London
(Cf. p. 230)

Fig. 622. "Theseus," from the eastern pediment of the Parthenon
British Museum, London
(Cf. p. 232)

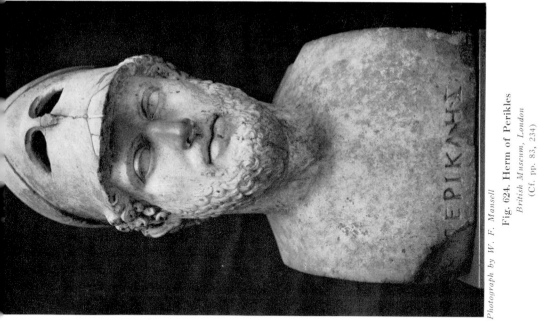

Fig. 624. **Herm of Perikles**
British Museum, London
(Cf. pp. 83, 234)

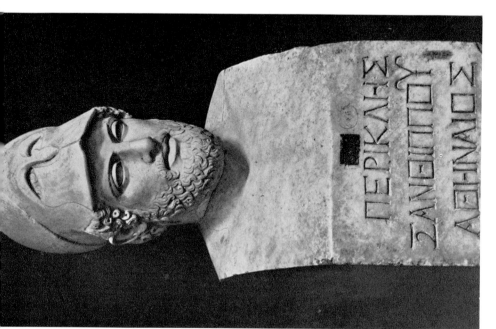

Fig. 623. **Herm of Perikles**
The Vatican, Rome
(Cf. p. 234)

Fig. 625. Detail of a bronze statuette of a warrior
(cf. Fig. 127)

Musée St. Germain-en-Laye

(Cf. p. 236)

Fig. 626. Head of Fig. 627 (from a cast)

Fig. 627. Amazon

Capitoline Museum, Rome

(Cf. p. 236)

Fig. 629. Bronze herm of Hermes Propylaios
Metropolitan Museum of Art
(Cf. p. 238)

Fig. 630. Head of the Dionysos
by Alkamenes, on a coin of Athens
(enlarged)
E. T. Newell Collection, New York
(Cf. p. 238)

Fig. 628. Herm of Hermes Propylaios
Musées d'Antiquités de Stamboul (Constantinople)
(Cf. p. 238)

Fig. 631. Dionysos, by Alkamenes, on a coin
of Athens (from a cast, enlarged)
Bibliothèque Nationale, Paris
(Cf. p. 238)

Fig. 633. Head of Nemesis
by Agorakritos
British Museum, London
(Cf. p. 241)

Fig. 635. Head of a woman, from the
base of the statue of Nemesis by
Agorakritos (from a cast)
National Museum, Athens
(Cf. p. 242)

Fig. 634. Nemesis, on a coin of Paphos
(from a cast, enlarged) (cf. p. 242)
British Museum, London

Fig. 636. Pan and the Graces (cf. p. 243)
Capitoline Museum, Rome

Fig. 638. Maenad
Metropolitan Museum of Art
(Cf. p. 243)

Fig. 637. Nike by Paíonios (three-quarters view)
Olympia Museum
(Cf. pp. 63, 101, 244)

Fig. 639. The "Hertz" head
Palazzo Venezia, Rome
(Cf. p. 245)

Fig. 640. Profile view of Fig. 639
(from a cast)

Fig. 641. Head of the same type
as that shown in Fig. 639
The Vatican, Rome
(Cf. p. 245)

Fig. 642. Fragment of the head
of the Nike by Paionios
(cf. Fig. 637)

Olympia Museum

(Cf. p. 244)

Fig. 643. Artemis, by Strongylion, on a coin of Megara
(from a cast, enlarged)

British Museum, London

(Cf. p. 246)

Fig. 644. Inscribed base of the bronze statue of the wooden
horse by Strongylion

On the Akropolis, Athens

(Cf. p. 246)

Fig. 645. Doryphoros, from Pompeii
Museo Nazionale, Naples
(Cf. pp. 56, 248)

Fig. 646. Head of the Doryphoros
Corinth Museum
(Cf. p. 248)

Fig. 647. Profile view of Fig. 646

Fig. 648. Bronze herm of the Doryphoros
Museo Nazionale, Naples
(Cf. p. 248)

Fig. 649. Relief of the Doryphoros (from a cast)
National Museum, Athens
(Cf. p. 248)

Fig. 650. Diadoumenos, from Delos
National Museum, Athens
(Cf. pp. 57, 178, 249f.)

651. Terracotta statuette of the Diadoumenos

Metropolitan Museum of Art

(Cf. pp. 249f.)

Fig. 652. Head of the Diadoumenos

Metropolitan Museum of Art

(Cf. pp. 249f.)

g. 653. Head of Hera, on a coin of Argos
(slightly enlarged)

*T. Newell Collection, American Numismatic Society,
New York*

(Cf. p. 251)

Fig. 654. Hera, on a coin of Argos (from a
cast, enlarged)

British Museum, London

(Cf. p. 251)

Fig. 655. Amazon, from Rome
Staatliche Museen, Berlin
(Cf. p. 251)

Fig. 656. Head of an Amazon
(from a cast) (cf. p. 252)

In the Metropolitan Museum of Art

Fig. 657. Hera and Hebe, on a coin of Argos
(from a cast, enlarged)

(Cf. p. 254)

Photograph by W. F. Mansell

Fig. 658. "Westmacott Athlete"

British Museum, London

(Cf. p. 252)

Fig. 660. Eiren...

Fig. 659. Eirene and the Infant Ploutos

. 661. Eirene and the Infant Ploutos, on a coin
of Athens (from a cast, enlarged)

British Museum, London

(Cf. p. 257)

Fig. 662. Head of Fig. 663
before restorations

Fig. 663. Ploutos

The Albertinum, Dresden

(Cf. p. 258)

Fig. 664. Hermes and the Infant Dionysos, by Praxiteles
Olympia Museum
(Cf. pp. 58, 104, 180, 259)

Fig. 666. Satyr with the infant Dionysos
From Pompeii
(Cf. p. 260)

Fig. 667. Foot of the Hermes by Praxiteles (see Fig. 664)
(Cf. p. 260)

Fig. 665. Head of the Hermes by Praxiteles (see Fig. 664)
(Cf. p. 259)

Fig. 668. Reconstruction of the Aphrodite of Knidos: body of the Vatican
figure, the Kaufmann head, and some restorations (from a cast)

(Cf. pp. 59, 261)

Fig. 669. Torso of Aphrodite in the
Musée Cinquantenaire, Brussels, with a
cast of the head in the Glyptotek Ny
Carlsberg, Copenhagen
(Cf. p. 261)

Fig. 670. Aphrodite
The Magazzini of the Vatican, Rome
(Cf. p. 261)

Fig. 671. Head of Aphrodite
The Kaufmann Collection, Berlin
(Cf. p. 262)

Fig. 672. Aphrodite, on a coin
of Knidos (from a cast)
Bibliothèque Nationale, Paris
(Cf. p. 261)

578

Fig. 673. Apollo Sauroktonos, on a coin
of Nikopolis (from a cast, enlarged)
British Museum, London
(Cf. p. 262)

Fig. 674. Eros on a Roman coin of Parion
Staatliche Museen, Berlin
(Cf. p. 263)

Fig. 675. Bronze statuette of the
Apollo Sauroktonos
Villa Albani, Rome
(Cf. p. 263)

Fig. 676. Apollo Sauroktonos
The Vatican, Rome
(Cf. pp. 58, 262)

Fig. 677. Artemis, on a coin of Antikyra
(from a cast, enlarged)
Staatliche Museen, Berlin
(Cf. pp. 264, 268)

Fig. 678. Leto and Chloris, on a coin of Argos
(from a cast, enlarged)
British Museum, London
(Cf. p. 264)

Fig. 679. Apollo and Marsyas, relief from the Mantineia base
National Museum, Athens
(Cf. p. 265)

Fig. 680. Muses, relief from the Mantineia base
National Museum, Athens
(Cf. p. 265)

Fig. 681. Muses, relief from the Mantineia base
National Museum, Athens
(Cf. p. 265)

Fig. 684. Back view of Fig. 682

Fig. 683. Side view of Fig. 682

Fig. 682. Satyr
The Albertinum, Dresden
(Cf. pp. 58, 266)

582

Fig. 685. Aphrodite of Arles
The Louvre, Paris
(Cf. p. 267)

Fig. 686. Artemis of Gabii
The Louvre, Paris
(Cf. p. 265)

Fig. 687. Head of a girl, from the altar
of Kos (profile view)
(Cf. p. 269)   *Musées d'Antiquités de Stamboul (Constantinople)*

Fig. 688. Front view of Fig. 687, with
restorations
(Cf. p. 269)

Fig. 689. Lower half of a female figure
from the altar of Kos (cf. p. 269)
Musées d'Antiquités de Stamboul (Constantinople)

Fig. 693. Head of a warrior, from the temple at Tegea (from a cast)

Tegea Museum

(Cf. pp. 81, 270)

Fig. 692. Head of Herakles, from the temple at Tegea (from a cast)

Tegea Museum

(Cf. pp. 81, 270)

Fig. 694. Apollo, on a coin of Nero
(from a cast, enlarged)
British Museum, London
(Cf. p. 275)

Fig. 695. Apollo, on a coin of
Alexandria Troas, enlarged
E. T. Newell Collection, New York
(Cf. p. 274)

Fig. 696. Atalante, from the eastern pediment of the temple at Tegea
(from a cast) (cf. p. 270)
Tegea Museum

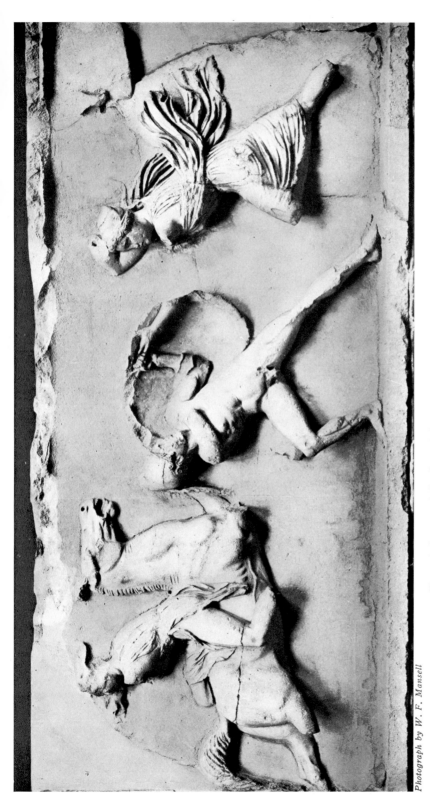

Fig. 697. Contest of Greeks and Amazons, from a frieze of the Mausoleum

British Museum, London

(Cf. pp. 112, 131, 173, 272)

Fig. 698. Contest of Greeks and Amazons, from a frieze of the Mausoleum

British Museum, London

(Cf. pp. 66, 131, 173, 272)

Fig. 699. Contest of Greeks and Amazons, from a frieze of the Mausoleum

British Museum, London

(Cf. pp. 131, 173, 272)

700. Head of a charioteer, from a frieze of the
Mausoleum

British Museum, London

(Cf. p. 273)

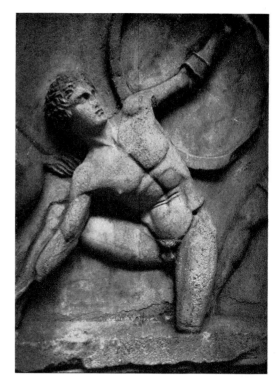

Fig. 701. Greek warrior. Detail of Fig. 699

(Cf. p. 273)

Fig. 702. Detail of head of Fig. 701

(Cf. p. 273)

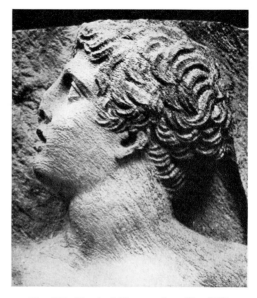

Fig. 703. Head of Hermes (see Fig. 705)

(Cf. p. 273)

Fig. 705. Sculptured drum from a column of the temple of Artemis at Ephesos
British Museum, London
(Cf. pp. 58, 105, 273)

Fig. 706. Apollo
Musée d'Art et d'Histoire, Geneva
(Cf. p. 275)

Fig. 707. Herakles (from a cast)
Lansdowne Collection
(Cf. pp. 180, 276)

Fig. 708. Head of Meleager
The Garden of the Villa Medici, Rome
(Cf. p. 276)

Fig. 709. Maenad
The Albertinum, Dresden
(Cf. p. 276)

Fig. 711, Nereid, akroterion of the temple of Asklepios

Fig. 710, Nereid, akroterion of the temple of Asklepios at Epidauros

Fig. 712. Nike, akroterion(?) of the temple of Asklepios
at Epidauros (cf. pp. 104, 278f.)
National Museum, Athens

Fig. 713. Nike, akroterion of the temple of Asklepios
at Epidauros (cf. pp. 64, 104, 278f.)
National Museum, Athens

Fig. 715. Relief of Asklepios, from Epidauros
National Museum, Athens
(Cf. p. 279)

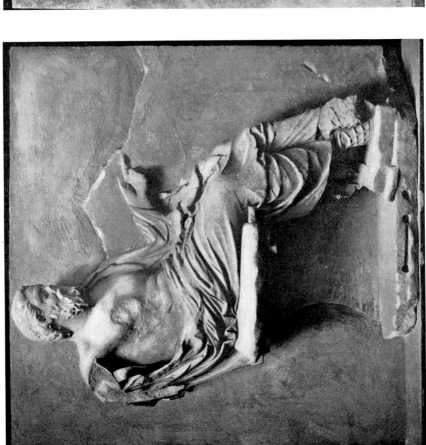

Fig. 714. Relief of Asklepios, from Epidauros
National Museum, Athens
(Cf. p. 279)

Fig. 716. Amazon, from the western pediment
at Epidauros

National Museum, Athens

(Cf. pp. 278f.)

Fig. 717. Front view of statue shown
in Fig. 716 (from a cast)

(Cf. p. 279)

Fig. 718. Torso of an Amazon, from the pediment of the
temple at Epidauros

National Museum, Athens

(Cf. p. 278)

Fig. 719. Torso of a woman, probably from
the pediment at Epidauros

National Museum, Athens

(Cf. p. 278)

Fig. 720. Contest of Greeks and Amazons, from a frieze of the Mausoleum

No. 1006, British Museum, London

(Cf. pp. 112, 131, 280)

Fig. 721. Contest of Greek and Amazon, from a frieze of
the Mausoleum

No. 1016, British Museum, London

(Cf. pp. 112, 131, 280)

Fig. 722. Amazon, from a frieze
of the Mausoleum

No. 1017, British Museum, London

(Cf. p. 280)

Fig. 723. Horseman approaching a tripod, base of a statue by Bryaxis

National Museum, Athens

(Cf. p. 281)

Fig. 724. Inscription on the statue base of Bryaxis (see Fig. 723)

(Cf. p. 281)

Fig. 725. Nike
National Museum, Athens
(Cf. pp. 281–282)

Fig. 726. Side view of Fig. 725
National Museum, Athens

Fig. 727. Fragment of a female figure
from the base of the statue of
Nemesis at Rhamnous
National Museum, Athens
(Cf. p. 282)

Fig. 728. Group from the frieze of the Erechtheion
Akropolis Museum, Athens
(Cf. p. 282)

Fig. 729. Contest of Greeks and Amazons, from a frieze of the Mausoleum
British Museum, London
(Cf. pp. 112, 131, 282)

Fig. 730. Contest of Greeks and Amazons, from a frieze of the Mausoleum
British Museum, London
(Cf. pp. 131, 282)

Fig. 731. Head of Apollo, perhaps after the statue
by Bryaxis, on a coin of Antiochos IV, Epiphanes

E. T. Newell Collection, New York

(Cf. p. 283)

Fig. 732. Apollo, perhaps after a statue
Bryaxis, on the reverse of the coin, Fig.

(Cf. p. 283)

Fig. 733. Asklepios, statue by Thrasymedes
on a coin of Epidauros (from a
cast, enlarged)

Staatliche Museen, Berlin

(Cf. p. 284)

Fig. 734. Ganymede and the Eagle, on
bronze mirror

Staatliche Museen, Berlin

(Cf. p. 286)

Fig. 735. Contest of Greeks and Amazons, from a frieze of the Mausoleum

British Museum, London

(Cf. pp. 131, 285)

Fig. 737. Ganymede and the Eagle

Fig. 736. Apollo Belvedere

Fig. 739. Apoxyomenos
The Vatican, Rome
(Cf. pp. 288f.)

Fig. 738. Agias
Delphi Museum
(Cf. p. 289)

Fig. 740. Head of Agias, profile view
(see Fig. 738)
(Cf. p. 289)

Fig. 741. Head of Agias, front view
(from a cast)

Fig. 742. Head of the Apoxyomenos
(see Fig. 739; from a cast)
(Cf. p. 288)

Fig. 743. Profile view of Fig. 742 (from a cast)

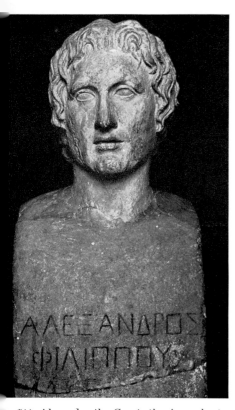

Fig. 744. Alexander the Great, the Azara bust
The Louvre, Paris
(Cf. p. 292)

Photograph by W. F. Mansell

Fig. 745. Alexander the Great
British Museum, London
(Cf. p. 292)

Fig. 746. Alexander (cf. p. 292)
From *Musée Guimet, Paris*
on deposit in The Louvre

Fig. 747. Portrait of Alexander, on a coin
of Babylon, enlarged
331–319 B.C.
(Cf. p. 292)

Fig. 748. The "Alexander sarcophagus"
Musées d'Antiquités de Stamboul (Constantinople)

Fig. 749. Farnese Herakles
Museo Nazionale, Naples
(Cf. p. 289)

Fig. 750. Herakles, on a coin of
Amastris, enlarged
Museo Archeologico, Florence
(Cf. p. 290)

Fig. 751. Statuette of Herakles
British Museum, London
(Cf. p. 290)

Fig. 752. Base of the statue of Poulydamas by Lysippos
Olympia Museum
(Cf. p. 291)

g. 753. Statuette of the Tyche of Antioch
The Vatican, Rome
(Cf. p. 295)

Fig. 754. Bronze statuette of the Tyche
of Antioch
Metropolitan Museum of Art
(Cf. p. 295)

Fig. 755. The Tyche of Antioch,
on a coin of Tigranes
(from a cast)
British Museum, London
(Cf. p. 295)

Fig. 756. Amykos(?), on a
coin of Lakedaimon, enlarged
British Museum, London
(Cf. p. 306, note)

Fig. 757. Demosthenes
Glyptotek Ny Carlsberg, Copenhagen
(Cf. p. 297)

Fig. 758. Head of Anytos, from the temple
at Lykosoura
National Museum, Athens
(Cf. p. 302)

Fig. 759. Head of Artemis, from the
temple at Lykosoura
National Museum, Athens
(Cf. p. 302)

Fig. 760. Head of Demeter, from the
temple at Lykosoura
National Museum, Athens
(Cf. p. 302)

Fig. 761. Profile view of Fig. 760

Fig. 763. Bronze herm of Dionysos, signed by Boethos
Museum of Beirut, T...

Fig. 762. Boy strangling a goose, after a work by Boethos
The Glyptothek, Munich

Fig. 764. Crouching Aphrodite after
Doidalses

National Museum, Rome

(Cf. p. 298)

Fig. 765. Head of Athena probably by
Euboulides

National Museum, Athens

(Cf. p. 303)

Fig. 766. Agon perhaps by Boethos
(see fig. 762)

Museum of Bardo, Tunis

(Cf. p. 300)

Fig. 767. C. Ophellios signed by Dionysios
and Timarchides

Museum of Delos

(Cf. p. 304)

Fig. 658. Laokoon-Gruppe

Fig. 771. Belvedere Torso
The Vatican, Rome
(Cf. pp. 61, 306)

Fig. 770. Bronze statue of a boxer
Museo Nazionale delle Terme, Rome
(Cf. pp. 61, 306)

Fig. 772. Farnese Bull
Museo Nazionale, Naples
(Cf. p. 301)

Fig. 773. Youth signed
by Stephanos

Albani Collection, Rome
(Cf. pp. 182, 305)

Fig. 774. Athena Parthenos (both arms are
restored) signed by Antiochos

National Museum, Rome
(Cf. p. 306)

Fig. 775. "Elektra and Orestes" signed by Menelaos

National Museum, Rome
(Cf. p. 305)

INDEX TO THE ILLUSTRATIONS

INDEX TO THE ILLUSTRATIONS

(The numbers refer to figures)